Brief Contents

Detailed Contents

10 Excerpts from the 9/11 Commission Report: Intelligence   176

List of Figures, Maps, and Tables

Preface

I believe it is essential for students to have a basic understanding of some of the most fundamental concepts in the international relations literature. The chapters of this text present thumbnail definitions of two dozen essential concepts in the field. One could easily add another dozen or so, and there may be some who would take out a few. But the list is a good start. You will find short definitions of "state," the "nation," "power," the "balance of power," "public opinion," "international law," and so forth. Taken alone, these definitions will likely help you to understand more clearly some of the material you will find in other readings and your instructor's lectures. They are the building blocks of the literature.

But since the concepts are derived from observing history, and since history becomes understandable through the concepts, I felt the best way to understand the ideas is to present an illustration in the form of a historical case study. The case studies are mostly stories of important events or problems in the twentieth and twenty-first centuries. Most of the events I select took place after the end of the Second World War (1945), and several are quite recent. But in order to make sure the cases are significant and are likely to be meaningful for years to come, I have focused on material that has its roots in decades-old and even centuries-old antecedents. Thus, the case study on the situation in the former Yugoslavia begins with a description of the region in the Middle Ages. The chapter on sweatshops describes the dawn of the Industrial Revolution. The discussion of the "Great Debate" over the general direction of U.S. foreign policy harks back to previous "great debates" in the 1920s and 1930s.

The material you read, however, is more than a mere compendium of information. It offers you the ingredients to create theories and begin to test hypotheses. You will see enough different events and developments that you will be able to begin developing your own generalizations. By looking across the cases and combining concepts, students are in a position to get the most from this text. They will be engaged in the most fundamental activity of the profession. They may even develop new theories and generalizations that will allow you to better understand some new event that no one has yet foreseen.

ORGANIZATION

The text is presently organized around a logical and relatively typical presentation of key concepts. However, several alternatives are available. I suggest two others. One could review the cases not in terms of the concepts but strictly in terms of the cases and present them chronologically. I would suggest the following sequencing:

Pre-1960: Cases 2, 11
1960–1980: Cases 4, 6, 7, 11, 14, 18
1980–2000: Cases 1, 3, 5, 8, 9, 10, 12, 13, 14, 15, 16, 17, 18, 19

It would also be possible to use this text in a course on comparative politics by focusing on particular regions. For example, the cases could be organized along the following lines (note that some chapters cover more than one region):

U.S. Foreign Policy: Cases 2, 3, 4, 5, 6, 7, 9, 10, 11, 12, 16
Europe: Cases 1, 2, 8, 9, 12, 16, 18
Latin America: Cases 4, 11, 17
Asia: Cases 2, 7, 12, 16, 17
Africa: Cases 11, 13, 14, 17
Middle East: Cases 5, 6, 9, 10

It is also clear that certain issues and events can be understood by looking at particular groupings of chapters. For example, the problem of international terrorism is addressed not only in Case 9, but also in Cases 1, 5, 8, 10, and 13. Likewise, the question of human rights is addressed not only in Case 14, but is also prominently featured in Cases 1, 7, 8, 11, 12, 13, 16, 17, 18, and 19.

NEW TO THE FIFTH EDITION

This fifth edition makes this linkage between theory and history more explicit and dynamic by providing students with a new section: "Thinking Theoretically." In these units, I consider the competing utility of two different theories with regard to the case in question. While brief, these commentaries allow students not only to better understand how historical developments can be interpreted in different ways, but also help clarify the purposes of the theories and the methods whereby they may be tested. I anticipate that they will serve as a jumping-off point for class discussion, essays, assignments, or exam questions.

Most of the cases have undergone significant revision in light of recent major developments. The chapter on the Persian Gulf War has been transformed into a comparative case study since we can now juxtapose the 1990–1991 intervention with the 2003 intervention. Insights from the Iraq War also inform Case 11 on U.S. intervention and Case 3 on the Great Debate over the future of U.S. foreign policy—with far greater attention to the so-called "neo-con" position. Naturally, the case on al Qaeda has been appropriately updated as well. Some cases have been dropped from this edition due to their declining relevance and the emergence of other cases that illustrate the concepts they were intended to exemplify.

The text also includes several new cases, each of which is designed to draw more attention to events in the developing world. These cases do not shy away from looking closely at some of the most troubling developments of our time: the Rwanda genocide and efforts to hold the génocidaires accountable, human trafficking and sexual slavery, and pandemics. Students will not only learn from these new cases the basic facts but will also be able to consider how Western powers—and Westerners generally—may be involved in either the problem or its solution. In addition, a chapter on regionalism in the developing world shows how countries in these regions are attempting to solve their own problems.

Taken together, the text provides numerous resources for faculty to help students think critically and creatively about world events, international relations theory, and policymaking. Whatever your emphasis in the classroom, you will find this text will complement and enhance outcomes.

I hope that readers will find this text to be a useful reference work for purposes beyond the classroom, as many readers of the first edition have told me they have done. The background provided here to contemporary problems does not change, although naturally its interpretation does. As new problems emerge in new parts of the world, this background will give the reader an advantage in appreciating the sources of these problems.

ACKNOWLEDGMENTS

I would like to extend thanks to a number of individuals who helped bring about this fifth edition. Vikram Mukhija, Lucy Silberman, Elizabeth Fogarty, and the staff at Longman were supportive from the outset and provided valuable advice and direction. I would also like to thank the reviewers of this edition for their sound advice: Debra DeLaet, Drake University; Jon Timothy Kelly, West Valley College; Cameron Thies, Louisiana State University; and Michael Colomaio, Alfred State College. Here at Brigham Young University, I would like to thank W. Chris Harvey for his able research assistance without which the manuscript would have been many months behind schedule. And finally, I thank my wife Rebecca for putting up with all the work I brought home in connection with this project.

KEN STILES

TO THE STUDENT

It is easy to be overwhelmed by the pace of events in the world and confused about their significance. Each day seems to bring new announcements of impending war or heightened alert. It might even be tempting to simply refuse to deal with it all and retreat to a cocoon of ignorance. But the stakes are too high to settle for this. We owe it to ourselves to make some effort to understand what is happening, even if we may not always be able to predict it.

So—where do we start? To begin, we must reach some agreement on what it is we're talking about. Simply observing world affairs is not enough, because there is so much noise and commotion. After all, how do we know whether a group of men in uniform carrying guns is an army, a militia, a terrorist group, or a gun club? And if that group of uniformed individuals begins walking toward another town, killing people in their path, are we witnessing a revolution, a war, a terrorist incident, or a gang war? Most events in world affairs have little meaning in and of themselves. It is only after observers agree among themselves on the concepts they all will use to describe and categorize events that we can begin communicating with each other. Thus concepts and their definitions are fundamental to the study of world affairs.

Once we have begun to label world events, we can look at different events and make comparisons. If we have decided that a group of armed men attacking a village is an act of war because of certain mitigating circumstances, then we can look for other instances of armed attack to see how they differ and how they are the same. For example, are more troops involved in one incident? Are they better armed? Are they moving more swiftly and with greater efficiency? Is the number of victims higher? Are the troops more confident and cheerful? Can an observer determine what the goals of the armies are?

Once we can compare different events, we can begin the process of looking for patterns. In some cases, this can be done by simply taking a few examples and studying them in depth. One can also take a large number of cases and draft numerical or statistical summaries. By laying out these numbers or these cases, it might be possible to identify coincidences or sequences of events and/or conditions. For example, we may find that large numbers of troops go on the march immediately after a prolonged drought or famine. We may note that where the people vote to choose their leaders, few troops ever march. We may find that wars often occur in the same place for what appears to be the same purpose over time. And so forth.

Identifying coincidences and sequences of events is the beginning of many explanations. Theories are simply systematic forms of explanation linking various events and conditions in a logical way. We may begin with a general set of rules and principles ("humanity can learn from its mistakes," "the powerful force themselves on the weak," "freedom breeds peace" . . .) and from them derive our theories (wars will tend to diminish in number over time, powerful states tend to create empires, democracies will usually not fight each other . . .). Or we may simply observe patterns and begin to generalize—which is to say, develop general rules and theories that may apply to new situations. For example, some have noted that the city-states of the Greek peninsula in the days of Athens and Sparta bear interesting similarities to the Cold War era.[1,2]

At some point, these broad generalizations will need to be put to the test, either with detailed case-study work or with broader comparative studies. This can be done by deriving "testable hypotheses" from the theories and then returning to the facts and events to see whether our predictions are correct. For example, a liberal thinker may believe firmly that democracies are inherently more peaceful for a variety of reasons (some ideological). From this, she may derive a simple hypothesis that states with democratic governments (defined, let's say, as a state where the people vote for a national legislature in free and fair elections) will not go to war with each other. The next step would be to identify all the wars in history, or at least back to the Age of Enlightenment era, when modern democracy emerged, and then classify all the various types of governments of the warring parties. This done, it would be a rather simple thing to count how many democracies were at war with each other compared to nondemocracies. It may be useful to conduct a statistical test to make sure that a low number can't be explained by the fact that there are simply few democracies (if there are only two democracies and fifty nondemocracies, the fact that they didn't go to war may be a fluke). Once all this is done, the findings will either support or disconfirm the hypothesis, which in turn may cause us to have different opinions of the underlying theory.[3]

By the time you finish reading this, you will not only have been exposed to some of the key concepts in the discipline, which should help you understand both history and current events, but you will also have studied the two World Wars, the Cold War, the post–Cold War era, the process of colonialism and decolonization, economic expansion and environmental decay, and human rights. While I urge you to take a conventional course on the history of world civilization and the twentieth century, this text provides a useful overview.

---

[1] Dingman, Robert V. "Theories of, and Approaches to, Alliance Politics." In Paul Gordon Lauren, ed. *Diplomacy: New Approaches in History, Theory, and Policy* (New York: Free Press, 1979): 245–266.
[2] Evangelista, Matthew. "Issue-Area and Foreign Policy Revisited." *International Organization* 43 #1 (Winter 1989): 147.
[3] Maoz, Zeev, and Bruce Russett. "Normative and Structural Causes of Democratic Peace, 1946–1986." *American Political Science Review* 87 #3 (September 1993): 624–639.

PART

1

FUNDAMENTAL CONCEPTS

CASE 1

Yugoslavia's Dismemberment: Anarchy

INTRODUCTION

Anarchy is the condition that the world faces, according to most international relations scholars. Anarchy means the absence of a central, controlling, governing authority. Anarchy is not necessarily equivalent to chaos or violence, however. Peace and anarchy may exist simultaneously, which is generally the case in the international system.

Anarchy implies that if a state is to be safe, it must seek out its own allies, build up its own armies, and play the diplomatic game carefully. No one can be depended upon to rescue it from attack. This need for "self-help" explains much of the "balance of power" dynamic discussed in Case 3.

The opposite of anarchy is world government. In this condition, states need not fear for their safety, because a higher legal and political authority will come to their rescue. Inside states, we hope that no anarchy occurs, as it would indicate a breakdown of central authority (Somalia comes to mind). Internationally, a central government is mostly the vision of idealists. For all its symbolic presence, the United Nations is clearly not a world government. And for all the pressures against it, national sovereignty remains the rule in international life. Thus we live in a world of legal equals that have no overriding authority to settle disputes.

The case of Yugoslavia is useful for understanding anarchy not because of the high levels of violence found there, but because of the role that the international community played in recognizing new states and protecting their new-found independence as well as the rights of individuals living in the region facing extermination. As we will see, nothing that happened in Yugoslavia escaped international scrutiny, and the world community responded with all the resources it could muster, from economic sanctions to military intervention and a war crimes trial. Is it possible that Yugoslavia illustrates the end of anarchy?

For years, Yugoslavia was at the center of major power struggles for control over southern Europe. The Ottomans, Hungarians, and Austrians each took a turn at Balkan domination. Sarajevo entered the history books as the spot where World War I began. Much of the post–World War I settlement at Versailles was inspired by an international desire to provide justice and peace to the Balkans. The breakup of the Yugoslav Federation during the 1990s illustrated the limits of anarchy in some ways, even as it revealed the failures of international law. As civil war was transformed into international conflict with the secession and recognition of an increasing number of the country's republics, an ever-growing international military presence attempted to restore peace. At the same time, the international community used the Yugoslav experience to reinstate the principle of war crimes guilt, thus paving the way for the establishment of the first permanent International Criminal Court (see Case 10). Thus, Yugoslavia is a case of both balance of power run amok and an international system attempting to create order.

The atrocities of the wars in the former Yugoslavia have been embedded in the international consciousness thanks to the work of war crimes prosecutors, journalists, and government- and UN-sponsored fact-finding missions. We have heard stories of summary executions of civilians, mutilations of enemy soldiers, concentration camps, and the use of rape as a weapon of war. These wars also included aerial bombardment of residential zones, economic sanctions, and diplomatic isolation imposed by Western forces, each painfully damaging in its own way.

KEY FIGURES
YUGOSLAVIA'S DISMEMBERMENT

Slobodan Milosevic   President of Serbia, 1987–2000. He is generally considered responsible for the wars that took place in the Yugoslavian region during the 1990s. He died while on trial for war crimes at the Hague.

Josip Broz Tito   President of Yugoslavia, 1946–1980.

Vojislav Kostunica   President of Serbia, 2000–present. He won elections and international support, leading to Milosevic's resignation.

Radovan Karadzic   Local leader of the Bosnian Serbs. Currently in hiding as an indicted war criminal.

Louise Arbour   Chief Prosecutor of the ICTY. She pursued Milosevic's arrest and prosecution.

Bill Clinton   U.S. President, 1993–2001. He deployed U.S. troops to Bosnia under NATO.

Richard Holbrooke   U.S. diplomat who spearheaded the Dayton Accords.

Alija Itzebegovic   Leader of the Bosnian Muslims.

Franjo Tudjman   President of Croatia, 1990–1999.

Warren Christopher   U.S. Secretary of State, 1993–1997.

Boutros Boutros-Ghali   UN Secretary General, 1991–1996. He questioned Western interest in Yugoslavia in contrast to its neglect of Rwanda.

George H. W. Bush   U.S. President, 1989–1993. He supported UN operations in Bosnia.

CHRONOLOGY
YUGOSLAVIA'S DISMEMBERMENT

1444
The Ottoman Empire defeats the Serbs at the battle of Varna.

1806
Serbians establish an independent kingdom. The Ottomans later reassert a degree of control.

1848
Croatia takes Austria's side in the rebellion against Hungary.

1871
A Croatian rebellion against Austria is unsuccessful.

1877
The Treaty of San Stefano establishes an independent Serbia and Montenegro.

1878
European powers revise the largely Russian San Stefano Treaty, leaving Serbia under Austrian rule.

1912
Balkan forces expel the Ottomans from the region, precipitating a two-year struggle for territory in the region.

1914
Austrian Archduke Ferdinand is assassinated in Sarajevo by a Serbian nationalist, sparking the outbreak of World War I.

1918
The Kingdom of the Serbs, Croats, and Slovenes is proclaimed after the end of World War I.

1929
A dictatorship is imposed in response to ethnic unrest.

1941
The Nazis conquer the Balkans. Croat fascists (Ustase) join forces with them.

1946
Tito is elected leader of the newly proclaimed Yugoslav Socialist Republic under Soviet sponsorship.

1971
Tito suppresses a Croatian uprising.

1980
Tito dies, leaving a leadership void. Eventually, a rotating presidency is established that shares power among the various republics.

1981
The central government suppresses an Albanian uprising.

1990
Bosnia, Slovenia, Croatia, and Macedonia declare independence and hold elections.

1991
Violence erupts as Serbian forces clash with Croatians. The war continues until 1992.

1992
Violence erupts in Bosnia between Serbs and Croat/Muslim forces. The war lasts until the Dayton Accords are signed in 1995.

1993
The International Criminal Tribunal for the former Yugoslavia founded.

1995
Serbs overrun Srebreniza, a UN-declared safe haven. NATO forces attack Serb artillery in Sarajevo.

November 21 The Dayton Accords are signed, ending the war and leaving Bosnia divided into Serb and Muslim sectors with NATO acting as a buffer.

1997
Kosovo Liberation Army forces attack Serb outposts. Serbia attacks.

1999
NATO bombs Serb installations to protect Kosovars. Serbia withdraws.

2000
Elections in September yield a victory for Milosevic's opponent, Kostunica. Street protests prompt Milosevic to resign.

2001
Milosevic is extradited to the ICTY.

2002
Milosevic's trial begins.

2003
Moderate Serb Prime Minister Zoran Djindjic is assassinated.

2004
Violence erupts in Kosovo. United States imposes economic sanctions as punishment for failure to surrender ICTY indictees.

2006
Slobodan Milosevic dies in his cell in the Hague on March 12.

HISTORY TO 1918

To a certain extent, the history of ethnic relations in Yugoslavia has followed a common pattern: increasingly mobilized linguistic and religious communities are overwhelmed by a foreign invader; the communities either collaborate or resist; the invader becomes increasingly unable to maintain control of the fringe territory; a new invader unseats the previous power, which gives the local community the opportunity to develop a new political arrangement (*Economist*, August 23, 1992, 36). In the process, differences among the communities become exaggerated and rivalries based on the different experiences emerge.

The earliest Balkan peoples arrived near the dawn of man and were organized at the family, clan, or tribe level. It was not until the early Middle Ages that nations became a force to be reckoned with. Bulgaria reached its zenith during the tenth century, Croatia dominated in the eleventh century, and Bosnia and Serbia were each independent kingdoms of some note in the fourteenth century. Although these moments of glory may seem quaint episodes from the modern perspective, they became embedded in the concept of "rightful heritage" that continues today: "In the nineteenth century the national leaders, looking back on this period, tended to consider the maximum extension of their medieval kingdoms as the natural historical boundaries for their nations" (Jelavich 1983 1, 27).

By the fifteenth century, the Balkans were the battleground of empires, much like Poland to the north. Contact with numerous powerful empires left its imprint on Balkan society and spirit (see Map 1.1). In each region the population represented a fusion of original inhabitants with subsequent invaders, an amalgamation achieved through military conquest by a stronger group, the absorption of one people by another owing to the weight of numbers, or the acceptance of another language because of the cultural attraction offered by a more advanced civilization (Jelavich 1983 1, 27).

By 1500, the Muslims had established firm control over the leaders of the Balkan peoples, forcing them to embrace Islam and submit to the "Porte," as the central government was called. The Ottoman hold continued through the seventeenth century, when Russian and Hapsburg (a central European dynasty embracing a wide variety of nationalities) armies seized and controlled fringe territories. In other cases, such as Serbia, local Muslim strongmen emerged, exercising considerable independence without sanction from the Porte. In Croatia, the Hapsburgs, though dominant, permitted the surviving Catholic elites to exercise considerable discretion and power over the domain. Orthodox Serbs remained considerably organized, thanks largely to geography and the tenacity of the Orthodox hierarchy.

During the second half of the eighteenth century, war raged across the region, particularly in Bosnia and Serbia, where local Serbs rebelled against despotic Muslim leaders with the Porte endorsement. By 1806, the Serbs, successful on the battlefield and far from the Porte's power, established an independent kingdom (Jelavich 1983 1, 196).

Croats repeatedly sought greater autonomy and status within the Hapsburg empire, demanding control of newly acquired territories to the south and east. Croat nationalism began to emerge by 1830. They resented Hapsburg attempts to "divide and rule" by offering some benefits to a few without extending them to the people at large (Cohen 1992, 369). The unrest boiled over into full-fledged rebellion in 1848, and again in 1871. Croatia was granted additional powers, but not independence (Jelavich 1983 1, 206).

Map 1.1 Balkan medieval kingdoms with a breakdown of ethnic divisions

Source: Adapted from Barbara Jelavich, *History of the Balkans: 18th and 19th Centuries* (New York: Cambridge University Press, 1983). Reprinted with the permission of Cambridge University Press.

The conflict was exacerbated by the active involvement of Russia, the Hapsburgs, and other continental powers that were eager to bring stability and their presence to a volatile, strategic region. The Treaty of San Stafano (1877), provided for an independent Serbia and Montenegro as well as a huge Bulgaria under Russian occupation. The Congress of Berlin in 1878 was called by the other European powers to adjust this Russian power play and settled on a much smaller Bulgaria and Bosnia-Herzegovina's inclusion in the Hapsburg Empire (Jelavich 1983 1, 358). The problem of Macedonia was finessed by simply leaving it under Ottoman control—the last major bastion of Muslim power. Increasingly Balkan peoples understood that they could achieve more by joining together, but the years of conquest and division had left profound animosities. Serbs considered Bosnia and Macedonia their rightful heritage, based largely on medieval and ethnic considerations. Croats felt largely the same way about Bosnia. The Muslim population of Bosnia was never considered "authentic" by Serbs or Croats, coming as it did as a product of Ottoman imperialism (Djilas and Mousavizadeh 1992, 26). Not only were these antagonisms ethnically based, but it soon became clear that concrete balance-of-power considerations made suspicion and apprehension rational attitudes. None of the Balkan states had the capacity to ensure its own safety, and any alliance between neighbors could tip the balance against a lone state. Hence competing experiences combined with outside powers, perceptions of national heritage, religion, language, and security concerns to prevent a lasting bond among the nations (Armour 1992, 11).

In 1908 the traditional leadership in the Ottoman Empire was overthrown by the "Young Turk" revolt. These young colonels were determined to bring a sense of national unity to all the empire's colonies. The Balkan states saw the move as a concrete threat to their hard-earned independence and for the first time organized a strong alliance. The alliance was so confident that in 1912 it launched an attack against Turkish forces and succeeded in pushing them virtually off the continent. Ironically, it was as a result of the alliance's success that the most tragic episode of Balkan relations began. The question of territorial compensation aroused intense disagreement because each nation felt its military victories had earned it more spoils of war than it was slated to receive.

World War was sparked by a gunman in Sarajevo, a member of a Serbian nationalist group, who shot the Austrian Archduke Ferdinand in July 1914. Austria declared war on Serbia, Serbia allied with Russia, Russia declared war on Austria, Austria allied with Germany, and so on. Four years and 16 million deaths later, the war ended.

As the defeated Hapsburg and Ottoman Empires were dismantled, many new nation-states were formed. Even before the war ended, Croats and Slovenes were organizing a united Yugoslavia. A Yugoslav Committee was formed which then prepared a draft constitution providing for Serbian participation. When the proposal was forwarded to the Serbian monarchy, it was accepted almost immediately. "Thus the organization of the Yugoslav state was primarily the work of national committees, and the initiative came from the Hapsburg South Slavs" (Jelavich 1983 2, 147). The proposal had to be validated in London, where the territory was formally mapped. On December 1, 1918, the Kingdom of the Serbs, Croats, and Slovenes was officially proclaimed (Cohen 1992, 369).

1918 TO 1980

The first attempt at Yugoslav federation failed after ten years, when the largely nationality-based parliament demanded more autonomy for the various regions than the central government in Belgrade was willing to concede (see Map 1.2). Serbs in Belgrade hoped to instill a sense of national unity, but these efforts merely exacerbated tensions (Cohen 1992, 370). "The basic problem of the state was that, despite the hopes of some intellectuals and political leaders before 1914, a Yugoslav nationality did not come into existence" (Jelavich 1983 2, 151).

Questions of language use, representation in the government, and self-rule became extremely intense in the late 1920s. In 1929, following violent demonstrations in Zagreb, King Alexander dismantled the parliamentary institutions and imposed a form of dictatorship on the country. He was assassinated in 1934, and his successor brought back some of the democratic structures, only to see his country overwhelmed by German Nazi forces in 1941.

The wartime experience of Yugoslavia has been suggested as a cause of the present antagonism. One reason is that the Catholic Croatian region was treated very differently than the Orthodox Serbian areas. Croatia was granted independence and membership in Axis-led international organizations. This diplomatic status and newfound autonomy, after years of failed attempts, was greeted warmly by many Croats. The Catholic hierarchy gave firm instructions to the clergy to serve the new rulers. In the words of the Zagreb archbishop: "These are events . . . which fulfill the long dreamed of and desired ideal of our people. . . . Respond readily to my call to join in the noble task of working for the safety and well-being of the Independent State of Croatia" (MacLean 1957, 88). The Ustase movement, a fascist Croatian group based in Italy, undertook a systematic and egregious rule of terror. Serbs who resided in Croatia were the primary targets, and they "suffered greatly at the hands of the Croatian fascists" (Cohen 1992, 371). According to the current Bosnian Serb leader, some 700,000 Serbs were killed from 1941 to 1945 at Croatian Catholic and Muslim hands, prompting him to vow, "We will never again be history's fools" (Karadzic 1992, 50).

Meanwhile, Josip Broz-Tito, leader of the outlawed Communist Party, organized a highly effective resistance movement in the mountains around Serbia and Bosnia. Many peasants with weapons were ready to take to the mountains, as their forefathers had done so many times before.

By the end of the war, tensions were extremely high among the various groups. Partisans regularly rounded up and shot Croatian fascists. One incident reveals the depth of animosity:

> As the Ustase were being led off to execution, a peasant woman rushed into the middle of them and began scratching and hitting at them, screaming all the time. The Partisans had difficulty pulling her off them. Then the shots rang out and she again rushed forward, this time among the corpses, dancing in the blood. "A-ah!" she gasped, dripping with sweat and blood. It seemed the Ustase had slaughtered all her sons. (MacLean 1957, 156)

Map 1.2 Nationalities of Yugoslavia showing ethnic groups, 1919

Source: Barbara Jelavich, *History of the Balkans: 18th and 19th Centuries; 20th Century* (New York: Cambridge University Press, 1983), vols. 1 and 2. Reprinted with the permission of Cambridge University Press.

Fearful of such reprisals, one particularly large group of Ustase surrendered to the British in the closing days of the war, only to be sent back to the partisans. Reports indicate that between 40,000 and 100,000 of them were killed within days (Jelavich 1983 2, 272).

Tito organized a government among the partisans, although a royal government-in-exile in London had the support of the United States and Great Britain. To consolidate his political support in Yugoslavia, Tito declared Macedonia, previously a province of Serbia, a full-fledged republic in the future Yugoslavia, a status that did, and still does, profoundly disturb Greece to the south and Bulgaria to the east. Tito received Soviet support and recognition and moved early after the war to join the emerging Soviet bloc as a socialist state. An ill-fated USSR-inspired attempt at a Balkan federation failed by 1948, which contributed in part to the eventual separation of Yugoslavia and the Soviet Union.

Tito embarked on a unique and solitary path toward socialism based on decentralized worker organizations, tolerance of nationalities, and intense socialist propaganda campaigns (Jelavich 1983 2, 388). He hoped that socialist solidarity and idealism, combined with dynamic economic growth and prosperity, would lead to a pan-Yugoslav nationalism. But throughout all of Yugoslav history, ethnic tensions remained high. As put by Jelavich:

> With the loosening of the central bonds, more authority was transferred to the capitals of the republics, the majority of which had been, and still were, strongholds of fervent nationalist sentiments. When disputes arose over economic or political questions, the local leaders tended to dust off the old flags and symbols and return with enthusiasm to the battles of the past. . . . (Jelavich 1983 2, 388)

Tito and his government felt compelled in 1971 and again in 1981 to use force to suppress first Croatian and later Kosovo Albanian demands for greater autonomy and more national rights. Through it all, Tito continued to appeal to the people's socialist solidarity to overcome these political disputes. In the final analysis, however, Marxism failed as an integrative force in Yugoslavia (Braun 1983, 37). Tito died in 1980 without a clear successor. As would be seen in the 1990s, with the removal of the communist state, "all that remained was the nation, and the ideology of nationalism" (Hayden 1992, 43).

AFTER TITO

The decade of the 1980s brought economic hardship and lack of central leadership in Yugoslavia, which together fostered nationalist demands in Croatia. The League of Yugoslav Communists failed to maintain cohesion, even though after forty years many party officials, military commanders, and government agents were firmly entrenched in the federal bureaucracy (Cohen 1992, 370). By 1987, Slobodan Milosevic emerged as the sole Serbian leader, resentful that Croatians and others had encroached on federal authority:

Through his brash articulation of Serbia's political discontent, and particularly his populist mobilization of Serbian ethnic consciousness at mass rallies—sometimes referred to as "street democracy"—Milosevic challenged the oligarchic Titoist style of managing the "national question" and also provoked a sharp nationalist backlash from Yugoslavia's other republics and ethnic groups. (Cohen 1992, 371)

The winds of democracy swept through Yugoslavia in the tumultuous fall of 1989. Between April and December 1990, each republic held elections. In Slovenia, Croatia, Bosnia, and Macedonia, new democratic parties were elected, while former Communists were returned to power in Serbia, Montenegro, and Vojvodina.

> Although the elections of 1990 were an impressive exercise in regime transition, the results left the country even more politically fragmented than it had been during the last days of Communist rule. Thus, whether born-again Communists or non-Communists, both the newly elected political authorities and the bulk of the opposition forces in all regions of Yugoslavia were committed to programs of regional and ethnic nationalism that seriously challenged the power of the federal system. (Cohen 1992, 371)

Milosevic, following an undemocratic election, spearheaded efforts to preserve the federation with Serbia at the center and found considerable support among the federal power elite. He proposed a "modern federation," which would preserve the size of the military and the dominance of the Communist Party. In the meantime, he supported efforts by Serbs who resided outside of Serbia to exercise self-determination while maintaining their potential rights to citizenship in Serbia proper.

The question of ethnic rights for minorities came to a head later in 1990, when the Croatian assembly approved a constitution that failed to specifically mention protection of the rights of Serbs living in Croatia. This move was repeated across the nation. As put by Hayden:

> The solution found in the various Yugoslav republics was the creation of systems of a constitutional and legal structure that guarantees privileges to the members of one nation over those of any other residents in a particular state. (Hayden 1992, 41)

Serbians living in Krajina, a Croatian city where Serbs are in the majority, began demonstrating against Croatian authority and seized control of government bureaus and facilities. In early 1991, the Croatian government moved to suppress the unrest.

WARFARE IN SLOVENIA AND CROATIA

During the first part of 1991, Slovenia and Croatia moved toward outright independence, and the legitimacy of the shared federal presidency was challenged throughout the country. In March, when the Croatian delegate was scheduled to take his seat at the head of the table, the Serbian delegation protested his ascension and in May vetoed it altogether (New York Times, May 16, 1991, A1).

While attempts were made to preserve the federal structure, irreconcilable demands and fast action toward independence and diplomatic recognition in Slovenia and Croatia frustrated the efforts (New York Times, June 7, 1991, A5). Meanwhile, U.S. Secretary of State James Baker urged national leaders to preserve the federation, a statement that the military apparently interpreted as "a green light for military intervention should secession occur" (Cohen 1992, 373). When the Croatian and Slovene parliaments approved independence resolutions on June 26, 1991, the George H. W. Bush administration announced its "regret" for such "unilateral action" and warned of a "dangerous situation" (*New York Times*, June 27, 1991, A1). On June 28, Yugoslav army tanks battled Slovene troops that had taken control of border posts. Slovenia defeated the incursion and held firm to independence in spite of several offers for increased autonomy in the old federation. When Yugoslav troops began to make new inroads, European Community (EC) officials offered to mediate the dispute. By early July, EC mediators managed to identify the terms of a settlement, but when a cease-fire was accepted in August, it became clear that many soldiers in the field had no loyalty to the Belgrade government, prompting the EC mediators to declare that the Yugoslav army units were "out of control" (*New York Times*, August 30, 1991, A3).

In Croatia, violence first erupted in Zagreb and then quickly spread across the region inhabited by Serbs. Early on, the tactics used by both sides strayed far from traditional rules of war. Serb fighters used Croatian civilians as human shields when attacking Croatian outposts, forcing the defenders to shoot at relatives (*New York Times*, July 31, 1991, A1). On the other side, Serbian soldiers with Croatian relatives agonized over orders to shoot (*New York Times*, October 1, 1991, A1). The Yugoslav defense minister, Veljko Kadijevec, negotiated several cease-fires with the Croats during these months, only to be dismissed by an impatient Milosevic.

By the end of the initial phase of hostilities in March, some 10,000 were dead and 500,000 were homeless. The fighting intensified in the fall and continued through most of 1992. Vukovar was described as a "wasteland" in November after eighty-six days of shelling and aerial bombardment (*New York Times*, November 21, 1992, A1). By December, the military actions lost most of their strategic content and took on the form of vendettas. Reports of unconfirmed atrocities became commonplace by early 1992.

The international community was ill prepared to intervene in this situation, coming as it did during the collapse of the Soviet Union and the general restructuring of international institutions and practices. The EC wanted desperately for this situation to be resolved without military intervention, even of peacekeepers, and the EC lost several diplomats in the skies of Croatia in their efforts to mediate a peaceful settlement. NATO forces were unable to intervene because the treaty prohibited the use of the forces outside the member countries' collective borders. The CSCE (Council for Security and Cooperation in Europe) was untested and required unanimity in its decision making, and the UN was happy to let regional organizations take the first crack before intervening (Cohen 1992, 373). It was not until September that the Security Council began to issue a series of resolutions condemning Serbian and Yugoslav army support of Serbian militiamen in Croatia.

At any rate, the Western response was tepid at best. In spite of Germany's insistence, the EC did not officially extend diplomatic recognition to Croatia until January 1992 (nearly one month after Germany), and the United States waited until the spring. These delays hampered attempts to treat the problem as an international, rather than civil, conflict. Some have argued that this inaction helped bring on the war (Mastnak 1992, 11).

Over several months beginning in November, the UN Security Council deliberated a proposal to send a group of peacekeeping forces to monitor a future cease-fire in Croatia. This force, originally pegged at 10,000, was ultimately increased to 14,000 and was deployed strategically not only in the Serb-inhabited zones of Croatia ("pink zones") but also in Belgrade and Sarajevo. Wanting to assure himself that the UN troops would not be in serious danger, the new secretary general, Boutros Boutros-Ghali, waited until a cease-fire held for several days. This did not happen until March, following Croatian, Serb, and eventually Serb Croatian support (although in the case of Serbs living in Croatia, supporters of the peacekeeping operation had to force out an intransigent leadership; *New York Times*, February 22, 1992, A1). The troop arrival on March 16 marked the end of civil war in Croatia for the time being. Unrest erupted again in early 1993 but was contained.

WARFARE IN BOSNIA

No sooner had peacekeepers arrived in Croatia than a full-scale war broke out in Bosnia-Herzegovina, which so dominated international affairs that the Croatian struggle paled in comparison. The war generated 2 million refugees and 140,000 dead or missing (11,000 died in Sarajevo alone). The scale of atrocities approached World War II proportions, introducing a new concept in international discourse: "ethnic cleansing." Bosnian leaders declared their independence from the rest of Yugoslavia in October 1991, and a referendum was scheduled for early March 1992. Ethnic Serbs, who make up roughly one-third of the Bosnian population, protested the formation of an independent state where they would be outnumbered by their erstwhile enemies, and they boycotted the vote. On March 1, 1992, the country overwhelmingly approved independence. Within a month, Serb irregulars were fighting in the streets of Bosnia with the support of the local leader, Radovan Karadzic. After firing on pro-independence demonstrators, Serb sharpshooters were forced to flee the country, and a large guerrilla force formed in the mountains surrounding Sarajevo and beyond. Serbian leaders in Bosnia received considerable support from the Serbian government, which by late April had declared itself, along with Montenegro, Vojvodina, and a reluctant Kosovo, a new Yugoslav federation.

The international community acted swiftly to grant recognition to Bosnia and within one month had moved to include it in the community of nations, although some feared that this speed was as unwise as the delays had been vis-à-vis Croatia (Cohen 1992, 374). Discussion of deploying peacekeepers began almost immediately, but Boutros-Ghali slowed things down by pointing out that the level of violence in Bosnia posed a grave danger to any future deployment. He also rejected a call from Bosnian Muslim President Alija Itzebegovic for an "intervention force" on the grounds that it would require "many tens of thousands" of troops in a very dangerous situation (*UN Chronicle*, September 1992, 8). In May, Boutros-Ghali withdrew most of the UN observers from Sarajevo, although he ultimately approved Cyrus Vance's recommendation to increase the force already there from 10,000 to 14,000.

The scale of destruction in Bosnia far exceeded that in Croatia. The artillery barrage against Sarajevo continued virtually uninterrupted for the next year, sometimes with as many as 3,000 shells falling on the city in a single day. Serbs moved quickly to gain control of Bosnian territory, and by summer, with only one-third of the population, Serbs controlled nearly three-fourths of the territory, cutting off access to several towns and villages populated by Muslims in the eastern region of the country. The refugee population grew at the rate of 30,000 per day in the early months of the war.

After some hesitation to take sides (particularly on the part of Russia—a historic Serbian ally), the UN Security Council began in May 1992 to condemn not just the war and its associated atrocities but specifically Serbia and the Serbs of Bosnia. The United States and EC nations imposed economic and diplomatic sanctions against Serbia and Montenegro in April, expanding them in May, and the French, British, and American representatives on the Security Council raised questions about Yugoslavia's continued membership in the UN (in September that membership was revoked, in spite of serious legal questions; "Current Development" 1992, 832). On May 30, the Security Council placed blame for the violence squarely on Serbia and called for sanctions on the basis of Chapter VII of the UN Charter (*New York Times*, May 31, 1992, A1).

The focus of UN efforts in Bosnia was to provide humanitarian assistance to the besieged Muslims in Sarajevo and other towns and villages that were cut off from food and fuel supplies. The Sarajevo airport, overrun by Serb gunmen, was eventually opened thanks to Security Council intervention and diplomatic activity, including a personal visit by François Mitterand, president of France (*New York Times*, June 29, 1992, A1). The Serbs continued to block access to more remote villages on the grounds that even humanitarian assistance had a concrete military impact, which prompted the Security Council to pass a resolution in late June allowing military escorts for humanitarian aid convoys. When this failed, the Security Council approved the use of "all necessary means"—a phrase taken from the Gulf War—to ensure that aid reached its destination (*Economist*, August 15, 1992, 37–38). Although the UN avoided direct confrontation, in March 1993 the rather innovative tactic of air drops delivered significant amounts of food. Perhaps the most heroic figure in the war was General Phillippe Morillon, commander of UN forces in eastern Bosnia, who made saving Srebreniza his personal quest. Entering the Muslim enclave despite shelling and inadequate food, he defied the Serbian troops to attack the helpless city. Even this effort largely failed, however, because many Muslims were eager to abandon the city (against Bosnian Muslim military leaders' hopes) and the secretary general was growing weary of Morillon's grandstanding (*New York Times*, April 8, 1993, A5).

Eventually, the UN became actively involved in evacuating Muslims from such cities as Srebreniza. UN intervention raised disturbing questions about its complicity with Serbian "ethnic cleansing," a practice that involved deliberate depopulation of

Muslim-dominated regions. Ethnic cleansing involved not only simple removal of persons by the thousands but also mass executions and even large-scale rape to alter the gene pool of those who remained behind (*New York Times*, May 22, 1992, A1). The Serbs were soundly condemned by the Security Council, the General Assembly, and the Human Rights Commission. Reports of not only ethnic cleansing but also death camps prompted charges of "war crimes" and the approval in September of the creation of a war crimes tribunal along the lines of the Nuremburg Trials (see Case 10). In a conference held in London in August, Acting Secretary of State Lawrence Eagleburger warned Serb delegates:

> [W]e should, here at this conference, place squarely before the people of Serbia the choice they must make between joining a democratic and prosperous Europe or joining their leaders in the opprobrium, isolation, and defeat which will be theirs if they continue on their present march of folly. (U.S. State Department, September 1992, 1)

It was not just one group that was guilty of atrocities, however; other developments took place during the first months of the war. To begin, Croats and Muslims were guilty of atrocities and ethnic cleansing as well. For example, in early June, Bosnian Muslims and Croats who lived in Bosnia were reported to have rounded up whole villages and killed the inhabitants. Radovan Karadzic, the Bosnian Serbs' leader, was convinced that Muslims were working for years to dominate the country through means of population control:

> The Bosnian Muslims want, ultimately, to dominate, relying on a very high birthrate. They even wanted to move some Turks from Germany to Bosnia to help build their Islamic society. Since such a strategy of domination would be at the expense of Bosnian Serbs, we have resisted it by protecting our own villages. . . . We have not been fighting to gain territory. We have been fighting for the principle that there will be three autonomous communities in Bosnia-Herzegovina in order that no one of the three dominates the other. . . . We are fighting to protect ourselves from becoming vulnerable to the same kind of genocide that coalition waged upon us in World War II when 700,000 Serbs were killed. Today, Serbs would be 60 percent of the population of Bosnia if this genocide had not been committed. We will never again be history's fools. (Karadzic 1992, 50)

In addition, numerous Serbs opposed violence. In late May, tens of thousands demonstrated in the streets of Belgrade against Slobodan Milosevic and called for his resignation. In the village of Gorazde, an ethnically mixed community, Serb residents were angry with Karadzic's policy of ethnic cleansing. When asked about his remarks that Serbs and Muslims are inherently hostile, they responded: "Remarks like that are simply stupid. . . . Serbs and Muslims have lived in the same valleys, used the same roads, worked in the same places, and intermarried throughout history. Now Karadzic wants to tear us apart" (*New York Times*, March 9, 1993, A5).

Serbian parliamentary leader Milan Panic, a longtime resident of the United States, pressed for a liberal solution to the Yugoslav problem and even ran a strong campaign for president until his defeat and eventual ouster in the fall. He portrayed the situation this way:

> I look at all this a little like a family feud. One family happens to be mine, the Serbs. They happen to live across the river in Bosnia. But they are my family, they are Serbs. To ask Serbs from one side of the river not to help Serbs on the other side is not fair. . . . Now I'm not saying send the army. But we need to help each other, to protect each other. (Panic 1992, 49)

The struggle in Yugoslavia was far from simple because it involved the mutually exclusive goals of territorial integrity and self-determination for a multiethnic state (Woodward 1992, 54). When past experience is overlaid on such a Gordian knot, it is no surprise that there are enough virtue and blame for all.

Peace negotiations under American and European auspices began in earnest in early 1993 with the so-called Vance–Owen plan (named after its diplomatic creators), which would have divided the country into ten more or less ethnically homogeneous areas. Negotiators representing the Muslim and Serb governments expressed strong interest in the plan, but it was ultimately rejected by the Yugoslav parliament in Belgrade under the leadership of Milosevic. Gradually, plans that focused on dividing the country along lines of actual military occupation seemed more realistic and became the foundation for the Dayton Accords.

In 1995, Serb forces stepped up their offensive in spite of NATO threats of retaliation. They overran two safe havens, Srebreniza and Zepa, in the summer and continued shelling Sarajevo. Negotiations for a peace settlement began in earnest in August, shortly before a mortar attack on Sarajevo cost the lives of nearly forty Muslims who were waiting in line at a market on August 28. Two days later, NATO followed through on its threat of aerial bombardment and maintained the shelling until September 14, at which time the tentative agreement to begin full-scale negotiations solidified (the bombing probably did not help move forward the peace process and ran the risk of backfiring; Malanczuk 1997, 414).

Beginning in late September, an extended, secret negotiation took place at Wright-Patterson Air Force Base near Dayton, Ohio. Alija Itzebegovic, Slobodan Milosevic, and Franjo Tudjman signed the agreement with U.S. Secretary of State Warren Christopher on November 21, 1995, signaling both an end to the fighting and the division of Bosnia into two quasi-states: the Serbian Republic centered in Pale and a Muslim-Croat Federation centered in Sarajevo. Although Bosnia is still formally a unified country and the Sarajevo regime is represented in the United Nations, in fact the country has been divided ethnically—one of the goals of the ethnic cleansers.

The Dayton Accords have been implemented primarily by NATO troops from France, the United Kingdom, and the United States, who divided the country into areas of supervision, much like Germany after World War II. The force of roughly 40,000 has encountered periodic resistance and has been criticized for failure to aggressively pursue those accused of war crimes, but in all it has performed as well as expected in preserving stability in the region.

WARFARE IN KOSOVO

Ironically, the structure of the Dayton Accords inadvertently sowed the seeds of a new conflict in the Balkans, this time in Kosovo (Judah 2000, 125). Kosovo, formerly an autonomous republic inside Serbia, is inhabited primarily by ethnic Albanians who have fairly strong ties to the nation of Albania to the south (see Map 1.3). A Serb minority complained of abuse by Albanians in the late 1980s, and in response the Belgrade government rescinded the region's autonomy. Over several years, opposition groups began to coalesce in Kosovo, most aiming for at least a restoration of home rule if not independence, although they differed on the means to be employed to achieve either goal. Ibrahim Rugova, the Kosovar president elected in 1992, consistently favored a peaceful, negotiated settlement, whereas the Kosovo Liberation Army (KLA) took a more radical approach. After the Dayton Accords, Rugova and many Kosovars realized that a peaceful approach would never attract the attention of Western diplomats and was therefore doomed.

Beginning in 1997, KLA attacks against Serb military and police installations in Kosovo prompted retaliatory actions that began a tit-for-tat cycle of escalating violence. It is unclear to what extent the KLA was hoping for Serb reprisals, but it is

Map 1.3 Yugoslavia after the Dayton Accords

Source: Viktor Meier, *Yugoslavia: A History of Its Demise* (New York: Routledge, 1999). Reproduced by permission of Taylor & Francis Books UK.

easy to imagine that a lesson from the Bosnian experience was that Serb atrocities were likely to ultimately prompt NATO intervention (which was Kosovo's only real hope for independence; Ignatieff 2000, 28).

Western diplomats were slow to focus attention on Kosovo. In the meantime, the collapse of the Albanian government of Sali Berisha in 1997 created an opportunity for KLA fighters to consolidate their strongholds in Albania near the Kosovo border and to increase their stockpile of small arms (Judah 2000, 128). By 1998, sporadic violence was the norm in Kosovo. The United States ultimately dispatched Richard Holbrooke, the master diplomat who spearheaded the Dayton Accords, to forge a truce between the factions. In October, Milosevic, under threat of NATO aerial bombardment, agreed to pull back his police and military forces and allow international observers to monitor human rights conditions in Kosovo (*Economist*, October 17, 1998, 53). In January, however, a Serb reprisal that left forty-five ethnic Albanians dead brought an end to the deal. Western diplomats brought Milosevic to Rambouillet, near Paris, to force a peace treaty between Serbs and Albanian Kosovars, again under threat of bombing. The agreement called for NATO deployments in and around Kosovo and the withdrawal of Serb forces, while preserving the fig leaf of Serb sovereignty over the region. Ultimately, Milosevic considered this too great a violation of his country's independence and decided to take his chances on surviving a bombing campaign. As put by Judah, "He was going to risk the bombs and go for broke" (Judah 2000, 227). Milosevic was counting on the collapse of NATO resolve in the face of CNN reports of child victims and such. He also counted on Russian support in the corridors of power.

On March 22, 1999, NATO began a bombing campaign that intensified as it went on for 78 days. While the bombs fell, Serb police forced Albanians out of Kosovo in the hope of more easily exposing the remaining KLA fighters (Ignatieff 2000, 41). Nearly one million refugees flooded Albania, Macedonia (which was already protected by a UN force), and Bosnia (where Milosevic hoped war would break out again). The bombardment did little to protect the KLA, however, and Serbs regained control of numerous towns and roads. The Serbs were unable to completely dislodge the guerrillas, and the diplomatic collapse did not take place as Milosevic had predicted.

All his calculations had failed. NATO had not split, he was unable to spark new wars in Macedonia and Bosnia and, in the end, the Russians had proved unwilling or unable to help him (Judah 2000, 279).

On June 10, 1999, following Milosevic's agreement to Western demands, the NATO bombardment was called off and NATO troops from neighboring Bosnia began to take up positions around the Kosovar capital with UN Security Council approval.

WAR CRIMES TRIBUNAL

In the background of the Yugoslav situation beginning in 1993 was the prospect that those responsible for atrocities would wind up on the docket in the Hague. The International Criminal Tribunal for the former Yugoslavia (ICTY), though starting slow, began to issue indictments for war criminals in 1994 and started its first trial in mid-1995. The first conviction was handed down for Dusko Tadic two years later. Gradually, during 1998 and 1999, an increasing number of those indicted (more than sixty, including leaders of the Pale and Belgrade governments) either surrendered or were captured and arrested by NATO forces in and around Bosnia. The pace of the trials and convictions picked up, and as of mid2000, ten had been convicted and nearly forty were in custody awaiting imminent trial.

Critics point out that NATO forces have been slow to go after those indicted, often leaving them alone even when they know their whereabouts. Even more serious are charges of complicity by the Belgrade government in providing asylum to many of those indicted. The indictments against Milosevic in May 1999 meant that he was a prisoner in his own country (the decision to issue the indictment was prompted in part by a fear on the part of Chief Prosecutor Louise Arbour that Milosevic would flee to Belarus or some other safe haven).

With the fall of the Milosevic regime in 2000, the new president, Vojislav Kostunica, was pressured by the West to transfer him to the Hague Tribunal. Under threat of aid being cut off, Kostunica relented and, in defiance of Serbian nationalists, surrendered Milosevic to the ICTY. The Tribunal finally had its star suspect in custody. The trial itself began amid chaotic media attention on February 12, 2002, after a flurry of confusing and disjointed statements by Milosevic, who refused to recognize the authority of the trial. His plea of "not guilty" was entered on his behalf by the Tribunal. The charges against him include genocide, murder, extermination, torture, plunder, and cruel treatment of civilians, stemming from Serbia's actions in Croatia, Bosnia, and Kosovo. Following months of meandering and often confusing and inflammatory testimony, at a point when it seemed to some that trial might never end, Milosevic was found dead in his cell on March 12, 2006. Reaction to his death was naturally mixed, with one man on the street in Vrajne, Serbia, commenting "He was a big Serb. Maybe he made a few mistakes. . . ." On the other hand, Richard Dicker of Human Rights Watch lamented that his death was "a terrible setback first and foremost for the victims of horrific crimes in the former Yugoslavia, and because it deprives the tribunal of a chance to render a verdict on his true role" (*New York Times*, March 12, 2006). At the same time, many feel justice was done—at least in a cosmic sense.

CONCLUSION: WHITHER YUGOSLAVIA?

Have the great powers of the late twentieth century done any better at bringing peace and justice to the Balkans, or have they simply manipulated local conflicts for strategic ends? Although NATO intervention halted the bloodletting in Bosnia and no doubt helped prevent the spread of warfare during the Kosovo crisis, the conflict has always been on Western (specifically U.S.) terms. This has often meant delayed and minimal intervention. The Bosnia conflict, after all, cost nearly 250,000 lives before NATO became directly involved. Even the UN admits that the international community failed in its effort to protect the citizens of Srebreniza and other safe havens (United Nations 1999). Likewise, intervention in Kosovo did little in the short run to protect ethnic Albanians but created instead an opportunity for Serb aggression. Conversely, Western intervention has sometimes been precipitous for strategic reasons, as with Germany's sudden recognition of Slovenian and Croatian independence without regard for the security implications. Even more uncharitably, one could interpret the entire Western initiative in the Balkans as an attempt to both shore up and extend NATO influence in southern Europe (Gervasi 1998, 20). Certainly an important loser in all of this strategic jockeying has been Russia.

Since 2003, the Kostunica government has adopted a less conciliatory attitude toward the West. Nationalism appears to be resurgent and the government has resisted Western pressure to cooperate. The United States imposed economic sanctions in April 2004 over the government's refusal to extradite a number of ICTY indictees. Ratko Mladic, for example, is reported to be living in Serbia, although local leaders deny this (*Los Angeles Times*, August 1, 2004, A14). The country has also experienced a number of profound disturbances. In 2003 the Serbian prime minister, reformer, and unifying figure Zoran Djindjic, was assassinated and in March 2004 new violence erupted in Kosovo, resulting in over thirty deaths (*The Times of London*, March 19, 2004, A11). Throughout this period there has been no progress on negotiations over the status of Kosovo. And finally, in May 2006, Montenegrins voted to secede from Serbia—completing the countries dissolution.

The Western initiative has nevertheless been somewhat measured and constrained compared to past great power machinations. The decision to act through the UN to a considerable degree validates the norm of multilateralism. Likewise, the decision to establish a war crimes tribunal was intended to make clear that more than strategic considerations were at stake. As put simply by Senator Joseph Biden, "I think we did the right thing in our seventy-eight day air campaign, and we succeeded. The war against Milosevic was of great consequence" (Biden 1999). At the Hague, 161 persons were charged with war crimes in connection with the Balkan crisis, and as of May 2006, 94 trials have concluded, resulting in 46 convictions. Is it possible that with respect to the Balkans at least, the international community has overcome international anarchy? This conclusion may be all the more intriguing when we consider the relative peace and prosperity we are currently witnessing in the new, democratic Serbia.

 DEBATE TOPIC

Does Yugoslavia demonstrate the capacity of states to set aside power politics and instead ensure that "right" wins out over "might"?

PRO

Those who believe that the handling of Yugoslavia's problems bodes well for a future international system argue as follows: (1) Most major powers were reticent about becoming involved, but were persuaded to intervene to halt human rights atrocities. (2) The international community acted with considerable unity in a variety of institutions (UN, NATO,

(*continued*)

(*continued*)

ICTY). (3) International actions in Yugoslavia helped set a precedent for other initiatives, including the International Criminal Court.

CON
Those who believe little has changed point out: (1) Americans and Europeans intervened only because Yugoslavia has strategic importance—unlike Rwanda. (2) Germany saw recognition of new former-Yugoslav republics as an opportunity to increase its influence in the region, in spite of European objections. (3) The West has been markedly unenthusiastic about pursuing known war criminals for fear of disrupting the strategic balance.

THINKING THEORETICALLY

Conventional wisdom about Yugoslavia holds that hostilities between Serbs and Croats and Muslims were inevitable, the product of hundreds of years of antagonism unleashed by the death of Tito. But some of what we find in this case study challenges that. Two alternative theories might be worth exploring. One is rational choice—the other is institutionalism.

Rational choice assumes that actors calculate the costs and benefits of their options before selecting the one that gets them closest to their goals. In the actions of characters like Slobodan Milosevic and Radovan Karadzic we see evidence of shrewd calculation. Note, for example, that Milosevic was careful never to take on more than one enemy at a time. First he attacked the Croats, then the Muslims in Bosnia, and finally the Kosavar Albanians. Although he failed in each fight, he gave himself the best opportunity by never confronting all the separatists at once. Likewise, we see how Milosevic and Karadzic carefully manipulated public opinion by stirring up old hatreds—or even creating new ones with lies and myths.

Institutional theories bring to our attention the structures of Yugoslavia's government as a key factor. The failure to find a single individual to replace Tito led to the awkward rotating presidency described in the case. This contributed a sense of frustration and alienation by most of the leaders of the various republics. Add to this the natural desire for self-determination at a time when every former Soviet Republic had obtained its independence, and it is easy to see why dismemberment became a logical and predictable outcome—even setting aside issues of ethnic hatred and historical animosity.

QUESTIONS TO CONSIDER

1. How does one judge the merits of a nation's demand for self-determination? At what point does such a demand become the concern of the international community? What criteria do the international community use to grant or deny the demand?

2. To what extent should justice take precedence over stability and peace? To what extent do the needs of ethnic communities justify the use of force to alter the political status quo?

3. What force ought to be used by the international community to remedy injustices? How much voice should the great powers have in deciding and implementing these choices?

WEBSITES

The official Web site of the government of Yugoslavia: **www.gov.yu**
Official Web site for the war crimes tribunal: **www.un.org/icty/**
Updates on the Milosevic trial: **www.un.org/icty/glance/casestatus.htm**

U.S. Agencies That Maintain Information Updates

CIA: **www.odci.gov/cia/publications/factbook/bk.html**
State Department: **www.state.gov/www/regions/eur/**
Defense Department: **www.dtic.mil/bosnia/index.html**

Other Databases

www.kosovo.com
www.bosnia-online.com
www.centraleurope.com

REFERENCES

Armour, Ian. "Nationalism vs. Yugoslavia." *History Today* 42 (October 1992): 11–13.

Biden, Joseph. "Bosnia and Kosovo: Lessons for U.S. Policy." Director's Forum, Woodrow Wilson International Center for Scholars, July 22, 1999.

Braun, Aurel. *Small-State Security in the Balkans* (Totowa, NJ: Barnes & Noble Books, 1983).

Cohen, Leonard J. "The Disintegration of Yugoslavia." *Current History* 91 #568 (November 1992): 369–375.

"Current Development—UN Membership of the 'New' Yugoslavia." *American Journal of International Law* 86 #4 (October 1992): 830–833.

Djilas, Aleska, and Nader Mousavizadeh. "The Nation That Wasn't." *New Republic* (September 21, 1992): 25–31.

The Economist (August 15, 1992): 37–38.

The Economist (August 23, 1992): 36.

The Economist (October 17, 1998): 53.

Gervasi, Sean. "Why Is NATO in Yugoslavia?" in Sara Flounders, ed., *NATO in the Balkans: Voices of Opposition* (New York: International Action Center, 1998): 20–46.

Hayden, Robert. "Yugoslavia: Where Self-determination Meets Ethnic Cleansing." *New Perspectives Quarterly* 9 #4 (Fall 1992): 41–46.

Ignatieff, Michael. *Virtual War: Kosovo and Beyond* (New York: Metropolitan Books, 2000).

Jelavich, Barbara. *History of the Balkans: Vol. 1: 18th & 19th Centuries; Vol. 2: 20th Century* (New York: Cambridge University Press, 1983).

Judah, Tim. *Kosovo: War and Revenge* (New Haven, CT: Yale University Press, 2000).

Karadzic, Radovan. "Salvation Is a Serbian State—Interview." *New Perspectives Quarterly* 9 #4 (Fall 1992): 50–51.

Los Angeles Times, August 1, 2004, A14.

MacLean, Fitzroy. *The Heretic: The Life and Times of Josep Broz Tito* (New York: Harper, 1957).

Malanczuk, Peter. *Akehurst's Modern Introduction to International Law*, 7th ed. (New York: Routledge, 1997).

Mastnak, Tomas. "Is the Nation-State Really Obsolete?" *Times Literary Supplement*, August 7, 1992, 11.

Meier, Viktor. *Yugoslavia: A History of Its Demise* (New York: Routledge, 1999).

New York Times, May 16, 1991, A1.

New York Times, June 7, 1991, A5.

New York Times, June 27, 1991, A1.

New York Times, July 31, 1991, A1.

New York Times, August 30, 1991, A3.

New York Times, October 1, 1991, A1.

New York Times, February 22, 1992, A1.

New York Times, May 22, 1992, A1.

New York Times, May 31, 1992, A1.

New York Times, June 29, 1992, A1.

New York Times, November 21, 1992, A1.

New York Times, March 9, 1993, A5.

New York Times, April 8, 1993, A5.

New York Times, March 12, 2006, A1.

Panic, Milan. "The Future Is Forgetting—Interview." *New Perspectives Quarterly* 9 #4 (Fall 1992): 47–50.

Stavrianos, L. S. *The Balkans: 1815–1914* (New York: Holt, Rinehart & Winston, 1963).

The Times of London, March 19, 2004, A11.

UN Chronicle (September 1992): 8.

United Nations. "Kosovo: Recovering from Ravage." *UN Chronicle* #4 (December 1999): 54–55.

U.S. State Department Dispatch Supplement, September 1992, 1.

Wachtel, Andrew Baruch. *Making a Nation, Breaking a Nation: Literature and Cultural Politics in Yugoslavia* (Stanford, CA: Stanford University Press, 1998).

Woodward, Susan. "The Yugoslav Wars." *Brookings Review* 10 #4 (Fall 1992): 54.

Yugoslavia (Stanford, CA: Stanford University Press, 1998).

Sino–Soviet–American Relations: The Balance of Power

INTRODUCTION

As major powers seek security in international affairs, they have several options: increase their military capability beyond the level of any potential adversaries, declare neutrality, or align with other countries to combine their military strengths. The last option is the essence of the balance of power: As nations seek security by forming alliances, the international system will be composed of coalitions that balance one another. This is not to say that every state will remain in a given coalition, but that overall the arrangement of alliances will tend toward a stalemate. Advocates of the balance of power emphasize that this arrangement is both inevitable and beneficial because it prevents any one state from conquering the world. Opponents point out that the balance of power has failed to prevent world wars in the past and that it is based on the amoral principle that "might makes right."

In the past, the story of world affairs has often been told as the story of great power alliances. European history, in particular, consists largely of a string of strategic and tactical agreements between monarchs and emperors, cemented through treaty, marriage, territorial transfers, and so forth. Rarely did any question of whether a particular alliance was "moral" or "right" arise—just whether it was advantageous or prudent. The result has been a string of strange pairings between democracies and dictatorships, kingdoms and republics.

This situation began to change at the beginning of the twentieth century, when ideology began to emerge as an important defining trait of states. With the entry of the United States into World War I, President Woodrow Wilson could claim (however speciously) that the struggle pitted freedom against oppression (he conveniently ignored the fact that Great Britain, France, and the United States were on the same side as the despotic Tsarist Russia). Since then, it has become increasingly important for alliances to have a greater purpose than to merely offset the power of a threatening state. Rather, they must also advance some overarching cause, such as democracy, socialism, or divine destiny. Pragmatic realists seem to be on the defensive in their advocacy of alliances of convenience.

Throughout the Cold War, the three major powers—the United States, the Soviet Union, and the People's Republic of China (PRC)—were often torn by the desire to make alliances meaningful while at the same time behaving pragmatically to defend against would-be enemies. The result has been a series of often surprising alignments.

KEY FIGURES
SINO–SOVIET–AMERICAN RELATIONS

Josef Stalin   Soviet Communist Party leader, 1928–1953. He introduced collectivization and industrialization policies in tune with his view of socialism. Stalin allied with Nazi Germany at the beginning of World War II, then with the Allies after Hitler's attack on Russia in 1942. After the war, his actions in Eastern Europe and elsewhere contributed to the emergence of the Cold War.

Mao Zedong   Leader of the Chinese Communist Party and the Chinese Revolution in 1949. He led China from 1949 to 1976, taking it through various phases of development and crisis.

Harry Truman   U.S. President, 1945–1953. He presided over the outbreak of the Cold War. His "Truman Doctrine," defending pro-U.S. and democratic regimes with force, shaped U.S. policy toward the Soviet Union and China for many years.

Nikita Khrushchev   Leader of the Soviet Communist Party, 1953–1964. He undertook a number of economic and political reforms that liberalized life in Russia to some extent while also challenging the West.

John F. Kennedy   U.S. President, 1961–1963. He dealt with repeated Soviet challenges to U.S. power in Cuba, Berlin, Vietnam, and elsewhere. He helped inaugurate détente after the Cuban Missile Crisis.

Richard Nixon   U.S. President, 1969–1974. Although an ardent anti-Communist as a member of the House of Representatives and Vice President, he adopted a pragmatic, strategic approach while in office. He is credited with consolidating détente and establishing relations with China.

Leonid Brezhnev   Soviet Communist Party leader,1964–1982. He enjoyed a businesslike relationship with Richard Nixon, although the USSR's relations with China soured during his rule.

Mikhail Gorbachev   Soviet Premier, 1985–1991. He undertook radical political and economic reforms that resulted in the introduction of a pro-Western democratic government in Moscow, democratization of Eastern Europe, the end of the Cold War, and the collapse of the Soviet Union.

Deng Hsiao Ping   Leader of the PRC beginning in 1976 with the death of Mao. While maintaining strong Communist Party control over China, he introduced market reforms that helped accelerate the country's development and opening to the rest of the world.

Jimmy Carter   U.S. President, 1977–1981. He formally recognized the PRC as the only government of China and signed the SALT II arms control treaty with the USSR. The Soviet invasion of Afghanistan in 1979 prompted him to impose sanctions on Russia and increase U.S. military spending.

Henry Kissinger   Senior U.S. foreign policymaker under Presidents Nixon and Ford, serving as National Security Adviser and Secretary of State. His realist approach to international affairs guided a pragmatic, unsentimental U.S. foreign policy that improved relations with both the Soviet Union and China.

Ronald Reagan   U.S. President, 1981–1989. A well-known anti-Communist, Reagan imbued his first term with anti-Russian and anti-Chinese rhetoric, expanded the military, and eschewed arms control. During his second term, he presided over a more conciliatory approach that contributed to major arms control agreements with Moscow, the collapse of the Berlin Wall, and the end of the Cold War.

Hu Jintao   President of China beginning in 2002. He was elevated to the Politburo in 1993 by his mentor, Deng Hsiao Ping, presumably because he held reformist credentials, although this has not always been clear to observers.

CHRONOLOGY
SINO–SOVIET–AMERICAN RELATIONS

1945
At the close of the Second World War, Russia, the United States and China are victorious allies.

1945–1947
The Soviet Union conspires with local Communists in Eastern Europe to install sympathetic regimes across the region.

1947
In response to threats from Communist rebels against pro-U.S. forces in Greece and Turkey, Harry Truman announces his plans to provide direct military and economic assistance. This new policy is dubbed the "Truman Doctrine."

1948
West Berlin is cut off from the rest of Germany by a road and rail blockade. Over 18 months, the United States supplies the city by air.

1949
The Soviet Union successfully tests an atomic bomb. Mao Zedong's People's Liberation Army takes power in Beijing as the Nationalist government begins its exile in Taiwan. NATO is formed. The Warsaw Pact is formed shortly thereafter.

(continued)

(*continued*)

1950

North Korea, with Soviet encouragement, invades South Korea in hopes of unifying the country under communism. China later joins the fight on the side of the North Koreans.

1953

The Korean War armistice ends the fighting without resolving the conflict.

1954

The PRC shells the Taiwanese islands of Quemoy and Matsu. The United States threatens nuclear retaliation. The incident is repeated in 1958.

1956

Soviet military forces invade Budapest and replace the West-leaning government of Hungary.

1959

Sputnik, the first human-made satellite, is launched by the Russians, prompting a decades-long "space race."

1961

The East German government erects a concrete wall around West Berlin to prevent East Germans from emigrating.

1962

Cuba allows the deployment of Russian nuclear weapons, prompting a U.S. blockade of the island. The weapons are withdrawn after tensions come close to the breaking point. Mao Zedong repudiates the Soviet version of socialism.

1963

A U.S.–Soviet "hotline" is installed to prevent lapses in communication during a crisis.

1964

The Tonkin Gulf Resolution inaugurates a period of significant U.S. military involvement in Southeast Asia. China tests an atomic bomb.

1968

The USSR deploys troops to Prague to suppress reformist movements in Czechoslovakia.

1968–1969

China and Russia engage in sporadic border clashes.

1969

SALT I is signed by the United States and Russia, signaling the beginning of détente.

1971

Nixon visits China.

1979

The United States and Soviet Union sign SALT II. The United States formally recognizes the PRC. The Soviet Union invades Afghanistan.

1981

Ronald Reagan assumes office. He refers to the Soviet Union as an "evil empire" and begins a dramatic increase in military spending.

1983
Reagan unveils the military's Strategic Defense Initiative, dubbed "Star Wars" by the press.

1985
Mikhail Gorbachev becomes Chairman of the Communist Party of the Soviet Union and almost immediately begins a series of economic and political reforms at home and in Eastern Europe. Russia announces a unilateral moratorium on nuclear testing.

1987
The United States and Russia sign the Intermediate-Range Nuclear Forces Treaty, the first nuclear arms reduction treaty.

1989
Gorbachev signals to Eastern European governments that political reforms are acceptable. In rapid succession, following the dismantling of the Berlin Wall in November, each socialist government in Eastern Europe falls amid protests and street demonstrations. The Warsaw Pact is dissolved.

1990
A coup attempt in Moscow is thwarted by Russian President Boris Yeltsin, and Mikhail Gorbachev is reinstalled as his ally. They negotiate the dismantling of the Soviet Union into its fifteen republics. The Soviet flag is lowered on December 25, 1990.

1991
The United States and Soviet Union are allies in the Persian Gulf War.

2002
Russia joins NATO as a junior member.

2003
The United States and the United Kingdom invade Iraq. Russia, China, France, and Germany object, bringing these countries closer together.

THE SUPERPOWER "TRIANGLE" AND ALIGNMENTS

John Stoessinger opined:

> Machiavelli would have taken considerable pleasure in the dynamics of Sino–Soviet–American triangular relations in our time. During the 1950s, China and the Soviet Union were allies, and the United States feared the menace of a monolithic Sino–Soviet threat. In the 1960s, after the Cuban missile crisis had ushered in a détente between the Soviet Union and the United States, China began to fear the specter of Soviet–American collusion. And in the 1970s, the Soviet leaders began to worry that the Chinese and Americans might be getting along too well. Each of the three powers has had its turn at being frozen out by the other two. (Stoessinger 1990, 257)

The tenuousness of superpower relations is symptomatic of the balance of power. To understand changes in relations among these countries, it is not enough to know the ins and outs of diplomatic language, protocol, and individual personalities. It is also not enough to understand the cultural heritage, historical habits, and ever-changing perceptions of world leaders. Instead, one should focus on how each nation has tried to increase its security by adjusting its relations with a pair of enemies. This adjustment is the essence of the balance of power.

Little naturally links the United States, the Soviet Union, and the People's Republic of China (PRC). In fact, it was not until the twentieth century that meaningful contacts developed among the three nations, at a time when each was already a major global power. The historical circumstances that have forced these three nations to take on the burden of world leadership seem to have been largely beyond their control. Because of this fact, the response of the countries' leaders to these political choices can be more clearly attributed to strategic concerns than to habit, tradition, or heritage.

Each of the three nations has viewed itself as a model for the rest of the world. China's sense of cultural superiority was boundless until the twentieth century, when Western barbarians began to exact humiliating concessions for trade. The Russian empire has consistently viewed itself as a model of efficiency and sophistication, although its views of the West have been generally sympathetic. The United States, with its feelings of "Manifest Destiny," has long considered its role as a model of democracy and scientific progress to be unquestioned. The Communist revolutions in Russia and China had the effect of accentuating ideological differences and feelings of uniqueness and superiority.

At the turn of the century, the United States attempted to mediate a dispute between Western powers intent on trading with China and anti-Western Boxers with its "Open Door" policy, but in the end it sided with the Westerners (Stoessinger 1990, 25). The United States refused to accept the outcome of the October 1917 Bolshevik Revolution and joined an international force to overthrow the new Russian regime in 1919. The Chinese were largely uninterested in Russia, although the Great Wall provided little insurance that the influence of the northern barbarians could be contained for long.

By the 1930s, however, relations among the three nations had grown generally warm. The Soviets provided support for both the Nationalist government in Beijing and the Communist Party forces under Mao Zedong. In 1933, after the Soviet Union had demonstrated political and economic resilience through the Great Depression and America had not, the United States was more favorably disposed toward working with the socialist behemoth on equal terms. Their budding friendship was temporarily strained by Stalin's decision to sign a nonaggression pact with Hitler in 1939. Americans actively supported the beleaguered Chinese National government in its failed efforts to prevent conquest of Manchuria (northern China). When Hitler invaded Russia in 1941 and Japan attacked Pearl Harbor a few months later, the three superpowers-to-be suddenly and quite unexpectedly found themselves on the same winning side in World War II.

The story of how these three World War II allies evolved into a nuclear triangle is the great diplomatic saga of our time.

MAJOR INCIDENTS

Outbreak of the Cold War and U.S.–PRC Tensions

On March 12, 1947, President Harry Truman addressed a joint session of Congress and requested $400 million to support regimes in Greece and Turkey against Soviet-backed insurrections. Without explicitly naming the Soviet Union, Truman declared:

> It would be an unspeakable tragedy if these countries, which have struggled so long against overwhelming odds, should lose the victory for which they sacrificed so much. Collapse of free institutions and loss of independence would be disastrous not only for them but for the world. Discouragement and possibly failure would quickly be the lot of neighboring peoples striving to maintain their freedom and independence. (McCormick 1986, 59)

With that statement, all pretense of cordial postwar relations with the Soviet Union was dropped and the Cold War began in earnest. The 1945–1947 period had witnessed the "gradual disengagement" of the Soviet Union from its Cold War alliance with the United States (Ulam 1971, 102). Fueled by a persistent fear of invasion from Europe, Soviet leaders acted to consolidate control over the Eastern European territories liberated by the Red Army in the closing months of World War II. The response from the West was slow; the Truman administration held out a great deal of hope for the United Nations to act as a vehicle for restoring postwar order.

Soviet attitudes toward the United Nations were disturbing. The "Baruch Plan" to bring all nuclear weapons under international control was rejected by the Soviets in 1946, as were countless resolutions in the Security Council, where the Soviet veto prevented action. Americans deeply resented this frustration of a great cause and began to question Soviet commitment to peaceful coexistence. The fact that Stalin was carrying out an extraordinarily intense reindustrialization program at the time did little to comfort the West.

Soviet forces and pro-Soviet leaders in East Germany became alarmed during 1948 at the collapse of the East German mark specifically and the vulnerability of the economy generally. In response, Soviet forces were dispatched to seal off West Berlin from Western products and prevent emigration by rail or road. The United States then embarked on an eighteen-month airlift that supplied so much food and other materials that prices for the goods fell below East Berlin levels. The worst fears of Soviet intentions were confirmed, and events demonstrated the importance of American leadership, technology, and boldness. The Soviet decision not to shoot down the aircraft also illustrated the limits to Soviet power and belligerence.

At that time, U.S. policy was heavily influenced by the thoughts of George Kennan, a senior expert on Russia, who coined the word *containment*. Kennan's call for diplomatic maneuvering to undermine the Soviet bloc suggested ways to pull apart the East European coalition through selective pressure, enticements, and determined resoluteness. He added the recommendation to act quickly to shore up collapsing pro-U.S. governments in Western Europe by providing massive economic aid and a strong military presence. In 1948, the Marshall Plan aid from the United States, which amounted to some $12 billion over five years, became available to Western Europe. In 1949, the United States helped to form the North Atlantic Treaty Organization (NATO), a military alliance aimed at preventing further Soviet expansion in Europe. NATO members moved quickly to restore German sovereignty and military might, and thousands of American soldiers were deployed to Germany. The Soviets responded by organizing the Warsaw Pact and maintaining a large military force in the East European theater.

In September 1949, the Soviet Union detonated its first atomic weapon, thereby ending the U.S. nuclear monopoly. The effect of this event was primarily psychological, in that the Soviets then lacked the means to deliver the weapon to a target. It was at this time that the U.S.–Soviet nuclear arms race began, however.

The Chinese Revolution in 1949 represented the culmination of a fifteen-year Communist insurrection that had weathered assassinations, mass arrests, a "Long March" to regroup forces, and Japanese invasion. Mao Zedong received Soviet support, although he had sought American backing, and almost immediately turned to the Soviet Union once victory was achieved. The Soviets responded by providing large numbers of military, economic, and industrial advisors, whose aim was the establishment of a large-scale industrial plant in China and the inclusion of the Chinese Communist Party in the Soviet-dominated Comintern—the umbrella organization of all Communist parties worldwide. Mao was quick to embrace Soviet support and formed what appeared to be a united front against imperialist capitalism. For its part, the United States denounced the Cultural Revolution and preserved formal diplomatic ties with the exiled Nationalist government, now based on the island of Taiwan.

The formation of what appeared to be a united Communist bloc covering the entire Eurasian continent from Warsaw to Beijing gave a special urgency to the U.S. containment strategy. The document designated NSC-68 took the original ideas of Kennan and tilted them toward a blatantly military strategy of direct confrontation (Gaddis & Diebel 1987, 6). The result was a readiness on the part of the United States to respond to Soviet "mischief" with proportional force. This primarily reactive policy prompted U.S. interventions in Korea, Vietnam, and Cuba over the next fifteen years.

The jury is still out on the question of who started the Cold War. Soviet behavior in Eastern Europe can easily be interpreted as aggressive, especially when combined with Soviet support for the Western European Communist parties that came close to taking power in the late 1940s. Given Soviet apprehensions about the vulnerability of the USSR's western borders, however, the policies are easy to explain and even justify. From the Soviet perspective, U.S. attempts to shape the world through the United Nations, the Marshall Plan, and the rearming of Germany seemed no less threatening. After all, the United States had delayed its entry into the European theater by two years in World War II (Soviets expected an American landing by 1942), it had detonated an atomic weapon and in the process cut the Soviets out of the peace process in the Far East, and it had participated in an invasion of the Soviet Union in an attempt to reverse the Bolshevik Revolution.

Much as in a family feud, the question of who started the conflict may be immaterial once the fight is on. We can, however, gain some interesting insights into the nature of the balance of power. One can easily argue that when two powers exist on the world stage without rival, they will tend to fear each other and therefore each will protect itself against the other (Waltz 1979). Once this process has begun, it is nearly impossible to distinguish "prudent preparations for potential conflict" on the one hand, from "openly hostile actions" on the other. One cannot tell by looking at it whether a nuclear missile is "offensive" or "defensive" after all.

Cold War I: 1949–1962

With the stage set for an enduring three-way conflict among the United States, the Soviet Union, and China, all three nations were preparing for a possible outbreak of hostilities. On June 25, 1950, equipped with Soviet-made weapons and supported politically by China, North Korean forces crossed the postwar dividing line of the 38th parallel to invade and ultimately annex the U.S. ally South Korea. The United States called for multilateral action against the North Koreans, which was organized in the United Nations (the Soviet delegation was boycotting the Security Council to protest the continued occupation of the China seat by the Taiwanese Nationalists and so was not able to veto the proposal). American ships were already on their way and within days began pushing back North Korean forces, which had taken control of roughly seven-eighths of the total South Korean territory. General Douglas MacArthur led the counteroffensive and, with the dramatic invasion at Inchon behind the front lines, succeeded in pushing back the invaders to the original frontier by late September. After MacArthur's demand for surrender went unheeded, the General Assembly authorized the invasion of North Korea by UN forces.

With the tables turned, the North Korean forces quickly fell back until the UN armies threatened to enter China, Korea's neighbor. Despite Chinese threats not to approach the border, UN forces came within miles of China and prompted the People's Liberation Army to enter the fray. Chinese intervention in the Korean War raised the very real possibility of full-scale world war in late 1950. MacArthur was sacked by President Truman precisely because he had ignored Truman's warnings to avoid accidental escalation. The front moved back into South Korean territory and eventually stabilized near the 38th parallel. Peace talks dragged on as both sides hoped for a military breakthrough. An armistice was eventually signed on July 27, 1953, after some 450,000 casualties on the South Korean side, of which 150,000 were Americans, and an estimated 2 million casualties on the North Korean/Chinese side (Chai 1972, 86).

In the beginning of the Korean War, U.S. ships were maneuvered into the Formosa Straits between mainland China and Taiwan to discourage would-be aggression by the PRC against the Nationalist government on the island. Throughout the 1950s and 1960s, both governments remained adamant in their claims that the other side had no right to govern any part of China. The United States repeatedly acted to prevent aggression, but by so doing precipitated bellicose responses from Beijing. The U.S.–Taiwan Mutual Defense Assistance Agreement of 1951 confirmed China's fears that the United States sought domination of the entire Asian continent from this foothold (Camilleri 1980, 32). With the formation of the South-East Asian Treaty Organization (SEATO), which encircled China, Beijing had sufficient evidence to seek a preemptive strike to reassert its control over the region.

China began shelling some of the Taiwanese fortresses on the islands in the Formosa Straits in late 1954. In response, the United States demanded a cessation of hostilities, implicitly threatening U.S. intervention with atomic weapons. This U.S. policy of "brinkmanship" surfaced again in 1958 after Chinese shelling was renewed. The Chinese, meanwhile, were ambivalent. In 1956, China declared its interest in improved relations with the West in the context of the Third World Bandung Conference. The goal of disengaging the United States from the region had clearly failed, but concerns about precedents and appearances prevented a public capitulation on the issue. The result was simmering Sino–American hostility, which was exacerbated by the U.S. entry into the Vietnam War in the mid-1960s.

During the 1950s, the U.S.–Soviet Cold War was in full swing. Although the Eisenhower administration offered tentative olive branches (his "Open Skies" proposal would have permitted free access by each nation's reconnaissance aircraft to the other's airspace), confrontational rhetoric dominated the debate. John Foster Dulles, the U.S. secretary of state, strongly advocated a "perimeter containment" strategy, which led to the formation of numerous regional alliances (containment) in areas surrounding the Soviet Union. Minor skirmishes were to be treated as major tests of resolve. The enemy was seen as an insidious, pervasive, single-minded force bent on world domination. This perspective was codified in the 1957 "Eisenhower Doctrine" declaring U.S. support for any victim of "armed aggression from any country controlled by international Communism" (Spanier 1988, 101). We should note, however, that U.S. intervention stopped short of helping nations already within the Soviet sphere, such as Hungary in 1956, where an anti-Soviet uprising was quelled with tanks.

The Soviets, on their side, viewed any American efforts at self-defense as inherently provocative. The rearmament of Germany beginning in 1950, the establishment of anti-Soviet alliances, the dramatic era of the Korean War–U.S. military buildup, and the detonation of the hydrogen bomb in 1952 all seemed to convey the attitude that the United States was preparing to conquer the world. With the economic aid provided to Western Europe in the context of European integration and the isolation of the Soviet economy, Moscow had evidence that the United States also aimed to cripple the socialist world financially.

By 1960, Americans were close to panic following a chain of Soviet achievements: the Soviet detonation of a hydrogen bomb in 1953, the test of the first intercontinental ballistic missile in 1957, and the shocking success of the Sputnik satellite in 1957. Fidel Castro's successful revolution in Cuba in 1959 prompted the United States to intervene in what would be later called the "perfect failure"—the Bay of Pigs. A group of U.S.-backed Cuban exiles attempted an amphibious invasion to overthrow Castro's regime, only to be captured at great public embarrassment to the Kennedy administration (Higgins 1987). The downing of a U–2 reconnaissance aircraft in 1960 scuttled an important peace conference being planned at the time, and the Berlin Wall crisis of 1961 severely tested the mettle of newly elected President John F. Kennedy.

This is not to say that the entire period was a catastrophe. On the contrary, many felt that with the death of Joseph Stalin in 1953, his successor Nikita Khrushchev would bring a new warmth to U.S.–Soviet relations. A number of early summits and agreements confirmed this hope. Khrushchev became the first Soviet leader to visit the United States when he attended a summit there in 1959. Talks concerning the disposition of Germany continued throughout the decade, albeit with no resolution. American intervention to prevent the fall of Egypt's left-leaning Gamel Nasser during the 1956 war with Israel did much to convince Third World revolutionaries that the United States was capable of impartiality.

The culmination of these Cold War tensions was also the crucible for change. The Cuban Missile Crisis, which took place over a two-week period in October 1962, brought the two superpowers to the brink of full-scale nuclear confrontation (see Case 4). Kennedy estimated at the height of the crisis that the chances of all-out war were "between one out of three and even" (Allison 1999, 1). Ostensibly an attempt by the Soviet Union to offset the tremendous American advantage in nuclear weaponry, the deployment of Soviet medium-range nuclear missiles in Cuba was deemed provocative by the Kennedy administration, and their removal became the object of a tense confrontation. The Soviets demanded, after stonewalling for a week, U.S. assurance that Cuba would never again be attacked and that U.S. weapons deployed in Turkey would be dismantled. Kennedy placed a naval blockade around the island in an attempt to buy time and prevent completion of the missile project, only to find that by day 13 the missiles were apparently operational. An American reconnaissance aircraft was shot down over Cuba, and the United States prepared to implement plans for an all-out attack and invasion against Cuba. Only at the last moment did word come from Moscow, in the form of conflicting cables, that the Soviets would accept a settlement.

While the world breathed a sigh of relief, the immediacy of nuclear war led leaders on both sides of the Cold War to seek new arrangements and agreements to prevent a serious confrontation from happening again. From 1963 through 1979, the United States and the Soviets (later joined by the Chinese) entered a period of relative "détente" or relaxation of tensions. Although the Vietnam War interrupted this trend, the pattern is nonetheless visible (Stoessinger 1990, 207).

Détente I: 1963–1979

Almost as soon as the Cuban Missile Crisis was over, Kennedy and Khrushchev (soon to be replaced by Lyndon Johnson and Leonid Brezhnev) began to build bridges. The "hotline" was established in 1963 as a permanent communication link between the United States and the Soviet Union (although a Norwegian's plow once severed it!), and the problem of rapid communication in times of crisis was essentially solved. An above-ground nuclear Test Ban Treaty was also signed, ending the environmentally catastrophic practice of testing nuclear weapons in the atmosphere.

Perhaps the most significant development during this period, aside from the gradual rapprochement between East and West, was the severing of relations between erstwhile comrades in the Soviet Union and the PRC. Although the Sino–Soviet alliance had clearly been as much a marriage of convenience as an ideological alliance, the breakup largely resulted from differences in philosophy and priority. Mao's revolutionaries had long placed Third World liberation ahead of all other international objectives and did not hesitate to burn bridges with the United States in their efforts to liberate colonies and spread socialism. The Soviet Union, on the other hand, had learned that it was partly dependent on Western support and goodwill to succeed in the world and was inclined to favor warmer relations. This difference in attitude became more pronounced after the Cuban Missile Crisis, when China found itself allied with more and more radical regimes in the Third World as decolonization moved into full swing and as the Soviets mended fences with the West.

Another key factor in the rupture was China's resentment of the influence exerted on its political and economic life by a Soviet Union long intent on reproducing itself. Soviet economic advisors urged Chinese leaders to implement a full-scale industrialization program based on steel, machines, and other heavy industry. This plan collided with the largely agrarian context in which the Chinese Revolution had flourished. The Great Leap Forward, a program of intense modernization of the Chinese economy, was initiated as much to achieve economic objectives as to assert Chinese autonomy. Furthermore, Mao objected to the rather tentative Soviet reforms under Khrushchev, which introduced more market-oriented policies. Chinese leaders felt that the Soviets had essentially sold out the revolution and that China alone held the torch of true socialism.

In 1962, Mao declared that the leaders of the Soviet Union were now "revisionists"—a withering attack from an ideological perspective that aimed at undermining Soviet leadership of international communism. In 1963, China condemned the Test Ban Treaty, which pointedly left it out as a "non-nuclear power." In 1964, the country tested its first atomic weapon, as if to thumb its nose at what it saw as a U.S.–Soviet alliance forming against it (Yahuda 1982, 30). By the late 1960s, the Soviets and Chinese engaged in border skirmishes that threatened to escalate as the Soviets spoke of preemptive strikes against Chinese nuclear installations. Ultimately, it was the United States that intervened to defuse the conflict.

The Vietnam War created new tension in what by the mid-1960s was clearly a three-way relationship. American support for the South Vietnamese government deeply troubled China, although China's relations with the North Vietnamese were cool at best, stemming from Hanoi's rejection of Chinese claims on Vietnamese territory. The Soviet Union, having supported Ho Chi Minh and the North Vietnamese revolution, was forced to provide support for China again throughout the Vietnam War. China was thus in the enviable position of watching its two enemies fight it out with each other, all the while hoping the violence could be contained to a modest level. During this period of relative security, the Cultural Revolution was begun to purify China's society of Western influences, although the result was the elimination of many of the nation's most accomplished intellectuals. The events so disgusted

Western observers that Chou En-Lai felt forced to render a weak explanation six years later on the occasion of Henry Kissinger's first visit to China (Kissinger 1979, 751).

The escalation of U.S. involvement in Vietnam from a handful of troops and advisors in 1964 to more than 500,000 personnel by 1969 was so gradual that it never, in and of itself, constituted a serious threat to global stability. It was not until the war began to wane, following Lyndon Johnson's decision in 1968 to begin troop withdrawals, that uncertainty entered the picture. Richard Nixon's attacks on Cambodia; the "Vietnamization" of the war, through which poorly motivated South Vietnamese soldiers were put in charge of the fighting; the popular unrest at home; and the on again-off again peace talks in Paris combined to give the closing years of the Vietnam War an unreal dimension that was separate from the "real" world of superpower diplomacy. An illustration of this was Beijing's crucial invitation to the United States to send a high-level representative in 1971. Henry Kissinger went to Pakistan and secretly on to China (absent on the pretense of catching the flu!), where preparations were made for Nixon's historic trip. All of this activity took place against the backdrop of intensified American air attacks in North Vietnam and a secret invasion of Cambodia.

Nixon's visit to China came in late February 1972 and resulted in a rather ambiguously worded statement known as the Shanghai Communique. The statement pledged an effort toward normalization of relations and supported the notion of "One China," although it left unclear who should govern this entity—the PRC or Taiwan (Kissinger 1979, 1085). Nixon's visit to China was followed in May by the first-ever visit by an American president to Moscow, where the Strategic Arms Limitation Talks (SALT I) were accepted in principle. Each of these agreements came in spite of ongoing disputes between the superpowers over conflicts with China, India, and Pakistan; between North and South Vietnam (although the Paris Peace Accords ended U.S. involvement in the war in January 1973); between Israel and Arab nations (Anwar Sadat expelled Soviet advisors from Egypt in July 1972, five years after they had supported his country during the Six-Day War); and in Cambodia and elsewhere.

The period of détente was perhaps best known for the general warming of relations between all Western nations and the East. Willy Brandt, Chancellor of West Germany during the mid-1970s, established solid ties with the German Democratic Republic to the East (see Case 1). The Helsinki Accords were signed in 1975 and pledged all European nations, East and West, to safeguard human rights and civil liberties. The United States, under Jimmy Carter, continued these trends by strengthening the arms control agreements made under SALT I and extending full diplomatic recognition to the PRC, now under the leadership of Western-oriented Deng Hsiao Ping in 1979. In short, there seemed to be every reason to hope that the United States had established an era of understanding and cooperation.

Cold War II: 1979–1985

The year 1980 stands out as a critical turning point in the Cold War because it was in January of that year that the Soviet Union for the first time invaded a neutral country with its own troops. It would be another nine years before the troops were withdrawn, and during this period East–West relations slipped back into Cold War patterns.

Following the Afghanistan invasion, Jimmy Carter declared, "My opinion of the Russians has changed more drastically in the last week than in the previous two and a half years" (Stoessinger 1990, 232). Soviet motives for the invasion remain difficult to understand, although the immediate reason was to shore up an embattled ally in a strategic region. The fall of the Shah of Iran in 1979 had facilitated the spread of radical Islamic fervor throughout the region and jeopardized Russia's long-term quest for a warm-water port, access to oil reserves, and proximity to Pakistan and India. Perhaps also the Soviets estimated that the benefits of U.S. rapprochement were at a zenith and could only go downhill. The Soviet Union imposed martial law in Poland in response to worker unrest, and with the election of President Ronald Reagan in late 1980, détente was over. The Carter Doctrine, which pledged U.S. action against any attempt by an "outside power" to control Middle East oil, was the new agenda. (The Carter Doctrine later formed the basis for George H. W. Bush's Gulf War actions.)

The Reagan administration chose this time to strengthen U.S. power at home and to improve ties with Beijing abroad. Sino–American relations were never better. China imposed diplomatic sanctions against Moscow and joined the United States in its containment of Soviet expansionism (Stoessinger 1990, 106). Reagan expanded the arms buildup begun by Carter, even at the cost of an overwhelming fiscal deficit, and engaged in military interventions in Nicaragua, Lebanon, and Afghanistan. SALT II was abandoned and Reagan's aggressive rhetoric ("evil empire," "plan for Armageddon") alarmed Europeans without chasing away their support. Margaret Thatcher and Helmut Kohl were united in condemning Soviet aggression and, acting against extraordinary public pressure, permitted the deployment of a new generation of medium-range nuclear missiles in Europe.

Reagan offered rather unrealistic arms control proposals, which resulted in a stalemate and ultimately a Soviet walkout at the Strategic Arms Reduction Talks (START) and Intermediate-Range Nuclear Forces (INF) talks. The Strategic Defense Initiative (SDI) was proposed in 1983 with the goal of enveloping the United States in a protective shield of high-tech weapons aimed at incoming Soviet missiles. Reagan proposed repeatedly to abandon the research program in exchange for deep unilateral Soviet arms cuts.

It was not until the emergence of Mikhail Gorbachev on the world scene that Cold War II began to change course.

Détente II: 1985–1991

The story of the second wave of détente, culminating in the collapse of the Soviet Union itself, is probably familiar and so bears only a cursory review. Suffice it to say that Reagan embraced the new, youthful, and apparently open-minded Soviet leader with open arms. He noted that Gorbachev was not a typical Communist, but rather someone with whom the United States could work (Nathan & Oliver 1989, 483). A number of summits were arranged, and by 1987 the INF Treaty, the first-ever arms reduction agreement, was signed.

Strategic arms talks took much longer to resolve, with Gorbachev repeatedly asking the United States to abandon SDI unilaterally. It was not until the Soviet empire was crumbling during the Bush administration's watch that a far-reaching strategic arms reduction treaty was signed. Before the ink was dry (and prior to ratification by the Senate), a new, more profound agreement was signed with the new Russian Republic under the leadership of Boris Yeltsin. Other agreements to dramatically cut chemical weapons stockpiles and ban their production, implement significant cuts in conventional (nonnuclear) weapons deployed across Europe, and form an eventual U.S.–Soviet "alliance" against Iraq in the Persian Gulf War of 1990–1991 demonstrated an entirely new era of cooperation. With the Soviets leaving Afghanistan and releasing control over all East European states in 1989, thereby permitting the reunification of Germany in 1990, the Cold War was well and truly over. Rehabilitation of the defeated erstwhile enemy became the pressing issue of peacetime, much as it was after the defeat of Nazi Germany and Imperial Japan in 1945.

What was the Chinese orientation to the Americans and Russians in this new context? The well-known Tiananmen Square massacres of 1989 dealt a serious blow to the emerging democracy movement that had swept across China under Deng. The immediate result was the imposition of sanctions against China by the United States and Western Europe, although most of these were either allowed to lapse or reversed by 1992. Chinese relations with the Soviet Union improved significantly during the Gorbachev era. The Soviets supported a UN-mediated withdrawal of Soviet-backed Vietnam from China-backed Cambodia—a process that has not entirely succeeded at this writing. A Sino–Soviet summit took place in 1989 (the first since 1956) as "Russia wooed and China cooed" (Rourke 1990, 44). China became concerned about the closeness of U.S.–Soviet relations during the Gulf War but stopped short of vetoing a critical UN resolution permitting armed intervention against Iraq.

Post–Cold War Era: After 1992

Since the breakup of the Soviet Union in 1991, the strategic triangle has been far more difficult for analysts to understand. Economic factors seem to predominate now. It is thus increasingly difficult to know which pair of countries is experiencing strain or harmony because trade and investment not only serve as indicators of good relations but also generate friction and can be used as potential weapons. Russia received billions in aid from the West, particularly through the International Monetary Fund (too much, according to both Russian and IMF accounts). This largesse generated considerable resentment, however: In Russia, nationalists and Communists objected to the "neoimperialism" implicit in this economic dependence; in the West, officials grew increasingly impatient with the inefficiencies and corruption of the Yeltsin regime. For China, economics has become the focal point of national planning, which has produced annual growth rates of close to 10 percent for much of the 1990s. Maintaining a strong trade relationship with the United States has significantly helped China control its balance of payments. Americans have shown increasing resentment of the unbalanced trade relationship with China, and Congress resisted granting the country "normal trade relations" status until 2000. Considerable doubt remains as to whether China will become a full-fledged member of the World Trade Organization. China's mixed record in human rights further complicates U.S. willingness to work closely with Beijing.

On the security front, the relationship among the three countries is also ambiguous. Officially, relations are good, but at the same time each country is acutely aware of the potential threat that the others pose. Consequently, the game is more "shadow boxing" than outright rivalry. Each country is engaged in efforts to enhance its military preparedness, although Russia is clearly lagging in this regard. During the 1990s, China detonated a number of nuclear warheads, resisted cooperating in the nonproliferation regime, openly threatened Taiwan's election campaign in 1999 (to which the United States at times responded with military deployments of its own), and was involved in illicit military technology transfers—both by spying on U.S. nuclear facilities and by selling technology to Pakistan and other Asian countries. The United States has maintained high levels of defense spending in the past ten years, although it has also dismantled a number of bases and units and has moved forward to implement START II nuclear weapons reductions (along with Russia, although both have encountered resistance in their respective legislatures). In addition the United States has continued to improve weapons based on stealth technology and has undertaken a new initiative to improve its antiballistic missile defense capability, purportedly to protect against isolated attacks from rogue states such as North Korea. Dramatic U.S. support of regional military intervention, particularly in Yugoslavia (both Bosnia and Kosovo), was resisted by Russia. Perhaps most directly threatening was the decision taken by the United States in 1995 to expand NATO by including Poland, Hungary, and the Czech Republic, a move that met with considerable Russian opposition ("Eastern Cheers" 1997, 5). Yeltsin spoke of a "cold peace," and at a summit meeting in mid-2000, both Russian and Chinese leaders warned the United States of the dangers of generating tensions through its antiballistic missile defense plans ("At CSCE Summit" 1995, 8).

Although it is too early to say that the United States is becoming isolated by Russia and China and that the latter are forging a strong alliance, those developments would hardly be surprising. Realists would predict that the second- and third-ranking powers in any international system would naturally unite to offset the power of the preeminent state. As China becomes more economically powerful and Russia regains its financial footing, we can expect to see both act with considerably less deference to Washington's wishes. In the spring of 2001, for example, the United States deployed one of many spy planes along the Chinese coast to intercept various electronic communication signals. Unlike in past incidents, the Chinese air force intercepted one plane and accidentally made contact, forcing it to land in Chinese territory. Rather than return the plane and simply write off the incident, Beijing opted instead to castigate the United States for recklessly violating its territory and proceeded to detain the crew and dismantle the aircraft. After weeks of negotiation, the United States agreed to issue a "quasi-apology" for the incident and the crew was released. The plane was later returned—in several crates. . . .

The September 11, 2001 terrorist attacks altered the superpower relationships, at least temporarily. Both Moscow and Beijing made it very clear that they viewed the attacks as a threat to civilization itself and pledged unlimited support for the United States. They all joined in the war against terrorism, with the United States leading the way in Afghanistan. Except for a United States decision to withdraw from the Anti-Ballistic Missile (ABM) Treaty, which was greeted with dismay by Russian President Vladimir Putin in early 2002, there are few signs that the latest era of good feelings has diminished significantly. The decision in early 2003 to invade Iraq damaged U.S. relations with Russia and China, both of which blocked a resolution approving the action in the UN Security Council. The result was a clear rapprochement between Moscow and Brussels, which followed a very friendly meeting between Vladimir Putin and Hu Jintao, the new Chinese premier. China, for its part, has continued to object to U.S. support for the Taiwanese government— particularly military assistance. This said, China's membership in the World Trade Organization, beginning in 2001, along with Russia's imminent membership, are indicative of a generally positive relationship between the three major powers (*China Daily*, 2004). They are further united on fighting terrorism (the Bush administration has given Moscow considerable lee-way in its war in Chechnya) and limiting nuclear proliferation (China has actively worked to persuade North Korea to halt its drive to possess nuclear weapons—although there are rumors that it helped Pakistan and others obtain nuclear technology).

One could argue that the most serious threats to the relationship are economic. Russia's economic weakness continues to be a drain on the world economy and its indebtedness threatens to strain relations. For its part, China's remarkable economic growth is seen as both a serious challenge and an irresistible opportunity by Westerners in general and Americans in particular (*New York Times*, December 6, 2004, special Business Day issue). In this sense, the relationship between the superpowers bears some remarkable similarities to the interaction between the United States, Europe, and Japan—a mixture of economic rivalry and competition over global status, amid a generally nonviolent strategic backdrop—what Joseph Nye and Robert Keohane called "complex interdependence" (Keohane & Nye 2001).

THE BALANCE OF POWER TRIANGLE

As we mentioned, the balance of power theory assumes that major powers, in the pursuit of increased security and influence, will combine forces with other nations that share the same enemies. These alliances will shift frequently over time as different nations develop greater capacity to wage war and thereby become a new threat. Overall, no single country will rise above the rest, and every major power's essential identity will be preserved (or at least the basic number of major players will remain stable).

Does this pattern of behavior hold true in our case? First, we will discuss the nature of a three-way balance of power, usually referred to as tripolarity. Four alliance patterns are possible in a tripolar system, as illustrated in Figure 2.1:

MÉNAGE À TROIS

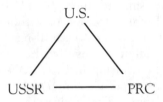

Example: Gorbachev Era

UNIT VETO

Example: 1962

MARRIAGE

Example: 1950s

ROMANTIC TRIANGLE

Example: 1972 (Nixon in China,
Nixon in Moscow)

————————————— Amity
- - - - - - - - - - - - - - - - - Hostility

Figure 2.1 The tripolar system's possible configurations
Source: Adapted from Lowell Dittmer, "The Strategic Triangle: A Critical Review." In J. Kim Ilpong, ed., *The Strategic Triangle* (New York: McGraw-Hill, 1987).

(1) a very cordial "ménage à trois," in which all major powers cooperate with one another; (2) the "unit veto" system, in which none of the players cooperates; (3) the intermediate stages of a "marriage," in which one player ("odd man out") is positioned against the other two; and (4) the "romantic triangle," in which one player ("pivot") has good relations with each of the others, which are antagonistic to each other (Dittmer 1987).

Figure 2.1 also gives examples of the possible alliances in a tripolar system. The "marriage" and "romantic triangle" arrangements have numerous examples and deserve more attention. Segal and the contributors to his volume (1982) generally credit China with best understanding the nature of the "triangle" and with taking the most active role in changing its nature over time. After all, it was China that attempted to mend fences with the Eisenhower administration and ultimately invited Nixon to Beijing. And it was China that severed relations with the Soviets against Moscow's wishes.

The United States demonstrated some diplomatic sophistication beginning in the mid-1960s, particularly during the Nixon administration, when it abandoned twenty years of ideological principles in favor of an improved strategic position by warming up to China and working with the Soviets (perhaps trusting them both too much). One can hardly imagine two more unlikely individuals to meet with Chinese leaders in Beijing than Richard Nixon and Ronald Reagan, both passionate Cold Warriors from the outset!

Under Gorbachev, the Soviet Union maneuvered itself into something close to a pivot position when it continued to work closely with the Chinese during the Tienanmen Square period as U.S.–Chinese relations cooled significantly. This move represented a departure for the Soviets, who tended to view the "China Factor" with some contempt—particularly in the presplit days when the Chinese were viewed as mere pupils.

CONCLUSION

By the 1960s, all superpowers were clearly cognizant of the tripolar dynamics in which they were enmeshed and made some effort to jockey for the best position— namely, the pivot role. Barring diplomatic success, each player at least attempted to avoid being locked in the least desirable position—"odd man out." For example, one can attribute China's eagerness to open diplomatic relations with the United States in the late 1960s to Beijing's perception of significantly improved U.S.–Soviet relations and the fear of being "left out"—even if its actions resulted in giving extraordinary influence to the United States. Likewise, Gorbachev knew that combining his good relations with the United States with improved ties to China could ultimately put him in the pivot position, although this scenario never materialized.

Today, the relationship between the three is beginning to resemble a more normal, nonviolent rivalry where the likelihood of war between any of the three is increasingly unlikely. This is not to say that military posturing is irrelevant. All three states are working to upgrade their strategic military capability. But overall, rivalry is expressed more in terms of trade, diplomatic status, regional influence, and so forth. Russia continues to reach out to its neighbors and resists the expansion of NATO, albeit in subdued ways. China for its part is beginning to form economic pacts with countries in the region (*New York Times*, November 30, 2004, A5). This said, neither is attempting to forge new military alliances or deploy troops overseas—although this describes the policy of the United States which in recent years must be seen as the most aggressive and expansionist of the three.

DEBATE TOPIC

Ultimately, the key issue in this case study is whether international politics is best approached from a pragmatic, unsentimental perspective (or whether values and ideology should play a part).

PRO

Those who support a realist approach have made the following points: (1) "Ideologies change—interests don't." It is best to always be practical because beliefs and attitudes might change at any moment. (2) Ideology gets in the way of useful relationships—both economic and strategic. (3) Ideology can drive a state to greater degrees of violence and aggression than mere pragmatism.

CON

Those who challenge the "balance of power" make the following arguments: (1) The point of politics should be to make life better for individuals; engagement with human rights violators is therefore wrong. (2) International relations based only on convenience are inherently unstable and unpredictable, carrying a greater risk of violence. (3) International affairs is evolving toward a more principled approach based on law; the balance of power means regression.

THINKING THEORETICALLY

Not all realists agree. There is a significant split among realists—going back to the 1970s—with respect to the need to appreciate the subtleties of diplomacy and strategic choice. Traditional realists such as Hans Morgenthau and Henry Kissinger argue that diplomats make a tremendous difference, and when faced with complex situations can turn a crisis into either calamity or triumph, depending on their skills. Structural realists generally dismiss the importance of individuals. Further, they question whether it is necessary to know much at all about the major powers on the international scene, except their relative capabilities.

The long history of the tripolar balance of power between the United States, USSR/Russia, and the PRC should provide a useful test of these two approaches. In fact, it is clear that knowing the nuclear weapons capability of each country can allow us to predict when they will behave confrontationally, seek alliances, or strategically pit one adversary against another. Then again, structural realism might just have easily predicted a longstanding alliance between the Russians and Chinese since together they could never quite match American capabilities. The fact that Nixon and Kissinger were able to exacerbate the split between them during the 1970s can probably best be attributed to the clever maneuvers the United States undertook. It is perhaps not surprising that Henry Kissinger behaved in ways that were consistent with his own version of realist theory—and in turn proved himself correct.

QUESTIONS TO CONSIDER

1. What does the future hold for this great power triangle? With the demise of the Soviet Union and the end of East–West antagonism in the European theater, is China the ultimate "odd man out" from here on? Or will the United States now play that role as China and Russia strive to balance power?

2. To what extent were forces other than balancing power significant in determining alignment choices by the superpowers? Did ideology make a difference? What about perceptions?

3. To what extent were the needs of humanity served by the tripolar relationship? Were people on the planet safer? More free? Better fed? What does this tell us about politics and morality?

WEBSITES

Several universities and NGOs maintain websites with background material on security-related matters.

George Washington University National Security Archive: **glws.circ.gwu.edu/~nsarchiv**

American Foreign Policy Council: **www.afpc.org**

National Center for Policy Analysis: **www.ncpa.org**

Center for American–Eurasian Studies and Relations: **www.eurasiacenter.org**

REFERENCES

Allison, Graham. *Essence of Decision: Explaining the Cuban Missile Crisis*, 2nd ed. (New York: Addison Wesley Longman, 1999).

"At CSCE Summit, Yeltsin Warns of 'Cold Peace.'" *Current Digest of the Post-Soviet Press* 46 #49 (January 4, 1995): 8–9.

Camilleri, Joseph. *Chinese Foreign Policy: The Maoist Era and Its Aftermath* (Seattle: University of Washington Press, 1980).

Chai, Winberg. *The Foreign Relations of the People's Republic of China* (New York: Putnam's Sons, 1972).

China Daily. "WTO Performance called 'outstanding.'" New York, November 17, 2004, p. 11.

Dittmer, Lowell. "The Strategic Triangle: A Critical Review" in J. Kim Ilpong, ed., *The Strategic Triangle* (New York: MacGraw-Hill, 1987): 17–33.

"Eastern Cheers, Russian Jeers, American Silence." *Bulletin of the Atomic Scientists* (January/February 1997): 5–7.

Gaddis, John Lewis, and Terry L. Diebel, eds. *Containing the Soviet Union* (New York: Pergamon-Brassey's, 1987).

Higgins, Trumbull. *The Perfect Failure: Kennedy, Eisenhower and the CIA at the Bay of Pigs* (New York: Norton, 1987).

Keohane, Robert O. and Joseph Nye, Jr., *Power and Interdependence*, 3rd ed. New York: Longman, 2001.

Kissinger, Henry. *White House Years* (Boston: Little, Brown, 1979).

McCormick, James M., ed. *A Reader in American Foreign Policy* (Itasca, IL: Peacock, 1986).

Nathan, James A., and James K. Oliver. *United States Foreign Policy and World Order*, 4th ed. (Glenview, IL: Scott, Foresman, 1989).

New York Times, November 30, 2004, A5.

New York Times, December 6, 2004, special Business Day issue.

Rourke, John T. *Making Foreign Policy: United States, Soviet Union, China* (Pacific Grove, CA: Brooks/Cole, 1990).

Segal, Gerald, ed. *The China Factor: Peking and the Superpowers* (New York: Holmes & Meier, 1982).

Spanier, John. *American Foreign Policy Since World War II*, 11th ed. (Washington, DC: Congressional Quarterly Press, 1988).

Stoessinger, John G. *Nations in Darkness: China, Russia, and America*, 5th ed. (New York: McGraw-Hill, 1990).

Ulam, Adam B. *The Rivals: America and Russia Since World War II* (New York: Viking, 1971).

Waltz, Kenneth. *Theory of International Politics* (Reading, MA: Addison-Wesley, 1979).

Yahuda, Michael. "China and the Great Power Triangle." In Segal, ed., *The China Factor* 26–41.

CASE 3

U.S. Role After the Cold War: The National Interest

INTRODUCTION

"National interest" is an incredibly elastic concept—capable of stretching to encompass any potential foreign threats for which an overzealous internationalist wants to prepare. It can also shrink to cover only life-threatening dangers on your doorstep. Because of the concept's malleability, we could easily dismiss it as a mere rhetorical flourish. Beneath the rhetoric, however, lies a fundamental question of what really matters in American foreign policy. Drawing the line between vital interests and peripheral preoccupations is the great question of our time.

Historically, "national interest" has come to include increasingly more issues. In the early days of the nation-state, it was possible to say the national interest was nothing more than the monarch's interests: "I am the state," Louis XIV once declared to no one's objection. As states came to be based on popular sovereignty, however, the interests of the citizenry as a whole had to be taken into account. The happiness of the people—which included economic vitality, agricultural prosperity, a sense of confidence and security, and so forth—became the principal end of national policy. It even extended to the security of citizens living outside the territory of the state. Most powerful states have been quick to intervene—often militarily—when their citizens come under attack overseas (see Case 13). The most powerful ones even try to anticipate potential threats, taking steps to mitigate them in advance, perhaps by creating a "buffer zone" of friendly governments along the border or by moving troops overseas to facilitate quick deployment at great distances.

Each time a state expands its definition of the national interest, it must face a cost–benefit calculus: How much happiness and security do my people demand, and how much can they afford? Chances are high that no state will be able to do everything it takes to make its citizenry absolutely secure, so compromises are inevitable. In the history of the United States, decisions about these compromises have occasionally become a matter of broad and heated debate, as we will see.

KEY FIGURES
U.S. ROLE AFTER THE COLD WAR

Dwight D. Eisenhower   U.S. President, 1953–1961. He promoted an internationalist policy but generally eschewed the United Nations.

George H.W. Bush   U.S. President, 1989–1993. He involved the UN in U.S. policy more deeply than had past U.S. Presidents.

Bill Clinton   U.S. President, 1993–2001. He maintained the multilateralist policies of George Bush.

James Baker III   U.S. Secretary of State, 1989–1993. He cautioned George W. Bush against a unilateral, preemptive strike against Iraq.

George W. Bush   U.S. President, 2001–present. He has generally promoted a unilateralist approach.

Colin Powell   U.S. Secretary of State, 2001–2005. He warned George W. Bush of the risks involved in unilateral military operations.

Donald Rumsfeld   U.S. Secretary of Defense, 2001–2006. He promoted and directed the Iraq invasion.

Paul Wolfowitz   U.S. Deputy Secretary of Defense, 2001–present. He helped author the Defense Planning Guidance in 1992 under the first President Bush, calling for preemptive strikes against potential enemies, as opposed to mere containment of threats.

Richard (Dick) Cheney   U.S. Vice President, 2001–present. He consistently advocated preemptive strikes.

Charles Krauthammer   Syndicated columnist. He is known as a supporter of the "hegemonic imperative."

Ross Perot   Businessman, frequent presidential candidate, and supporter of the "national interest" approach.

Patrick Buchanan   Journalist, frequent presidential candidate, and supporter of the "national interest" approach.

Jesse Helms   U.S. Senator from North Carolina, 1972–2003, and Chairman of the Senate Foreign Relations Committee. He often opposed multilateralism.

Joseph Nye   Harvard University political scientist who has promoted multilateralism.

Bruce Russett   Yale University political scientist who advocates multilateralism.

THE "GREAT" DEBATE

Americans have not always accepted the U.S. role as leader of the free world. Prior to the entry of the United States into World War I, for example, most opinion makers in the country agreed that the United States should remain aloof from

European troubles. After the war, U.S. membership in the League of Nations and the establishment of a standing army were rejected by Congress. Meanwhile, the White House and State Department had grown attached to American leadership and repeatedly advanced its necessity. At the heart of this debate was the question of whether American idealism—its quest for peace and justice—should push the country into a leadership role in world affairs (exporting idealism, as it were) or whether it should avoid all "entangling alliances" (to use George Washington's phrase). This debate was ultimately resolved with the Japanese attack on Pearl Harbor.

After the collapse of the Berlin Wall, the dismantling of the Warsaw Pact, and the dissolution of the Soviet Union, the U.S. foreign policy establishment found itself without a clear purpose. The question of what to do in the next century gripped policy analysts in a dramatic way. Such publications as *Foreign Affairs*, *Foreign Policy*, *National Interest*, *National Review*, and the *Atlantic Monthly*, to name but a few (see also Kegley & Wittkopf 1992; Schmergel 1991; Lynn-Jones 1991; Lynn-Jones & Miller 1992), devoted considerable space to a single question: What should be the guiding principles of U.S. foreign policy in this new era? We will review the major points of this debate by organizing the various proposals into three general categories: the "national interest" approach, the "hegemonic imperative" school, and the "multilateralist" position.

NATIONAL INTEREST

The "national interest" position, often espoused by politicians seeking the votes of unemployed steel or textile workers, aims at defining national interest in narrow terms. John F. Kennedy's pledge on behalf of the American public in 1961 to "bear any burden" in the cause of freedom rings hollow to analysts who see a declining U.S. economy and an urban and even suburban social infrastructure in shambles, where problems of the outside world seem trivial at best. To the 1972 McGovern Democrats' call of "Come Home America," many neoconservatives add the refrain "America First." As put by Charles Krauthammer, "[T]he internationalist consensus is under renewed assault. The assault this time comes not only from the usual pockets of post-Vietnam liberal isolationism (e.g., the churches) but from a resurgence of 1930s-style conservative isolationism" (Krauthammer 1990/91, 23).

Republican Patrick Buchanan and Democrat Tom Harkin made "America First" a prominent campaign theme during the 1992 presidential election, and numerous analysts have written extensively about the need for relative retrenchment in U.S. foreign policy. Alan Tonelson argued that the George H. W. Bush administration's attachment to Cold War activism was misguided and neglected the simple fact that U.S. power must be founded on a strong domestic society and economy. "The contrast between American victories in the Cold War and the Gulf War, and growing domestic social and economic decay shows that the traditional benchmarks for evaluating United States foreign policy are sorely inadequate" (Tonelson 1992, 145). William Pfaff argued that, as the world system becomes more complex and unpredictable, U.S. capability will be based as much on inner strength and resistance to instability abroad as on the ability to project power beyond the country's borders (Pfaff 1990/91). Paul Kennedy and Arthur Taylor, in testimony on Capitol Hill, argued that the only way to stop the decline of U.S. strength is by redirecting resources from international commitments to domestic retooling and reinvigoration (U.S. Congress 1990).

Most national interest authors emphasize the need for the United States to withdraw from nonessential international obligations. The *Atlantic Monthly*'s July 1991 cover story criticized the failures of internationalism, which, in the authors' view, was out of step with the American public and had led to wasting billions of dollars on problems of only remote importance to the U.S. citizenry (Tonelson 1991). They urged a renewed emphasis on programs that directly benefit the United States, although they did not dismiss all international activities. "An interest-based foreign policy would tend to rule out economic initiatives deemed necessary for the international system's health if those initiatives wound up siphoning more wealth out of this country than they brought in" (Tonelson 1991, 38).

In the tradition of avoiding "entangling alliances" (Hendrickson 1992), the new national interest would exclude international commitments that involve long-term and open-ended obligations, on the grounds that these limit U.S. flexibility and self-reliance. Such analysts see no further need for our involvement in NATO given the dissolution of the Warsaw Pact, as well as U.S. maintenance of military bases across the world, and call for a large-scale withdrawal of troops. Furthermore, they question the merits of an overwhelming nuclear missile deterrent in the face of the collapse and democratization of the United States' principal nuclear adversary, the Soviet Union, and call for unilateral disarmament (Krasner 1989).

During the 1990s, the national interest position focused on U.S. involvement in UN activities and payment of dues to the agency. Following the gruesome deaths of U.S. marines in Somalia, Senator Jesse Helms of the Senate Foreign Relations Committee blocked U.S. participation in other UN missions (Sterling-Folker 1998, 287). Congressional leaders also blocked the payment of UN dues until the United States nearly lost its voting rights (Tessitore & Woolfson 1999, 300).

Some national interest advocates emphasize the need for reducing oil dependency and import dependency generally, while others focus on the need to control foreign investment flows into the country to preserve U.S. control of critical resources, industries, and even symbolic entities such as Rockefeller Plaza and the Seattle Mariners. Protectionism, investment controls, export promotion, and maintenance of an undervalued currency are among the international economic policies consistent with this approach.

Analysts who accept the national interest approach emphasize the primacy of American sovereignty; however, liberals and conservatives disagree on what in America needs fixing. Liberal neoisolationists stress repairing urban decay, alleviating poverty, fighting racism, and rebuilding schools. Neoconservatives, in contrast, seek reductions in government regulations and handouts to the poor, and a reversal of the decline of "family values." Conservatives dismiss liberal isolationism as merely a ploy "to spend the maximum amount of money on social programs at home and the minimum abroad" (Kristol 1990, 20).

Although the national interest approach seems particularly appealing during tough economic times, the Bush administration and liberal internationalists outside government argued strongly against it. Such retrenchment, so the logic goes, will take the United States down the well-worn path toward isolation, xenophobia, and ultimately the collapse of the modern world order. Richard Nixon argued that the choice between domestic resurgence and international activism is a false one. "We do not face a choice between dealing with domestic problems and playing an international role. Our challenge is to do both by setting realistic goals and by managing our limited resources" (Nixon 1992, 277–278). Antiisolationists argue that even a limited retrenchment from international obligations, whether collective or unilateral, could lead to an increase in America's insecurity as renegade states, reactionary dictatorships, and protectionism abroad flourish and undermine U.S. interests.

HEGEMONIC IMPERATIVE

Many feel that the United States is still, both by duty and by right, the leader of the free world. With the collapse of the Soviet Union, we no longer need to worry about an overwhelming threat to our security. But with that collapse go much of the order and stability of the international system and the risk of new, unforeseen dangers (Gaddis 1987; 1991). As pointed out by Chairman of the Joint Chiefs Colin Powell, none of the troop deployments during the George H. W. Bush administration (Panama, Persian Gulf, Somalia) were anticipated at the time of his inauguration—a fact that reinforces the need for the country to be prepared for threats to peace, no matter how remote they may seem (U.S. Congress 1992, 367).

Many like-minded authors argue that the United States has the capability to lead and lacks only the will. Joseph Nye, an antideclinist, disagrees with President Bush's lament that the United States lacks not the will but the wallet by saying that the reverse is true: In terms of what we can afford as a nation, we are far too tight-fisted in dealing with global problems (Nye 1990). Richard Cooper argued before Congress that the United States must not shrink from global responsibilities for fear of what it will cost (U.S. Congress 1990). Alexander Haig echoed the sentiment, pointing out that it is up to the executive to promote a domestic consensus about the need for American leadership abroad and then to act on that consensus (Haig 1991).

There is a further sense from many authors that the United States has the right not only to lead but also to act unilaterally. Although they pay some lip service to multilateral institutions, they imply that the United States has the best ideas, the strongest institutions, and the natural gifts required to create world order. Charles Krauthammer pointed out: "American preeminence is based on the fact that it is the only country with the military, diplomatic, political and economic assets to be a decisive player in any conflict in whatever part of the world it chooses to involve itself" (Krauthammer 1990/91, 24). Coupled with this assumption of preeminence comes a disdain for the cumbersome mechanisms of the United Nations and the assumption that the UN will never have effective enforcement powers. This tone has been criticized as vain "triumphalism."

During the 1990s, U.S. dominance came to be seen almost as a birthright. The Clinton administration worked to preserve U.S. power through a variety of maneuvers aimed at rewarding countries that had accepted a subordinate position and co-opting those that had not (Mastanduno 1997). The United States, furthermore, has returned to some old, romantic notions of spreading democracy worldwide (Ikenberry 1999). Foreign aid, military deployments, and other initiatives are increasingly designed to strengthen liberal regimes and punish autocrats. Many governments have begun to fear that the United States is "throwing its weight around" with no regard to the implications of its actions. This attitude was at the heart of the debate over UN authorization of the American attack on Iraq in 2003.

Some analysts suggest that the U.S. leadership role is merely an extension of old Cold War attitudes and behaviors, as if the Soviet Union had never collapsed. Richard Lugar declared, "Americans must demonstrate staying power and the ability to master and prolong the peace" (Lugar 1992). Many call for maintaining alliances, defense spending, and nuclear weapon arsenals at roughly constant levels in anticipation of future conflicts.

In their exuberance, some have gone so far as to declare the end of international conflict. With the end of the Cold War, so the thinking goes, we are at the conclusion of the grand struggle between liberalism and authoritarianism—the "end of history" itself (Fukuyama 1989). Given this situation, we may find ourselves well and truly in an age without the threat of global war. Naturally, some have steered clear of such dramatic predictions and contented themselves with pointing out the unique nature of America's position in the world, with a call for continued leadership and international engagement (Huntington 1989).

The "errors of endism" are probably obvious enough but bear repetition here. Sanders has warned that attachment to a "unipolar myth" will quickly lead to frustration by those who ignore the reality of the diffusion of power in the last few years. This frustration with America not always getting its way may in turn lead to nationalist retrenchment, with equally serious consequences (Sanders 1991).

The most extreme version of the presumption of American global leadership emerged in the 1980s from the Project for a New American Century led by William Kristol, a student of Leo Strauss. He was joined by Richard Perle, Paul Wolfowitz, Dick Cheney, and others who would feature prominently in the administration of George W. Bush (see below). Harking back to the words of Teddy Roosevelt, these writers emphasized the need for American "greatness." The United States should lead—not necessarily to make the country safer or the world better, but for the sake of leadership itself. As put by Anne Norton, "It is not threats that should incite war, but opportunity" (Norton 2004, 191). Rather than advocating cautious gradualism and prudence, this group called for quick, decisive blows that would establish American preeminence. It entails:

> . . . enthusiasm for innovation, for intervention, for utopias. Nothing can wait, everything must be done now. No one need be consulted, for local custom and established preferences must fall before the rational force of liberal (yes, liberal) values. Liberal values require not the consent of the governed, but the force of arms. (Norton 2004, 191)

We will see that this attitude has colored the Bush administration's bold initiatives in security affairs.

In economic affairs, the question is whether the United States is using its position of dominance for good or for ill. An established tradition in international relations literature holds that for the world to enjoy open markets and free flows of ideas and money across international borders, it takes a "hegemon." A hegemon, in this context, is a powerful, benevolent nation that can provide money, markets, and technology to weaker countries as an inducement to them to lower international barriers (Gilpin 1987). In 1944, the Bretton Woods system was set up by the United States and the United Kingdom as a framework for this sort of bargain. The United States was successful in persuading most nations of the world to join the pact but in the 1980s began increasingly to ignore its provisions.

In the 1990s, even though the U.S. economy was growing at the rate of nearly 4 percent per year, the Clinton administration adopted a fairly combative approach to international trade and economics generally. It cut back on foreign aid, negotiated the North American Free Trade Agreement (NAFTA), which took advantage of the United States' strong position relative to Canada and Mexico, and repeatedly pressured Japan to allow increased amounts of U.S. imports with specific targets for market shares in semiconductors, autos, and automobile parts (Mastanduno 1997). Although the United States concluded the Uruguay Round negotiations of the General Agreement on Tariffs and Trade (GATT) in 1994, it did so by employing very harsh tactics, threatening to pull out at several junctures if its demands were not met. The United States increasingly makes use of dispute settlement panels and threats of unilateral sanctions against what it considers unfair trading partners, even at the expense of security agreements (Maswood 1997, 534). Throughout, U.S. policymakers stress that they are merely trying to promote liberal economics through U.S. leadership—the essence of hegemony.

More subtle are the debates among would-be supporters of U.S. hegemony concerning the goals of U.S. leadership. On the one hand, some feel that U.S. internationalism should be firmly rooted in American idealism and that the nation should devote its energies to supporting and sustaining democracy and human rights. For example, candidate Bill Clinton argued for, among other things, sanctions against China for its repression of students in 1989; support for Somalis, Kurds, and Bosnians fighting against authoritarian enemies; and admission of Haitian refugees into the United States on humanitarian grounds (see also DLC 1991).

On the other hand, many feel that the United States need not be a crusader. Its international engagement should be based on a sort of expanded self-interest, they argue. A stable world order is good for America because it minimizes surprises, allows for methodical planning, and usually results in economic prosperity. The object of U.S. foreign policy should be to discourage instability by supporting the status quo, particularly where existing regimes are already pro-United States. Krauthammer and others stress that the great enemy is no longer an organized opposition but rather disorder itself. They emphasize the need to contain this "chaotic sphere" in international relations by controlling the spread of weapons, intervening in civil wars before they spread, maintaining existing troop deployments in an effort to respond more rapidly to crises, and otherwise taking on the burden of enforcing international law—unilaterally if necessary (Krauthammer 1990/91; Gaddis 1991). Nowhere in this discussion, however, is there any mention of U.S. compliance with international law if such compliance undermines U.S. interests.

The George W. Bush administration has begun to formulate what has been dubbed the "Bush Doctrine." Simply put, it means that, particularly where terrorist threats are concerned, the United States should not wait until the attacks occur to retaliate, but rather seek out plotters and strike preemptively. This philosophy underpins the decision to attack Iraq in advance of its attacking U.S. interests directly. Presumably, this action would be taken not by seeking international approval through the UN, but as part of America's role as global hegemon. As put by Director of Policy Planning in the State Department, Richard Haass:

> We're not looking to turn international relations in 2002 into the Wild West. We understand that restraint and rules still need to be the norm. But there may well be a place for exceptions. You have to ask yourself whether rules and norms which have grown up over hundreds of years in one context are adequate to changing circumstances. (*Chicago Tribune*, September 4, 2002)

Prior to the September 11, 2001 terror attacks, senior members of the Bush administration had called for a more "muscular" foreign policy involving preemptive strikes against America's threats. Paul Wolfowitz, while serving in the first Bush administration, spearheaded the drafting of the Defense Planning Guidance, calling for preemptive strikes against potential enemies as opposed to the mere containment of threats. He was joined by Richard Perle and other "Vulcans" who favored an activist role for the United States in reshaping the world. As explained by Daalder and Lindsay:

> This group argued that the United States should actively deploy its overwhelming military, economic, and political might to remake the world in its image—and that doing so would serve the interests of other countries as well as the United States. They were less worried about the dangers of nation-building and more willing to commit the nation's resources not just to toppling tyrants, but also to creating democracies in their wake. (Daalder & Lindsay 2003, 47)

In September 2002, President Bush released the annual National Security Strategy. In it, he promoted a vision of American leadership that is expansive and dramatic. In order to reshape the balance of power in the world so as to "favor human freedom," the United States must be willing to confront those who would acquire weapons of mass destruction for radical purposes. "[A]s a matter of common sense and self-defense, America will act against such emerging threats before they are fully formed. . . . [W]e will not hesitate to act alone, if necessary, to exercise our right of self-defense by acting preemptively" (Daalder & Lindsay 2003, 123). As he put it more directly in a speech to the West Point graduating class in June 2002, "[W]e must take the battle to the enemy, and confront the worst threats before they emerge. In the world we have entered, the only path to safety is the path of action" (Prestowitz 2003, 22).

The strategy has broad support in American society, which helps explain why the invasion of Iraq was very popular. Even with the failure to find the weapons of mass destruction (a key rationale for the invasion) and the difficulties in suppressing the insurrection, a slim majority still approves of the decision to go to war.

Critics, on the other hand, stress the alienation these policies have prompted around the world. Not only have the enemies of the United States been galvanized by the new policy of preemption, but most of the nation's allies are uncertain of the government's intentions. As put by T. D. Allman, "Although from a very great distance, George W. Bush looked like an acceptable representative of the American nation, as he drew closer, the smirk about the mouth, the hostile glint in the eyes, became apparent. These, combined with the rippling of ire of his response to even the more well-reasoned unwillingness to line up behind him and America 100 percent, no questions asked, angered and frightened people" (Allman 2004, 151). As a result, the Bush Doctrine became a campaign issue in 2004 with Democratic nominee John Kerry taking on the multilateralist standard.

MULTILATERALISM

The differences between the multilateralist and hegemonic approaches are rather subtle but nonetheless profound. To begin, most multilateralists are skeptical of the argument that the United States has either the capability or the prerogative to lead the world. Foremost among their concerns is the fact that the world is no longer bipolar and will never be unipolar. At best, the world is tripolar, with Germany, Japan, and the United States at three opposite poles (Tarnoff 1990). With the end of the Cold War, raw military might has become largely obsolete. We live in an age of economics. As pointed out by Fred Bergsten, "The central task in shaping a new American foreign policy is to set priorities and select central themes. Those choices must derive from America's national interests, which have shifted sharply in the direction of economics" (Bergsten 1992, 4).

The economic issue has led many to urge a collaborative U.S. policy based on close cooperation among the United States, Japan, and Europe (via Germany) (U.S. Congress 1990). The tripartite arrangement will go the farthest to promote open markets, liberal monetary policy, and free investment activities (Tarnoff 1990). Analysts emphasize the need to work through multilateral institutions, such as GATT and the International Monetary Fund (IMF), and to create yet more, stronger rules and enforcement mechanisms to preserve open markets (Aho & Stokes 1990/91). They assume that a failure to continue expanding free trade will lead quickly to a rapid retreat into protectionism.

This urge to "go multilateral" stems not only from an acceptance of the U.S. decline into parity (or at least the rise of Europe and Japan), but also from a hope that security concerns will continue to remain back-burner issues in the future. Some have pointed out that democracies do not go to war with each other, concluding like the "endists" that the threat of global conflict is virtually over (Jervis 1992). War has become less likely because of the nature of states, and it has become less profitable and therefore less attractive to rational actors interested in maximizing gains over losses (Kaysen 1991). The implication of these developments is that we have reached a point when collective security may finally be a feasible method for dealing with all international conflict—a solution that would eliminate the need for American unilateralism. Russett and Sutterlin feel that now is the time to give the UN the authority and capability to intervene actively in conflict situations not only to "keep" the peace but also to "make" it. The success of the UN in the Persian Gulf War:

> . . . can enhance the United Nations' ability not just to restore the status quo as it existed prior to a breach of the peace, but also to change the parameters of the global order to something more favorable than existed under the prior status quo. In this it may even go beyond the vision of the U.N. founders. (Russett & Sutterlin 1991, 82)

In the Clinton administration, Secretary of State Madeleine Albright and Vice President Al Gore were noted for their enthusiasm for the multilateral approach. Their propensity to urge an assertive U.S. leadership role, including a military one, has been described as "assertive multilateralism" (Sterling-Folker 1998, 284). A draft presidential directive—PRD-13—called for a broader and more dynamic UN role, including a standing UN army and a willingness to place U.S. troops under UN command. Though no longer U.S. policy as early as 1994, this position was assailed by Republican critics and remained an issue into the 1996 presidential campaign.

Although it is assumed that the UN will continue to be supportive of U.S. goals of promoting democracy, spreading free trade, and enforcing international law, there is an implicit acknowledgment that in the future the United States must accept that it will not always get its way. Former U.S. envoy to the UN, Daniel Patrick Moynihan, deplores the fact that the United States has a bad habit of giving lip service to the letter of international law without complying with its spirit. We sign the Optional Clause of the World Court, thereby showing our support for rendering its decisions binding, and then we deny their validity on technical grounds when they go against us. We draw up a UN Charter that pledges our support for establishing a UN-commanded standing military force, and then we refuse to allow U.S. troops to participate in peacekeeping operations. It is time, so the multilateralists say, to play by all the rules, not just those we like (Chace 1992).

It may seem ironic that multilateralists, while accepting the fact of American decline, believe that American idealism can now be adopted as the global standard. The hope is that, given the core values of fairness and tolerance, a weaker United States will actually live in a manner closer to its own rhetoric. On the down side, multilateralists fear that American decline and increased great power parity may create an urgent need to institutionalize idealism quickly. Failure to do so may lead to a collapse of the precarious consensus we now enjoy.

Critics of multilateralism come from many corners. Neoisolationists fear that multilateralism will become yet another way to "sell the farm" to foreign interests. Yielding to international pressures does not come naturally to most Americans, particularly those who deny any automatic or inevitable international role for the

United States. They do not see the need for continued international involvement as a prerequisite for national renewal, and they see multilateral institutions as an impediment to national strength, not a help.

Unilateralists deny the inevitability of U.S. decline and feel that multilateralism, though acceptable when applied to other nations, should not be U.S. policy. They point to the economic troubles experienced by Europe and Japan in the second half of 1992 as evidence that nothing is inevitable about their ascendance. They further point to the paralysis of the European Community in the face of full-scale civil war in Yugoslavia as evidence that the United States should not expect international leadership from Brussels or Berlin. The UN has been incapable of enforcing international law, and international economic institutions have more often than not provided a cover for unfair trading practices by the United States' economic rivals, so the logic goes. Thus, although the unilateralists share the multilateralists' internationalism, they emphasize leadership. Furthermore, they share with the neoisolationists the view that the United States should never voluntarily submit to international law if this law is dysfunctional and runs contrary to U.S. interests (however defined).

CONCLUSION

If you, the reader, are still a bit uncertain about where you stand on the question, do not be dismayed. Even the experts have to hedge a bit. Former Secretary of State James Baker, a unilateralist at heart, emphasized the need for the United States to share both burdens and powers with its allies via multilateral institutions (U.S. Congress 1992). Joseph Nye likewise seems to straddle the fence on whether the United States should take control of global institutions or be more of a team player (U.S. Congress 1990). Even military analysts who seem most readily inclined to accept unilateralism have paid lip service to the UN.

Some neoisolationists are still quick to acknowledge that there might be a role for some U.S. troops overseas (as a trip wire, perhaps) and caution against the dangers of a too-rapid demobilization (Hyland 1990; Brzezinski 1991). They will accept that although weapons manufacturing is no longer essential, maintenance of production lines, jobs, and even technological research may continue to have a place in a peacetime economy. Even the threat of protectionism is seen by many as merely a bargaining strategy to persuade other nations to open their markets and embrace true free trade.

The record of the Clinton administration was mixed, and the door remains open to future presidents to adopt any number of courses of action. Although assertive multilateralism is on the shelf for now, given George W. Bush's basic skepticism of UN intervention, the United States has a record of supporting multilateral ventures.

The disasters that took place on September 11, 2001, prompted a strong and virtually unanimous response from policymakers and legislators on both sides of the aisle. The war against terror became the new, defining focus of U.S. foreign policy, playing much the same role as anticommunism during the Cold War (*Chicago Tribune*, September 6, 2002). The United States was determined to lead the fight, without direction from the rest of the world (although U.S. officials were careful to obtain UN approval first). Operation Enduring Freedom in Afghanistan was very much an American operation, as was the establishment of the Karzai government after the defeat of the Taliban.

It was not until the summer of 2002, when Bush administration officials leaked plans to invade Iraq and replace Saddam Hussein, that some voices of dissent and concern were raised. Perhaps most troubling to Bush was the opposition of loyal Republicans who served in the Senate and had previously supported his father. James Baker opined that a military strike, while well intentioned, was ill advised without a UN resolution to back it up (Baker 2002). Senior Democrats have gone on record against the proposal. Even after the war's successful outcome in April 2003, some questions arose as to whether ignoring international law was necessary.

Thus a new debate has begun, focused on the limits of the Bush Doctrine of unilateral, preemptive strikes. It seems to be having some effect, since in September 2002 the White House indicated some willingness to consider a debate in Congress and at the UN prior to launching an attack. It may be useful to dust off the pages of the Great Debates of the past as the United States attempts to find its way through a post–September 11 world.

The invasion of Iraq, discussed in detail in Case 8, provides a laboratory to test the validity of these various approaches. National interest advocates were split on the issue, since they disagreed on whether Iraq posed a clear and present danger to the U.S. homeland. Once it was clear there were no stockpiles of weapons of mass destruction, they concluded that the effort was a waste of precious resources that would have been better spent protecting U.S. territory and moving against al Qaeda targets. Needless to say, advocates of the hegemonic imperative were the authors of the policy, although some have been surprised at how difficult the operation has proved to be. Troop levels and budget expenditures have been far higher than anticipated. The insurgents, once dismissed as "dead-enders" by Secretary of Defense Donald Rumsfeld, have become the focus of concerted military operations. And multilateralists are resisting the urge to say "I told you so." Secretary of State Colin Powell, an unlikely multilateralist, resigned his position with few regrets, other than his inability to stop Vice President Dick Cheney and the other "Vulcans" from their ill-advised purposes (Woodward 2004, 129).

 # DEBATE TOPIC

Is the current war against terror best carried out as a multilateral or unilateral strategy?

PRO

A supporter of the multilateralist approach would likely argue as follows: (1) Because terrorism violates the rules of civilization itself, fighting it is inherently multilateral. Only supporters of terrorism would object. (2) Because terrorism is ubiquitous, only a global approach will be successful. The difficulties involved in the war in Iraq provide ample evidence of this. (3) The United States is a relative newcomer in the fight against terrorism, and it could benefit from undertaking joint operations with states such as the United Kingdom, Germany, Italy, and Israel which have far more experience.

CON

Supporters of a unilateral approach have pointed out: (1) The September 11 attacks were aimed solely at the United States, so it is incumbent on the United States to respond directly, with or without the rest of the world's support. (2) Only the United States has the capability of projecting force worldwide, and it will therefore be expected to lead an antiterror campaign. (3) Because so many countries sponsor and tolerate terrorism, it is best not to depend too much on international collaboration, but to move forward unilaterally. The refusal of France and Russia to join in the war in Iraq is ample evidence of this.

QUESTIONS TO CONSIDER

1. If you were an advisor to the president, what would you recommend?

2. What basic values can you identify in relation to each of the perspectives on post–Cold War U.S. policy? With which values are you most comfortable and why?

3. Can one make a "rational" decision about such issues when so much is tied up in values, perceptions, beliefs, and assumptions? Or are these part of rationality itself?

WEBSITES

Well-Known Foreign Policy "Think Tanks"

The Brookings Institution: **www.brook.edu/fp/fp_hp.htm**

Council on Foreign Relations: **www.cfr.org**

Foreign Policy Association: **www.fpa.org**

Foreign Policy Institute: **www.sais-jhu.edu/centers/fpi/index.htm**

Heritage Foundation: **www.heritage.org**

Institute for Policy Analysis: **www.ifpa.org**

United Nations Association of the United States: **www.unausa.org**

REFERENCES

Aho, Michael, and Bruce Stokes. "The Year the World Economy Turned." *Foreign Affairs* 70 #1 (1990/91): 160–178.

Allman, T. D. *Rogue State: America at War with the World.* New York: Nation Books, 2004.

Baker, James, "The Right Way to Change a Regime." *New York Times*, August 25, 2002.

Bergsten, Fred. "The Primacy of Economics." *Foreign Policy* 87 (Summer 1992): 3–24.

Brzezinski, Zbigniew. "Selective Global Commitment." *Foreign Affairs* 70 #4 (Fall 1991): 1–20.

Chace, James. *The Consequences of the Peace: The New Internationalism and American Foreign Policy* (New York: Oxford University Press, 1992).

Chicago Tribune, September 4, 2002.

Chicago Tribune, September 6, 2002.

Daalder, Ivo, and James Lindsay. *America Unbound: The Bush Revolution in Foreign Policy*. Washington, D.C.: Brookings Institution Press, 2003.

Democratic Leadership Council (DLC). *The New American Choice: Opportunity, Reponsibility, Community*. Resolutions Adopted at the DLC Convention, Cleveland, Ohio, 1991.

Fukuyama, Francis. "The End of History?" *National Interest* 16 (Summer 1989): 3–18.

Gaddis, John Lewis. *The Long Peace: Inquiries into the History of the Cold War* (New York: Oxford University Press, 1987).

Gaddis, John Lewis. "Toward the Post–Cold War World." *Foreign Affairs* 70 #2 (Spring 1991): 102–122.

Gilpin, Robert. *The Political Economy of International Relations* (Princeton, NJ: Princeton University Press, 1987).

Haig, Alexander. "The Challenges to American Leadership." In Schmergel, Greg, ed., *U.S. Foreign Policy in the 1990s*: New York: Palgrave, 1991: 34–46.

Hendrickson, David. "The Renovation of American Foreign Policy." *Foreign Affairs* 71 #2 (Spring 1992): 48–63.

Huntington, Samuel. "No Exit: The Errors of Endism." *National Interest* 17 (Fall 1989): 3–11.

Hyland, William. "America's New Course." *Foreign Affairs* 69 #2 (Spring 1990): 1–12.

Ikenberry, John. "Why Export Democracy?" *Wilson Quarterly* #3 (Spring 1999): 56.

Jervis, Robert. "The Future of World Politics: Will It Resemble the Past?" In Sean Lynn-Jones and Steven E. Miller, eds., *America's Strategy in a Changing World*. Cambridge: MIT Press, 1992: 3–37.

Kaysen, Carl. "Is War Obsolete? A Review Essay." In Sean Lynn-Jones and Steven E. Miller, eds., *The Cold War and After: Prospects for Peace*. Cambridge: MIT Press, 1991: 81–103.

Kegley, Charles, and Eugene Wittkopf, eds. *The Future of American Foreign Policy* (New York: St. Martin's, 1992).

Krasner, Stephen. "Realist Praxis: Neo-isolationism and Structural Change." *Journal of International Affairs* 43 #1 (1989): 143–160.

Krauthammer, Charles. "The Unipolar Moment." *Foreign Affairs* 70 #1 (1990/91): 23–33.

Kristol, Irving. "Defining Our National Interest." *National Interest* (Fall 1990): 16–25.

Lugar, Richard. "The Republican Course." *Foreign Policy* # 86 (Spring 1992): 86–98.

Lynn-Jones, Sean, ed. *The Cold War and After: Prospects for Peace* (Cambridge, MA: MIT Press, 1991).

Lynn-Jones, Sean, and Steven Miller, eds. *America's Changing Strategy in a Changing World* (Cambridge, MA: MIT Press, 1992).

Mastanduno, Michael. "Preserving the Unipolar Moment: Realist Theories and U.S. Grand Strategy After the Cold War." *International Security* 21 #4 (Spring 1997): 49–88.

Maswood, Javed. "Does Revisionism Work? U.S. Trade Strategy and the 1995 U.S.–Japan Auto Dispute." *Pacific Affairs* 70 #4 (Winter 1997): 533–555.

Nixon, Richard. *Seize the Moment: America's Challenge in a One-Superpower World* (New York: Simon & Schuster, 1992).

Norton, Anne. *Leo Strauss and the Politics of American Empire.* New Haven: Yale University Press, 2004.

Nye, Joseph. *Bound to Lead: The Changing Nature of American Power* (New York: Basic Books, 1990).

Pfaff, William. "Redefining World Power." *Foreign Affairs* 70 #1 (1990/91): 34–48.

Prestowitz, Clyde. *Rogue Nation: American Unilateralism and the Failure of Good Intentions* (New York: Basic Books, 2003).

Russett, Bruce, and James Sutterlin. "The U.N. in a New World Order." *Foreign Affairs* 70 #2 (Spring 1991): 69–83.

Sanders, Jerry. "Retreat from World Order: The Perils of Triumphalism." *World Policy Journal* 8 #2 (Spring 1991): 227–250.

Schmergel, Greg, ed. *U.S. Foreign Policy in the 1990s* (New York: St. Martin's, 1991).

Sterling-Folker, Jennifer. "Between a Rock and a Hard Place: Assertive Multilateralism and Post–Cold War U.S. Foreign Policy Making." In James Scott, ed., *After the End: Making U.S. Foreign Policy in the Post–Cold War World* (Durham, NC: Duke University Press, 1998), 277–304.

Tarnoff, Peter. "America's New Special Relationships." *Foreign Affairs* 69 #3 (Summer 1990): 67–80.

Tessitore, John, and Susan Woolfson, eds. *A Global Agenda: Issues Before the 54th General Assembly of the United Nations* (Lanham, MD: Rowman and Littlefield, 1999).

Tonelson, Alan. "Prudence or Inertia? The Bush Administration's Foreign Policy." *Current History* 91 #564 (April 1992): 145–150.

Tonelson, Alan. "What Is the National Interest?" *The Atlantic Monthly* (July 1991): 35–52.

U.S. Congress, House. *The Future of U.S. Foreign Policy in the Post–Cold War Era.* Hearings before the Committee on Foreign Affairs, 102nd Congress, 2nd Session, 1992.

U.S. Congress, House. *U.S. Power in a Changing World.* Special Report 28-802 prepared for the Committee on Foreign Affairs, 101st Congress, 2nd Session, 1990.

Woodward, Robert. *Plan of Attack.* New York: Simon & Schuster, 2004.

CASE 4

The Cuban Missile Crisis: Rationality

INTRODUCTION

When making a decision, we typically know in advance what we want. We consider the facts at hand, come up with a few alternative courses of action, imagine what might happen if we pick each one, and then choose the alternative that gets us what we wanted in the first place. This is the epitome of what is meant by rationality. Any other method is not purely rational, although the result is not necessarily wrong or bad. We sometimes make choices based on habit or tradition, or we feel driven by our emotions. Our analysis of the situation and consideration of alternatives may be cursory. Anyone who has ever worked on a committee knows that groups rarely make decisions based on a careful calculation of costs and benefits—they typically go for the least common denominator. And this tells us nothing about putting the decision into practice.

Scholars have learned that if they assume rationality on the part of the people they study, it is possible to predict how different decision makers will address similar situations, which in turn allows us to anticipate numerous events. The field of game theory attempts to explain how rational actors interact with one another. When an actor faces a decision the outcome of which depends on what another actor decides, it is often possible to design a matrix that shows the range of outcomes. You can select the alternative that each actor will choose based on these outcomes and the goals each actor brings. For example, where two players face the option of cooperating or not cooperating, but where cooperating opens up the possibility of losing something of considerable value, one can predict that the actors will likely shun that option (this helps to explain everything from an international arms race to marital infidelity).

With respect to the Cuban Missile Crisis, we see two sets of actors. On the one hand, we have the "game" of superpower relations where each country plays a game of "chicken" with the other. On the other hand, we have the interactions between domestic decision makers within each country (presidents, advisors, generals, and so forth). As we explore the story of the Cuban Missile Crisis, consider whether the various players are behaving "rationally"—that is, identifying goals, exploring options, selecting the "best" option, and seeing it fully implemented.

KEY FIGURES
THE CUBAN MISSILE CRISIS

John F. Kennedy   U.S. President, 1961–1963. It was his responsibility to set U.S. policy with respect to detection and removal of Soviet missiles in Cuba in 1962.

Nikita Khrushchev   Soviet Premier, 1953–1964. He led the Soviet Union to both deploy and withdraw nuclear missiles in and from Cuba.

Fidel Castro   Leader of the Cuban government since 1959. He sought Soviet protection following the failed Bay of Pigs invasion.

John Scali   American newsman. He was used for back-channel negotiations with Aleksandr Feklisov.

Aleksandr Feklisov (Fomin)   Soviet KGB operative based in Washington, D.C.

Anatoly Dobrynin   Soviet Ambassador to the United States, 1962–1986.

Selected Members of ExComm

Robert F. Kennedy   Attorney-General of the United States, 1961–1964. As the brother of President Kennedy, he always had influence in shaping national policy in many areas. He conducted the meetings of the Executive Committee.

Dean Rusk   U.S. Secretary of State, 1961–1963.

George Ball   Undersecretary of State, 1961–1966.

John McCone   Director of Central Intelligence Agency, 1961–1965.

McGeorge Bundy   National Security Advisor, 1961–1966.

Robert McNamara   U.S. Secretary of Defense, 1961–1968. He discounted the threat presented by the Russian missiles.

Llewellyn Thompson   Ambassador-at-Large, 1962–1966. Former U.S. Ambassador to the Soviet Union, he was the only Russia expert on ExComm.

CHRONOLOGY
THE CUBAN MISSILE CRISIS

1959
Fidel Castro takes power in Cuba at the head of a Communist revolution.

1960
John F. Kennedy is elected to be the youngest president in U.S. history.

(continued)

(*continued*)

1961

The Kennedy administration withdraws support for Cuban exiles who suffer defeat at the Bay of Pigs. Castro demands additional military support from the Soviet Union to defend against future U.S. attacks.

1962

June   Soviet Premier Nikita Khrushchev comes away from his summit meeting with Kennedy unimpressed.

September   The Soviet Union begins deploying nuclear missiles in Cuba.

October 15   American U-2 aircraft detect Soviet activity in Cuba.

October 16–20   ExComm deliberates, ultimately recommending a blockade first, and an invasion second.

October 22   Kennedy announces his plan to the nation by televised address.

October 23   Kennedy orders the blockade against Cuba. Later that day, Adlai Stevenson presents photos of the Cuban sites to the UN Security Council.

October 24   Russian vessels turn away from the blockade, prompting Dean Rusk's "eyeball to eyeball" comment.

October 26   A conciliatory message is sent by Khrushchev, followed shortly thereafter by a more intransigent demand for the withdrawal of U.S. missiles from Turkey.

October 27   The "Trollope Ploy" is formulated in response to two conflicting Russian messages. The conciliatory message is treated as a genuine compromise and largely accepted.

October 28   Khrushchev agrees to withdraw the missiles from Cuba. Kennedy secretly agrees to withdraw U.S. missiles from Turkey.

November 19   Removal of Soviet missiles from Cuba is complete.

RATIONALITY AND THE CUBAN MISSILE CRISIS

Almost as soon as it was resolved, the October 1962 Cuban Missile Crisis became the object of scholarly attention. It was one moment, suspended in time, when the earth's survival hung in the balance. President John F. Kennedy himself is reported to have estimated that the chances of a nuclear war were "between one out of three and even" (Allison 1999, 1). Fidel Castro felt the odds were 20:1 that a U.S. invasion of Cuba was virtually inevitable, and he urged Nikita Khrushchev to launch a full-scale nuclear strike in retaliation. Given the extreme danger and risk of the situation on the one hand and its successful conclusion on the other hand, this episode in world history has become a popular case study of conflict management and crisis decision making. Because of the ease of hearing from actual participants in the crisis, particularly since the end of the Cold War, and the voluminous documentary evidence available to scholars (including secret tapes of White House meetings), analysts have considerable details to study.

We will focus on what the Cuban Missile Crisis teaches us about how policy is developed and implemented in a crisis. A crisis, as defined by Charles Hermann (1969), is a problem that combines the elements of surprise, salience, and urgency. In other words, the problem erupts with little warning, directly threatens a high-priority value, and must be resolved quickly to avoid negative consequences. From another point of view, a crisis is "coercive diplomacy" used by an adversary to blackmail or intimidate a nation into submission without the direct use of force (Craig & George 1990). Avoidance of bloodshed is the primary concern in such situations, even though the risk of war is usually extremely high.

Hermann assumes that in a crisis situation, decisions are made at the top levels in a bewildering "pressure cooker" environment. Issues of lesser importance are set aside, all energy is put into gathering facts and alternatives, and stress levels are high. Conditions are ideal for intensive and creative problem solving as the combined energy and talent of some of the most able men and women in the country are brought to bear on a single issue. Of course, the reverse can also happen when decisions based on few facts must be made quickly by people with a great deal to lose. The actual outcomes depend on many factors, including the personalities, perceptions, and decision-making styles of the key participants, the degree of contingency planning that preceded the crisis, and the organization of the decision-making unit itself. To the extent that information is made available, options and objectives are clearly and creatively articulated, and the implications of various choices are thoroughly understood, the likelihood of a sound decision increases.

Before determining whether the decisions made during the Cuban Missile Crisis meet our ideal standard, we will review the history of the event.

THE CUBAN MISSILE CRISIS

Precursors

In 1960, John F. Kennedy ran for president on a platform of narrowing the "missile gap" between the USSR and the United States. Upon reaching office, he was surprised to learn that, according to the CIA, the missile gap was larger than he expected—but it was in America's favor. Soviet leaders were acutely aware of the U.S. advantage in number, quality, and deployment of nuclear missiles, however, and were considering options to achieve a balance.

In 1959, Fidel Castro became the leader of Cuba and in 1961 declared himself unabashedly Marxist, to the dismay of American defense planners. His presence in the hemisphere represented a "bridgehead of Sino–Soviet imperialism and a base for Communist agitation" (Ferrell 1985, 362). U.S. agents made several attempts on Castro's life in these early years, and in 1961, the United States helped orchestrate a failed amphibious invasion of Cuba aimed at overthrowing the regime. Conserva-tives in Congress accused Kennedy of being "soft on Communism."

These events, combined with a disastrous U.S.–USSR summit meeting in June 1962 that gave Khrushchev the impression that Kennedy was a political light-weight, set the stage for the Soviet decision to deploy nuclear missiles in Cuba in May 1962 (Fursenko & Naftali 1997, 179). By deploying missiles, Khrushchev hoped to achieve a nuclear balance, protect Cuba from U.S. invasion, and keep Castro in the Soviet camp (rather than defecting to the more radical China). He wanted to deploy several medium-range missiles, along with defensive antiaircraft batteries, between May and November 1962 without revealing his plans to the United States. Once the installations were in place, Khrushchev hoped the United States would feel obliged to accept this change in strategic balance (Gartoff 1989, 23; Trachtenberg 1985, 163).

U.S. officials suspected Soviet intentions and tried to get information through both open and secret channels. Each time they met with firm denials. It was not until October 15, 1962, that the United States had proof of Soviet activities: photo-graphs of Soviet nuclear installations in Cuba taken by an American U-2 spy plane. The Cuban Missile Crisis had begun.

The Crisis Erupts

Early the next morning, Kennedy was presented with the information from the photographs by his national security advisor, McGeorge Bundy, who stressed the seriousness of the situation: The Soviets now had the capability to attack more than half of the United States, including Washington, D.C., with only a few minutes' warning. The president was astonished by the report. As put by Robert Kennedy, the president's brother and U.S. Attorney General, "[T]he dominant feeling was one of shocked incredulity" (Kennedy 1969, 27). President Kennedy determined during that first meeting that some forceful response was incumbent upon the administra-tion, although not all agreed. (Secretary of Defense Robert McNamara wondered aloud whether this discovery constituted, in and of itself, a mortal danger.) Nonetheless, given the political climate at home and worldwide, Kennedy deter-mined that this situation qualified as a crisis.

By that evening, a group that came to be known as the ExComm (Executive Committee of the National Security Council—even though it included individuals who did not belong to the council) was organized by the president and was generat-ing options for responding to the news. Potential actions included blockade or quarantine, surgical air strike followed by invasion, diplomatic overtures and negoti-ation, talks with Castro, and leaving things alone (Sorenson 1965, 735). Although everyone acknowledged that air strikes followed by invasion were the only means of being sure the missiles were removed, most did not want to pursue that option as a first alternative. The diplomatic option was ruled out as too timid and passive. Ulti-mately, the air strike/invasion option and the blockade option were deemed the only viable responses, and the blockade was considered far weaker under the circum-stances.

For nearly a week, the ExComm deliberated to develop a final operational plan that could win unanimous approval. As time went on, the air strike option was set aside for two principal reasons. First, if done without warning, an air strike would be seen by the rest of the world as a "Pearl Harbor in reverse" (as put by John McCone, the director of the CIA; Fursenko & Naftali 1997, 226) or as an unprovoked attack against an unprepared enemy. Second, the air strike option was never guaranteed success by military planners, in part because no air strike is ever guaranteed and because the missiles were considered "moveable targets" and therefore able to be relocated without warning. The blockade, in its favor, was a less "final" solution. The United States could rather easily escalate its response if a blockade failed. Also, a blockade was considered a fairly forceful reaction—an act of war according to international law. It might be enough to force the Russians to back down and negotiate a settlement. A blockade could not, in itself, remove the missiles, however. And the ExComm had to consider what to do if the Russians attempted to run the blockade. The crisis might simply be relocated rather than solved.

By Friday evening, October 20, President Kennedy had made the decision to impose a blockade, citing the advantage of giving Khrushchev more time to consider the implications of the situation (Sorenson 1965, 691). Kennedy readily acknowledged that "there isn't a good solution . . . but this one seems less objectionable" (National Archives 1988, 7). The decision was made formal on October 22, when Kennedy spoke to the nation in a televised address. He announced the existence of the missiles, his intent to see them removed, and the approach he intended to use to do that. He made sure to keep his options open. He underlined the gravity of the problem for both American and Soviet audiences:

> My fellow citizens: let no one doubt that this is a difficult and dangerous effort on which we have set out. No one can foresee precisely what course it will take or what costs or casualties will be incurred. . . . The path we have chosen for the present is full of hazards, as all paths are—but it is the one most consistent with our character and courage as a nation. (National Archives 1988, 10)

The Blockade Aftermath

Over the next four days, the situation worsened. Khrushchev, alarmed to learn that the Americans had discovered his missiles, was relieved when he learned of the blockade. He considered the blockade the policy of a weak leader, and he intended to take advantage of it. He ordered the Cuban installations accelerated and instructed ships carrying nuclear equipment to move quickly to beat the blockade. Only at the last minute, once the blockade was in place, were other Russian ships ordered to halt (prompting Secretary of State Dean Rusk to make the famous remark: "We're eyeball to eyeball and I think the other fellow just blinked!"). At the same time, Khrushchev moved to ensure his direct control over the nuclear missiles that were operational to prevent an accidental launch (fearing Castro's impulsiveness).

Meanwhile, the United States began a diplomatic assault against Russia in the Organization of American States (OAS) and the UN Security Council, where virtually every nation approved the U.S. response and demanded a withdrawal of Soviet missiles (Blight 1990, 17). Robert Kennedy undertook back-channel negotiations through Georgi Bolshakov as well as front-door meetings with Anatoly Dobrynin, the USSR's envoy in Washington, both to determine Russian thinking and to communicate American resolve (Fursenko & Naftali 1997, 249–252). Perhaps most important, the Kennedy administration mobilized active-duty and reserve personnel and moved a half-million troops with accompanying equipment into the south Florida area. It sent every possible signal that an invasion force was prepared to act at any moment. (This helps explain Castro's alarm.)

Khrushchev also used a variety of channels to communicate his intentions. He communicated through an American businessman in Moscow, through journalists, and through KGB agents in Washington. Ultimately, a letter was delivered through Alexander Fomin (a code name for Aleksandr Feklisov) to John Scali, a reporter with ties to the Kennedy administration. The initial proposal involved removal of the missiles by the USSR in exchange for a promise to respect Cuban sovereignty by the United States. While the ExComm was formulating a response to this message, it received a second message via Radio Moscow adding the caveat that Jupiter missiles—American medium-range missiles based in Turkey—also be removed.

The administration did not know what to believe after receiving conflicting proposals at almost the same time. If they had known that Fomin was acting on his own initiative, the confusion would have been even greater (Garthoff 1989, 80). Add to this the downing of an American U-2 over Cuba at the same time (October 27, 1962), and it was frankly impossible to know what was taking place. (The downing was not even authorized by Moscow; Garthoff 1989, 91.) For that matter, the United States was guilty of sending mixed signals of its own. It had ordered the constant over-flight of the Arctic region by bombers with nuclear weapons, and one of them strayed into Soviet airspace at about this time. In fact, Khrushchev was very personally involved in the formulation of proposals, and the second proposal to remove missiles from Turkey came when he considered an invasion of Cuba less likely (Garthoff 1989, 82).

Negotiating the Resolution

The ExComm made two decisions on Saturday, October 27. The first was to make final preparations for an invasion of Cuba to begin on Monday (Blight 1990, 18), and the second was to draft a formal response accepting the conditions detailed in Khrushchev's first proposal. This latter move was suggested by Soviet expert Llewellyn Thompson and was nicknamed the "Trollope Ploy." Thompson also exerted considerable energy to convince a downhearted President Kennedy to implement the plan. In addition to drafting a message to be sent to Khrushchev, Kennedy dispatched his brother Robert to present the American position as well as to offer a "sweetener": secret removal of the Jupiter missiles over a five-month period.

On October 28, Khrushchev's response accepting these terms was received at the White House. The Cuban Missile Crisis was at an end. By November 19, much to Castro's chagrin, the missiles had been dismantled and removed.

ANALYSIS OF THE DECISION TO BLOCKADE CUBA

Although several critical decisions were made at various points prior to and during the crisis, two are easiest for American audiences to study: (1) Kennedy's decision to reveal the existence of the missiles and impose a blockade and (2) Kennedy's decision to accept the terms of the first Khrushchev letter and ignore the second message. To determine whether these two decisions by Kennedy were "rational," we should consider his goals, assess the quality of the search for options and their respective outcomes, and check whether the final choice promised to achieve his original goals. To the extent that the decision-making process comes close to this ideal model, we can say that it was rational (Allison 1999, 33).

The decision to impose a blockade was reached after roughly four days of intensive deliberations in the White House. Within twelve hours of learning about the missiles, Kennedy had assembled a collection of individuals chosen for their authority over certain key areas of foreign policy and their subject-matter expertise. He called in the secretaries of state and defense, the director of the CIA, the national security advisor, and the joint chiefs of staff (chaired by Maxwell Taylor). Douglas Dillon, secretary of the treasury; Theodore Sorenson, presidential counsel; Pierre Salinger, press secretary; and Robert Kennedy were also included, though more for their relationships to President Kennedy than for their policy roles. Six other men from the State and Defense Departments were brought in for their expertise, and Lyndon Johnson, the vice president, was permitted to join the group. The ExComm met regularly, sometimes for ten hours at a time (not all members met all the time). The group had no obvious seniority system, although Robert McNamara and Robert Kennedy informally led the discussions.

The ExComm structure has been praised as a nearly ideal form for crisis decision making, in that the individuals were present, as Sorenson later put it, "on our own, representing the president and not individual departments" (Sorenson 1965, 679). Furthermore, as the days wore on, the group met without the president, divided into smaller caucuses, and otherwise ignored traditional rank and protocol as they deliberated. Robert Kennedy commented, "It was a tremendously advantageous procedure that does not frequently occur within the executive branch of the government, where rank is often so important" (Kennedy 1969, 46). Specifically, the arrangement minimized the tendency for peer pressure to lead group members to take a more hard-line approach than would normally be the case ("groupthink"; see Janis 1972). It also worked against any bureaucratic struggle over turf.

The first decision required was to determine whether the placement of missiles in Cuba was indeed a threat to national security. In fact, that question did not even come up until the evening of October 16, and then at the instigation of McGeorge Bundy—not the president. McNamara made it clear that he did not consider the new missiles a threat. The joint chiefs unanimously disagreed ("White House" 1985, 184). Kennedy dismissed McNamara's assessment, although he did not necessarily agree with the joint chiefs either. He was more concerned about conservatives in Congress who, he felt, would likely have him impeached if he ignored the missiles.

Once the problem was identified, the process of clarifying the goals and options began, though not necessarily in that order. Early on, Kennedy determined, with general approval, that the missiles must be removed but that the use of force should be a last resort. Kennedy weighed not only U.S. security concerns but also the response of the American public and NATO allies. The Europeans, he surmised, would not be especially alarmed at the presence of Soviet missiles in Cuba because they lived every day with the prospect of a Soviet attack from the Ukraine and eastern Russia. Kennedy kept in mind that a trade-off of Cuban missiles for Jupiter missiles would seem eminently reasonable to U.S. allies ("October 27, 1962" 1987/88, 58). As the crisis evolved, avoiding global nuclear war was likely the highest priority on Kennedy's mind and shaped his willingness to ignore Soviet provocations.

McNamara was the first to clearly articulate three options for dealing with the crisis: (1) a "diplomatic" option involving public declarations, consultations with allies, UN resolutions, and other gestures aimed at condemning and publicizing the Soviet move; (2) a "middle course" of aggressive surveillance and interdiction (read: blockade) of new weapons bound for Cuba; and (3) a "military" option with several variants ranging from air strikes on narrowly selected targets (missile launchers and installations) to a broad-ranging series of attacks on all Cuban military facilities followed by an amphibious invasion ("White House" 1985, 182). Other ideas were mentioned, including taking retaliatory measures, doing nothing at all, and somehow persuading Castro to expel the weapons (Sorenson 1965, 682). Beyond these general categories of action, the ExComm questioned the specific implementation of each approach at length. Should an air strike be preceded by a public ultimatum, or should it be a surprise? Should diplomatic initiatives include a specific ultimatum and a deadline for withdrawal? Should an exchange of missiles in Turkey (which President Kennedy had once ordered removed) be offered up front to persuade the Soviets to settle the problem quickly? Should the nuclear arsenal be put on alert and forces mobilized? What contingencies should be made for a likely Soviet move in Berlin?

By the evening of October 16, the choices seemed to have been whittled down to two: blockade and diplomacy versus air strikes and invasion. When the president seemed to be leaning toward an air strike, McNamara essentially halted the discussion: "I think tonight we ought to put down on paper the alternative plans and probable, possible consequences thereof in a way that State and Defense could agree on, even if we disagree and put in both views. . . . [T]he consequences of these actions have not been thought through clearly" ("White House" 1985, 189). His suggestion was accepted, and the group split into two committees, each drafting the pros and cons of different options. Heavy emphasis was placed on extrapolating the outcomes and implications of each action, including the variations of the actions. Exactly how will oncoming ships be treated at the blockade perimeter? What about submarines? Will the OAS, NATO, and UN support the United States? Should classified information regarding the missiles be divulged? How and where will the Soviets respond to air strikes? Will Berlin be affected? (It is interesting that the joint chiefs initially anticipated that there would be no

Soviet response to a U.S. air strike—a scenario Kennedy rejected.) Note this emotional exchange about the implications of an air strike between Undersecretary of State George Ball and McGeorge Bundy:

Ball: *This [surprise attack scenario] just frightens the hell out of me as to what's going beyond. . . .*
Bundy: *. . . What goes beyond what?*
Ball: *What happens beyond that. You go in there with a surprise attack. You put out all the missiles. This isn't the end. This is the beginning . . . ("White House" 1985, 194)*

This process of deliberation, development of options, extrapolation of possible outcomes, and assessment of risks, reactions, and secondary options proceeded for three full days, before a decision was made. At one point, the ExComm actually organized a sort of "moot court," assigning certain members to be advocates for particular policy options while others "cross-examined" them to identify weaknesses. The blockade ended up as the most attractive option. It at least had a chance of resolving the crisis, and at minimal cost. Deputy Secretary of Defense Roswell Gilpatrick explained, "Essentially, Mr. President, this is a choice between limited action and unlimited action, and most of us think that it's better to start with limited action" (Sorenson 1965, 693–695).

In reconsidering this decision-making ordeal, we see that the participants self-consciously and painstakingly went out of their way to be rational. Although the initial decision to declare the problem a crisis may have been rather poorly thought out, the decision to impose a blockade resulted from a very systematic, impartial, and thorough process. An alternative point of view is that President Kennedy manipulated the process from behind the scenes, and some evidence indicates that Robert Kennedy played the role of president-in-absentia. Also, one can ask whether the consideration of only a half-dozen alternatives to a situation that threatened the future of humankind was adequate. Herbert Simon and James March argue that in the best of all worlds, the most we can expect of organizational decision making is "satisficing": selecting the first option that satisfies the key elements of a solution, even though other options might have met a wider range of objectives (March & Simon 1958).

RESPONSE TO THE SOVIET OFFERS

Several days of rancorous debate in the UN Security Council and a number of close calls on the high seas east of Cuba preceded the exchange between the U.S. and Soviet governments of what seemed to be genuine offers at settlement. Three messages in particular arrived at the White House on Friday, October 26, and Saturday, October 27. Adding information about the downing of the U-2 on Saturday morning, one could say that four messages were delivered. The ExComm had to decide which of these conflicting messages to take seriously.

The most significant message delivered on Friday was a lengthy, disjointed letter from Khrushchev about the risks of nuclear war. He compared the crisis to a knot that he and Kennedy were pulling tighter and tighter each day. Unless they reversed their course, the only way to undo the knot would be to cut it. Buried in this message was the "germ of a reasonable settlement: inasmuch as his missiles were there only to defend Cuba against invasion, he would withdraw the missiles under UN inspection if the U.S. agreed not to invade" (Sorenson 1965, 712). At roughly the same time this message was received and translated, Alexander Fomin was communicating a similar proposal to John Scali on his own authority, although later reports indicate Fomin thought Scali was the one who put forward the proposal (Fursenko & Naftali 1997, 265). Combined, the two messages offered a way out of the crisis.

On Saturday morning, the Soviet news agency TASS announced that the USSR would be willing to withdraw its missiles from Cuba if the United States dismantled its missiles in Turkey. Although the message was sent publicly over the airwaves, Khrushchev did not intend to put any particular pressure on the United States; the channel was chosen simply to accelerate communication of the message (Fursenko & Naftali 1997, 276). Nevertheless, Khrushchev was well aware that this proposal was more demanding than the earlier one. It was simply a gamble on his part, though one based in part on informal talks between Robert Kennedy and Dobrynin. The effect of the second message was despondency at the White House. The growing sense of alarm and urgency was based in part on the mistaken notion that the Cuban weapons were not yet operational but soon would be. The White House feared that local Cuban commanders might take it upon themselves to order a launch without Moscow's approval.

The transcript of the ExComm meetings make it clear that President Kennedy was deeply shaken by Khrushchev's second letter:

> . . . We're going to be in an unsupportable position on this matter if this [the trade] becomes his proposal. In the first place, we last year tried to get the missiles out of [Turkey] because they're not militarily useful. . . . Number 2, . . . to any man at the United Nations or any other rational man this will look like a very fair trade. . . . I think you're going to find it very difficult to explain why we are going to take hostile military action in Cuba against these sites—what we've been thinking about. The thing that he's saying is, "If you'll get yours out of Turkey, we'll get ours out of Cuba." I think we've got a very tough one here. ("October 27, 1962" 1987/88, 366–367)

The president's advisors, arguing against the trade-off, pointed out that it would be undercutting a NATO ally and might undermine the entire alliance. This debate engendered a search for alternatives, although the pressure of time seems to have constricted the number of options considered. McNamara and others pushed for an immediate cessation of work on the missile sites and some form of warning and implicit threat to the Soviets to remove the missiles within forty-eight hours. From that point, it seems to have been assumed that air strikes would have to begin by Tuesday at the latest.

As the ExComm prepared a reply to the messages, the option of simply ignoring the second message was raised. The following pivotal exchange occurred between Llewellyn Thompson and President Kennedy:

JFK: . . . *[W]e're going to have to take our weapons out of Turkey. I don't think there's any doubt he's not going to retreat now that he's made that public, Tommy—he's not going to take them out of Cuba if we. . . .*
Thompson: *I don't agree, Mr. President. I think there's still a chance that we can get this line going [i.e., ignore the second letter].*
JFK: *He'll back down?*
Thompson: *The important thing to Khrushchev, it seems to me, is to be able to say, "I saved Cuba—I stopped an invasion."* . . . (*"October 27, 1962" 1987/88, 59*)

Some in the administration surmised that the second letter might have been written by the alleged "hawks" in Khrushchev's Politburo and that ignoring it might effectively elevate Khrushchev's status in his own government. We now know that this was merely wishful thinking and Khrushchev was, in fact, in firm control of the government at this time.

At any rate, the ExComm decided to issue a response that simply did not mention the Turkish missiles. At the same time, secret communications relayed in a meeting between Robert Kennedy and Dobrynin indicated a willingness by the United States to remove the Jupiter missiles at a later time. The ExComm continued to make detailed preparations for an air strike/invasion policy. The starting time for the attack was given as Thursday at the latest. The decision to ignore the U-2 downing was another U.S. effort to postpone the military option as long as possible.

The delay proved felicitous because Khrushchev's response arrived on Sunday morning. Was Khrushchev's cooperation the result of U.S. prudence, or were Kennedy administration officials simply lucky? In retrospect, much hinged on some communications that no one at the White House was aware of. A KGB agent who worked as a bartender at the National Press Club overheard a number of conversations between American journalists, including speculation by Warren Rogers that a U.S. invasion of Cuba was imminent. This information was communicated to Moscow along with reports of hospitals in Florida being warned to prepare for casualties and other rather disconnected observations that convinced Khrushchev on Friday that war was imminent (Allison 1999, 350). Although he had changed his mind in the interim, the downing of the U-2, unauthorized as it was, further alarmed Khrushchev and prompted him to accept the American response. He doubtless feared that the situation was spiraling out of control. Two recent revelations support this view. One is that Castro had actively encouraged the local Soviet commander to launch the missiles against the United States without seeking prior authorization from Moscow. The other is that on October 27, the commander of a Soviet submarine armed with nuclear weapons was seconds away from firing a nuclear-tipped torpedo at an American sub destroyer in retaliation for dropping depth charges when he was persuaded by his senior officers to desist (*Chicago Tribune* 2002). Khrushchev may have felt it was only a matter of time until a nuclear accident would force Washington's hand.

CONCLUSION

Thus, although the White House was operating on largely false assumptions and the messages that seem to have mattered most to Moscow were not the ones the administration deliberately sent, the outcome was a peaceful one. We should continue to ask whether the decision-making process was rational, however. Clearly, the White House believed that no action that could be seen as "final" ought to be taken if at all possible. This stalling ultimately proved to be the most prudent deliberate move. This policy was as much the result of Kennedy's frazzled emotional condition and fear of commitment, however, and could easily be considered "nonrational." Robert McNamara, in his popular 2003 documentary "The Fog of War," had a more succinct explanation: "It was luck that prevented nuclear war! . . . Rational individuals came *that close* to the total destruction of their societies."

Much of the Kennedy administration's decision-making process was based on flawed intelligence and therefore faulty assessments of Soviet behavior and intentions. This stemmed in part from the organizational structures and processes in place at the time. In addition, once decisions were made, they were often not carried out according to plan. The implementing agencies frequently filtered the instructions from the White House through their own standard operating procedures and institutional cultures.

As it happens, the most significant actions that the administration took involved the substantial preparations for war that were telegraphed to Moscow on a daily basis. In retrospect, it was perhaps this state of readiness that made the deepest impression on the Soviet leadership and prompted them to take the other messages coming from Washington seriously. Warnings, blockades, speeches at the UN, and so forth, carried a powerful punch when placed against the backdrop of hundreds of thousands of Marines and soldiers gathering in Florida.

Interestingly enough, the Cuban Missile Crisis signaled the beginning of a long and winding process of superpower détente. Having faced a nuclear exchange, both Moscow and Washington took steps over the next few years to prevent such a crisis from recurring. The "hotline" was installed in 1963 to allow the heads of each government to communicate at any time. Major arms control agreements and military safeguards were negotiated during both Lyndon Johnson's and Richard Nixon's administrations between 1963 and 1972. Thus, although the world can fault the superpowers for bringing it to the brink of annihilation, we can take comfort from the fact that important lessons were learned and acted upon.

 DEBATE TOPIC

His handling of the Cuban Missile Crisis catapulted John F. Kennedy to heroic status. Does he deserve the credit he has been given?

PRO

Kennedy apologists routinely cite the following points: (1) Kennedy single-handedly promoted the blockade solution as a way of helping the Soviets save face. (2) Kennedy overcame objections from both the military and the diplomatic corps (including his brother Robert) to maintain this course once adopted. (3) Kennedy carefully constructed a decision-making structure that promoted brainstorming and "buy in."

CON

Those who question Kennedy's stature point out the following: (1) The blockade solution actually heightened risks by alerting the Soviets to U.S. intentions without removing the missiles in itself. (2) Kennedy did not assert control of intelligence gathering and the implementation process until after serious mistakes were already made. (3) Kennedy was the beneficiary of numerous strokes of luck that were beyond his control (and even knowledge).

 # THINKING THEORETICALLY

Although the case aims at illustrating rationality in decision making, the fact is that there is just as much evidence for as against this theory. Let us consider two completely different alternative explanations. Institutionalists would be quick to point out—as did Graham Allison many years ago—that most if not all of the decisions taken by both American and Russian officials were driven by bureaucratic dynamics: the imperfect quest for information, the limited search for options, the selection of "least bad" alternatives and their flawed implementation. But there is another approach that may be less familiar to the student. Constructivists argue, among other things, that the values one holds near and dear can direct choice by privileging certain ideas and making other options taboo. Consider the Kennedy's response to the military options presented before him: he wasn't so much concerned about their effectiveness as their legitimacy. He did not want to go down in history as the president that launched a massive surprise attack against a small, Third World country. This fear of losing his reputation was closely tied to his perception of his own and the American people's values about what is right and wrong—regardless of whether what is wrong might be effective.

QUESTIONS TO CONSIDER

1. To what extent were decision makers during the Cuban Missile Crisis motivated by habit, prejudice, emotion, or other nonrational impulses? Would other people in the same situation have reached the same decisions?

2. To what extent did group dynamics and social pressures influence the ExComm's decision making? Would these individuals have reached the same decisions alone?

3. How did the stress and pressure of crisis decision making affect the search for alternative options? Would the players have come to the same conclusions if they had had several weeks or months to think them through?

4. How effectively were the decisions implemented? Did any unanticipated outcomes follow from the decisions taken?

WEBSITES

Audio recordings of ExComm meetings: **www.hpol.org/jfk/cuban**
National Security Agency's record: **www.nsa.gov:8080/docs/cuba**
Documents on the crisis: **www.mtholyoke.edu/acad/intrel/cuba.htm**
More crisis documentation: **www.gwu.edu/~nsarchive/nsa/cuba_mis_cri/moment.htm**
"Fog of War" documentary Web site presenting Robert McNamara's lessons:
    http://www.sonyclassics.com/fogofwar/

REFERENCES

Allison, Graham. *Essence of Decision: Explaining the Cuban Missile Crisis*, 2nd ed. (New York: Addison Wesley Longman, 1999).

Blight, James G. *The Shattered Crystal Ball: Fear and Learning in the Cuban Missile Crisis* (Savage, MD: Rowman and Littlefield, 1990).

Chicago Tribune, October 14, 2002, p. 3

Craig, Gordon, and Alexander George. *Force and Statecraft* (New York: Oxford University Press, 1990).

Ferrell, Robert, ed. *The Twentieth Century: An Almanac* (New York: World Almanac, 1985).

Fursenko, Aleksandr, and Timothy Naftali. *"One Hell of a Gamble": Khrushchev, Castro and Kennedy, 1958–1964* (New York: W. W. Norton, 1997).

Garthoff, Raymond. *Reflections on the Cuban Missile Crisis*, rev. ed. (Washington, DC: Brookings Institute, 1989).

Hermann, Charles. "International Crisis a Situational Variable." In James Rosenau, ed., *International Politics and Foreign Policy* (New York: Free Press, 1969): 113–137.

Janis, Irving. *Victims of Groupthink* (Boston: Houghton Mifflin, 1972).

Kennedy, Robert. *Thirteen Days: A Memoir of the Cuban Missile Crisis* (New York: W. W. Norton, 1969).

March, James, and Herbert Simon. *Organizations* (New York: Wiley and Sons, 1958).

National Archives. *The Cuban Missile Crisis: President Kennedy's Address to the Nation, October 22, 1962* (Washington, DC: U.S. Government Printing Office, 1988).

"October 27, 1962: Transcripts of the Meetings of the ExComm." *International Security* 12 #3 (Winter 1987/88): 30–92.

Sorenson, Theodore. *Kennedy* (New York: Harper & Row, 1965).

Trachtenberg, Mark. "The Influence of Nuclear Weapons in the Cuban Missile Crisis." *International Security* 10 #1 (Summer 1985): 135–163.

"White House Tapes and Minutes of the Cuban Missile Crisis." *International Security* 10 #1 (Summer 1985): 171–203.

PART

2

INTERNATIONAL SECURITY

CASE 5

The Persian Gulf War: Capabilities and Influence

INTRODUCTION: POWER

Central to the debate over the best definition of power is how a nation's power capabilities are converted into actual influence. A nation is often described as "powerful" when it has a large military establishment, sizable natural resources, and a large and well-educated population, among other things. These features are more properly described as "capabilities," and they may or may not translate into "influence" in terms of changing or preserving the international system. An army two million strong and several thousand nuclear warheads did not bring American victory in the Vietnam War, and many feared that the overwhelming advantage of the U.S.-led coalition in the Persian Gulf War would likewise be for naught. Control of oil was an advantage for Iraq, but, paradoxically, control of oil consumption turned out to be a more significant asset for the United States and the West.

Resources are certainly vital to a nation's power. As pointed out by Rothgeb, they provide (1) the impression of power (which may be enough in and of itself to bring about compliance with your wishes), (2) expanded vehicles for influencing others (bribery, boycotts, invasions, and so forth), and (3) resistance to others' efforts at influencing your own policies (oil stockpiles protect against embargoes, for example) (Rothgeb 1993, 192).

This is not to say that capability is sufficient to generate influence. Much depends on how this power is utilized in day-to-day, dynamic situations. Military threats that are not credible or are poorly communicated will probably not deter undesired action. If a nation's capabilities are exaggerated, then the country may enjoy a false sense of security until a crisis unravels everything.

The reader is invited to pay especially close attention to the way power is used in a crisis where stakes are high and "all necessary means" are brought to bear. The number of players in the Gulf War was quite large, and their interests and power varied dramatically. To what can we attribute George H. W. Bush's success in assembling an anti-Iraq coalition with countries in Western Europe, the Middle East, and many other regions? How significant was the UN's involvement? Could this alliance

November 6   President George H. W. Bush announces a large increase in troop strength.

November 29   The UN Security Council sets a deadline for Iraqi withdrawal from Kuwait.

1991
January 17   Coalition forces launch air strikes against Iraqi forces in and around Kuwait.

January 20   Coalition forces achieve air superiority.

January 26   Iraqi forces begin releasing Kuwaiti oil into the Persian Gulf.

February 23   Coalition forces launch a ground strike against Iraqi forces.

February 28   Iraqi forces surrender.

May   U.S. troops are withdrawn from Kuwait. Kurds rebel against Saddam Hussein's regime.
A "no-fly" zone is created in northern Iraq to discourage Iraqi attacks against rebels.

1992
A "no-fly" zone is created in southern Iraq. UN weapons inspectors are rebuffed in Baghdad.
Paul Wolfowitz directs drafting of Defense Planning Guidance, calling for preemptive strikes
against potential enemies, as opposed to mere containment of threats.

1998
The United Kingdom and the United States launch air strikes against Iraqi weapons installations. Iraq bars UN weapons inspectors.

2002
The U.S. proposes an invasion of Iraq to overthrow Saddam Hussein's regime. The White
House consistently argues that Iraq is rebuilding a stockpile of weapons of mass destruction
and had ties to al Qaeda and the September 11 terror attacks.

September 17   President Bush releases the National Security Strategy which clarifies the
new "Bush Doctrine" of preemptive strikes.

October 11   The U.S. Senate, by a vote of 77–23, approves a resolution granting President
Bush the authority to use force to disarm Saddam Hussein.

2003
February 5   Colin Powell makes the case that Iraq has weapons of mass destruction before the
UN Security Council. France and Russia are unmoved and continue to oppose a new
resolution.

March 19   Cabinet members approve the plan of attack.

March 20   Air campaign begins, described as "shock and awe." The 1st Marine Division
enters Iraqi territory the next day and quickly advances toward Baghdad.

April 9   A statue of Saddam Hussein is toppled in downtown Baghdad, symbolizing the end
of his government. Hussein himself would eventually by found in a spider hole on December
13. The collapse of Hussein's regime leads to large-scale looting of government facilities.

(*continued*)

(*continued*)

May 1   George W. Bush lands a jet on the deck of the USS Abraham Lincoln to celebrate "mission accomplished." U.S. casualties number 138.

July 22   Udai and Qusai, Saddam's sons, are killed in a shootout in Mosul.

August   More than 110 are killed in two truck bombs in Baghdad and Najaf.

October   David Kay, the U.S. weapons inspector, issues the first of several reports indicating that no weapons of mass destruction had been found in Iraq. In January 2004, he acknowledges an intelligence failure.

May   After uprisings in Najaf and Fallujah, a truce is announced. Sadr City in Baghdad continues to see unrest directed by Moqtada al-Sadr.

2004
June 28   Sovereignty is formally transferred to Iraqi nations, with Iyad Allawi as leader of the new government.

September   American casualties in Iraq pass the 1,000 mark.

November   American forces attack Fallujah to break the back of the Iraqi insurgency. Insurgents are routed in house-to-house combat, but Abu Musab al-Zarqawi escapes.

2005
January 30   Elections for the Transitional National Assembly bring roughly eight million voters to the polls and hand victory to the Shia United Iraqi Alliance.

April   Kurdish leader Jalal Talibani is named president and Shia leader Ibrahim Jaafari becomes the prime minister.

August   A draft constitution is produced by the assembly without Sunni support. It is later approved overwhelmingly in a referendum.

December 15   Iraqis vote for a permanent government. The Shia United Iraqi Alliance wins a plurality, but must wait until May 2006 before it can negotiate formation of a coalition government led by Jawad al-Maliki.

THE FIRST PERSIAN GULF WAR

On August 2, 1990, the Iraqi army, fourth largest in the world, led by more than 4,000 tanks, poured across the Kuwaiti border to overrun a nation roughly the size of Connecticut. One might ask, given the ultimate outcome, why did Saddam Hussein do it? To answer this question, one must understand both the circumstances of the invasion and the character of the Iraqi regime and its leader. A longtime member of the Baathist political movement, Saddam Hussein began his career as a torturer for the short-lived Baathist regime that governed Iraq from 1958 to 1963. Upon its return to power in 1968, the party rewarded Hussein's loyalty and energy with the position of deputy chairman of the Revolutionary Command Council, where he set about ensuring that the party would never again be victimized by factional infighting as it had in 1963. Within a few years, he emerged as the de facto leader of the state and, with the wealth he derived from oil following the 1973 price hike, covered himself with riches and power. He assumed the presidency in 1979 and immediately purged the upper ranks of the party, often carrying out the executions personally and with great publicity (Miller & Mylroie 1990, 45).

The legacy of Hussein's rule is well known. Several villages populated by ethnic Kurds in the northern regions of Iraq were attacked with chemical weapons during the 1980s on the grounds that they sought a separate statehood. The Shia Muslim majority of Iraq (as opposed to the minority Sunni to which Hussein belonged) was a frequent target of Saddam's internal attacks because of their support for the radical Ayatollah Khomeini in neighboring Iran. His relations with Kuwait, Syria, and Saudi Arabia were also tense.

Kuwait had a reputation for arrogance borne of its record-breaking wealth. Many Arabs resented the Kuwaiti practice of hiring other Arabs for the most menial jobs they were not willing to do themselves and then denying the workers any political or civil rights. It was widely believed that Kuwaitis were siphoning oil from the Rumaila oil field in Iraqi territory (*New York Times*, September 3, 1990, A7). And Kuwait, to whom Iraq owed billions, regularly exceeded its OPEC-imposed production quota to reap unfair profits at OPEC's expense.

In the months leading up to the invasion, the U.S. position was mixed—a problem that dogged George H. W. Bush during his 1992 presidential reelection campaign. U.S. envoy to Iraq, April Glaspie, was accused of telling Saddam Hussein in June that territorial disputes between Arab neighbors were strictly a regional matter, hinting that the United States would stand on the sidelines. Although this has been denied (*New York Times*, March 21, 1991, A17), rumors persisted through 1992. According to a CIA official, the United State knew as early as January 1990 that Iraq was prepared to attack Kuwait (*New York Times*, September 25, 1991, A18). It was not until Iraq spoke openly in July 1990 of military action against both Kuwait and the United Arab Emirates that the United States signaled its willingness to intervene by deploying combat ships to the Gulf (*New York Times*, July 25, 1990, A1).

THE DIPLOMATIC PHASE: AUGUST 2, 1990–JANUARY 16, 1991

Within a week of the invasion of Kuwait, Iraqi forces began to amass on the Saudi Arabian border to the south. In order to deter an Iraqi attack on the enormous Saudi oil fields, the United States sought and obtained permission to deploy the 82nd Airborne Division along the border. With this "trip-wire" force in place, the United States began to expand its size in order to withstand an assault in case Iraq decided to attack after all. At the same time, President George Bush sought the support of other countries, focusing especially on powerful European allies and Arab countries most directly threatened by Iraq in the hope of pressuring Saddam Hussein to withdraw from Kuwait.

The UN Security Council was active in the days and weeks following the invasion, passing a dozen resolutions that included issuing a sweeping condemnations of the Iraqi "breach of the peace," demanding a restoration of the situation to pre–August 1, 1990 conditions (Resolution 660), and setting up extensive economic and diplomatic sanctions in the hope they would force Iraq to leave Kuwait (Resolution 661). These sanctions were to be enforced by the U.S.-led coalition through sea power (Resolution 665). Ultimately, in a dramatic show of unity, the foreign ministers of the Security Council members approved Resolution 678 on November 29, 1990, which authorized nations to enforce all preceding sanctions "by all necessary means"—a clear signal that military intervention had the UN's blessing. Resolution 678 was in a sense a sign of the failure of diplomatic efforts by James Baker of the United States, Tariq Aziz of Iraq, and Eduard Schevardnadze of the USSR to reach a settlement on the Kuwaiti problem.

Until late October, American and European diplomats held out hope that some compromise could be reached between Iraq and Kuwait that would avert the need for further war. Economic sanctions were imposed throughout the period. According to Tucker, "those sanctions were almost completely successful in stopping Iraqi oil exports, and Iraqi imports were reduced by 90 percent. These economic sanctions were unprecedented in modern history" in their severity (Tucker & Hendrickson 1992, 101). By late August, the Western powers, Japan, and the Soviet Union were essentially speaking with one voice. By the end of September, 250,000 troops from this combined force were deployed in Saudi Arabia.

The Soviets, unwilling to join the coalition itself, were especially active in seeking a compromise between the parties in the crisis. Up to the day before the beginning of the ground offensive, Soviet emissaries were pressing for a deal that would prevent war to no avail. "Although the American-led coalition had the capability to do as it threatened, the Iraqi government apparently believed that it possessed the military muscle needed to neutralize any moves by the coalition. Thus, Iraq largely ignored the American threats made in the fall of 1990 and the winter of 1991" (Rothgeb 1993, 101).

American demands, which were more modest in the early weeks of the crisis, became more and more inflexible as the U.S. military presence grew. Bob Woodward of the *Washington Post* has argued that the decision to rely entirely on military force was made as early as late October and that all diplomatic moves from that point were largely posturing and rhetoric (Woodward 1991). Others have argued that, given White House priorities, the military option was far preferable to either maintaining the sanctions or withdrawing (Mintz 1993).

On November 6, a few days after the midterm election, George Bush announced his decision to double U.S. troop strength in the Gulf, from roughly 250,000 to over 500,000—half of America's active-duty combat forces. The decision to rely on military solutions, as fate would have it, soon revealed itself to be irreversible—and perhaps this was the intention of the president. Thus it was, with a UN-imposed deadline for Iraqi compliance with all UN resolutions of January 15, 1991, that the region was poised for war.

THE AIR WAR PHASE: JANUARY 17–FEBRUARY 23, 1991

Those who watched the events unfold on television will long remember the beginning of the air war on Baghdad early in the morning of January 17 (3:00 A.M. local time). President Bush appeared on television to declare the beginning of the attack as well as its purpose, making frequent references to the U.S. invasion on D day 1944: "The liberation of Kuwait has begun."

The tactic in the air war was fairly simple: destroy all targets that could conceivably support the Iraqi war effort. As a result, not only such things as radar installations, military airfields, and bunkers, but also electrical power plants, highways, water treatment facilities, and commercial airports were on the list of targets. Within less than a week of bombing, Baghdad had no water or electricity (*New York Times*, January 20, 1991, A1). Early attacks were carried out primarily by Tomahawk cruise missiles and Stealth fighters, which were launched from ships offshore and could hug the ground and pass below radar. Although Iraq eventually responded with antiaircraft artillery, the defense of Baghdad was anemic at best, and after the first few hours, Iraqi air defenses were essentially "blind" (*New York Times*, January 17, 1991, A1).

Iraq responded the next day with Scud missile attacks on Israel, a move aimed at widening the war and undermining Arab support for the United States. In an unprecedented show of restraint, Israel refrained from retaliating against Iraqi targets. U.S. bombers attempted to destroy Iraqi Scud launchers with only partial success. The A-10 "Warthog" was now brought in for its slow, low-level flying abilities, and the operations moved toward destroying the Republican Guard and other ground troops in Kuwait (*New York Times*, January 20, 1991, A1). At home, the war began to take on a surrealistic feeling. Emphasis on technical details of missile targeting led some to describe this as the "Nintendo War" (Florman 1991). Daily reports of targets destroyed and images from cameras mounted on missile nose cones seemed like so many graphics from a video game (see Map 5.1). Estimates of Iraqi civilian casualties vary, but the general consensus is that 7,000 were killed as a direct result of the bombing (Hooglund 1991, 4). Troop losses during this phase of the war seem to have numbered around 75,000. The condition of Iraqi soldiers captured and of refugees coming into Jordan gave visible evidence of widespread disease and malnutrition in the Iraqi capital and on the front lines.

THE GROUND WAR PHASE:
FEBRUARY 24–FEBRUARY 28, 1991

In the middle of February, new deadlines were set, new ultimata laid down, and new battle plans set in motion. On February 24 (4:00 A.M. local time), U.S.-led troops and tanks stormed southern Iraq and Kuwait in a dramatic sweep from the west through miles of barren desert (see Map 5.1). In what was dubbed the "Hail Mary" operation—an allusion to a last-ditch pass by a football quarterback into a crowd of

Map 5.1 Map of the Gulf War (1991)
Source: Michael Dockrill, *Atlas of Twentieth Century World History* (New York: HarperPerennial, 1991),
114–115.

receivers in the end zone—U.S. General Norman Schwartzkopf ordered the deployment of troops originally massed on the Kuwaiti border to positions stretching 150
miles westward along the Saudi–Iraq border. Marine forces were kept in the waters
off Kuwait City, thus forcing the Iraqis to maintain a strong presence and leave their
rear relatively unguarded. U.S. and British divisions stormed into the desert, performing a pivoting maneuver at and around Kuwait, thereby completely isolating

Iraqi troops stationed in the area. The tank battle that ensued was extremely lop-sided, in that only American tanks were equipped with targeting systems that allowed them to fire while moving at full speed and through dust and smoke. "We're meeting the enemy, and we're not having any trouble destroying him," said the military spokesman on Tuesday after thirty-six hours of fighting (*New York Times*, February 26, 1991, A1).

Within forty-eight hours, nearly all of southern Iraq and most of Kuwait were in coalition hands, and Iraqi soldiers were surrendering by the battalion. Tens of thou-sands of fleeing Iraqi troops lined the road leading northward out of Kuwait City, many of them with Kuwaiti hostages. Coalition jets targeted the troops as if they were still part of the fighting.

After 100 hours of fighting on the ground and the expulsion of Iraqi forces from Kuwait, President Bush officially announced a cessation of hostilities on February 28, 1991.

THE INTER-WAR PERIOD: MARCH 1991–MARCH 2003

A wide range of problems fell to the coalition governments with the end of the war. Saddam Hussein's forces destroyed oil tanks and set 500 oil wells on fire, leading to an oil spill of some 6 million barrels (Canby 1991, 2). Iraqi forces moved to suppress uprisings in Kurdistan and in Shia-dominated cities in the south. Finally, the ques-tion of Iraqi weapons and general compliance with UN resolutions dealing with war reparations and boundary guarantees are yet to be finally resolved. The environmen-tal catastrophe following the Gulf War served to destroy not only the region's wildlife but also the Kuwaiti regime's credibility. Countless delays, largely the result of bureaucratic incompetence in Kuwait, prevented the speedy extinguishing of fires at the 500 wells. It took a total of fifteen months to finally put out all the fires—but at least five months of this time were largely wasted. The regime has struggled with the question of restoring its stature ever since, the most recent development being the formation of a strong antimonarchy movement in the parliament, a move that may be throttled by a regime still unsure of its tolerance for dissent.

U.S. troops left the region by May, although the humanitarian crisis in north-ern Iraq following the displacement of thousands of Kurds reached epidemic pro-portions shortly after the end of the war. Some 300,000 Kurds were killed by Iraqi troops, both before and after the war, through systematic razing of Kurdish villages. Ultimately, to protect and provide for these people, a zone of Iraq north of the 36th parallel (roughly 20,000 square miles) was declared a sanctuary by the UN and patrolled by peacekeeping forces (*New York Times*, May 19, 1991, A8). To the south, Shia Moslems rebelled against Hussein and were suppressed, not only imme-diately after the war but throughout 1991. Not until the summer of 1992 did the UN act to impose a no-fly zone over the southern regions of Iraq (south of the 32nd parallel). This had the effect of eliminating the more wanton aspects of Iraqi reprisals, and it also led to a more permanent role for U.S. pilots charged with enforcing the rule.

The destruction of Iraqi weapons precipitated several violent and nearly disastrous encounters between Iraqi officials and UN inspectors throughout 1992. Given the task of destroying all Iraqi weapons of "mass destruction" by the Security Council, the UN inspectors went into Iraqi nuclear weapons laboratories and other extremely sensitive sites (*New York Times*, July 25, 1991, A1). UN inspectors were toyed with as early as 1992 and as recently as 1998. In retaliation for obstructing weapons inspections in 1998, the United States and United Kingdom launched punitive air strikes in December. This prompted the Hussein regime to ban inspectors all together. News reports indicated that Hussein had secretly managed to obtain the necessary materials to assemble three nuclear warheads in spite of it all (Tessitore & Woolfson 1999, 49).

By the late 1990s, the coalition that had organized the Gulf War counteroffensive had splintered. Russia and China were joined by France in their efforts to end the economic sanctions against Iraq, which had already cost the country tens of billions in lost oil revenues and were increasingly linked to deteriorating health and nutrition levels among Iraqi children. A growing number of nonprofit organizations began to mobilize against the sanctions, including the Iraq Action Coalition, which posted a website and began a petition drive in the United States. Ramsey Clark, former U.S. attorney general, founded the International Action Center and joined UNICEF and the UN's Food and Agriculture Organization to deplore the effects of sanctions on children (Clark 1998). As of mid–2000, the stalemate between the prosanctions and antisanctions forces seemed unbreakable.

ENTER THE VULCANS

Shortly after the election of George W. Bush in November 2000, the president-elect was given an international affairs orientation. In it, neoconservative idealists such as Richard Perle, Paul Wolfowitz, and the Vice President-elect Dick Cheney, explained their vision of a democratic Middle East, anchored by a post-Saddam Iraq. Although other senior Bush administration officials, including Secretary of State Colin Powell and National Security Advisor Condoleezza Rice were more cautious, the message was clear: Saddam should have been removed back in 1991. For them, the question was not whether the United States would remove him, but when and how. Paul Wolfowitz urged a more aggressive U.S. foreign policy across the board, introducing a serious discussion of "preemption"—the launching of military strikes to discomfit America's enemies (PBS 2004).

The terror attacks on September 11 2001 prompted serious deliberations in the White House about retaliation. All agreed that strikes against Afghanistan were called for, but that an attack on Iraq should be postponed, at least until the Afghan situation was settled (Woodward 2004, 25). That said, senior members of the administration continued to argue that Saddam Hussein had links to al Qaeda and thereby to the 9/11 attacks, although the only evidence was the alleged presence in Baghdad of a shadowy figure: Abu Musab al-Zarqawi. It was a link that Colin Powell was never willing to assert. This said, the impression left by U.S. policymakers in the run-up to the war was so strong that on election day 2004, the vast majority of those voting for Bush believed Saddam had been involved in the September 11 attacks (Pew/CFR 2002).

As the war in Afghanistan began to wind down in late 2001, the president's attention turned to Iraq. On December 28th, General Tommy Franks, Commander of the Central Command, laid out several scenarios for removing the Saddam Hussein regime (Woodward 2004, 53–60). The message was clear: Saddam posed a serious and immediate threat to the United States, and the United States could take him out—even if acting alone—with acceptable casualties. The administration began preparing the public for an extension of the war against terror in the January 2002 State of the Union address by declaring that al Qaeda was only part of the problem. Iraq, Iran, and North Korea made up the "axis of evil" bent on threatening the United States and its allies around the world. In April, Bush announced on British television that he had decided that Saddam must go. "The worst thing that could happen would be to allow a nation like Iraq, run by Saddam Hussein, to develop weapons of mass destruction, and then team them up with terrorist organizations so they can blackmail the world. I'm not going to let this happen" (Woodward 2004, 120).

By July 2002, Bush administration war planning was becoming clear to the outside world (*New York Times*, July 29, A1). Secretary of Defense Donald Rumsfeld strongly favored a highly mobile, high-tech force with a small number of troops (roughly 200,000) that would quickly strike from Kuwait, leapfrogging towns along the Euphrates on its way to Baghdad. Planning had moved beyond the hypothetical stage.

It was at this point that Colin Powell intervened. He spoke with President Bush about the dangers of occupying a country. "You are going to be the proud owner of 25 million people. You will own all their hopes, aspirations and problems. You'll own it all" (Woodward 2004, 150). This was privately called the "Pottery Barn rule"—you break it, you own it. Powell pressed the president to wait until he had worked to bring together a coalition worthy of the name as well as a UN Security Resolution that explicitly authorized the use of force. His intervention, while largely unwelcome, was successful. Bush spoke in harsh terms to the UN in September 2002, making clear his exasperation with Saddam's obstructionism and his concern about the threat he posed to the world. At roughly the same time the White House published the National Security Strategy laying out the "Bush Doctrine" of preemptive strikes against threats to the country, a policy strongly favored by neoconservatives but condemned by international legal experts as reckless (Boyle 2004, 149; Tiefer 2004, 189). The White House also succeeded in October in persuading Congress to pass a resolution authorizing the use of force against Iraq (by a vote of 77–23 in the Senate).

The Security Council passed a strongly worded resolution a few weeks later, prompting the Iraq regime to once again permit weapons inspectors on site. The action, however, created more confusion as the Iraqi government received mixed reviews from weapons inspectors under the director of Hans Blix. The ambiguities of the situation were enough for some Security Council members to argue that war should be postponed as long as possible. It also did not help the debate that France and Russia stood to make substantial gains from the survival of Saddam's regime by way of oil contracts that had been negotiated years earlier. Donald Rumsfeld did little for his part to mend relations by dismissing France and Germany as "old Europe" in contrast to such new NATO members as Poland and Hungary which had adopted a more pro-U.S. position (Purdum 2003, 67).

After months of posturing by Security Council members, Colin Powell gave them a detailed presentation, reminiscent of the Adlai Stevenson presentation during the Cuban Missile Crisis. In this case, however, France, Russia, China, and Germany were unpersuaded on the need to end sanctions and launch a military strike. The February speech included satellite photos, tapes of intercepted telephone conversations, and even a simulated vial of anthrax to make the point that Saddam had weapons of mass destruction in spite of eleven years of sanctions. The implication was obvious: sanctions do not work and therefore force is necessary. Another implication was clear: you're either with us or against us. Bush's policy was not aimed at compromise or accommodation of criticisms. There was more political benefit to be gained by clearly identifying adversaries (Allman 2004, 209).

France and Russia announced their intention to use their veto to block any new resolution, however, and so the issue was taken off the agenda. The United States would have to settle for the support of Britain, Spain, Australia, Poland, and a handful of other countries in its war in Iraq.

THE WAR IN IRAQ

In a meeting on March 19, 2003, Bush's "war cabinet" (Rumsfeld, Powell, Cheney, Tenet, Rice, and General Franks) approved the plan of attack that had emerged from more than a year's planning. On March 20th, U.S. aircraft launched what it called a "shock and awe" air campaign designed to disrupt and demoralize the Iraqi high command. The next day, an invasion force of 183,000, supported by another 150,000 in the region, moved northward from Kuwait (a northern front was not possible because Turkey had refused to participate) and quickly seized ground (see Map 5.2). The southern city of Basra was surrounded and then taken by British forces early on while American troops moved up the Euphrates River.

Resistance was lighter than expected, although the Republican Guard did not surrender as hoped. Militias, formed prior to the invasion, launched attacks against the thinly stretched lines of troops (Hersh 2004, 258).

In spite of a few setbacks, the coalition forces moved into Baghdad itself in early April and on April 9th American troops were pulling down a statue of Saddam Hussein in the heart of the city. The Iraqi army had "melted away." On May 1st, in spite of warnings against chest-thumping, George W. Bush celebrated the "end of major hostilities" by flying a jet onto the deck of the aircraft carrier USS Abraham Lincoln off the coast of San Diego, California. His stirring speech, replete with references to D day and other heroic moments, was delivered under a massive banner declaring "Mission Accomplished."

Map 5.2 The 2003 Invasion
Source: Compiled from various *Washington Post* maps.

Paul Bremer was appointed Administrator of the Coalition Provisional Authority (CPA) on May 6th, taking the place of General Jay Garner as the civilian leader, answerable to Donald Rumsfeld. He quickly established a command center in one of Saddam's principal palaces in downtown Baghdad, surrounding the area with a security perimeter known as the "Green Zone" where coalition forces and CPA staff could operate without fear of attack. Other parts of Baghdad and Iraq were designated "yellow" and "red" zones—the latter being off-limits to all but heavily protected troops. Although most of the country has been safe, several insurgent groups emerged over the course of the occupation, leading to intense battles for control in places like Fallujah and Sadr City—a neighborhood of Baghdad dominated by Moqtada al-Sadr, a radical Shia cleric with aspirations of national power. Casualties of coalition forces continued to rise throughout 2003, with more killed in December than in March or April (see Figure 5.1).

As time went on, the red zones increased in size and number, until by early 2004 whole cities were off-limits to U.S. troops. Coalition troops carried out organized attacks in Najaf, Fallujah, and Sadr City during 2004, killing thousands of insurgents. In Sadr City, the stand-off between Moqtada al-Sadr's forces and the coalition was ultimately settled through the intervention of Grand Ayatollah Ali al-Sistani who brokered a cease-fire and the withdrawal of Sadr's militia from holy sites. In early 2004, in addition to suicide bombings (which killed over 700 in the first half of 2004 alone), roadside bombs, mortar and grenade attacks, and open battles, insurgents began to resort to kidnappings of foreigners. By the end of September, 140 foreigners had been kidnapped and paraded before the world press, many of them later beheaded. The actions served to undermine the coalition as some of the smaller

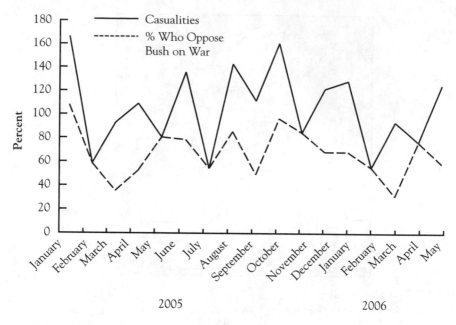

Figure 5.1 Trends in the war—casualties and public support

contributors began to withdraw their forces. The end result was a continued strong military presence of roughly 150,000—a level far higher than had initially been planned by Bush administration. The announcement in February that intelligence on weapons of mass destruction was almost entirely flawed shook the American public's confidence in the abilities of the Bush administration (some critics referred to WMDs as "weapons of mass delusion"; Allman 2004, 309). With more than 130 deaths in April and the discovery of torture being committed by U.S. troops in prisons such as that at Abu Ghraib (apparently with the tacit approval of senior commanders and Washington officials), talk of "quagmire" became increasingly common in the United States (Thomas 2004). A solid majority (58%) opposed the administration's handling of the war, although this figure would decline by the end of the year (and did not prevent President Bush's reelection in November).

News on the war was not entirely negative, however. The UN Security Council, thanks in part to an increased willingness on the part of the Bush administration to moderate its language, showed itself willing to accept the CPA's legitimacy in Iraq and offered its help in preparing for elections in January 2005. On June 28th, sovereignty was formally (if not practically) transferred to a new Iraqi regime under Prime Minister Iyad Allawi, a moderate Shia who has proved capable of generating support from Iraqis and Americans alike. Saddam's capture in December 2003 no doubt went far to reassure Iraqis that his regime would not reemerge. Likewise the removal of insurgent bases in cities such as Fallujah in late 2004. And while some soldiers were responsible for abuse and torture, others, including Lt. Gen. David Patraeus, were successful in implementing "hearts and minds" programs that enhanced the reputation of the American military (Nordland 2004).

The current status of the war in Iraq (May 2006) is ambiguous at best. There is evidence on both sides of the question of whether this was a mistaken enterprise. Clearly the Iraqi people are able to shape their government as never before, having twice in one year voted for national assemblies. The press is relatively free and parties from across the political spectrum are active and vocal. On the other hand, the failure to form a government for four months following the December 2005 elections signals deep fissures among the political elite that will require heroic efforts to reconcile. These fissures are exacerbated by ever-rising violence on the ground. Not only are al Qaeda affiliated terrorist groups active (see Case 9 on al Qaeda), but numerous militia groups tied to Saddam Hussein and various religious and ethnic groups are increasingly bold and dangerous. In some cases, neighborhoods and towns are forming their own protection forces, some of which have devolved into death squads. The violence has escalated to the point that most experts and journalists describe the situation as a "civil war." American casualties have topped 3,000 and a majority of Americans are opposed to the war. Saddam Hussein's execution in January 2007 was met with outrage in Sunni communities. There are few who still harbor optimism regarding Iraq's immediate future.

CONCLUSION

What do the two Gulf Wars tell us about the nature of power, as understood in terms of both capability and influence? Much depends on one's assessment of the extent of coalition victory. Clearly the immediate aims of dislodging Iraq from Kuwait and Saddam from Baghdad were achieved, although only by resort to force. In spite of Iraq's almost complete dependence on oil exports, the sanctions did not have the effect of changing the government's policy in Kuwait or inducing Saddam to step down (although no one will ever know whether they might have eventually worked).

On the other hand, the formation of the coalition in the first Gulf War was a remarkable victory, especially given obvious tensions between Security Council members manifested in the second Iraq war. Saddam learned that defiance is less useful than strategic ambiguity (Cooper, Higgott, & Nossal 1991). The coalition also enjoyed a degree of political legitimacy that is rare thanks to the approval of United Nations bodies throughout the operation (Russett 1994), something that was obviously lacking in the case of the 2003 invasion.

Dissenting voices have pointed out that the war failed to dislodge the Iraqi regime or protect its political opponents (Byman 2000), which in turn motivated many senior Bush officials to call for a preemptive strike in 2003 to finish the job. But the failure to locate weapons of mass destruction or clearly link Saddam to 9/11 has led many to conclude that the end of the first war was perhaps more successful than had been originally thought.

DEBATE TOPIC

Was the Bush administration correct to attack Iraq in 2003 as part of its war on terror?

PRO

(1) Saddam had demonstrated the capacity to build and use weapons of mass destruction. Even if he didn't have them, he would soon. (2) After twelve years of sanctions, it was clear that Saddam would never leave peacefully. (3) The United Nations resolutions gave the administration more than enough legal authority to undertake the mission—the Security Council's recognition of the CPA validates this view. (4) Iraq is much closer to being a peaceful, democratic regime than ever before.

CON

(1) Saddam represented little more than a paper tiger, easily contained—as he had been for twelve years. (2) The war in Iraq is a costly distraction from the war on terror and homeland defense. (3) The United States is ill-equipped to govern a country where it is seen largely as an alien presence. (4) Iraq has become a haven for Islamic terrorists who will continue to use it as a base to attack American forces in the region and American interests abroad.

THINKING THEORETICALLY

It is only fair to allow Marxists another opportunity to demonstrate their relevance. This time we will pit them against the Constructivists and Postmodernists. Where the Iraq War is concerned, Marxists would argue that the quest for oil security is driven first and foremost by the demands of the oil industry—which is dominated by U.S. firms. They stand to gain tremendously from the policy—and in fact their profits have been hitting record levels since the invasion. In addition, the move sustains automobile manufacturers, plastics and petrochemical industries, and all those industries that rely on inexpensive oil—including shipping firms and so forth. Add to this the corrupt ties between firms such as Halliburton and the Bush administration and it is easy to see why Marxist theorists feel vindicated by what is happening in Iraq.

Postmodernists argue that what is really happening is a re-definition of the world in light of apocalyptic religious visions held by senior Bush administration officials. They are so thoroughly convinced of the rightness of their cause that—like the Crusaders before them—they cannot grasp why anyone but traitors would express dissent. They therefore lash out at the press for reporting on casualties, lambaste academia for its pessimistic forecasts, and ignore public opinion when approval ratings drop below 35%. In their reality, the war is a great success and will go down in history as the turning point in the victory of Christian democracy over Islamic autocracy.

QUESTIONS TO CONSIDER

1. Was the Gulf War a legitimate and/or moral use of American power? What about the 2003 invasion?

2. To what extent was resorting to military force a sign a weakness or strength?

3. Did the Gulf Wars achieve the political objectives of the Bush administrations? To what extent were international and domestic public opinion a deciding factor in how Bush prosecuted the war?

4. Does the Gulf War and the 2003 invasion help you to decide when military force should and should not be used? Are there causes worth fighting for?

WEBSITES

General Gulf War and 2003 invasion information:

www.historyguy.com/GulfWar.html

www.pbs.org/wgbh/pages/frontline/shows/iraq/etc/cron.html

www.desert-storm.com

www.nmhschool.org/tthornton/mehistorydatabase/united_states_in_iraq.htm

Advocacy Groups:

www.iraqaction.org

www.iacenter.org

REFERENCES

Allman, T. D. *Rogue State: America at War with the World* (New York: Nation Books, 2004).

Boyle, Francis A. *Destroying World Order: U.S. Imperialism in the Middle East Before and After September 11* (Atlanta: Clarity Press, 2004).

Byman, Daniel. "After the Storm: U.S. Policy Toward Iraq Since 1991." *Political Science Quarterly* 115 #4 (Winter 2000): 493–520.

Canby, Thomas Y. "After the Storm." *National Geographic* (August 1991): 2–35.

Clark, Ramsey, ed. *The Children Are Dying: Reports by the UN Food and Agriculture Organization* (New York: International Action Center, 1998).

Cooper, Andrew, Richard Higgott, and Kim Nossal. "Bound to Follow? Leadership and Followership in the Gulf Conflict." *PSQ* 106 (1991) : 391–410.

Florman, Samuel. "Engineers and the Nintendo War." *Technology Review* 94 #5 (July 1991): 62.

Hooglund, Eric. "The Other Face of War." *Middle East Report* (July–August 1991): 3–13.

Hersh, Seymour. *Chain of Command: The Road from 9/11 to Abu Ghraib.* New York: HarperCollins Publishers.

Miller, Judith, and Laurie Mylroie. *Saddam Hussein and the Crisis in the Gulf.* (New York: Random House, 1990).

Mintz, Alex. "The Decision to Attack Iraq." *Journal of Conflict Resolution* 37 #4 (December 1993): 595–619.

New York Times, July 25, 1990, A1.

New York Times, September 3, 1990, A7.

New York Times, March 21, 1991, A17.

New York Times, September 25, 1991.

Nordland, Rod. "Iraq's Repairman." *Newsweek* July 5, 2004, pp. 22–30.

PBS. "Frontline: The War Behind Closed Doors—Chronology" available at http://www.pbs.org/wgbh/pages/frontline/shows/iraq/etc/cron.html.

Pew/Council on Foreign Relations. "Americans Thinking About Iraq, But Focused on the Economy." October 2003. Available at http://www.peoplepress.org/reports/display.php3?/PageID=646.

Purdum, Todd S. *A Time of Our Choosing: America's War in Iraq* (New York: Times Books, 2003).

Rothgeb, John G., Jr. *Defining Power: Influence and Force in the Contemporary International System* (New York: St. Martin's Press, 1993).

Russett, Bruce. "The Gulf War as Empowering the United Nations." In John O'Loughlin, Tom Mayer, Edward Greenberg, eds. *War and Its Consequences: Lessons from the Persian Gulf War.* (NY: HarperCollins Publishers, 1994): 185–197.

Tessitore, John, and Susan Woolfson, eds. *A Global Agenda: Issues Before the 54th General Assembly of the United Nations* (Lanham, MD: Rowman and Littlefield, 1999).

Tiefer, Charles. *Veering Right: How the Bush Administration Subverts the Law for Conservative Causes.* (Berkeley: University of California Press, 2004).

Thomas, Evan. "The Vietnam Question" *Newsweek*, April 19, 2004, pp. 28–35.

Tucker, Robert W., and David C. Hendrickson. *The Imperial Temptation: The New World Order and America's Purpose* (New York: Council on Foreign Relations, 1992).

Woodward, Robert. *The Commanders* (New York: Simon & Schuster, 1991).

Woodward, Robert. *Plan of Attack* (New York: Simon & Schuster, 2004).

CASE 6

The Camp David Accords:
Individuals in Foreign Affairs

INTRODUCTION

"At a moment of crisis, the quality of a nation's leader can be decisive" (Gergen 2000, 12). This is the conclusion of David Gergen, who served under four presidents between 1970 and 2000. On the other hand, many scholars have questioned whether the personalities of world leaders really matter once one factors into the equation such things as the distribution of power among states, the domestic politics that create and constrain leaders, and the role of bureaucrats and advisers—not to mention the men and women in the field who must carry out any decision (Hermann & Hagan 1998, 124).

Ultimately, the best way to frame the issue is not whether individuals matter but when. At this point, there is a broad consensus that certain conditions may increase the importance of certain individuals. For one thing, a crisis environment typically amplifies the role of the executive in a government, since it is typically necessary to respond to the problem quickly and decisively rather than subject the issue for debate in the legislature or the press (Hermann 1972; Holsti 1989). Presidents earn their salaries during crises, as John F. Kennedy learned in October 1962 and George W. Bush in September 2001. In addition, the personality of an individual matters more where that person has considerable power due to the job itself. Where the leader is endowed with the authority to act alone, s/he is able to allow his or her biases, worldviews, and background to influence a decision more so than when her or she is a member of a committee or is required to submit decisions for approval by another body. The personalities of dictators thus express themselves more clearly than those of senior advisors to an assistant secretary of state (Hermann & Hermann 1989).

*This case includes substantial portions reprinted from Linda B. Miller, "Shadow and Substance: Jimmy Carter and the Camp David Accords," #433R Pew Case Studies in International Affairs, © 1988 by the Pew Charitable Trusts, revised 1992 by the Institute for the Study of Diplomacy, Georgetown University.

Finally, the personality of the individual may express itself depending on the type of personality. Ambivalent, modest leaders who seek advice and consensus may have little clear influence on a decision, even when endowed with authority to act unilaterally. On the other hand, leaders with a clear vision for the future and who enjoy wielding power may be able to shape policy—even when their job description does not lend itself to such influence (Preston 2001, 252). Consider, for example, the considerable influence enjoyed by Henry Kissinger during the Nixon years when the White House deliberately worked to sideline the State Department and control foreign affairs directly. As put by Harvey Starr, ". . . in the case of Henry Kissinger, individuals did count. Kissinger had the official position [National Security Adviser], the unofficial 'clout,' and the opportunity to shape and execute policy in an important era of American foreign policy" (Starr 1980, 467). Conversely, Nixon's Secretary of State, William Rogers, remains little more than a footnote due to his refusal to assert himself.

The story of the Camp David Accords is largely a story of several strong personalities taking advantage of and even creating their own historic opportunity. Henry Kissinger, Jimmy Carter, Anwar Sadat, and Manachem Begin each enjoyed considerable formal power (enhanced by a proclivity for secrecy), relatively strong personalities and visions for the future, and a crisis atmosphere in which to operate. As we discuss the case, ask yourself whether the outcome might have been different had a different cast of characters been involved.

KEY FIGURES
THE CAMP DAVID ACCORDS

Henry Kissinger   National Security Advisor, 1969–1975; U.S. Secretary of State, 1973–1977. He played a pivotal role in creating a stalemate between Egypt and Israel following the Yom Kippur/Ramadan War.

Jimmy Carter   U.S. President, 1977–1981. He is credited with bringing Sadat and Begin together to work out a settlement to the Egyptian–Israeli conflict.

Menachem Begin   Prime Minister of Israel, 1977–1983. A conservative who fought with Jewish guerrillas in the 1940s, his nationalist credentials made it easier for him to persuade the Israeli people of the benefits of the Camp David Accords.

Anwar Sadat   President of Egypt, 1970–1981. He reversed the pro-Soviet policies of his predecessor and made overtures to the West and to Israel. He was assassinated by Muslim fundamentalists in 1981.

Golda Meir   Prime Minister of Israel, 1969–1974.

Yitzhak Rabin   Prime Minister of Israel, 1974–1977, 1992–1995. He reached a preliminary agreement with Yasser Arafat on Palestinian control of the occupied territories. He was assassinated in 1995 by Jewish nationalists.

Yitzhak Shamir   Prime Minister of Israel, 1986–1992.

Shimon Peres   Prime Minister of Israel, 1984–1986, 1995–1996. He served in numerous capacities in the Israeli government and repeatedly negotiated with its adversaries.

Yasser Arafat   Leader of the Palestinian Liberation Organization (PLO) and later the Palestinian Authority.

Benjamin Netanyahu   Prime Minister of Israel, 1996–1999.

Ehud Barak   Prime Minister of Israel, 1999–2001.

Ariel Sharon   Prime Minister of Israel, 2001–2006.

Hosni Mubarak   President of Egypt, 1981–present.

Bill Clinton   U.S. President, 1993–2001. He helped sponsor the Oslo and Madrid Accords between Israel and the PLO and hosted Camp David II.

CHRONOLOGY
THE CAMP DAVID ACCORDS

1948
The State of Israel is declared. A war almost immediately ensues between the new Jewish government and surrounding Arab states.

1956
The Suez War pits Israel against Egypt over control of the Suez Canal.

1967
The Six-Day War takes place between Israel and its Arab neighbors.

1973
The Yom Kippur/Ramadan War between Israel, Egypt, and Syria ends in a stalemate. Henry Kissinger intervenes to negotiate a cease-fire and deployment of troops in a buffer zone.

1974
A cease-fire agreement between Israel, Egypt, and Syria is accepted by all parties.

1975
Preliminary and temporary agreements are signed by Egypt and Israel.

(continued)

(*continued*)

1977
Anwar Sadat meets Menachem Begin in Jerusalem.

1978
The Camp David negotiations begin. The apparent progress made earns Begin and Sadat the Nobel Peace Prize.

1979
Begin, Sadat, and Carter shake hands on the White House front lawn to celebrate the signing of the Camp David Accords, which provide for the gradual return of the Sinai peninsula to Egypt and guarantees of peace between Egypt and Israel.

1981
Anwar Sadat is assassinated. Hosni Mubarak succeeds him as president of Egypt.

1982
Israel invades and occupies southern Lebanon.

1987
The intifadah (Palestinian uprising) begins.

1988
The PLO renounces terrorism.

1991
The Persian Gulf War creates new alignments in the Middle East.

1992
Yitzhak Rabin is elected prime minister of Israel.

1993
The PLO and Israel accept the Oslo Peace Accords, which provide for a form of mutual recognition and phased transfer of land then under Israeli control to the new Palestinian Authority.

1994
Shimon Peres, Rabin, and Arafat are awarded the Nobel Peace Prize.

1995
Yitzhak Rabin is assassinated.

1998
The Wye River Accords are signed in Washington.

1999
Camp David II ends in deadlock.

2000
The second intifadah begins. Palestinian suicide bombers attack Israeli cities.

2001
Islamic fundamentalists attack the World Trade Center in New York and the Pentagon in Washington, D.C., creating a shift in Middle East alliances.

(*continued*)

2002
Israel seizes control of large segments of the West Bank that had been ceded to the Palestinian Authority, including Arafat's presidential compound. Jimmy Carter receives the Nobel Peace Prize for his years of peacemaking and election monitoring.

2003
Ariel Sharon is re-elected prime minister of Israel.

2004
January   Sharon announces his plan for unilateral withdrawal from the Gaza Strip. The controversial decision is ultimately approved by the Cabinet and the Bush administration.

November   Yassir Arafat dies in Paris following an illness.

2005
January   Elections in Palestine keep Fatah in power under President Mahmoud Abbas.

August   Israel completes pull out of troops and settlers from the Gaza Strip.

2006
January 5   Ariel Sharon has a stroke that puts him in a coma. Deputy Prime Minister Ehud Olmert assumes power.

January 26   Hamas wins parliamentary elections in Palestine. Western states begin applying economic and diplomatic sanctions against it.

March   Elections in Israeli bring a victory for Kadima, the party founded by Ariel Sharon.

HENRY KISSINGER AND THE 1973 WAR

Israel's lightning strike into Jordan, Syria, and Egypt in 1967 left Israeli troops and a growing number of settlers in power in the Golan Heights, the West Bank, the Gaza Strip, and the Sinai to the Suez Canal. None of these actions was recognized by the diplomatic community, and certainly not by the Arab states, which were determined to reverse Israel's gains. The Arab states seized their opportunity on October 6, 1973, during the Jewish Yom Kippur feast in Israel, when Egyptian and Syrian troops launched a coordinated surprise attack on Israel.

Unlike earlier Arab–Israeli wars, this battle did not produce a classic victory of West over East. To begin, Egypt had previously expelled its Soviet advisors in an ongoing effort to improve relations with the United States. ("Why has Sadat done me this favor?" Kissinger asked his aides; Sheehan 1981, 49.) Egypt was thus not acting as a Soviet surrogate. More important, the war did not go well for Israel. By the third day, it was clear that the Arab forces were well organized, were well armed, and were having moderate success. The Egyptians had reclaimed the Suez and a roughly ten-mile-deep adjacent strip in the Sinai. The Syrians reclaimed as much as one-third of the Golan, and Syrian forces pushed to within five miles of the Israeli border (Dockrill 1991, 109). Henry Kissinger took note of this rather unusual situation by endeavoring to "consolidate the stalemate":

> I believed that only a battlefield stalemate would provide the foundation on which fruitful negotiations might begin. Any equilibrium—if only an equilibrium of mutual exhaustion—would make it easier to reach an enforceable solution. (Kissinger 1982, 496)

From October 10 to November 9, 1973, Kissinger exerted considerable pressure on Israel to accept a ceasefire and a negotiated settlement. On October 11, President Richard Nixon accepted Kissinger's recommendation to send an airlift of military supplies to Israel, having failed to secure Egyptian acceptance of an immediate cease-fire. Shortly afterward, Arab members of OPEC imposed an embargo on the export of oil to the United States along with a unilateral quadrupling of crude oil prices.

The oil embargo intensified Kissinger's efforts to reach a negotiated settlement of the war, and he sought the support of the Soviet Union. On October 22, UN Security Council Resolution 338, cosponsored by the two superpowers, demanded the immediate cessation of hostilities and the beginning of a peaceful settlement (along the lines of a two-state solution called for in UN Security Council Resolution 242). The resolution did not stop the fighting, and Israeli armies swarmed across the Suez, effectively cutting off Egypt's Third Army on the eastern bank. The Soviet Union came close to intervening directly to support Egypt, but American warnings and a dramatic rise in its nuclear preparedness (DEFCON) caused the Soviets to refrain. The United States simultaneously exerted pressure on Israel to pull back from the Egyptian front to allow Egypt's forces to be re-supplied. Israel was reluctant to agree, given the considerable diplomatic leverage on Egypt this military posture commanded.

With each passing day, Kissinger became more and more directly involved in negotiating a peaceful settlement of the Suez dispute. On November 7, while in Cairo, he secured the support of President Anwar Sadat of Egypt for a six-point program that provided for Third Army relief, prisoner exchange, and a future peace conference in Geneva. This has been considered a major turning point in Egyptian policy because it was the first time Sadat was willing to accept something less than full Israeli withdrawal to the 1967 lines (Kalb & Kalb 1974, 510). It was also the beginning of a break in the Arab alliance, although this outcome was more unintended than deliberate. On November 9, Israel agreed to the plan after the United States gave assurances that it would monitor the re-supply effort for the Third Army. The model of Israeli concessions conditional on major guarantees by the United States was repeated again and again during later talks.

Israel and Egypt were still far apart on two main issues: "nonbelligerency" and exchange of prisoners. The Israelis sought from Egypt a firm commitment to peaceful relations, whereas Egypt wanted to maintain strong ties to other Arab states. Egypt was also reluctant to engage in a full-scale exchange of prisoners until it could be assured that Israeli forces would withdraw from Egyptian territory west of the Suez Canal.

A third issue that still divided Israel and Egypt involved Palestinian rights and self-determination. Kissinger hoped to set this problem aside and move forward instead on bilateral arrangements between Israel and each of its enemies. Nonetheless, a conference was organized to study the general problem of the occupied territories as well as to finalize plans for troop disengagement in both the Sinai and the Golan. In this context, Kissinger sought the participation of Syria, Jordan, and Saudi Arabia as well as Israel and Egypt.

The December Geneva conference met with little enthusiasm. Although Israel, Egypt, and Jordan accepted invitations delivered jointly by the Soviets, Americans, and UN, Syria and Saudi Arabia declined on the grounds that Israeli withdrawal should precede any conference. Israel opposed UN participation, but the United States insisted, so Kissinger agreed to lessen the secretary general's role to that of symbolic figurehead. Israel refused to permit Palestinian representatives at the conference, which Egypt regretted but accepted. Throughout the preliminaries, all the Arab nations except Egypt seemed to assume that the United States was able to change Israeli attitudes with the wave of a hand—in reality, it seemed at times that the reverse was more accurate. Nevertheless, running throughout this process as a subtle prod to Arab attentiveness and flexibility was the implicit threat of U.S. military intervention.

The conference itself was largely symbolic rather than substantive, and it did not lead to any larger negotiations or even to talks between Israel and Jordan. In fact, by January what Kissinger hoped would become an ongoing negotiation process in Geneva was superseded by what became "shuttle diplomacy." On January 12, while meeting with Sadat in Cairo, Kissinger accepted Sadat's invitation to act as a go-between to Israeli Prime Minister Golda Meir. The arrangement suited all the parties: not only did it give Sadat a superpower in Egypt's camp, but it also calmed Israeli fears that its concessions would make it more vulnerable. Kissinger himself received extraordinary publicity from the process.

The process of diplomacy led to a rather rapid reconciliation of the conflicting demands of the major parties. By mid-January, agreement was reached on an immediate Israeli troop withdrawal and Egyptian troop redeployment. On January 17, 1974, the agreement was signed, providing for a thin line of Egyptian forces on the east bank of the Suez Canal, while Israeli troops withdrew to a line roughly six miles to the east. Following a proposal by Israeli Defense Minister Moshe Dayan, a UN contingent was deployed in the narrow buffer zone between the forces, and troops near the buffer zone were lightly armed (Sheehan 1981, 65–66). This "five-zone" approach proved to be the recurring theme in all of the 1974–1975 disengagement talks involving Israel (see Map 6.1).

What role did Kissinger play in these negotiations? According to Touval, he was able to induce concessions without resorting to pressures. The incentives that the U.S. offered—economic aid to Egypt, and economic and military aid to Israel—do not appear to have been important causes for the parties" flexibility either. It was rather the pressure of circumstances in which Egypt and Israel found themselves that

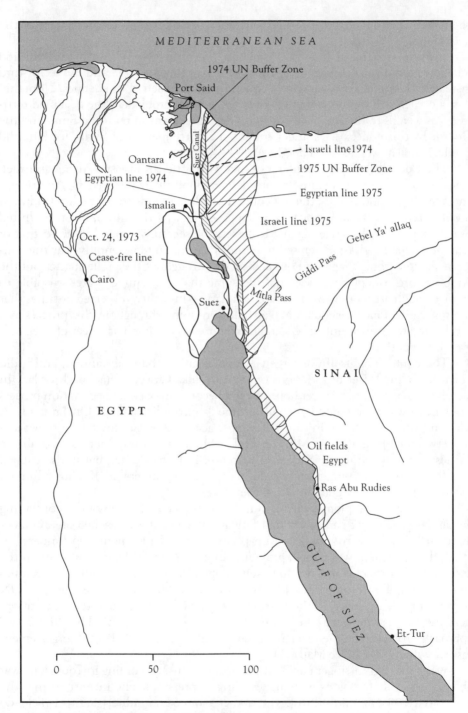

Map 6.1 1973–1975 Egyptian–Israeli troop withdrawal agreements
Source: Lester Sobel, ed. *Peace-Making in the Middle East* (New York: Facts on File, 1980).

made them eager to conclude a disengagement agreement rapidly. The mediator's contribution was, however, essential in suggesting compromises and in arranging the indirect transaction of commitments. This procedure helped to reduce Sadat's vulnerability to criticism from the opponents of the agreement, which a direct commitment to Israel might have entailed. And finally, by providing both parties with implicit and explicit guarantees, the mediator encouraged them to feel protected from some of the risks that they believed that their concessions entailed. (Touval 1982, 248).

Following this relatively easy success, Kissinger was drawn into two much more contentious processes: disengagement in the Golan and a second permanent Egyptian–Israeli disengagement in the Sinai. Because Syria simply did not trust the United States, Kissinger found it far more difficult to establish warm relations, unlike the rather easy warmth that developed between Kissinger and Sadat on the one hand and the near-infatuation between Kissinger and Meir on the other (Sheehan 1981, 72). Kissinger's first major contribution involved conveying prisoner lists to each party in late February and privately assuring King Faisal of Saudi Arabia that he would quietly work for Syria's interests. Formal talks were opened on March 18, the same day the oil embargo was finally lifted (over Syrian objections).

The key issues in these talks were rather simple. On the one hand, Israel did not want to withdraw its forces, which at the time were deep in Syrian territory— twenty-five miles from Damascus—beyond the territory it had occupied since 1967. On the other hand, Syria insisted on gaining considerable territory to prove that its war effort had been at least somewhat fruitful. The debate focused on the eastern town of Kuneitra (El Quneitra), which Israel firmly controlled but which was once a regional administrative center for Syria. Kissinger urged Israel to concede the city, or at least a sizable portion of it, and Israel relented. When it came to determining precisely where the Israeli troops would be deployed, the talks nearly broke down because Israel insisted on occupying three overlooking hills, to Syria's dismay. Israel also insisted on allowing settlers to harvest their crops around the town. Eventually, after Kissinger repeatedly threatened to walk out, the two parties settled on slightly deeper Israeli withdrawals in exchange for harvesting rights and a fairly strong UN presence in a buffer zone around the town (see Map 6.2).

On other issues, Syria refused to inhibit clandestine Palestine Liberation Organization (PLO) raids into northern Israel, even though Israel refused anything less than a guarantee that such attacks would cease. Kissinger intervened by pledging U.S. guarantees that any such attacks would be interpreted as a violation of the agreement, to which Israel could respond with all necessary means. The United States also provided considerable aid as an inducement (converting a $1 billion loan to a grant and sending military hardware).

Perhaps most interesting in these talks is how Kissinger made himself indispensable. He made the point that Israel would have a difficult time finding a better interlocutor than a Jew from the United States. He demonstrated even-handedness with Syria to prove to Damascus that he was the best available spokesman to Tel Aviv. He was able to keep the talks moving forward simply by threatening to go

Map 6.2 1967–1974 Israeli–Syrian troop withdrawal agreements
Source: Lester Sobel, ed. *Peace-Making in the Middle East* (New York: Facts on File, Inc., 1980).

home. On May 25, 1974, he went so far as to coauthor with President Hafez al-Assad of Syria a communiqué announcing the collapse of the talks and laying the blame on Israel (an important threat for Tel Aviv) when, on his way out the door, Assad said to him, "What a pity. We've come so far and not succeeded. Can't anything be done . . . ?" and urged him to try once more with the Israeli leadership (Sheehan 1981, 71). On May 29, Israel and Syria signed their disengagement treaty under Kissinger's watchful eye.

The second disengagement talks between Israel and Egypt stumbled from the start. The new government of Prime Minister Yitzhak Rabin was adamant about a peace treaty with Egypt, while Kissinger tried to convey the political dangers that such a move posed for Sadat vis-à-vis his Arab counterparts. Israel refused to abandon the strategic mountain passes Giddi and Mitla without guarantees. It sought access to Egypt's oil, U.S. aid, and U.S. weapons. Israel also wanted more participation in the rules surrounding the UN buffer troops. Israel's demands were so extreme and its position so obdurate that by the spring of 1975, Kissinger and other senior officials had concluded that the negotiations were dead. In a highly publicized "reassessment" of U.S. policy, Kissinger and President Gerald Ford implicitly accused Israel of stonewalling and threatening the talks. This ambivalence precipitated a "full-court press" by the Israeli lobby in the U.S. Congress, culminating in a letter signed by seventy-six members of Congress urging the Ford administration to maintain its commitment to Israeli security.

In this context, Israeli demands ultimately softened. Tel Aviv accepted the Egyptian offer of a "functional equivalent" to a peace treaty by pledging to solve all disputes by peaceful means. Egypt offered its oil to Israel at world market prices, and Israel was allowed a voice in decisions relating to the UN troops (particularly regarding their withdrawal, which in 1967 had been done unilaterally by Egypt). Israel also agreed to withdraw completely from the passes and allow U.S. and UN inspection of its deployment on the ground. Egypt explicitly (and Israel implicitly) agreed to abide by this treaty for at least three years, subject to annual review, thus creating de facto the Geneva conference arrangement Kissinger had originally hoped for. On September 1, 1975, the documents and corollary agreements were formally signed and Kissinger was hailed as a miracle worker.

In exchange for these agreements with Israel, the United States made what Sheehan describes as a "marriage": It promised to protect a wide range of Israeli interests, guarantee the security of Israel, and verify compliance with the treaties. The United States also promised to have no contact with the PLO so long as it did not renounce terrorism. Finally, the United States promised to veto any UN Security Council resolution that might undermine these various agreements. U.S. aid to both Israel and Egypt increased dramatically and proportionally.

CAMP DAVID

On September 5, 1978, President Anwar Sadat of Egypt and Prime Minister Menachem Begin of Israel and their delegations arrived at the U.S. presidential retreat in Maryland, Camp David, for a series of fateful meetings with President Jimmy Carter and his entourage. On March 26, 1979, the three leaders met on the front lawn of the White House to sign a peace treaty between Egypt and Israel. In the months that separated these widely publicized events, numerous obstacles between the countries arose and intensified; some crucial issues remained unresolved until the actual day of the signing. The entire undertaking was precarious at the time Carter reactivated his peacemaking initiative in August 1978 and remained so even after the documents were initialed and exchanged the next year. The story of these hopeful yet frustrating months is full of twists and turns that kept participants on the edge of failure and observers on the edge of their seats.

From the perspective of more than two decades after the accords were negotiated, the central issues that dominated the talks and their aftermath are clear. Would there be a bilateral accord between Egypt and Israel, linked vaguely (if at all) to an accord on the future of the West Bank and Gaza? Or would a comprehensive settlement address all facets of the Arab–Israeli conflict, from the status of Jerusalem and the Palestinians to elaborate security arrangements and normal relations among all the players (the approach Carter's advisors favored)? Furthermore, what should the United States offer and when should it secure the allegiance of Sadat and Begin to any agreements, as the two local leaders manipulated their own domestic constituents and the American public to gain better terms for themselves and their countries?

In November 1977, President Sadat paid his unprecedented visit to Jerusalem. His bombshell undercut U.S. plans for an international conference in Geneva. Carter was in danger of losing control over a process that had already aroused concerns in segments of the U.S. Congress and the American Jewish community. Some worried that Israel would be compelled to deal with the PLO or with a Palestinian state, and others were anxious about Syrian or Soviet meddling in the diplomatic process.

In the months of reassessment that followed Sadat's breakthrough trip, U.S. efforts concentrated on getting the Israelis and Egyptians to clarify their demands after bilateral talks at Ismailia stalled. Several of Carter's closest advisors "suggested moving toward a strategy of collusion with Sadat to bring pressure on Begin" (Quandt 1986, 163). Although Carter and Secretary of State Cyrus Vance flirted with this idea as a way of preventing the collapse of bilateral talks in the atmosphere of ill will and hostile rhetoric, they understood that it would not produce a lasting agreement and might worsen administration relations both with Begin and with the American Jewish community. Later, as America grew exasperated with Begin's rigidity, variations on this theme of U.S.–Egyptian collaboration reappeared in administration memos and dialogue. As 1978 proceeded, American officials became aware of the differing style of the two leaders: Sadat was eager for the dramatic gesture but not the tedious details of negotiations. Begin was insistent on dotting every i and crossing every t while lecturing his fellow politicians on Israel's security needs, its territorial claims, and the virtues of "autonomy" for the Palestinians rather than an independent Palestinian state or some form of federation of the West Bank and Gaza with Jordan.

Thus, in the second year of his administration, Carter, known for his own meticulous attention to detail, faced the choice of continuing to search for Israeli concessions on the West Bank and Gaza, perhaps more vigorously than Sadat himself would do, or striving to arrange a bilateral Egyptian–Israeli peace treaty based on the trade of Sinai for an end to belligerency. In seeking the second course—in deciding to work with Begin rather than against him—Carter adopted a posture consonant with the national objectives of Sadat and Begin and with public opinion on Resolution 242. When Carter issued his invitations to an unusual three-way summit in September 1978, he knew that he would have to promote interim arrangements for the thorniest issues—Jerusalem and the occupied territories.

Carter also knew that engaging the prestige of the U.S. presidency in such a venture was a high-risk enterprise that could backfire both domestically and internationally and might endanger other initiatives such as the SALT II agreement with the Soviet Union or congressional approval of the Panama Canal treaties. Stresses and strains with Egypt and Israel mounted as Sadat and Begin pressed their respective cases with the White House, Congress, the press, and U.S. public opinion (Spiegel 1985, Chapter 8). Keeping the diplomatic game going as the administration prepared to submit a Middle East arms package to Congress was the biggest challenge, especially because Carter was also working on relations with China. The president's growing involvement with the minutiae of diplomacy meant that Middle East political figures would not be satisfied dealing with lesser U.S. officials. Each complicated exchange of questions and answers among Washington, Cairo, and Jerusalem seemed to offer Washington two choices: either confront the parties by submitting American-drafted texts or retreat from an active role, with the possibility that the enterprise would bog down and Carter personally would be blamed.

Inviting Sadat, Begin, and their closest advisors to Camp David to explore the possibilities of an accord was one thing; keeping them there long enough and secluded enough to develop a general formula or framework for negotiations together with supporting details was quite another. Although Carter believed that gaining and keeping the trust of the two leaders and their negotiating teams were crucial, he did not anticipate that moving beyond opening positions would take a full ten days or more, far longer than the initial three days, or at most a week, that he had planned to devote to the summit. One reason for the length of the negotiations was the expressed desire of both Begin and Sadat to structure agreements with the United States before or, at the very least, alongside any they might conclude with each other. As Carter reports in his memoirs:

> I knew it was a good negotiation tactic by either Sadat or Begin first to reach agreement with me and then to have the two of us confront the third . . . I must admit that I capitalized on this situation with both delegations in order to get an agreement; it greatly magnified my own influence. (Carter 1982, 366)

Following ten days of successive one-on-one meetings with Begin and Sadat, Carter began to develop the essential feature of an agreement that would leave the Gaza and West Bank issues largely unresolved at Sadat's suggestion. On the eleventh day, Sadat threatened to leave—on the grounds that Israel would sign no agreements despite the tedious days of discussion and refining of terms. Impressed as he was with the efforts of two Israelis, Moshe Dayan and Ezer Weizman, to help bridge the gaps, Sadat nonetheless insisted that his advisors now counseled against signing an agreement with the United States alone if Israel could not be brought along. According to Carter's recollections, he approached Sadat, who was preparing to leave:

> I explained to him the extremely serious consequences of his unilaterally breaking off the negotiations: that his action would harm the relationship between Egypt and the United States, he would be violating his personal promise to me, and the onus for failure would be on him. I described the possible future progress of Egypt's friendships and alliances—from us to the moderate and then radical Arabs, thence to the Soviet Union. I told him it would damage one of my most precious possessions—his friendship and our mutual trust. . . . I told Sadat that he simply had to stick with me for another day or two—after which, if circumstances did not improve, all of us simultaneously would take the action he was now planning. (Carter 1982, 392)

The experience was most likely more jarring for Sadat than Carter presents it here. National Security Advisor Zbigniew Brzezinski remembers Carter explaining that he told Sadat his departure would mean "an end to the relationship between the United States and Egypt" (Brzezinski 1983, 272). In the end, Sadat agreed to stay, in part because Carter assured him that any tentative concession he might offer at Camp David, if not part of a treaty agreement, would not be taken as a starting point for future talks with Israel.

Significantly, neither Carter nor Brzezinski mentioned any promises of massive U.S. economic aid or military assistance to Egypt that may have induced Sadat to stay at Camp David. The practicality of such a pledge would become clearer in the future. Carter next turned to Begin and the Israelis to try to resolve the remaining differences. As the talks neared the crucial phase on such issues as Sinai settlements, oil, and the demilitarized zones, together with the connections between Sinai and the West Bank or Gaza, Begin's stage presence, frequently overshadowed by Sadat's flair for surprise and presumed outrage, emerged.

The Likud Party leader, whose ideological predilections differed from those of the Israeli Labour Party leaders with whom U.S. officials were accustomed to dealing over the years, was careful to leave himself a loophole on the issue of removing Israeli settlements from Sinai by stating that he would submit the matter to the Israeli parliament (Knesset) for a vote. In view of what would happen in later phases of interpretation and implementation, Carter was perhaps too persuaded of his own skill as a mediator at this stage: "I told him again and again that this proposal was totally unacceptable to Sadat, who insisted on a commitment to remove all Israeli settlers from his territory before any other negotiations could be conducted" (Carter 1982, 396).

Begin finally agreed to an accelerated Knesset review without the requirement of party loyalty, thus freeing Knesset members to simply vote their conscience. This commitment was enough for Sadat, who tended to lack interest in other details of the agreement. The issues of the West Bank settlements and the status of Jerusalem were addressed with an oral agreement on Israel's part to halt the construction of new settlements until a more formal resolution could be reached. As Carter put it after the talks were through:

> After the Israelis left, Vance and I agreed that we had a settlement, at least for Camp David. There was no doubt that Sadat would accept my recommendations on the issues we had just discussed with Begin. What the Knesset might decide was uncertain, but I was convinced that the people of Israel would be in favor of the overall agreement, including the withdrawal of the settlers from the Sinai. . . . I intended to try in every way possible to shape world opinion and to get the American Jewish community to support this effort. (Carter 1982, 397)

Carter's persistence paid off. An agreement was reached, even though the final tradeoffs were specific only with reference to the Sinai and they downgraded the link between the bilateral accord and the future of the occupied territories, including Jerusalem. Begin could take pride in the arrangements calling for normalization of relations with Egypt. Sadat had attained what no other Arab leader had the courage to seek—the return of occupied territory through negotiations with Israel, even though the basic formula guaranteed Egyptian national aims at the expense of wider Arab demands concerning the Palestinians. Furthermore, Sadat had suc-ceeded in having the United States play the role of "full partner." Ironically, the price he would pay for that accomplishment would be additional demands for con-cessions (see Map 6.3).

The thirteen days at Camp David had produced a framework outlining transi-tional arrangements for the West Bank and Gaza, an agreement by Egypt and Israel to sign a peace treaty within three months, and a specific plan for the return of the Sinai to Egypt with demilitarized zones and international policing of strategically sensitive areas. The issue of linkage might arise again, but for the time being, Begin's loose formulas had prevailed.

The post-conference haggling over who agreed to what, though predictable, threatened to heighten misunderstandings. Trust began to dissipate as the conflict-ing positions of Egypt and Israel hardened on the settlements and on linking a bilat-eral treaty to prospects for the West Bank and Gaza. Carter, sensing urgency, found it difficult to comprehend the domestic political problems Sadat and Begin faced. He was well aware of his own problems, with the midterm elections scheduled for November 1978. He was also aware that Begin was a master at using Israeli domestic constraints as a way to drag out the negotiations. Begin was often tougher than his advisors, whereas Sadat was often more accommodating. American policymakers openly considered an overture to the PLO as a way of pressing Israel harder, but Carter demurred, citing the 1975 U.S. pledges to Israel on the subject as a test of American credibility.

Perhaps more important as the months passed after Camp David, both Begin and Sadat knew that Carter's influence had peaked in 1978 and that as the 1980 U.S. presidential election approached, he would be entangled elsewhere. Begin sought a deceleration of the process to avoid granting Palestinians any additional rights, while Sadat hoped for a measured pace toward eventual linkage with independence for the occupied territories. Cyrus Vance approached Jordan and Saudi Arabia to enlist their support for some eventual Palestinian autonomy accord, although he was also aware that this had not been made explicit in the Camp David language.

In the context of these conflicting interpretations and hidden agendas, Carter learned of Israel's intention to increase the number of settlements in the West Bank, in violation of the oral agreement at Camp David:

It [was] obvious that the negotiations [were] going backwards. . . . I told Cy [Vance] to withdraw from the negotiations at the end of this week, to let the technicians take over, and let the leadership in Israel and Egypt know that we are through devoting full time to this nonproductive effort. It [was] obvious that the Israelis [wanted] a separate treaty with Egypt; they [wanted] to keep the West Bank and Gaza permanently . . . and they [used] the settlements (on the West Bank) and East Jerusalem issues to prevent the involvement of the Jordanians and the Palestinians. (Carter 1982, 409)

Map 6.3 1979–1982 Egyptian–Israeli troop withdrawal agreements
Source: Lester Sobel, ed. *Peace-Making in the Middle East* (New York: Facts on File, 1980).

By December 1978, Carter was close to throwing in the towel. The three-month deadline for an Egypt–Israel peace treaty set at Camp David would not be met. For Carter, the confluence of U.S. domestic politics—the 1980 election—and international politics—the tumultuous Iranian revolution then unfolding—meant that an Egyptian–Israeli peace treaty must come soon, if at all. "I decided to pursue with my top advisers the possibility of my going to Egypt and then to Israel—getting together with Sadat and making my strongest appeal to the Israelis. My main purpose would be to remind them what they would be giving up if the treaty were lost" (Carter 1982, 415).

Prior to the trip, Carter met with Begin in Washington and managed to create a treaty text that was "barely acceptable to the Israelis but did not quite comply with the key points on which Sadat was insisting. . . . " Upon hearing news of the treaty and Carter's upcoming trip to the Middle East, Sadat "was overjoyed" (Carter 1982, 416). Before leaving Washington, Carter was careful to prepare Sadat, who was delighted to welcome the president to Egypt. Carter warned him that additional concessions would be needed:

> The language may not be exactly what you want, but the target date issued and the "priority of obligations" issue are such that you can accept them and legitimately claim victory. You may or may not completely agree with me on the nuances of the exact words but, in any case, the differences are minimal when compared to the overall strategic considerations which you and I must address together. (Carter 1982, 417)

If the Camp David formula could be preserved, the details might be completed quickly while Carter was on the scene in the region. When Sadat did accept what the Israeli cabinet had approved, Carter was encouraged, yet Begin, in keeping with his previous modus operandi, told the president on his arrival in Israel that "he [Begin] could not sign or initial any agreement." As Carter wrote:

> I would have to conclude my talks with him, let him submit the proposals to the cabinet, let the Knesset have an extended debate, going into all the issues concerning the definition of autonomy, East Jerusalem, and so forth, and then only after all that would he sign the documents.
>
> I couldn't believe it. I stood up and asked him if it was necessary for me to stay any longer. We then spent about 45 minutes on our feet in his study. I asked him if he actually wanted a peace treaty, because my impression was that everything he could do to obstruct it, he did with apparent relish. He came right up and looked into my eyes about a foot away and said that it was obvious from the expression on his face that he wanted peace as much as anything else in the world. . . . (Carter 1982, 421)

The final breakthrough that permitted plans for signing of the treaty to go forward came when Carter returned to Cairo from Israel with agreements in hand that committed him to asking Congress for substantial aid in relocating Israeli bases from

Sinai and provisions for the United States to compensate Israel for giving up Sinai oil. Also spelled out were steps to be taken if Egypt violated the treaty.

After Carter's return to Washington, amid preparations to receive Sadat and Begin in triumph, Vance, Dayan, and others strove to wrap up all the details in time for the signing. As Vance recalls, it was a close call:

> Inevitably, there were last-minute hitches. For several days prior to Begin's arrival I had discussions with Dayan on the U.S.–Israeli memorandum of agreement, as well as on the oil supply agreement and the U.S. financial and military assistance package that had been agreed to in Jerusalem. The President also met Sadat and Begin to work out the precise details of the accelerated Israeli withdrawal from that portion of the Sinai containing the oilfields. The final details concerning Israeli access to Sinai oil remained an issue right down to the end. They were not finally resolved until Sadat and Begin agreed in a meeting in the residence of Ashraf Gorbal, the distinguished and extremely able Egyptian ambassador in Washington. At that time Sadat guaranteed to the Israelis the right to bid for Egyptian oil at the world market price on a permanent basis, thus removing the last major stumbling block to the signing ceremony. We did go down to the wire on one or two minor details. . . . (Vance 1983, 252)

On March 26, 1979, then, the signatures were placed on the document and an arduous process, begun by Henry Kissinger in 1973, was completed. The implementation of the agreement, including the continuation of discussion on Palestinian autonomy, was spotty. The Israeli army left the Sinai within the prescribed deadline—a remarkable example by Egypt of winning back territory through the pen rather than the sword. Autonomy talks for the Palestinians, however, were almost immediately overwhelmed by nationalist pressure in Israel and the revolution in Iran. More than a decade later, Camp David may seem to be less of an achievement than it was. If so, it is because Egyptian–Israeli peace is now taken for granted in the midst of rising political extremism in the region as a whole. That peace is perhaps the finest tribute to the thirty-ninth president: other politicians come and go with less to show for their labors than Jimmy Carter.

MIDDLE EAST PEACE SINCE CAMP DAVID

With Carter voted out of office in November, the Middle East peace process halted. Egypt paid dearly for its peace with Israel. It was castigated by other Arab states. Sadat was assassinated in 1981, thus removing one of the most conciliatory Arab leaders in history. Israel invaded Lebanon in 1982, which precipitated the deployment of peacekeeping troops in Beirut by President Ronald Reagan, the evacuation of PLO headquarters, and the movement of thousands of troops across the Middle East. The PLO initiated the bloody "intifadah" in 1987—a mass uprising that continues to this day and in turn has spurred increased Israeli repression in the West Bank and Gaza. In 1988, the PLO renounced terrorism and quietly recognized

Israel's right to exist, thus allowing the United States to undertake direct talks with PLO representatives. Throughout the 1980s, however, the Israeli position hardened and the United States found itself more and more at odds with Tel Aviv over everything from Israeli police repression in East Jerusalem to increased Soviet Jewish settlements in the West Bank.

It was not until the Persian Gulf War in 1991 that major shifts occurred in Middle East political alignments. During the war, many Arab countries sided with the United States and therefore implicitly with Israel. Israel also broke with precedent by not retaliating against Baghdad following repeated Scud missile attacks. Within a year of the war, the United States and the Soviet Union, under the leadership of Secretary of State James Baker and Foreign Minister Eduard Scheverdnadze, organized a new multilateral Middle East peace conference amid skepticism, ambivalence, and only a modicum of hope. The seating at the conference of a joint Jordanian–Palestinian delegation made possible the first direct talks between Israelis and Palestinians in forty-three years. In spite of this historic breakthrough, however, the negotiations plodded along unsuccessfully for nearly two years. Even the election in June 1992 of Yitzhak Shamir's Labour Party—traditionally more flexible on the issues of land for peace and Palestinian rights—had little effect.

On August 31, 1993, in the eleventh round of what seemed to be almost pointless negotiations, Israel and the PLO announced a surprise. As a result of extended secret talks, they had concluded a deal that provided for mutual recognition and self-rule for Palestinians in parts of the West Bank and Gaza. Within two weeks, Shamir and Arafat were shaking hands in front of the White House and American senators were dining with a former terrorist. President Bill Clinton was quick to take credit, if only by virtue of his intentions, even though the Norwegian government had a more direct role in facilitating the secret talks by discreetly providing good offices. More agreements signed in May and September of 1994 sealed the progress achieved. In October 1994, Jordan and Israel signed a peace agreement settling numerous outstanding issues.

CONCLUSION

The assassination of Yitzhak Rabin in Israel in 1995 and the subsequent election of Benjamin Netanyahu in mid-1996 derailed the peace process for another two years. Ultimately, in October 1998, at the Wye River complex near Washington, under the guidance of Secretary of State Madeleine Albright and President Bill Clinton, the Israelis and Palestinians committed to a timetable to complete the peace process—the withdrawal of Israeli forces from the West Bank and Gaza, the sovereignty of Palestine, and the disposition of Jerusalem. The process moved slowly until the election of Ehud Barak as Israel's prime minister in May 1999. He won on a campaign of bringing peace to the region and immediately began settling differences with his neighbors to the north (Israel withdrew its forces from Lebanon after an eighteen-year occupation and began peace talks with Syria) and his Palestinian rivals. Although an intense round of negotiations at Camp David in July 2000 (dubbed Camp David II) ended in failure, the process clarified what elements are needed for a final settlement—namely, resolution of the status of Jerusalem, compensation and repatriation of refugees, Israeli recognition of Palestinian statehood, and Palestinian security guarantees for Israel.

Today, the situation in the Middle East is as tense as ever. On September 28, 2000, Ariel Sharon, an Israeli leader much despised in the Palestinian community, paid a visit to the al-Aqsa mosque on the Temple Mount. The next day, Palestinians began systematically rioting and attacking Jewish targets, using both rocks and rifles. The Israeli government responded with rockets and missiles. In spite of intervention by Bill Clinton, the violence continued throughout the month of October until more than 300 Palestinians and Jews had been killed in what was dubbed the "al-Aqsa intifadah." By early November, the violence had begun to subside and Arafat and Barak were attempting to cement a cease-fire with President Clinton's help. Ehud Barak's failure to stem the violence or reach a settlement with the Palestinians contributed to his resounding defeat in elections in February 2001. The new prime minister, none other than Ariel Sharon, promised a hard line in talks.

Since the terrorist attacks on September 11, 2001, conditions in the Middle East have worsened considerably. Although Arafat was quick to condemn the attacks and continued to renounce terrorism, an increasing amount of violence was perpetrated on Jews in Israel and the West Bank. Suicide bombings became the favored tactic and cost hundreds of Israeli lives. With each attack, reprisals were administered by an increasingly belligerent Israeli government. The George W. Bush administration supported Sharon's policy as part of the war against global terrorism.

In March 2002, the Israeli government invaded Arafat's compound in Ramallah and proceeded to seize control of numerous Palestinian towns in the West Bank that had previously been turned over to the Palestinian Authority. Arafat remained holed up in his offices for days while Israeli soldiers swept the region for suspects. Although the troops were later withdrawn, the hostility between the two camps continues to be extremely high. As of this writing, there is no prospect of peace in Palestine.

In 2003, Ariel Sharon was re-elected as prime minister and instituted plans for a unilateral withdrawal of Israeli settlements from the Gaza Strip and West Bank. Although the announcement could have been seen as a step forward in the peace process, it was widely criticized as a repudiation of the Oslo Accords and the legitimacy of the Palestinian regime. At the same time, in an effort to curtail suicide bombings in Israel, the Sharon government began building a wall around the West Bank territories—a move that was condemned by the International Court of Justice in late 2004. On the other hand, the question of Palestinian governance was thrown into disarray with the death of Yassir Arafat in November 2004 following an illness. Throughout this period, the United States was virtually mute (Jimmy Carter's receipt of the Nobel Peace Prize in 2003 was probably intended as a criticism of the U.S. role in the Middle East under Bush).

Since 2004, negotiations have continued to face impediments. Israel has proceeded with unilateral withdrawal from Gaza as a signal that it considered negotiations with Palestinians futile. This view was validated to some extent with the election by Palestinians in January 2006 of the radical Hamas Party. Its denunciation of Israel and past support of terrorism made it an unlikely candidate for talks, and instead made it the target for economic and diplomatic sanctions by Israel and most Western governments. Finally, the incapacitation of Ariel Sharon in the same month (he was comatose following a stroke) left the country essentially leaderless—a problem that was partly remedied by the victory of Sharon's newly-founded Kadima party in March elections and assumption of power by Ehud Olmert.

What does this story tell us about the power of individuals? It is clear that had Kissinger not applied his ample diplomatic skill to freeze the military stalemate in 1974, there would have been no reason for a peaceful settlement in 1979. Likewise, without Anwar Sadat's heroic initiative toward Israel, the peace process would not have occurred. And finally, Jimmy Carter's vision and tolerance were essential to the successful conclusion of the talks. As predicted, strength of personality, crisis conditions, and substantial power and authority combined to increase the significance of the actors' personalities in the outcomes.

Or did they? The fact of the matter is that while personalities appear to have mattered, this was true only to an extent. They were also constrained by domestic politics and other conditions. Anwar Sadat paid for his daring move with his life. And although his successor, Hosni Mubarak, was able to continue his work, he was not able to expand upon it to any great extent and has struggled to contain the fundamentalism that took Sadat's life. Manachem Begin left office shortly after Camp David, the breakthrough notwithstanding. And subsequent Israeli prime ministers have had to walk a fine line between confrontation and appeasement due to conflicting domestic pressures. Yasser Arafat and his Fatah Party found their popularity plummet among Palestinian voters as they reached out to Israeli leaders. Needless to say, it is doubtful that the new Hamas government will be coming forward with new peace initiatives in the near future. Even Jimmy Carter found that his Camp David success did little to prevent his electoral defeat in 1980.

Furthermore, these actors functioned within an international context that was not of their creation. It is clear that Jimmy Carter could not have performed his role had he presided over a country other than the United States. No other state had a record of support to Israel—a key to bringing Begin on board—or the military and financial resources to guarantee the agreement. Likewise, Israel and Egypt were uniquely positioned as relatively equal rivals, each with the capacity to launch devastating attacks against the other—and to repel them. Had Israel entered into talks with Lebanon, the outcome would have no doubt been very different due to the power imbalance. And so, while it is clear that personalities mattered in this account, the reader should also ask whether they would have mattered as much had domestic and international conditions been significantly different.

DEBATE TOPIC

Does it matter who Americans choose as their president?

PRO

Democratic theory and common sense tell us that the selection of the chief executive is important, but this is particularly true when the nation faces serious challenges overseas. Since crises are, by definition, unexpected, it is only logical to assume that there may be a crisis during any random four-year period of any president's term. And since American presidents are endowed with tremendous power and resources, American citizens bear an unusual responsibility to choose wisely their leader.

CON

American presidents, like all heads of state, are limited in their actions by the international and domestic system and the resources at their disposal. Ultimately, any president will be constrained by these conditions to do much the same as his or her predecessor or successor facing the same situations. Attacks require retaliation, peace initiatives deserve consideration, trade imbalances demand intervention, and so forth. And the bureaucracy, Congress, and even the courts remain in place to constrain or empower the leader. Ultimately, the choice of candidate is largely irrelevant.

THINKING THEORETICALLY

Feminists have a theory of international relations—more than one, in fact. In addition to arguments to explain why issues dealing with the status of women invariably remain secondary in international relations, feminists also argue that there is a "feminine" way of approaching world politics—even if this is carried out by men. Rather than emphasizing conflict and status, feminists argue that world politics could and should be dominated by cooperation—even nurturing—aimed at alleviating human suffering and promote freedom for the oppressed. One might ask, therefore, whether any of the leaders at Camp David were acting consistently with feminist theory. Of the three, it would seem that Anwar Sadat fell in this category, striving as he did to break with years of hostility for the sake of peace. He was directly assisted by Jimmy Carter, whose commitment to peace in the Middle East has been born out by his remarkable work and writings since his presidency—culminating in the awarding of the Nobel Peace Prize. This is not to say the players were not concerned about status and security—only that Sadat was willing to take tremendous risks for the sake of an ideal.

The clearly opposing theory would be realism. In this case, the achievement of a military stalemate in 1974 was key to creating an opportunity for negotiations, which in turn were supported by both the superpowers. The fact was that instability and violence in the Middle East did not serve either superpowers' interests in the long run, and locking in the status quo was the most desirable objective. On the other hand, it seems clear that a stalemate alone could not guarantee peace—this required the specific decisions of Sadat, Carter, and Begin.

QUESTIONS TO CONSIDER

1. What resources did Kissinger, Carter, and Clinton bring to bear on the negotiations by virtue of their position as U.S. leaders?

2. Did Kissinger and Carter make use of different personal, political, or diplomatic assets in their efforts? How did these affect the outcomes of their mediation?

3. To what extent did military matters and regional power relations affect the willingness of Israel, Egypt, and others to make concessions? Was this outcome predictable?

4. To what extent were the individuals interchangeable? Does this story provide clear evidence that personality matters more than other factors?

5. What makes for a good mediator, based on these experiences?

WEBSITES

Several universities maintain websites about Middle East peace processes in general and Camp David in particular: **www.ibilio.org/sullivan/CampDavid-Accords-homepage.html**
www.mfa.gov.il/MFA/Peace%20Process/Guide%20to%20the%20Peace%20Process/ Camp%20David%20Accords
www.cfcsc.dnd.ca/links/wars/mid.html
The Conference for Middle East Peace provides useful information and links:
www.jimmycarterlibrary.org/documents/campdavid/

REFERENCES

Brzezinski, Zbigniew. *Power and Principle* (New York: Farrar, Strauss and Giroux, 1983).

Carter, Jimmy. *Keeping Faith: Memoirs of a President* (Toronto: Bantam Books, 1982).

Dockrill, Michael. *Atlas of Twentieth Century World History* (New York: Harper-Perennial, 1991).

Gergen, David. *Eyewitness to Power: The Essence of Leadership from Nixon to Clinton* (New York: Simon & Schuster, 2000).

Hermann, Charles. *International Crises: Insights from Behavioral Research* (New York: The Free Press, 1972).

Hermann, Margaret, and Charles Hermann. "Who Makes Foreign Policy and How: An Empirical Inquiry." *International Studies Quarterly* vol. 33 #4 (December 1989): 361-387.

Hermann, Margaret, and Joe Hagan. "International Decision Making: Leadership Matters." *Foreign Policy* #110, Special Edition: Frontiers of Knowledge (Spring 1998): 124-137.

Holsti, Ole. "Crisis Decision Making." In Philip Tetlock, Jo Husbands, Robert Jervis, P. Stern and Charles Tilly, eds. *Behavior, Society, and Nuclear War* (New York: Oxford University Press, 1989): 8-84.

Kalb, Bernard, and Marvin Kalb. *Kissinger* (Boston: Little, Brown, 1974).

Kissinger, Henry. *Years of Upheaval* (Boston: Little, Brown, 1982).

Miller, Linda B. "Shadow and Substance: Jimmy Carter and the Camp David Accords." #433R Pew Case Studies in International Affairs, 1992.

Quandt, William B. *Camp David: Peacemaking and Politics* (Washington, DC: Brookings Institution, 1986).

Preston, Thomas. *The President & His Inner Circle: Leadership, Style and the Advisory Process in Foreign Affairs* (New York: Columbia University Press, 2001).

Sheehan, Edward. "How Kissinger Did It: Step-by-Step in the Middle East." In Jeffrey Z. Rubin, ed., *Dynamics of Third Party Intervention: Kissinger in the Middle East* (New York: Praeger, 1981): 44–93.

Sobel, Lester, ed. *Peace-Making in the Middle East* (New York: Facts on File, 1980).

Spiegel, Steven. *The Other Arab–Israeli Conflict* (Chicago: University of Chicago Press, 1985).

Starr, Harvey. "The Kissinger Years: Studying Individuals and Foreign Policy." *International Studies Quarterly* vol. 24 #4 (December 1980): 465-96.

Touval, Saadia. *The Peace Brokers: Mediators in the Arab-Israeli Conflict, 1948–1979* (Princeton, NJ: Princeton University Press, 1982).

Vance, Cyrus. *Hard Choices: Critical Years in America's Foreign Policy* (New York: Simon & Schuster, 1983).

CASE 7

Vietnam Homefront: Public Opinion

INTRODUCTION

Until several major powers became democratic, public opinion was important only to the extent that soldiers were willing to fight and citizens were willing to pay taxes without excessive pressure from the state. By the turn of the century, however, it was widely accepted that public opinion was crucial, even to nondemocratic governments. One can distinguish between fundamental and short-term public attitudes. Nationalism, a sense of duty toward the state, a feeling of community with compatriots, and confidence in the rightness of the national course tend not to vary significantly from month to month or year to year. These represent what may be called the "national character." On the other hand, public opinion polls demonstrate that the national mood and opinions about specific policies change dramatically from month to month—even minute by minute during a crisis. A successful leader will distinguish between these two and learn how to use them to his advantage. An unsuccessful one will kick against mass opinion at his peril.

War in a democracy is a hazardous endeavor for any politician seeking reelection. Although a democratic nation united in battle is an awesome force, democracies are uniquely prone to discouragement when wartime sacrifices seem to outweigh promised benefits. Politicians have been forced to break off an unpopular fight to save their political skins. Many argue that this is precisely what took place in the Vietnam era in the United States. Even today, Americans continue to experience a sense of deep personal ambivalence with regard to Vietnam. Could we have won the war? Was our cause just? Who was to blame for our failure? These doubts and questions were at the root of the public opposition to the war, which in turn contributed to the fall of two presidents and a dramatic change in our foreign policy priorities. As put by former Secretary of Defense George Ball:

> We have never recovered from the anger and divisiveness of the latter 1960s, and I find increasing evidence of the baleful mark left by our Vietnam experience on almost all aspects of American life. . . . (Ball 1982, 467)

To better understand both how public opinion was formed during the war and how this opinion may or may not have affected policy, we will briefly review the key events of the Vietnam War itself. U.S. involvement in Vietnam's civil war dates back at least to World War II and began in earnest in 1954, when the French colonists withdrew from Vietnam after their defeat at Dien Bien Phu. Ho Chi Minh, leader of the Vietcong Communist guerrillas since 1941, became the leader of the provisional North Vietnamese government in Hanoi, while a succession of largely unpopular governments emerged in Saigon with U.S. support. The rest of the story can be told most quickly with the simple chronology.

KEY FIGURES
VIETNAM HOMEFRONT

John F. Kennedy U.S. President, 1961–1963. He supported expanding U.S. military assistance to South Vietnam, although he became disillusioned with its government.

Lyndon Johnson Vice President, 1961–1963, and U.S. President, 1963–1969. He presided over the dramatic increase in U.S. military involvement in Vietnam, based in part on the Tonkin Gulf Resolution he persuaded Congress to pass. He eventually chose not to run for reelection in 1968 because of public opposition to his Vietnam policies.

Richard Nixon U.S. President, 1969–1974. He completed the American withdrawal from Vietnam and negotiated, with Henry Kissinger, the Paris Peace Accords. He also directed a series of massive bombing campaigns in Vietnam and Cambodia.

Henry Kissinger Senior advisor to Presidents Nixon and Gerald Ford as National Security Advisor and Secretary of State. He promoted a pragmatic approach to Vietnam that included both escalation and withdrawal.

Robert McNamara U.S. Secretary of Defense, 1963–1968. An early supporter of military intervention in Vietnam, he later testified before Senator Fulbright's committee that the effort was failing.

Dean Acheson U.S. Secretary of State, 1949–1953. He offered objections to the war beginning in 1967.

Clark Clifford U.S. Secretary of Defense, 1968–1969. He encouraged President Johnson to withdraw troops from Vietnam.

Ho Chi Minh Leader of the Vietnamese Communist Party, he governed North Vietnam from 1949 to 1969.

Nguyen Van Thieu South Vietnamese President, 1967–1975.

Ngo Dinh Diem Leader of South Vietnam from 1955 until his overthrow in 1963.

William Fulbright U.S. Senator from Arkansas. He helped pass President Johnson's Tonkin Gulf Resolution in 1964 and later conducted hearings critical of Johnson's conduct of the Vietnam War.

Barry Goldwater   Unsuccessful U.S. presidential candidate in 1964. He believed Lyndon Johnson was not going far enough to support South Vietnam.

Hubert Humphrey   U.S. Vice President, 1963–1969. He was an unsuccessful presidential candidate in 1968.

William Westmoreland   Commander of U.S. forces in South Vietnam, 1964–1968.

Eugene McCarthy   Unsuccessful U.S. presidential candidate in 1968. He opposed U.S. involvement in Vietnam.

Robert F. Kennedy   Former U.S. Attorney General and candidate for president in 1968. He opposed the war and was assassinated in 1968.

George McGovern   Unsuccessful U.S. presidential candidate in 1972. He opposed U.S. involvement in Vietnam.

Daniel Ellsberg   Defense Department official who resigned, and then released the Pentagon Papers to the *New York Times* in 1971.

Abby Hoffman   Antiwar activist.

Tom Hayden   Antiwar activist.

Walter Cronkite   Eminent news anchor. He came out against the war in Vietnam in 1968.

Martin Luther King, Jr.   Eminent civil rights leader. He came out against the war in Vietnam in 1968.

CHRONOLOGY
VIETNAM HOMEFRONT

1955
January   U.S. military advisors begin training the South Vietnamese army.

July   The Soviet Union and China begin providing aid to North Vietnam.

October   Ngo Dinh Diem becomes president.

1956
Diem begins a crackdown on Communist sympathizers (Vietminh).

1957
May   Diem and Eisenhower meet in Washington, D.C.

October   The North Vietnamese government helps organize a guerrilla army (Vietcong) in South Vietnam.

(*continued*)

(*continued*)

1959

May   The Ho Chi Minh Trail, running through Laos and Cambodia from Hanoi into South Vietnam, becomes an operational supply route for material for the Vietcong.

July   The first Americans die in Vietnam fighting.

1960

April   Universal military conscription is imposed in North Vietnam.

November   An unsuccessful coup attempt against Diem occurs amid growing protests over the regime in South Vietnam.

December   Civil war erupts in Laos, with Soviets supplying the rebels.

1961

May   The Geneva Conference on Laos leads to the creation of a neutral government.

Lyndon Johnson returns from a visit to South Vietnam with a recommendation for more aid to the Diem regime.

October   Maxwell Taylor and Walt Rostow recommend covert military aid after a visit with Diem, but Kennedy opts for more financial support.

1962

February   The United States organizes formal military support in South Vietnam and increases the number of advisors there from 700 to 12,000.

1963

January   The Vietcong score victories in battles with the South Vietnamese army; army unrest increases in the South.

May–June   Some Buddhist demonstrators are shot and others commit suicide by self-immolation.

August   The United States urges Diem to change his repressive policies and warns of a coup attempt.

November   General Duong Van Minh overthrows Diem in coup; Diem is assassinated.

December   U.S. advisors in South Vietnam number 15,000; U.S. aid in 1963 equals $500 million.

1964

January   General Nguyen Khanh seizes power in Saigon.

June   Robert McNamara and Dean Rusk encourage more support; the U.S. military plans a bombing raid against North Vietnam.

August   The Tonkin Gulf incident, involving purported North Vietnamese attacks on U.S. intelligence ships off the coast, leads to passage of the Tonkin Gulf Resolution, giving Lyndon Johnson significant powers to respond.

Autumn   Johnson rejects retaliatory bombing following Viet Cong raids against U.S. installations.

1965
February   Operations Flaming Dart and Rolling Thunder begin systematic bombing of North Vietnam.

General Khanh is removed by Phan Huy Quat in Saigon.

March   The first Marines land at Da Nang airfield.

June   Nguyan Cao Ky becomes the new prime minister, with Nguyan Van Thieu as South Vietnam's president.

July   In light of the defeats for the South Vietnamese army, Johnson authorizes the deployment of forty-four more battalions.

December   Johnson suspends the bombing campaign over Christmas to induce the North Vietnamese to negotiate.

U.S. troop strength reaches 200,000.

1966
January   Bombing of North Vietnam resumes.

Spring   The battles of Hue and Da Nang give the South Vietnam–U.S. forces major victories.

December   U.S. troop strength reaches 400,000.

1967
Spring   Johnson secretly corresponds with North Vietnamese officials on peace options; the North Vietnamese demand a halt to bombing prior to beginning negotiations.

August   McNamara testifies before Congress that the bombing campaign is ineffective.

October   A massive antiwar protest takes place at the Pentagon.

November   General William Westmoreland exudes confidence during a trip in the United States.

December   U.S. troop strength reaches 500,000.

1968
January   The Tet Offensive involving Viet Cong and North Vietnamese attacks on South Vietnamese cities, is repulsed but demonstrates the strength of the North Vietnamese forces to a surprised American audience.

March   Johnson decides to halt the war escalation and announces he will not run for reelection.

April   Paris peace talks begin between the United States and North Vietnam.

July   The Democratic convention in Chicago is the scene of antiwar demonstrations.

(*continued*)

(*continued*)

October   Johnson halts the bombing.

December   Troop strength peaks at roughly 540,000.

1969
January   South Vietnam is included in the Paris peace talks.

March   President Richard Nixon begins secret bombing of Cambodia.

June   Thieu and Nixon announce the withdrawal of 25,000 U.S. troops under the rubric of "Vietnamization."

October   A massive antiwar demonstration takes place in Washington.

November   The My Lai massacre is revealed.

December   U.S. troop strength is down to 480,000.

1970
April   Nixon reveals the covert attacks against Cambodia.

May   Four students are killed in an antiwar protest at Kent State University.

Autumn Nixon explores the possibility of simultaneous withdrawal with the North Vietnamese.

December   Troop strength is down to 280,000.

1971
March   Lieutenant William Calley is convicted of murder in connection with the My Lai massacre.

June   The Pentagon Papers are published, leading to an investigation of Daniel Ellsberg.

December   Troop strength is down to 140,000.

1972
January   Nixon reveals the secret talks between Kissinger and North Vietnamese officials (dating back to February 1970).

March   The North Vietnamese army attacks across the frontier.

April   Nixon approves the bombing of Hanoi.

August   Paris negotiations continue in spite of South Vietnamese resistance.

October   The United States and North Vietnam reach an accord; Thieu opposes it.

December   After the collapse of talks, the bombing raids resume.

1973
January   The peace accords are signed in Paris.

March   The last U.S. troops leave South Vietnam.

August   Congress forces the Nixon administration to halt the bombing of Cambodia.

November   Over Nixon's veto, Congress passes the War Powers Act.

1974
January   War is initiated again.

1975
January   The final North Vietnamese push begins.

March   Hue falls.

April   Saigon falls; South Vietnam ceases to exist.

*Karnow (1983, 670–686) provides the best chronology available.

PUBLIC OPINION AND VIETNAM

The American public generally favors presidents who deal decisively with foreign policy crises, even when their efforts fail. In the case of Vietnam, public support was not only strong but sustained until 1968. Following the Tet Offensive, the domestic consensus on the rightness of the U.S. war effort in Vietnam underwent a palpable shift, which directly affected the way the White House fought the war. To better understand this shift, we need to look at the chain of events that preceded and followed it.

TONKIN GULF AND RALLY 'ROUND THE FLAG

The Kennedy administration came to office with a call to sacrifice in the fight against communism. Kennedy referred to a "New Frontier" of progress and leadership. In the aftermath of the Sputnik shock, the "missile gap" scare, the fall of Cuba to communism, and other deeply troubling events, the country seemed to be on a war footing. Although Kennedy met with a setback in the failed invasion of Cuba at the Bay of Pigs, he captured the country's imagination with his firm stand against Moscow over the Cuban missiles (Kattenburg 1980, 210). Thus, for reasons of national pride and compassion for the citizens of "captive nations," as well as out of simple fear, the American public was favorably disposed in the early 1960s to undertake a crusade on distant shores (Levy 1991, 16). Although Vietnam had not yet entered the public consciousness, Kennedy and Vice President Lyndon Johnson could feel assured of the public's latent support.

After Kennedy's assassination in November 1963, Johnson came to power in the White House. His attitude was far less patient than that of Kennedy, who had tolerated the overthrow of South Vietnam's leader Ngo Dinh Diem after refusing to support the unpopular president. Johnson was more eager to score victories on the battlefield, where the Communist Vietcong insurgents, funded and supplied by North Vietnam, were making significant progress. Looking for a popular rationale for deploying more troops to the region, Johnson seized upon an incident in the Gulf of Tonkin. Two U.S. patrol boats had exchanged fire with North Vietnamese warships near the coast, prompting an outcry from the White House that was echoed on Capitol Hill. Johnson asked Senator William Fulbright to shepherd a resolution giving Johnson broad powers to retaliate immediately and in the future. The Tonkin Gulf Resolution was passed on August 7, 1964, by a vote of eighty-eight to two. As pointed out by Herring:

> From a domestic political standpoint, Johnson's handling of the Tonkin Gulf incident was masterly. His firm but restrained response to the alleged North Vietnamese attacks won broad popular support, his rating in the Louis Harris poll skyrocketed from 42 to 72 percent overnight. He effectively neutralized [hawkish Republican presidential hopeful Barry] Goldwater on Vietnam, a fact which contributed to his overwhelming electoral victory in November. (Herring 1986, 122)

Kattenburg explained, however, that this support was largely naïve because the American public did not fully understand the nature of the war that was under way.

> [T]he American people wanted to believe [the New Frontier rhetoric], and believe they did. When the number of U.S. military men increased from under 1,000 to about 15,000 in Vietnam in a little over six months, few people realized that the New Frontier had in effect started the process of extending U.S. borders to those of Indochina with Thailand. (Kattenburg 1980, 209)

Lyndon Johnson won an overwhelming victory against Goldwater in 1964, campaigning as the peace candidate (a position he reversed shortly after the election; Kattenburg 1980, 251). Support for the war was at 65 percent by late 1965, and with news of the bombing campaigns, public opinion was supportive (Mueller 1973, 119). This "spike" in public support is an illustration of the "rally 'round the flag" phenomenon, whereby large segments of the public express support for the president's policies in any crisis situation, regardless of the substance of the policies. Leslie Gelb argued that in spite of the emergence in 1965 of an antiwar movement, "the widespread belief that South Vietnam should not be lost to communism generated and sustained that war" (Gelb 1976, 103). Nevertheless, letters opposing the bombing campaign poured into Capitol Hill offices following the announcement (Herring 1986, 133). Overall, the signals sent by the public in the early stages of the war were contradictory and confusing. Political leaders could and did read into them what they wanted.

GROWING SKEPTICISM

During 1966 and 1967, Johnson's policy of escalation was in full swing. By the end of 1967, nearly half a million troops were deployed and nearly 10,000 had fallen in combat. Sustained bombing of the North, coupled with CIA covert operations, supported the Marines in the field. Vietnam was very much on the minds of Americans, to the point that it was viewed as the single most significant issue of the day by 1967. However, as the fight wore on, three different groups of Americans began to question the rightness of the war.

The first to defect was a group of already disenchanted individuals who later came to form the core of the antiwar movement across college campuses. We will say more about the peace movement later, but by 1965 it largely consisted of pacifists, leftists, and radicals but also included a growing number of housewives, moderate academics, and various celebrities. By mid-1965, antiwar groups could muster crowds of 15,000 and more (Levy 1991, 126). In November 1965, a major march in Washington, D.C., which hoped to appear respectable by including major mainstream figures, nonetheless deteriorated into a circus of sorts. It was not until the Fulbright hearings of early 1966 that dignified opposition could be articulated.

Of much greater significance to Johnson than antiwar demonstrations was the defection of several high-level policy advisors and members of Congress, who had previously supported the policy of escalation. Senator Fulbright began hearings on the war in the spring of 1966 with Senate Majority Leader Mike Mansfield's tacit support (Herring 1986, 172). At the hearings, the Senate Foreign Relations Committee questioned senior officials as well as prominent outsiders to the administration to make the point that the war had no clear objective or plan of action. In August 1967, Secretary of Defense Robert McNamara gave the committee much ammunition by stating that the intensive bombing campaign in the North not only was failing to achieve its objective of halting the supply of material to the South but likely would never succeed.

A group of senior unofficial advisors to Johnson, including such respected figures as former Secretary of State Dean Acheson, advised him privately in mid-1967 and publicly thereafter that the war could not be won and that he should look for a way out. The newly appointed Secretary of Defense Clark Clifford consistently encouraged Johnson to begin troop withdrawals and a general program of "Vietnamization"—turning over the prosecution of the war to local South Vietnamese forces (Karnow 1983, 559–562).

Most of these defections were by individuals who were firmly committed to U.S. leadership in the fight against communism. It wasn't that they opposed the New Frontier; they simply felt that Vietnam, with its largely illegitimate government, ill-defined battle fronts, and ambiguous context, ought not be the test case (Gelb 1976, 111).

Overall, as documented by Holsti and Rosenau (1984), elite opinion in the United States shifted dramatically against the war. Table 7.1 shows that 38 percent of the elites in the country began by favoring the war and ended by opposing it; only 16 percent consistently supported the war effort. If one adds the "ambivalent supporters," whose enthusiasm for the war clearly wanes, to the "critics," "converted critics," and "ambivalent critics," then three-fourths of the elites in the country were either critical or tending to be more critical of the war at its end than at its outset (Holsti & Rosenau 1984, 33). This kind of pressure from individuals who tended to play an active role in politics was overwhelming for Johnson.

Table 7.1 Classification of Attitudes on Vietnam

	Toward the end of U.S. involvement			
When the war first became an issue	I tended to favor a complete military victory	I tended to feel in between these two	Not sure	I tended to favor a complete withdrawal
I tended to favor a complete military victory	SUPPORTERS (n = 363, 15.9%)	AMBIVALENT SUPPORTERS (n = 346, 15.2%)		CONVERTED CRITICS (n = 867, 380.0%)
I tended to feel in between these two	CONVERTED SUPPORTERS (n = 128, 15.6%)	AMBIVALENTS (n = 128, 5.6%)		
Not sure				
I tended to favor a complete withdrawal		AMBIVALENT CRITICS (n = 63, 2.8%)		CRITICS (n = 378, 16.6%)

Source: Ole Holsti and James Rosenau, *American Leadership in World Affairs* (Boston: Allen & Unwin, 1984).

The third group that became disenchanted with the war was the "general" public—that poorly organized mass of opinion that pollsters constantly seek to measure and plot. Although the nature of public opinion prior to 1968 was uncertain, it seems that the U.S. public's perception changed slowly after 1965 from an initial and fairly general understanding that external aggression was being resisted by the South Vietnamese, to a largely unexpressed image of Vietnamese, both southern and northern, resisting the imposition by U.S. means of a type of U.S.-made order upon Vietnam (Kattenburg 1980, 244).

The press played some role in all of this. As early as 1963, it was reporting on the confusing nature of the war. Stanley Karnow criticized the corrupt regime of the Diem family in the mainstream magazine *Saturday Evening Post* (Levy 1991, 52), and visual reports from televised news media brought home the brutal and ugly nature of this conflict. The question of a "credibility gap" between official military projections and the reality of televised reports became the focal point of the debate on the war by 1968. Ultimately, the Tet Offensive tipped the balance ever so slightly against the war (see Figure 7.1 on public opinion).

TET SHOCK AND JOHNSON'S "RESIGNATION"

During the January 1968 lunar new year celebrations (called Tet) in Vietnam, the Vietcong and North Vietnamese Army (NVA) took advantage of a general lull in the fighting to launch an all-out offensive on every conceivable target in South Vietnam. The "Tet Offensive" brought Vietcong and NVA troops as far south as Saigon, outside the U.S. embassy complex there. Cities, airfields, and fuel depots were all targeted by the most visible and dramatic military operation of the war.

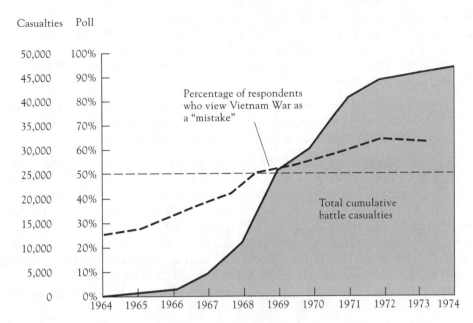

Figure 7.1 Americans' attitudes toward the Vietnam War and battle casualties.
Sources: Various issues of Gallup Poll annual editions.

All of this was covered in painful detail and was exaggerated to melodrama by the American media (Levy 1991, 145). Although the military engagement was clearly won by U.S.-led troops, the psychological effect of the event was to shock the American public into a realization that this war was far from over. Walter Cronkite, "the most trusted person in America," said on February 27, 1968, following an analysis of Tet, that it seemed "more certain than ever that the bloody experience of Vietnam is to end in a stalemate" (Karnow 1983, 547). Shortly thereafter, Martin Luther King, Jr., declared his opposition to the war. A majority of Americans for the first time agreed that U.S. involvement in Vietnam was "a mistake," although there was no consensus on how the country should extricate itself from the conflict (roughly half of those who opposed current policy felt the United States should escalate the war to finish the job, and roughly half felt troops should simply withdraw; Karnow 1983, 546). By 1968, the U.S. public seemed to agree that preserving South Vietnam was not vital to U.S. national interest (Kattenburg 1980, 244).

On the political front, the Tet Offensive coincided with the beginning of the 1968 presidential campaign. Although Johnson was assumed to be the party's nominee, he had failed to file as a candidate in time for the New Hampshire primary in March. A relatively unknown senator named Eugene McCarthy, running on an antiwar platform, inundated the state with an army of clean-cut college students and managed to secure just 300 votes less than write-in candidate Johnson in what was seen as the political upset of the decade. Certainly, all those who voted for McCarthy were not doves (three out of five, in fact, believed the United

States should escalate the effort in Vietnam; Kearns 1976, 354), but the event galvanized opposition to Johnson within the Democratic Party. Within a week, Senator Robert Kennedy had announced his candidacy for the presidency and declared his opposition to the war as the key issue of the race (Karnow 1983, 559). As put by Roche:

> The defection of Robert Kennedy was a decisive event in the anti-war saga. At last the anti-war forces had a senior, legitimate political figure who could not be written off as a Hanoi stooge or some species of eccentric. (Roche 1976, 131)

Lyndon Johnson had suddenly become what he feared most—the "war candidate." Furthermore, his visceral antipathy toward Robert Kennedy knew no bounds. He was haunted by Kennedy in his dreams (Kearns 1976, 264). Johnson immediately set out to draft a full-blown peace proposal, to be announced before the next round of primary elections in April. Finally, on March 31, Johnson announced a halt to the bombing of North Vietnam, a beginning of troop withdrawals, and his own decision not to run for reelection. The Tet Offensive, though failing to topple the South Vietnamese government, succeeded in felling a U.S. president.

During this stage, Johnson clearly was heavily influenced by public opinion. As stated by advisor William Bundy:

> My own impression—for what it is worth—is that the thrust of professional civilian advice would probably have been toward the most limited possible force increases, but that the change in bombing policy was greatly influenced—particularly in Secretary Clifford's actions and recommendations—by a sense of the progressively eroding domestic political support that was so dramatically evident to us all during the month of March. (Schandler 1977, 329)

The combination of elite and mass opinion (as expressed most concretely in New Hampshire) had a significant impact on the president's decision. What is less clear is the impact, if any, that the by-now large antiwar/peace movement was having.

THE PEACE MOVEMENT

The antiwar demonstrations of the 1960s and 1970s were among the most dramatic outpouring of public sentiment on a foreign policy issue in U.S. history. Roughly half a million people gathered in Washington, D.C. for the Vietnam Moratorium in October 1969. During the student protests following the Kent State/Cambodia incidents, 450 college campuses across the country were closed (Levy 1991, 155–159). In fact, the peace movement was strong among veterans of the war and even soldiers in Vietnam. Desertions rose to some 500,000 over the course of the war, and toward its end, many officers were reluctant to assign dangerous missions because of numerous incidents of "fragging" (assassination by another soldier) (Kattenburg 1980, 284). Estimates are that nearly 10 million of the 27 million draft-eligible men deserted, fled to another country, or obtained legal deferments to avoid service.

In general terms, the resistance of the youth of the country to the war effort went far to debilitate its prosecution but did not in and of itself alter government policy. In fact, Herring concludes:

Anti-war protests did not turn the American people against the war, as some critics have argued. . . . Public opinion polls make abundantly clear, moreover, that a majority of Americans found the anti-war movement, particularly its radical and "hippie" elements, more obnoxious than the war itself. In a perverse sort of way, the protest may even have strengthened support for a war that was not in itself popular. (Herring 1986, 173)

According to Gelb:

Passionate opposition and intellectual arguments, in the end, counted for very little and changed few minds. The argument that finally prevailed at the end of the Johnson Administration was the weight of dead Americans. (Gelb 1976, 112)

The antiwar movement was never centralized. It consisted of a wide variety of interests organized primarily at the local level at certain major universities and cities. The San Francisco Bay area, with the University of California at Berkeley as the focal point, was early on a key hub of the movement. Some of the important organizations associated with the antiwar movement were the Students for a Democratic Society (which later spawned a small terrorist group known as the Weathermen), the National Mobilization Committee to End the War, the Vietnam Moratorium Committee, and the National Peace Action Coalition. The principal elements of the movement were pacifist, radical, and anarchist in the early stages. Even the early leaders disagreed over methods and aims. It seems in retrospect that the only thing they shared was a disgust with the war. This problem would come back to haunt the more moderate elements of the movement in later years because it became apparent that antiwar activists were successful only to the extent that they focused exclusively on Vietnam (Levy 1991, 48). For example, when an effort was made to organize a massive antiwar demonstration in front of the Pentagon in October 1967, many were content to sing folk songs and sign petitions, while others in the group physically assaulted the military police (Levy 1991, 136).

This split became especially pronounced during the 1968 election campaign, when a large number of activists joined forces with Eugene McCarthy and Robert Kennedy to work for gradual change. In the meantime, anarchists and radicals, who called for an overthrow of the political system itself through civil disobedience and even violence, became more active (Brown 1976, 122). The contrast was vividly displayed during the tumultuous 1968 Democratic convention in Chicago.

On the floor of the convention, for those delegates whose credentials were approved—the fight, though acrimonious—was relatively formal. For the better part of a day, the convention delegates debated inclusion of an antiwar plank in the party platform, which was quickly countered by a plank supporting administration policy. When the vote was finally tallied, it demonstrated a profound split: 1,568 in favor and 1,041 against the proadministration policy (Levy 1991, 149).

Outside the convention hall, a large number of antiwar protesters assembled to confront, before a live television audience, the aggressive Chicago police force. As put by Shils:

> Hippies, pacifists, socialists, propagandists for a North Vietnamese and Vietcong victory came together and challenged the Chicago police. The provocation was deliberate and successful. The police responded as they were desired to respond, and the television services showed the entire country what the establishment was like— heavy-handed, monstrous, brutal, and incompetent. (Shils 1976, 57)

In a famous moment, the crowd, recognizing the cameras were rolling, began chanting "The whole world is watching!" Viewers at home were generally repelled by both sides of this confrontation, and it generated little sympathy for the antiwar movement.

The Nixon administration continued the policy of rapid troop withdrawal begun by Johnson in April 1968, and the peace movement lost some momentum. The urgency of changing government policy dissipated, and the movement returned to its more radical roots as moderates lost interest. The revelations in April 1970 that the administration had escalated the war by launching large-scale bombing raids in Cambodia and Laos, however, stirred a new enthusiasm for protest. Almost no campus was prowar by this time (Shils 1976, 56). Unrest broke out, most notably at Kent State University, where National Guardsmen, under the direction of Governor James Rhodes, fired into an unruly crowd with live bullets, killing four students. The outrage that followed the incident paralyzed the educational system of the country. For the first time, the public's sympathy was with the demonstrators (Kattenburg 1980, 278).

Did the peace movement change policy? Lyndon Johnson never appreciated the message that the activists conveyed, and he always felt unable to communicate with them. They did not seem to understand the feelings of self-sacrifice, devotion to country, and dread of communism that were so important to Johnson's generation. Likewise, Johnson feared the freedom, tolerance, and moral outrage spoken of by the students and activists.

Even leaders of the antiwar movement recognized that they achieved few of their goals regarding changing public policy (although this may be a function of unrealistic expectations).

THE NIXON ERA AND CONGRESSIONAL REASSERTION

Richard Nixon at one point claimed to have a "secret plan" to end the war in Vietnam. Just as Johnson had misled the public in the 1964 election, Nixon's claims were deceptive. The only plan was to escalate the violence while pursuing confidential contacts with the North Vietnamese (Levy 1991, 152). In fact, Nixon ended up dropping even more bombs on Indochina than Johnson had (Roche 1976, 135).

The reality that the war was not ending soon prompted an intensification of general opposition to the war. "Lou Harris observed that 'a literal race' was on between successive Nixon announcements of further troop withdrawals and a growing public appetite for faster and faster removal of troops from Vietnam" (Levy 1991, 161). Twenty-six percent of respondents thought that troop withdrawals were progressing too slowly in late 1969. In May 1971, that figure was up to 45 percent, and in November 1971 it had reached 53 percent. This increase in opposition paralleled the growth in cumulative casualty figures and mounting financial costs of the war. The mid-1971 publication of the Pentagon Papers, a collection of classified documents related to prosecuting the war, revealed a pattern of deception and secret escalation on the part of successive administrations (*New York Times* 1971, xi). The Cambodia revelations and the My Lai massacre of Vietnamese civilians by Lieutenant William Calley's unit all combined to create a new public consensus—this time in favor of rapid withdrawal regardless of the implications for South Vietnamese sovereignty (Kattenburg 1980, 258).

Nixon's general plan of "peace with honor" finally came to fruition shortly after the 1972 election with the Paris Agreement of January 1973. By then the public felt no remorse over the "loss" of Vietnam—only relief at the end of the conflict. When Saigon fell in mid-1975, President Gerald Ford did nothing to prevent it.

Congress had grown increasingly restive, adopting a variety of tactics to limit presidential prerogative. Following the Fulbright hearings in 1966–1967, several other committees followed suit—taking testimony from witnesses, traveling to Vietnam on fact-finding missions, and ultimately issuing antiwar resolutions aimed at curtailing the length and scope of the war. The Tonkin Gulf Resolution was repealed in late 1971, although an effort to prevent further military operations pending a formal declaration of war was defeated. Following a string of resolutions calling for withdrawal by a given deadline, Congress passed a bill banning all further military operations in Vietnam in 1973 (after the troops had already been withdrawn). In an effort to prevent future unilateral executive military interventions, Congress passed the War Powers Act over President Nixon's veto. The net result of congressional reassertion was a collapse of much of the power that had accreted to the White House over the period following World War II. The question of presidential war powers is still one of the most hotly debated constitutional issues of our time (note the Senate debate on the Gulf War in 1991).

CONCLUSION: CAN THE PUBLIC SHAPE POLICY?

The experience of Vietnam can teach several lessons to those wondering about the role of public opinion in foreign policy. At least as many questions are left unanswered, however.

The Vietnam experience demonstrates the limited impact of street activism in influencing national policy. To a certain extent, the reason for its ineffectiveness is that those who resort to mass demonstrations tend to be those who lack institutional power. That a large number of college students, many of whom could not even vote, failed to alter national policy through protest marches is therefore not surprising. Instead, the Vietnam experience demonstrates the significance of elite opinion in shaping national policy as well as the potential role of "mass opinion" in at least limiting the options a president might otherwise choose. The attentiveness with which successive presidents studied public opinion as well as their considerable efforts to shape it (including deception, obfuscation, and misrepresentation) are testament to the significance politicians attach to this amorphous social entity.

Because the Vietnam War created a moral conflict in the American public, opposition was never unambiguous. Those who favored continuing the war generally deplored its cost, while those who had come to favor withdrawal often regretted the loss of face and prestige it would cause. Congressional ambivalence throughout most of the war reflected this tension and prevented it from taking control. One could argue that even congressional assertion as expressed in the War Powers Act did more to legitimate presidential assertiveness than to limit it, particularly because the act has done little to hinder presidential freedom since 1973.

Did the expereince of the Vietnam War influence American willingness to commit troops overseas? Many have argued that the "Vietnam Syndrome" did precisely this and explains a reluctance to insert troops in Nicaragua in the 1980s, Rwanda in the 1990s, and Iran in 2000s, even though compelling political cases could be made for each. Rather, U.S. intervention has tended to be quick and "surgical" (consider the 1983 incursion into Grenada, the 1989 Panama operation, and the limited deployment in Afghanistan in 2001 in support of the Northern Alliance). Case 5 describes the 1991 Persian Gulf War which could be considered the "anti-Vietnam," employing as it did a decapitation strategy of more than a half million troops invading together to liberate Kuwait—what became known as the Powell Doctrine. The invasion of Iraq in 2003 was likewise intended to inflict "shock and awe" on the Hussein regime and prompt massive surrenders. Relatively few troops were deployed and few plans were made for postwar occupation and stabilization, with the result that coalition forces were ill-prepared for what became a protracted insurrection involving a mixture of former Saddam loyalists, foreign terrorists, and sectarian militias.

While there are naturally many differences between Iraq and Vietnam, talk of the Vietnam Syndrome has intensified and many wonder whether the United States will be able to extricate its troops from what appears an increasingly difficult situation (Greenberg 2004). Two-thirds of Americans opposed President Bush's handling of the war and three-fourths considered the costs to have outweighed the benefits as of May 2006 (Polling Report 2006). As of this writing (May 2006), American battle deaths are close to 2,500 with Iraqi deaths close to 35,000—and with no end in sight. It seems clear that the American people are demonstrating once again that they are not interested in long-term wars where the outcomes and purposes are uncertain (Solomon 2005). The implications for policymakers are increasingly obvious.

DEBATE TOPIC

Perhaps the most lasting legacy from the Vietnam War era is the changed relationship between the Congress and the White House with respect to waging war. The War Powers Act of 1974 was designed to curtail presidential power to deploy troops, while increasing congressional oversight. Is this good for the country?

PRO

Supporters of increased congressional oversight stress three points: (1) The United States is, first and foremost, a democracy, with the people exercising sovereign control over elected officials, typically through other elected officials such as Congress. The people cannot shirk this duty. (2) Presidents have often made strategic and tactical errors in choosing to deploy troops. Additional congressional involvement might enhance the quality of policy. (3) Presidents sometimes are able to deceive the public at large, but have a more difficult time deceiving Congress, given the greater access to information and expertise on Capitol Hill.

CON

Opponents of increased congressional oversight argue these points: (1) Questions of national security necessarily require some degree of secrecy. Increasing access to classified materials, which congressional involvement would entail, might put American lives at risk. (2) Foreign policy aims sometimes require stealth and surprise, both of which would be undermined by increased congressional involvement. (3) Members of Congress represent individual constituencies and often cannot see the "big picture" of the national interest.

THINKING THEORETICALLY

The period of the Vietnam War coincided with a considerable interest in Marxist theory in the United States and in most developed countries. While Marxist approaches have generally lost their appeal, it is interesting to consider why the Vietnam War might have contributed to their popularity. Marxists have quite a bit to say about imperialism, global exploitation, revolution, and so forth. They argued that the Vietnam War was primarily the result of a conspiracy between American militarists, political strategists, and high finance. Defense contractors in particular sought to expand the war in order to increase government orders for their wares, and business leaders wanted to open up markets for their goods in areas that have come under the control of Communist revolutionaries. The lack of interest on the part of American planners in the will of the Vietnamese people seemed consistent with this exploitative agenda.

Liberal thinkers would see the Vietnam War in a very different light. For one thing, the war was a tremendous waste of resources and wound up plunging the U.S. economy into a recession. Inflation soared for years and the United States for the first time lost its status as the undisputed champion in the world economy. The dollar was taken off the gold standard

(continued)

(continued)

and the country's trade policy became more protectionist. If anyone should have opposed the Vietnam War, it should have been the capitalists! Ultimately, it was these costs, combined with the shifting opinion of the American people generally, that led to the U.S. withdrawal from Vietnam—as liberal theory would have predicted. Only when you allow narrow political interests to interfere with the market do you end up with calamities. Proof of this is further shown in the far happier relationship between Vietnam and the United States today, thanks in large part by the inevitable switch from Communist measures to more open markets in Hanoi.

QUESTIONS TO CONSIDER

1. What was the relationship between the peace movement and society in general? Between the peace movement and the White House? How much influence did it really have over policy and shaping alternatives?

2. To what extent did Nixon and Johnson misjudge fundamental American attitudes? What are the apparent limits to patriotism in the United States?

3. What are the lessons of Vietnam in terms of the role of public opinion? How do they relate to the Bush administration's handling of the war in Iraq?

WEBSITES

Vietnam War Internet Project: **www.lbjlib.utexas.edu/scripts/johnson/simple.idq**
The Sixties Project: **lists.village.virginia.edu/sixties**
The Pew Center for the People and the Press: **http://www.people-press.org**

REFERENCES

Ball, George. *The Past Has Another Pattern* (New York: W. W. Norton, 1982).

Brown, Sam. "The Defeat of the Antiwar Movement" in Lake, ed., *The Vietnam Experience,* 120–127.

Gelb, Leslie. "Dissenting on Consensus" in Lake, ed., *The Vietnam Legacy* 102–119.

Greenberg, David. "Why Vietnam Haunts the Debate Over Iraq." Available at: hnn.us/articles/4778.html.

Herring, George C. *America's Longest War: The United States and Vietnam, 1950–1975,* 2nd ed. (Philadelphia: Temple University Press, 1986).

Holsti, Ole R., and James N. Rosenau. *American Leadership in World Affairs: Vietnam and the Breakdown of Consensus* (Boston: Allen & Unwin, 1984).

Karnow, Stanley. *Vietnam: A History* (New York: Viking Press, 1983).

Kattenburg, Paul. *The Vietnam Trauma in American Foreign Policy, 1945–1975* (New Brunswick, NJ: Transaction Books, 1980).

Kearns, Doris. *Lyndon Johnson and the American Dream* (New York: New American Library, 1976).

Lake, Anthony, ed. *The Vietnam Legacy: The War, American Society and the Future of American Foreign Policy* (New York: New York University Press, 1976).

Levy, David W. *The Debate Over Vietnam* (Baltimore: Johns Hopkins University Press, 1991).

Mueller, John. *War, Presidents, and Public Opinion* (New York: John Wiley & Sons, 1973).

New York Times. The Pentagon Papers (New York: New York Times Co., 1971).

Polling Report. "ABC News/Washington Post Poll. May 11-15, 2006." Available at: www.pollingreport.com.

Roche, John P. "The Impact of Dissent on Foreign Policy: Past and Future" in Lake, ed., *The Vietnam Legacy* 128–138.

Schandler, Herbert Y. *The Unmaking of a President: Lyndon Johnson and Vietnam* (Princeton, NJ: Princeton University Press, 1977).

Shils, Edward. "American Society and the War in Indochina" in Lake, ed., *The Vietnam Legacy* 40–65.

Solomon, Norman. "Beyond the Vietnam Syndrome." Anti-War.Com. Available at: www.antiwar.printthis.clickability.com, accessed on May 19, 2006.

Nationalism and the Russia–Chechnya Conflict: Nationalism and the Clash of Civilizations

INTRODUCTION

The nation is an essential building block of international society. A nation is a group of people who are more or less united around a common language, culture, religion, race, ethnicity, or some other identifying factor. It is almost entirely subjective, and the only way to determine whether a nation exists is to interview its members—other methods will probably fail. Nationalism is a political movement wherein members of a nation seek to express their identity by forming a separate political unit—a state. Chauvinism and xenophobia are the dark sides of nationalism—a feeling that one's nation is not only unique and special, but inherently superior to others, with the implication that other nations are either irrelevant or threatening. Self-determination is the legal concept that allows all nations the right to establish a state of their own—at least in principle.

As we consider the troubles in Chechnya—a territory within the Russian Federation—it is useful to imagine a hypothetical. Suppose the United States was made up of only 75 percent white English speakers. Suppose further that each of the various Native American tribes that inhabited the present territory of the United States back when the Pilgrims landed on Plymouth rock still retained their original powers, along with territory, representatives in the Congress, and so forth. Imagine that they also retained their old rivalries and mutual suspicions, such that periodic wars broke out in various segments of the country. Imagine the slaves that were liberated by the Civil War had all migrated to, say, the Rocky Mountains and now represented a powerful faction in the Congress. Also imagine that each of these actors retained their own languages, cultures, social structures, and so forth. Finally, imagine that the central government in Washington was being pressed to grant each of these groups full autonomy within a loose confederation and that federal troops were being attacked all around the country.

This bizarre-sounding scenario is not too far from the reality of Russian politics today. As a result of hundreds of years of conquest and dismemberment, the Russian Federation is a nation in name only. Even after the break up of the Soviet Union which spawned fifteen new states, the question of governing a multiethnic state remains. In Russia, there are at least forty-eight distinct ethnic groups, most of which have their own language, culture, religious traditions, social structures, and historical identities that make them as distinct from (and sometimes hostile to) each other as they are from the Russian majority. Note that our ignorance of their ethnic identity in no way diminishes its importance to those who possess it.

"CIVILIZATION" AS AN INTERNATIONAL RELATIONS CONCEPT

With the fall of the Berlin Wall in 1989 and the collapse of the Soviet Union in 1991, the Cold War came to an end. This prompted a number of international relations scholars to ask whether some new overarching conflict would replace the cold War as the defining struggle of our time. Samuel Huntington provided an interesting answer in the concept of a "clash of civilizations" (Huntington 1996). To Huntington, a civilization is more than a nation—it encompasses many nations and usually spans a continent. It refers to a grouping of people around core beliefs about how the world works and how mankind relates to it. It usually involves attitudes about the nature of God, man's capacity for independent action, the basic place of man in society, and so forth. It touches on questions of individualism vs. communitarianism, the scientific method vs. faith-based knowledge, freedom vs. structure, and so forth. Huntington identified seven such "civilizations": Western, Latin, African, Confucian, Hindu, Slavic, and Islamic.

These civilizations are by their nature in competition and conflict with each other, and the differences are irreconcilable. Whereas distance and lack of technology prevented these groups from interacting, they are now in almost constant contact. Where two civilizations abut each other, Huntington predicts the conflicts will be particularly intractable. This is apparent in Palestine, Bosnia, Kashmir, Afghanistan and other areas. The concept has also been used to explain Islamic terrorism in the West. It is clear that Osama bin Laden sees his role as a vanguard in the struggle between Islam and the West. He has used such terminology in explaining the September 11 attacks (CFR 2004).

While it may seem that the Islamic civilization has "bloody borders" (as once put by Huntington 1999), it is also clear that the concept of "civilization" raises as many questions as it answers. Why, for example, have most wars involved members of the same civilization? And why did so few of these types of conflict manifest themselves during the Cold War? Why can countries from different civilizations have long-standing warm relations? Those who challenge the "civilization" concept point out that Western culture has shown remarkable "portability" in the sense that the principles of the Enlightenment have been embraced by almost every society in the world. Francis Fukuyama has argued that Western culture is destined to expand globally by virtue of its vitality and inherent appeal (Fukuyama 1992). Bruce Russett and those who emphasize globalization as a means toward international cooperation point out that democracy, that most Western of institutions, has appeared in every region of the world (although it has admittedly had better success in some areas than others; Russett 1993). Still others stress the difficulties in spelling out exactly what is meant by "culture" and then applying that definition to the real world. The fact is that most societies embody several competing cultures—note that even in the United States there are "culture wars" that pit secularism against traditional religion. And once you've found a civilization, there is no guarantee it will stay put—culture is dynamic and ever-changing.

This said, the case of Chechnya seems to become more clear once we factor in cultural elements. Huntington himself has argued that Chechnya is an archetypal case of a clash of civilizations since we find a Slavic society trying to control a Muslim one. He therefore predicts that there is unlikely to be a negotiated settlement of this dispute any time soon.

A THUMBNAIL SKETCH OF THE CHECHEN PEOPLE

The roughly one million Chechens (a name assigned by Russian invaders—they call themselves Nokhchii; Dunlop 1998, x) have their roots in the Caucasus Mountains since the Stone Age (see Map 8.1). For centuries they lived here in relative isolation, organized in clans (teips) somewhat like the Scots. They nurtured a warrior culture dominated by men who encouraged family loyalty, although they also organized quasi-democratic structures similar to the Iroquois Nation encountered by American colonists 300 years ago. Each teip enjoyed equal status and no single leader dominated—except during military crises. Their military tactics involved small raiding bands and careful use of the topography of the region—which they naturally knew far better than any invaders (Dunlop 1998, 20).

It was not until the Middle Ages that the Chechen people became subject to a more powerful external actor: Islam. The religion spread to the Caucasus beginning around 600 A.D., but affected each national community differently. Those in Dagestan to the east developed a more orthodox and militant form of Islam, while the Chechens embraced a more mystical and magical style based on the teachings of itinerant Sufis (Fowkes 1998, 10). Thus, although Islam played an important role in the thoughts and emotions of the Chechens, it did little to unite them to the people of the surrounding area.

Map 8.1 Ethnolinguistic groups in the Caucausus region

KEY FIGURES
NATIONALISM AND THE RUSSIA-CHECHNYA CONFLICT

Aslambek Aslakhanov   Chechen member of the Russian Duma and rival to Kadurov. Offered a senior job by Putin to take him out of the running.

Shamil Basayev   Chechen rebel leader, described as a threat to the U.S. by Dept. of State. Not to be confused with the nineteenth-century militant of the same name.

Gen. Dzhokar Dudayev   Elected President of Chechnya by the National Congress of Chechen Peoples in 1991. Declared the independence of the oblast.

Yegor Gaidar   Opposition leader in mid-1990s, leader of Russia's Choice party.

Pavel Grachev   Minister of Defense.

Akhmad Kadyrov   Administrator of Chechnya prior to elections in 2003. A moderate Muslim legal expert, he opposed Russian occupation during the first Chechen War, but became a favorite of Vladimir Putin when he condemned Shamil Basayev's efforts at creating an Islamic state. He governed the area after the second Russian invasion, was elected President in 2003 and assassinated in 2004.

Khattab   Chechen rebel who tried to form alliances with al Qaeda.

(continued)

(*continued*)

Aslan Maskhadov   Chechen rebel leader, successor to Gen. Dudayev in 1996.

Vladimir Putin   Russian President, 1999–present.

Salman Raduyev   Chechen rebel leader.

Sergei Shakhrai   Deputy P.M. and a Cossack (ethnic rival of the Chechens) assigned to head up negotiations on Chechnya's future status.

Boris Yeltsin   President of the Russian Federation, 1991–1999.

CHRONOLOGY
NATIONALISM AND THE RUSSIA–CHECHNYA CONFLICT

1722
Peter the Great annexes Chechnya.

1791
Sheik Mansur is defeated after holding out against Russian troops for six years.

1817–1864
The Chechen War. Russians consolidate control over the region.

1922
USSR moves to consolidate control in Chechnya and the Caucasus.

1944
Soviet leaders in Moscow empty the region of Chechens, evacuating 400,000 to Central Asia.

1950s
Chechens are gradually permitted to return to Chechnya.

1985
Chechens appeal for union republic status. They are denied.

1991
Gen. Dzhokar Dudayev elected President of Chechnya by the National Congress of Chechen Peoples as the group declares the region's independence. Boris Yeltsin becomes President of the new Russian Federation after the dismemberment of the Soviet Union. Chechnya is not granted its independence, unlike the fifteen former Soviet Republics.

1992
Yeltsin assigns Sergei Shakhrai, the Deputy P.M. and a Cossack (ethnic rival of the Chechens) to head up negotiations on Chechnya's future status.

1993
Shakhrai forms the government of Umar Avturkhanov to replace that of Dudayev. Russia provides the new regime with weapons.

1994
Moscow–Grozny talks break down.

November   Yeltsin and the Security Council order an outright invasion of Chechnya by Russian troops. Russian Air Force begins attacks on Grozny. Roughly 100,000 would die during the first Chechen war. Russian troops storm Grozny.

1996
April   Gen. Dudavey is killed by Russian troops and is replaced by Aslan Maskhadov, who retakes the capital Grozny.

August   Alexander Lebed is dispatched by Yeltsin to negotiate a peace, leading to a postponement of a decision on Chechnya's final status until 2001.

1997
February   Aslan Maskhadov is elected president of Chechnya. What follows is a period of lawlessness dominated by a struggle between the warlords, organized in the Majlis-ul Shura (People's Council) and dominated by Shamil Basayez, and Maskhadov's government.

1999
September   Shamil Basayev launches attacks on apartment buildings in Moscow and elsewhere.

October   Russia invades Chechnya a second time.

December   Premier Vladimir Putin is elevated to the presidency by Yeltsin upon the latter's resignation. He is elected to the position in March.

2000
February   Russian forces control all of Chechnya. Akhmad Kadyrov is installed as interim leader.

June   First suicide bombing by Chechen rebels in Grozny kills two Russian special police.

July   Multiple suicide attacks kills scores of Russians in coordinated, synchronized attacks.

2002
October   Moscow theater attack involving "black widows"—Chechen suicide bombers who are survivors (widows, daughters, sisters) of Chechen terrorists who have been killed by Russian forces. Many carry slogans written in Arabic. The assault by Russian security forces includes a gas attack that kills all the hostage takers and 129 of the 800 hostages.

December   Suicide bomber kills 70 in Chechnya.

2003
July   "Black widow" kills herself and 15 others in a suicide bombing at a rock concert in Moscow. A total of 200 were killed in twenty suicide bombings across Russia in 2003.

(continued)

(continued)

March 23   Referendum in on Russian-drawn constitution for Chechnya—widely criticized as premature and manipulative. About 25,000 "permanently based" troops joined in the voting. Turnout was high and the proposals were approved by 96 percent.

August   Two Russian civilian aircraft are downed by Chechen rebels, resulting in ninety deaths.

September   Kadyrov forces seize opposition media prior to the presidential elections.

October 5   Presidential elections held in Chechnya. Akhmad Kadyrov, an Islamic law expert and Putin protege, wins in tainted vote.

2004
May 9   Akhmad Kadyrov is assassinated in a bombing that took more than a dozen lives.

June   Maskhadov leads a raid into Ingushetia, killing dozens of policemen.

August   Presidential elections held in Chechnya. Alu Alkhanov wins election in which his principal rival was removed from the ballot on a "technicality."

September   Chechen rebels seize a large elementary school in Beslan in southern Russia and take 1,000 students and teachers hostage. As rescue workers retrieved twenty bodies, an explosion erupted, causing children to run away in a panic. As the hostage-takers proceeded to gun down the fleeing children, Russian security forces opened fire. Twenty of the hostage-takers were killed (although perhaps that many escaped) and over two hundred hostages died.

October   Alu Alkhanov becomes president with Russian support.

2005
March   Separatist Chechen leader Aslan Maskhadov is reported killed by Russian authorities.

November   Russian-backed parties win local elections in tainted vote.

HISTORY OF CHECHNYA'S CONFLICT WITH RUSSIA TO 1990

Russia was an unwelcome intruder to the Caucasus in the sixteenth century when Ivan the Terrible first launched probing attacks in the hope of easily expanding his empire. It was Peter the Great, however, who invaded in the early 1700s and established Russian dominance for good. The region was annexed in 1722, although it would take Catherine the Great's efforts to subdue the region in the 1760s (Dunlop 1998, x).

Russia's intervention prompted a violent backlash by the Chechens who rallied behind Sheik Mansur. He led on the basis of religion and proved more successful as a preacher than a military commander. After holding off the Russians for six years, he was defeated in 1791. The new Russian ruler, Viceroy Aleksei Yermolov ruled with an iron fist, deporting, killing, and terrorizing opponents. In spite of this, the Chechen resistance persisted. The period 1817–1864 has been described as the Chechen War. Sheik Shamil, himself from Dagestan, obtained the support of the Chechens in his struggle against Russian imperialism. As a religious figure, he was able to appeal to Islam to mobilize large numbers of Chechens who were able to defeat the Russians in a number of pitched battles. His legacy has been mythologized and serves as a potent symbol of Chechen independence even today (Lieven 1998, 304). His life ended violently, however, as Russians hunted him down and, after killing him, expelled roughly 100,000 Chechens from the area. As many as 75,000 of these refugees later died in disease-infested camps. It has been estimated that Russians killed roughly half of the Chechen population over a period of one hundred years (Dunlop 1998, 20).

Chechens gradually migrated back to their homeland beginning in the 1860s and proved to be a useful ally to the Boshevik revolutionaries in 1917. It did not take long before Chechen demands for autonomy ended the alliance, however. By 1925, the Communists in Moscow had launched a pacification program reminiscent of czarist tactics. Once their power was established, the Russians attempted to remove key elements of Chechen culture, including the language (as well as Arabic script) and the religion. The army was called in once again to quell a rebellion in 1929 (Dunlop 1998, 59).

Rebellions occurred in 1939 and 1942. Frustrated by the distraction this caused to the war effort, Russians acted in 1944 with what can best be described as genocide. Roughly 400,000 Chechens were forcibly removed and relocated to central Asia. Many died in transit and as many as 150,000 died in the camps (Fleming 1998). Meanwhile, Ukrainians and Russians were brought in to take over the homes and farms of those who had been expelled. They proceeded to change the place-names, local histories, and everything that connected the Chechens to the area. After two hundred years, the Russians had finally subdued the Chechens. Or so it seemed.

With Stalin's death in 1954, the Chechens were permitted to gradually return to the region. They were not, however, permitted to occupy their homes and farms but instead had to settle for apartments in the cities where they were often a minority. Mikhail Gorbachev, however, was the first Soviet leader to show the Chechens the respect they craved. After his ascension in 1985, he received delegates from the region who requested greater autonomy. While they were granted additional rights and status, they were denied the thing they most sought: status as a union republic. As a mere autonomous republic, Chechnya had only limited autonomy from Moscow. More important is the fact that, once the Soviet Union collapsed, it was only the union republics that were granted full independence. Chechnya was not so lucky.

THE FIRST CHECHEN WAR: 1990–1996

Chechen leaders, beginning in November 1990, began to assert their own independence from Moscow. Duko Zavgayev, the Russian-appointed ethnic Chechen who presided over the area's Communist Party hierarchy, approved the formation of the

National Congress of the Chechen People (OKChN) in hopes of appeasing nationalist elements. General Dzhokar Dudayev, a Russian general, was elected its chairman. For the next nine months, Chechen leaders jockeyed for position in the fast-moving political environment. By August 1991, demonstrators demanded the removal of Communist Party leadership in favor of the OKChN committee. They prevailed on September 6, when Zavgayev resigned and turned power over to the committee under the leadership of Hussein Akhmadov and General Dudayev. On September 15, the party structure dissolved itself and was replaced with a pro-Moscow Provisional Supreme Council (VVS). Dudayev's forces announced the dissolution of the council three weeks later and went on to win parliamentary elections on October 27th. On November 2, 1991, the National Congress formally declared independence from Russia.

Boris Yeltsin, the new president of the Russian Federation, responded to the declaration by imposing martial law on the region (although this decision was reversed by the Russian Parliament). The military attempted to impose order by disarming Chechen fighters, but more often than not it was Russian soldiers who surrendered their weapons to the Chechens. Some estimate that Chechens collected almost 25,000 automatic rifles during 1992 (Lieven 1998, 64). The Russian troops were eventually withdrawn in June.

While Chechnya positioned itself against Moscow, it did little to secure the support of its neighbors. Ingushetia to the west, with which it shared many cultural traits, was disappointed in Grozny's lack of support for its territorial claims on neighboring Ossetia. This led the Ingush to side with Russia in the coming conflict. The regime in Grozny also alienated would-be allies in Georgia to the south by providing asylum to rebels who were fighting the regime in Tblisi. Some support flowed from Chechen expatriates living overseas, but to a large extent the Chechens were isolated against Russia (Lieven 1998, 97).

Throughout the 1992–1994 period, Dudayev fought off numerous contenders, relying increasingly on nationalist appeals and a confrontational foreign policy to secure public support. He also became increasingly dependent on the mafia and other gangster elements as his capacity to impose order throughout the region ebbed. Would-be challengers were as often as not divided against each other, which meant Dudayev could maintain control over the central government for the time being (Lieven 1998, 68). Ruslan Khasbutalov, for example, emerged in mid-1994 in the hope of overthrowing the regime, but when promised Russian support failed to materialize, he was defeated. Still other militant factions followed military leaders Aslan Maskhadov and Shamil Basayev.

As conditions in Chechnya deteriorated and guerrilla groups organized increasingly successful raids into Russian territory, the Yeltsin government made preparations to launch an all-out attack on Grozny—the first of several ill-fated military ventures. Yeltsin attempted to coordinate offensive operations with Dudayev's rivals, only to have repeated assaults go awry. On one occasion, opposition forces took their cue from Moscow and launched an assault on Dudayev's forces, only to pull back when Russian air support failed to come (Siren & Fowkes

1998, 110). Having failed to work closely with local militants, Yeltsin decided to launch a full assault using mechanized Russian divisions. Quick and easy victory was expected.

Beginning in early December 1994, Yeltsin attempted to coordinate a leaflet-drop on Chechnya to warn all parties to lay down their weapons. On December 11, Russians began bombing selected targets in the hope of stirring up a rebellion against Dudayev. The combination of these two actions had the reverse effect. All Chechen groups drew closer together, which prompted the spontaneous mobilization of hundreds of fighters in the mountains and left Russia facing a united, armed Chechen population for the first time since the 1940s. On December 18, 1994, Russian troops moved into northern Chechenya and on into Grozny with roughly 100,000 troops and 200 tanks.

The tanks met with determined resistance—the first of many instances when Chechen fighters would take advantage of their mobility, familiarity with Grozny streets, and canny tactics. The roughly 6,000 Chechen fighters in Grozny (of which only 3,000 were active at any one time) had only a few hundred well-trained fighters, but they had considerable supplies of weapons, often taken from Russian soldiers. Their weapon of choice was the antitank grenade launcher. Marksmen positioned themselves in the upper stories of apartment buildings and waited for the Russian tank columns to proceed single-file down narrow streets. A single shot at the first and last tanks in the column would immobilize the entire unit. The rest could be destroyed by less proficient fighters (Knezys & Sedlickas 1999, 19). In December, the Chechens were able to turn back the Russian army within two days. The Russians withdrew to the northern sections of Chechnya in January 1995. Conditions in Grozny continued to deteriorate, however, as refugees streamed out of the city, leaving behind the sick and elderly in squalor and fear. Russians reoccupied Grozny in late January after a period of sustained bombardment. The Chechens regained control of key buildings in June. Once it was clear that the fighting was stalemated, a cease-fire was agreed to in October. When fighting resumed in 1996, the Chechens were mostly on the defensive. In April, Dudayev was killed in a Russian rocket attack.

Under the direction of Shamil Basayev, Chechen fighters launched a counter-offensive in August 1996. Russians were targeted and pinned down in remarkably effective strikes. Eventually, the Russians were relieved, but not before it was made clear to Boris Yeltsin that a military victory was impossible. By the end of 1996, the Russian army had fully withdrawn from Chechnya.

THE SECOND CHECHEN WAR: 1997–2000

For nearly two years, Chechnya and Russia had an uneasy and often violent peace. With Russian troops gone, Chechnya held presidential elections that were won by one of the heroes of the war—former chief of staff Aslan Mahskadov. He attempted to carve out a more productive relationship with Moscow while pressing for independence at every opportunity. He and Yeltsin signed a formal peace agreement on May 13, 1997, described at the time with great optimism as the end of centuries of conflict.

From 1997 to 1999, order broke down in Chechnya. Militants carried out a string of terrorist attacks in Russia and Dagestan, culminating in the assassination of Russian General Gennadi Shipgun and the bombing of a Russian apartment building. Leaders in Russia were under pressure to put an end to the attacks and by the fall of 1999 were making plans to reinsert the military into northern Chechnya (Gordon 2000). Vladimir Putin (newly-appointed prime minister and soon-to-be president) put his reputation as a hard-liner on the line.

On August 8, 1999, Russian helicopter gun ships attacked Chechen militants who had infiltrated into Dagestan. As the fighting intensified, Russians attacked other areas in Chechnya and quickly occupied the northern half of the country. On October 3, Russians bombed Grozny in preparation for a land assault involving 100,000 troops. By November, Grozny had fallen into Russian hands and organized resistance had come to an end.

THE HISTORY SINCE 2000

Putin installed moderate Islamic legal scholar Akhmad Kadyrov to govern the province until elections could be held. Other Chechen leaders such as Aslan Maskhadov and Shamil Basayev were driven underground and began to adopt a more extremist philosophy. The influence of foreign Islamic terror networks increased once the Russian dominance was consolidated (Bowers, Derrick, & Olimov 2004).

The hopelessness of the situation for some Chechen separatists contributed to their adoption of suicide bombing as a weapon (Hilsum 2004). As early as mid-2000, just a few months after the Russian invasion, suicide bombers struck Russian troops in and around Grozny. The number and audacity of the attacks increased gradually until roughly fifty Chechen rebels, including a dozen women (so called "black widows" sworn to avenge the deaths of their husbands and brothers killed by Russian troops), seized a crowded Moscow theater in October 2002. Russian forces, frustrated by an extended stand-off, used a nerve agent to paralyze the attackers and their hostages (roughly eight hundred theater-goers and theater personnel). The dosage was incorrectly measured, however, and in addition to killing the hostage-takers, 129 of the hostages were also killed.

Vladimir Putin is determined to end Chechen resistance and has rejected any calls for a negotiated settlement. He described the Chechen rebels as lawless Islamic terrorists and his war in Chechnya as a front line in the battle against al Qaeda. What is perhaps ironic about his characterization is that, while probably not true in 1999 when the war broke out, it seems to be increasingly accurate. Foreign governments questioned the validity of this portrayal, but are generally muted in their criticisms of what have been widely described as draconian measures (Baev 2004, 343). President George Bush applauded Russian support in the war against al Qaeda following the September 11 attacks, while Europeans applauded Putin's opposition to Bush's war in Iraq in 2003. The result was considerable room for maneuver in his antirebel policy.

Putin sought to give legitimacy to the counterinsurgency measures by holding a series of elections in 2003 and again in 2004. In early 2003, the government in Moscow and the appointees in Grozny collaborated to draw up a new constitution. The result, however, was criticized by human rights activists as regressive in that it granted the region less autonomy than other parts of the Federation and required the use of the Russian language in official business (CRS 2004, 202). Tens of thousands of Russian troops were allowed to participate in the vote on the grounds that they were on permanent deployment. The elections themselves were only loosely monitored because of the precarious security situation (one of the reasons for international skepticism about their fairness) and the outcome was not widely respected. The reports of 96 percent approval for the constitution was too high to command respect (CRS 2004, 202). In October, Akhmad Kadyrov was elected with 81 percent of the vote, although important opposition candidates were either disqualified or induced to withdraw.

The measures did not, however, stem the violence. Chechen militants became increasingly violent against each other, the Russian military, and the Kadyrov regime. Kadyrov himself stopped counting the number of assassination attempts against him. In August 2003, two Russian commercial aircraft were downed within hours of each other, resulting in ninety deaths. Then in May 2004, Kadyrov himself was felled in a bombing that took a dozen of his staff and other bystanders. Finally, in September 2004, Chechens took hostage one thousand children, parents, and teachers in a school in Beslan in southern Russia. After three days, as ambulance workers came to extract the bodies of twenty victims of early violence, a melee ensued. Children and others ran for their lives as the hostage-takers opened fire. Russian forces returned fire, killing most of the rebels. The final death toll was well over two hundred, many of them children.

Given the violence on both sides, the prospects for a peaceful solution are remote. The Russian occupation seems to be coinciding with an increased role for Islamic militants in the region—something one author calls "Palestinization" (Khatchadourian 2003). Moderates are either killed or marginalized while extremists are locked in a battle of ideology, religion, and revenge. An estimated 100,000 Chechens and 25,000 Russians have died since 1994, while more than 250,000 Chechens are refugees. At least three thousand have been buried in fifty mass graves around the region. Thus far, no one has demonstrated the capacity to exercise authority in the area with any approximating civil rights or rule of law. As put by Nabi Abdullaev, "the Chechen conflict is not so much about who will govern Chechnya. It is about whether Chechnya will be governed at all" (2004, 333). Russia continues to pin its hopes on various leaders it has put forward and managed to get elected, but their status is weak among Chechens. Memorial, the Russian human rights group, has called for a negotiated settlement leading to Chechen independence. Although this may be the only solution to the on-going terrorism, it is doubtful that it will give the Chechen people peace and justice.

DEBATE TOPIC

Should Chechnya be independent?

PRO

Arguments in favor of independence typically refer to the following: (1) The principle of self-determination requires that each nation that wants to govern itself should be permitted to do so. (2) Governing Chechnya has proven nearly impossible for Russia, and so it would save itself a great deal of expense and grief by letting it go. (3) It will be impossible for Russia to control Chechnya without committing numerous human rights violations in the future.

CON

Those opposed point out: (1) Chechnya has demonstrated that it is incapable of governing itself, and so allowing it to become independent would only result in massive human rights violations. (2) Many who live in Chechnya do not want the country to be independent, and so it is not entirely clear what "self-determination" would lead to. (3) Allowing Chechnya to become independent will threaten the integrity of the Russian state and promote violence across the continent.

THINKING THEORETICALLY

The struggle between the Chechens and the Russians may be explained by the concept of nationalism, but two alternatives present themselves as well: realism and rational choice.

Realists would naturally focus on the imperative facing the government in Moscow to hold the line on separatists. Survival of the territory is paramount, according to realist theory, since without this a state's status will inevitably fall, leading perhaps to dismemberment as in Yugoslavia. Having already lost a large fraction of their territory in 1991, successive governments in Moscow could not ignore the explosive potential for further fracturing of the state. The Chechens, after all, are not the only alienated ethnic group in the Russian Federation. From a realist point of view, then, it matters little whether Chechens were Muslim or Russian Orthodox—it was their separatist impulses and the model they might have served that required brutal suppression.

Chechens also knew their goals. Granted, it's not always clear which Chechens were setting the goals, which might well account for the setbacks they've encountered. But clearly there was method to their actions—especially when it came to military tactics during the first Chechen War. Even the terrorist actions of more recent years seem calculated to provoke the type of Russian retaliation that will strengthen Chechen resolve and solidarity. In general terms, we have found in a number of cases in this text that writing off the actions of nationalist extremists as merely irrational violence might lead to trouble.

Questions to Consider

1. Are Chechens genuinely an extension of the Islamic world, given the many differences with other Muslim societies—Dagestan, in particular?

2. Which factors take precedence: Religion? Ethnicity? Historical grievances? Competition between elites?

3. How does Russia's policy in Chechnya compare with other cases of great power actions overseas, such as the Vietnam War, Iraq War, or other cases of major power intervention?

4. Is the rebellion in Chechnya primarily a nationalist movement or an extension of global Islamic terrorism?

Websites

Caucasus and Central Asia Program at UC Berkeley:
    http://ist-socrates.berkeley.edu/~bsp/caucasus/index.html
Chechnya News online: **http://www.chechnyanews.com/**
The Guardian Newspaper special coverage on Chechnya:
    www.guardian.co.uk/chechnya/0,,180787,00.html
Global Issues coverage of the conflict in Chechnya:
    http://www.globalissues.org/Geopolitics/Chechnya.asp
Human Rights Watch report on Chechnya: **http://www.hrw.org/campaigns/russia/chechnya/**

References

Abdullaev, Nabi. "Chechnya Ten Years Later," *Current History* (October 2004): 332–336.

Baev, Pavel K. "Instrumentalizing Counterterrorism for Regime Consolidation in Putin's Russia," *Studies in Conflict & Terrorism* vol. 27 (2004): 337–352.

Bowers, Stephen R., Ashley Ann Derrick, and Mousafar Abdulvakkosovich Olimov. "Suicide Terrorism in the Former USSR," *The Journal of Social, Political and Economic Studies* vol. 29 #3 (Fall 2004): 261–279.

Congressional Research Service (CRS). "Analysis of the Conflict: Elections and Pacification Efforts," *International Debates* (October 2004): 201–205.

Council on Foreign Relations (CFR). "Causes of 9/11: A Clash of Civilizations?" 2004, found at http://www.cfrterrorism.org/clash.html.

Dunlop, John B. *Russia Confront Chechnya: Roots of a Separatist Conflict.* (Cambridge: Cambridge University Press, 2004).

Fleming, William. "The Deportation of the Chechen an Ingush Peoples: A Critical Examination," in Fowkes, Ben, ed. *Russia and Chechnya: The Permanent Crisis* (London: Macmillan Press, 1998): 65–86.

Fowkes, Ben, ed. *Russia and Chechnya: The Permanent Crisis* (London: Macmillan Press, 1998).

Fukuyama, Francis. *The End of History and the Last Man* (New York: Free Press, 1992).

Gordon, Michael. "A Look at How the Kremlin Slid into the Chechen War," *New York Times*, February 1, 2000.

Hilsum, Lindsey. "The Conflict the West Always Ignores," *New Statesman* vol. 133 #4672 (January 26, 2004).

Hodgson, Quentin. "Is the Russian Bear Learning? An Operational and Tactical Analysis of the Second Chechen War, 1999–2002," *Journal of Strategic Studies* vol. 26 #2 (2003): 64–91.

Huntington, Samuel. *The Clash of Civilizations and the Remaking of World Order* (Norman: Oklahoma University Press, 1996).

Huntington, Samuel. "A Local Front of a Global War," *New York Times*, December 16, 1999: A31.

Khatchadourian, Raffi. "The Curse of the Caucasus," *Nation* vol. 277 #16 (November 17, 2003): 31–36.

Knezys, Stasys, and Romanas Sedlickas. *The War in Chechnya* (College Station: Texas A&M University Press, 1999).

Lieven, Anatol. *Chechnya: Tombstone of Russian Power* (New Haven: Yale University Press, 1998).

Russett, Bruce. *Grasping the Democratic: Principles for a Post–Cold War World* (Princeton: Princeton University Press, 1993).

Siren, Pontus, and Ben Fowkes. "An Outline Chronology of the Recent Conflict in Chechnya," in Fowkes, Ben, ed. *Russia and Chechnya: The Permanent Crisis* (London: Macmillan Press, 1998): 170–182.

CASE 9

Al Qaeda: Terrorism

INTRODUCTION

Before September 11, 2001, international terrorism was mostly an abstraction for many Americans—something the Israelis and British were forced to deal with, but not us. As long as we stayed home and minded our own business, we would be safe from international threats. After September 11, this illusion was shattered. Terrorism quickly became one of the country's top priorities. In the months following the September 11 attacks, as pointed out by President George W. Bush in his January 2002 State of the Union address, tens of billions of dollars of new spending were approved for homeland security, a vast international antiterror coalition was formed and new international laws adopted, and a war was fought and won in Afghanistan, resulting in the capture of thousands of al Qaeda operatives and the displacement of an entire regime (Bush 2002; *Christian Science Monitor* September 9, 2002, 1).

Defining terrorism seems easy when one considers such brazen acts of devastation. In practice, however, it is not always easy to categorize groups and actions neatly. Consider the following alternative definitions of terrorism:

> The unlawful use of force against persons or property to intimidate or coerce a government, the civilian population, or any segment thereof, in furtherance of political or social objectives. . . .
>
> Premeditated, politically motivated violence perpetrated against noncombatant targets by sub-national groups or clandestine agents. . . .
>
> The unlawful use or threat of violence against persons or property to further political or social objectives. It is generally intended to intimidate or coerce a government, individuals or groups or to modify their behavior or policies. . . . (Beres 1995, 3–4)

These definitions share several elements: 1. Terrorism involves violence—sometimes against civilian targets. 2. Terrorism has a political objective. 3. The terrorist expects that the political objective can be achieved by sowing fear. In most cases, terrorism is the act of an organized and politically motivated group that is expressing its profound dissatisfaction with the order of things, whether it be the occupation of territory by a foreign power, rule of a country by a racial minority, despotic government by a dictatorial regime, or something else.

Note that terrorism differs markedly from two other violent phenomena found in international life: international crime and warfare. International crime is conducted primarily for the purpose of accumulating wealth, and violence and political machinations are a means to that end. On the other hand, even where terrorists engage in garden-variety criminal activities, such as theft and drug-running, these actions are pursued to finance their political acts and agenda. Warfare involves state actors interacting with each other, and their actions are governed by codes of conduct and international law. Combatants must wear uniforms, refrain from targeting civilians, feed and protect prisoners, and so forth. The objective in war is to incapacitate the enemy, which is primarily a physical rather than a psychological goal (Tucker 1997, 67).

Terrorists share a great deal with guerrillas, who are usually better financed and organized but use many of the same tactics and have many of the same goals. Terrorists and guerrillas typically are both weaker than the governments they challenge and must therefore resort to hit-and-run attacks and other low-intensity tactics (bombings, assassinations, sabotage). Guerrillas differ in that they are always territorially based and are usually focused on seizing power to govern some land mass. Thus, the Peruvian Shining Path, the Tamil Tigers, and the ETA are interested in replacing existing governments in their homelands with their own members in Peru, Sri Lanka, and Spain, respectively. Their grievances are typically concrete and even understandable within the context of the state system and the goal of self-determination. Most countries in the world formed when some local group or nation sought to achieve independence from an alien government, and in almost all cases violence was part of the strategy. Many guerrillas who were successful have gone on to lead their countries as statesmen. Many of the prime ministers of Israel, for example, were guerrillas in their youth, as were Mao Zedong, Fidel Castro, and Nelson Mandela. One could even argue that George Washington was a guerrilla (he was portrayed as such by the British during the Revolutionary War).

Terrorists may also have concrete political goals, including replacing a government or controlling territory, but, as we have learned, this is not the only motivation. Terrorist organizations may have a broad set of goals that transcend controlling a particular state or region, and their membership may be drawn from many different nations. Their targets may include numerous states or nonstate actors across the globe, making them a genuine transnational threat.

Of the transnational terrorist organizations in the world, al Qaeda stands out and is therefore the focus of our study here. Al Qaeda is unusual in many respects, however, as we will make clear.

KEY FIGURES
GLOBAL TERRORISM AND AL QAEDA

Hasan al-Banna   1906–1949. He was the founder of the Society of Muslim Brothers in Egypt, a precursor to the Muslim Brotherhood that provided support to Osama bin Laden's al Qaeda in the 1990s.

Ayatollah Ruhollah Khomeini   1902–1989. He was the leader of the Iranian Revolution in 1978 that placed a revolutionary Shiite regime in power.

Sheik Omar Abdul Rahman   Leader of the Gama Islamiya (Islamic Group) in Egypt. With support from al Qaeda, his group carried out the first World Trade Center attack in 1993.

Osama bin Laden   Born 1957. Heir to a business fortune and Afghan mujahaddin, he was co-founder of MAK in 1984 and al Qaeda in 1988. His organization claimed responsibility for the attacks on the U.S. embassies in Tanzania and Kenya on August 7, 1998, and on the USS *Cole* in 2000. He has also been blamed for the September 11 attacks in the United States.

Hasan al-Turabi   Islamic leader of Sudan since seizing power in 1989. He provided safe haven to al Qaeda from 1991 to 1996 and has carried out a bloody civil war against Christian and animist separatists in the south.

Ayman Mohammed Rabi' al-Zawahiri   Egyptian Islamic cleric who emerged as the dominant religious authority of al Qaeda after the assassination of Abdullah Azzam in 1989.

Abu Musab al-Zarqawi   Islamic militant of Jordanian descent, active in Iraq, formally allied to al Qaeda since October 2004.

Muhammad Ibn Abdul Wahhab   Eighteenth-century Islamic cleric who developed a puritanical interpretation of Islam that became the foundation of the Saudi regime in Arabia.

Sheik Dr. Abdullah Azzam   1941–1989. A Muslim *ulama*, he was active in the Jordanian Muslim Brotherhood and founded the Afghan Service Bureau (MAK) with Osama bin Laden in 1984.

Mullah Mohammed Omar   Spiritual leader of the Taliban regime in Afghanistan. He worked closely with Osama bin Laden to impose an autocratic, puritanical rule on the country.

CHRONOLOGY
GLOBAL TERRORISM AND AL QAEDA

1744
Muhammad Ibn Abdul Wahhab joins forces with the future House of Saud, bringing a puritanical form of Islam to a position of power.

1916
The Sykes-Picot agreement between France and Great Britain consolidates European control over the Middle East, to the dismay of Arab leaders.

1928
Hasan al-Banna founds the Society of Muslim Brothers in Egypt.

(continued)

(*continued*)

1932
The House of Saud establishes control over the Arabian peninsula and rules following the dictates of Wahhabism.

1942
The Society of Muslim Brothers forms a militant "secret apparatus."

1949
Al-Banna is assassinated by the Egyptian government following violent attacks by his followers.

1964
Ayatollah Khomeini is expelled from Iran for sedition.

1979
The Soviet Union invades Afghanistan, sparking a guerrilla war. Ayatollah Khomeini seizes power in a popular uprising and begins to support fundamentalist Islamic militants in the region.

1983
Sharia law is imposed in Sudan.

1984
Osama bin Laden and Abdullah Azzam found the MAK to provide support to the Afghan mujahaddin. They later create training camps for local and Arab guerrillas.

1988
Bin Laden, Azzam, Mohammed Atef, and Abu Ubaidah al Banshiri found al Qaeda as a base of support to mujahaddin in Afghanistan and elsewhere. They join fundamentalist militant organizations in Egypt and Sudan to found the International Islamic Front for Jihad Against the Jews and Crusaders.

1989
Taking credit for expelling the Soviet Union forces from Afghanistan, bin Laden returns to Saudi Arabia, where he opposes the Saud family.

1990
U.S. troops are deployed to protect Saudi Arabia from Iraq, prompting bin Laden to declare the House of Saud to be "apostates" of Islam.

1991
Bin Laden is expelled from Saudi Arabia and moves the headquarters of al Qaeda from Peshawar, Pakistan, to Khartoum, Sudan, where he develops a close and profitable relationship with the ruling National Islamic Front.

1992
The first al Qaeda attack occurs. It is a largely unsuccessful attempt to kill American troops en route to Somalia by way of Yemen. In Algeria, the government, fearing gains by the fundamentalist Islamic Salvation Front, cancels elections. The country plunges into violence.

1993
The first World Trade Center attack occurs in February under the direction of Ramsi Yousef and Sheik Omar Abdul Rahman. Attacks against American soldiers in Somalia are carried out by al Qaeda–trained militants.

1994
Saudi Arabia revokes bin Laden's citizenship.

1995
Al Qaeda attacks Americans based in Saudi Arabia.

1996
Al Qaeda issues the first of three fatawa declaring jihad against Americans, the House of Saud, and Westerners generally.

1998
On August 7, two truck bombs explode at the U.S. embassies in Kenya and Tanzania, killing 234 and injuring nearly 5,000.

1999
Governments in the West and Middle East begin a systematic crack-down on al Qaeda militants. Osama bin Laden is placed on the FBI's "Ten Most Wanted" list. Some anti-Taliban Afghan clerics issue a fatwa against bin Laden, authorizing his assassination. Reports emerge that bin Laden suffers from kidney and liver disease.

2000
October 5   Suicide bombers attack the USS Cole in Yemen, killing 17 sailors.

December   The UN Security Council passes Resolution 1333, imposing sanctions on the Taliban pending bin Laden's extradition.

2001
September 11   Four aircraft are highjacked by teams of suicide bombers. Three are flown into the World Trade Center and the Pentagon. One aircraft is recaptured by passengers and crashes in western Pennsylvania (it is believed its destination was the Capitol in Washington, D.C.). Nearly 3,000 people are killed. The next day, the UN Security Council approves a resolution authorizing "all necessary means" to neutralize the terrorists responsible.

October–November   Northern Alliance fighters, with ground and air support from the United States, remove the Taliban from power in Afghanistan, killing hundreds of Taliban and al Qaeda fighters and taking hundreds more captive. Many, including possibly bin Laden, flee to Pakistan and other locations.

2002
March   Abu Zubaydah, al Qaeda's second-in-command, is arrested in Pakistan.

October   Al Qaeda is linked to an attack against a French oil tanker in Yemen and the killing of American military personnel in Kuwait and the Philippines. A major attack in Indonesia kills more than 180. The U.S. Congress authorizes President Bush to employ force against Iraq, which is linked to international terrorism by the administration.

2003
March   The United States and Britain attack Iraq. Among the reasons given is a link between Saddam Hussein's regime and the September 11 attacks, a claim that is later discredited.

(continued)

(continued)

2004

March   Ten bombs detonate on crowded commuter trains in Madrid, Spain, killing nearly two hundred. Al Qaeda is found responsible, although not until the voters in Spain turn out the sitting government in part over its support for the war in Iraq.

July   Ahmed Khalfan Ghailani, a top al Qaeda operative, is captured and interrogated in Pakistan.

September   In Russia, hundreds die in an attack on a school orchestrated by Chechen guerillas with al Qaeda ties.

2005

July   A series of attacks on public transportation in London kills over fifty. Islamic militants claim responsibility, although their ties to al Qaeda are unlikely.

2006

January   Osama bin Laden offers a cryptic truce to the West. He later recants.

ISLAMIC FUNDAMENTALISM

It is impossible to understand al Qaeda without knowing something of Islamic extremism. At its core, Islam is a conservative, family-centered, monotheistic faith that shares a great deal with Judeo-Christian religious tradition (Muslims generally feel a kinship with such "people of the book" and share a lineage to Abraham). Founded in the seventh century by the Prophet Mohammed (the story of his miraculous calling resembles in many ways the experiences of Moses and the Apostle Peter), Islam expanded quickly through the Middle East through both conversion and conquest. In its early days, its teachings on government and human rights were extremely progressive, since they encouraged democratic institutions, civil rights for women, and the empowerment of ordinary people (in contrast to the feudal and caste-based system of the day; al-Turabi 1987).

After the death of the Prophet and his immediate successors (the Caliphs), Islam experienced considerable splintering and decline. Today there is no single leader of the Muslim world (the *ummah*). Rather, numerous Islamic scholars (*ulama*), like theology professors or rabbinical scholars, spend their energies interpreting the Islamic holy writ (the *Qur'an*, giving revelations from the angel Gabriel to Mohammed, and the *Hadith*, stories and statements of Mohammed) and statements of earlier scholars.

A major schism occurred shortly after the death of the Prophet Mohammed and gave rise to two major Islamic movements: the Sunni and the Shi'a. From time to time, Islamic spiritualists (Sufi) and martyrs develop followings and become the source of other new schools and societies. The varieties of "Islams" are so diverse that what is permitted in some quarters is forbidden in others, sometimes leading to deadly arguments. Note, for example, the fact that every Muslim nation in the world

(with the exception of the secular government of Saddam Hussein in Iraq) unequivocally condemned the September 11 attacks and hundreds of ulama went on record
to declare terrorism to be an un-Islamic act (Schafer 2002, 18). This background is
mentioned to make it clear that Islam is a varied and complex religious movement
that defies easy generalization. One should add to this the fact that many Islamic
traditions have adopted and incorporated social traditions from particular regions
that existed long before Islam appeared. In Bangladesh, for example, Muslims continue to recognize Hindu castes in their day-to-day practice. The status and treatment of women varies dramatically across different Muslim communities, in part
due to local traditions.

Among these myriad branches and sects, a few have developed relatively
recently to challenge the mainstream. In the mid-1700s, in the wake of the European and Ottoman imperial conquests of North Africa and the Middle East, a few
began to challenge the prevailing Muslim orthodoxy. They argued that Muslims
had become lax and confused, having embraced too much of their Western
invaders' ways and/or perverting the ways of the Prophet. They took it upon themselves to cleanse the society through teaching, organizing, and, in a few cases,
violence. Muhammad Ibn Abdul Wahhab, for example, preached a puritanical
form of Islam that he thought was practiced by Muslims at the time of the Prophet
(Davidson 1998, 50). In 1744, he formed an alliance with the patriarch of the Saud
family to defeat what they considered polytheistic heresy among other Muslims.
The alliance succeeded for a time in conquering the Arabian peninsula and
reclaiming the holy cities of Mecca and Medina, only to be driven out by the
Ottomans (based in Turkey). The House of Saud reclaimed the territory over time,
and by 1932 it was able to establish an Islamic monarchy that ruled using the
Qur'an as its legal reference (*shariah* law). Osama bin Laden is a self-professed
Wahhabi (Wright 2001, 264).

In Egypt, where Western influence was pervasive, Hasan al-Banna emerged as a
teacher and activist. He organized the Society of Muslim Brothers in 1928 to urge
fellow Muslims to return to the pure tenets of the faith. He aspired to restore not
only the moral and social organization but also political structures of the earliest
period of Islam. The movement proved extremely popular and received support from
secular politicians, such as Gamal Abdel Nasser and Anwar Sadat, who took power
in the 1950s. It attracted a following among Muslims who were radicalized by the
creation of the state of Israel, although al-Banna was not especially militant himself.
The Society he founded provided health care, education, and other services (even a
Scouting program for youth) that were aimed at inculcating a respect for basic
Muslim values.

The Society also had a secret, military organization that engaged in assassination, leading to the murder of al-Banna by Egyptian authorities in 1949 (Davidson
1998, 26). His successor also failed to restrain the violent tendencies of the Brotherhood, and during the 1960s the organization was repressed. From the 1970s, it grew
in strength and served as an inspiration to so-called fundamentalist ("fanatically
puritanical" might be a better term), anti-Western movements across the region.
These sects included the Gam'a Islamiya (Islamic Group), led by the "Blind Sheik,"

Omar Abdul Rahman, who later collaborated with Osama bin Laden (Davidson 1998, 101; O'Ballance 1997, 19)

In 1978, Iran's Ayatollah Ruhollah Khomeini, a Shiite as well as a teacher and activist, led a popular uprising against the corrupt ruler Shah Reza Pahlavi. From his position at the helm of Iran, he was able to propagandize revolutionary Islamic fundamentalism by setting up Iran as a model, as well as provide shelter and direct support to revolutionary movements in the region and beyond (O'Ballance 1997). His regime was particularly instrumental in building Hezbollah (Party of God) in Lebanon in the early 1980s as a service organization with a strong military wing whose aim is the elimination of the state of Israel (Davidson 1998, 169).

OSAMA BIN LADEN AND THE FOUNDING OF AL QAEDA

It was in this context that Osama bin Laden came of age. One of the many children of a successful Saudi businessman, bin Laden studied engineering and Islamic law (his personal fortune has been conservatively estimated at $30 million; Gunaratna 2002, 19). In 1979, the Soviet Union invaded Afghanistan to establish a Communist regime on its southern border. Bin Laden was impressed by the strength of the resistance mounted by local Afghans, who came to be known as mujahaddin. He, along with Abdullah Azzam, began organizing various projects to bring relief supplies and war materiel to the mujahaddin in Afghanistan. In 1984, they organized the MAK (Afghan Service Bureau). They were part of a growing Arab presence in Afghanistan where, eventually, Islamic militants gathered from around the world (Huband 1998, 2). In the process of fighting together, these militants became increasingly radicalized as they saw the results of their struggle against the Soviet forces. When the Soviets withdrew in 1989, the mujahaddin, and bin Laden in particular, took full credit for their defeat (Wright 2001, 250). Furthermore, they took credit for the eventual collapse of the Soviet Union itself (bin Laden took personal offense at the West claiming credit for what was an Islamic victory; Gunaratna 2002, 22).

Hoping to capitalize on the energy of the Afghan movement, bin Laden and Azzam joined with Muhammed Atef and others to found al Qaeda (the Base) in 1988 as a mechanism for keeping militants in contact with each other, coordinating their actions against anti-Islamic forces, and providing training and supplies for this purpose. By 1989, several militants had been sworn in as the first cadre of al Qaeda fighters (Gunaratna 2002, 23). They established their headquarters in Peshawar, Pakistan, with the help of the ISI (CIA-equivalent) of Pakistan.

Azzam's views of the organization were somewhat more moderate than those of bin Laden, who had started training guerrillas as early as 1986. In 1989, Azzam was murdered by Egyptian radicals who later became leaders of al Qaeda (Gunaratna believes bin Laden conspired with Ayman Mohammed Rabi' al-Zawahiri in the attack; Gunaratna 2002, 25). After 1989, the movement became more intransigent and active.

Three other important developments stimulated the growth and orientation of al Qaeda. In August 1990, U.S. troops were deployed in northern Saudi Arabia at the invitation of the Saud royal family to defend the area from the Iraqi forces that had just invaded Kuwait. After the defeat of Iraq, the American troops remained. Bin Laden believed that the willingness of the Saud family to allow infidels into Saudi Arabia—the home of the two holiest sites of Islam (Mecca and Medina)—was a betrayal of the Prophet and an abdication of their sacred duty to protect the shrines. He labeled them as apostates and called for their destruction (Wright 2001, 265).

In 1991, the Saudi regime expelled bin Laden for sedition, but the Sudanese government soon welcomed him and roughly 500 militants (Wright 2001, 251). After moving the headquarters of al Qaeda to Khartoum, bin Laden took advantage of the government's hospitality to build several prosperous businesses and sign lucrative contracts, thereby significantly increasing the organization's assets and cash flow. In 1996, however, the Sudanese asked bin Laden to leave under considerable pressure from the United States and other Western states. By this time, the Taliban had seized power in Afghanistan and offered him safe haven.

While in Afghanistan, bin Laden's stature and power rose considerably. He developed a close relationship with Mullah Mohammed Omar and became highly influential in the regime. It was bin Laden who encouraged the Taliban to destroy giant Buddha statues in Bamiyan, to international outcry (Gunaratna 2002, 43, 62). Al Qaeda provided 2,000 militants (055 Brigade) to help the Taliban fight the Northern Alliance during the late 1990s, earning the respect and gratitude of the regime. It was from here that bin Laden issued three fatawa proclaiming it the duty of all Muslims to destroy the Saudi regime and to kill Americans, and Jews, and any Westerners who were blocking the establishment of puritanical Islam (these can be found in the appendix of Alexander and Swetnam 2001). It was also from Afghanistan that al Qaeda launched its most notorious attacks, against two U.S. embassies in Africa in 1998, against the USS Cole in 2000, and against the World Trade Center and Pentagon in 2001. These attacks, along with other minor strikes, killed a total of 3,300 individuals and injured more than 6,000.

The last attack, on September 11, 2001, began the most recent change in al Qaeda's fortunes. It prompted a massive retaliation by the United States and other states, including a global crack-down on al Qaeda's militants, finances, and sponsors, culminating in the defeat of the Taliban regime and the death and capture of thousands of militants in October and November of 2001.

DESCRIBING AL QAEDA

It is useful at this point to focus on the goals, structure, and financing of al Qaeda, so as to better illustrate the character of a major terrorist organization. It is important to underscore that al Qaeda is unique in several respects. To begin, it is uniquely transnational in structure and scope, including cells and operations in more than fifty countries with militants and financial backers in dozens of countries. It is also uniquely vitriolic in its orientation, surpassing even the militancy of other Islamic organizations (for example, the Saudi fundamentalist Advice and Reformation Committee announced that bin Laden's 1996 fatwa was merely a personal statement; Huband 1998, 115). It has been described as an "apocalyptic" organization, whose goal is primarily destruction and chaos in an attempt to usher in a new world, putting it on a par with Nazism (Herf 2002).

Al Qaeda's Goals

Bin Laden is a Wahhabi, taking an extremely puritanical approach to Islam. Only the Taliban embodied this view in its everyday practices, which included strict enforcement of dietary, moral, and other codes found in Islam. The Taliban, for example, viewed the place of women in society as extremely subordinate and inferior. Women were banned from schools and the business world and were not allowed to receive medical care from male doctors (since there were no female doctors, the implication was clear; Wright 2001, 264). Its absolutist view meant that not only infidels from other faiths, but also modern regimes that tolerated Western culture, were viewed as threats. Thus it is easy to understand why Anwar Sadat and Hosni Mubarak of Egypt were targeted by al Qaeda allies for assassination (the attempt was successful in the case of President Sadat). Likewise, attacks on Saudi leaders are consistent with this view.

The religious leaders of al Qaeda, especially Ayman Mohammed Rabi' al-Zawahiri, spend considerable energy working to legitimize their version of Islam to the world. This is done through religious instruction to the militants as well as through public pronouncements. The fatwa is used heavily as a religiously sanctioned call for action by all Muslims. Not only do al Qaeda clerics issue these from time to time, but in recent years bin Laden himself has been taking on the trappings of priesthood, naming himself "Sheik" and issuing fatawa (plural of fatwa) on his own authority (Wright 2001, 255). He has always endeavored to maintain a strict lifestyle so as to inspire piety and self-discipline in the ranks. Interestingly, bin Laden is one of the first Islamic militants to embrace terrorists of the Shiite school of Islam, in spite of the considerable hostility that has dominated Sunni–Shiite relations over the years. As a result, he has developed ties to both Iran and Lebanon's Ebola, much to the consternation of Western intelligence and defense agencies (Gunaratna 2002, case 3).

In "Join the Caravan," bin Laden urges all Muslims to take up the cause of jihad (struggle) against Jews and Christians (Zionists and crusaders) as an individual obligation (Gunaratna 2002, 87). Why join the jihad? (1) so that nonbelievers do not dominate; (2) because of the scarcity of manpower; (3) fear of hellfire; (4) fulfilling the duty of jihad and responding to the call of Allah; (5) following in the footsteps of pious predecessors; (6) establishing a solid foundation as a base for Islam; (7) protecting those who are oppressed in the land; (8) seeking martyrdom (Gunaratna 2002, 88).

A special problem for al Qaeda (and all Islamic militants) is the fact that the Qur'an and the Prophet's teachings specifically outlaw suicide and violence against innocents (particularly women and children). With respect to the ban on suicide, clerics have emphasized that the struggle requires the sacrifice of all things, including life itself. Those who take that ultimate step are assured "martyr" status and eternal bliss in heaven (there is even mention of women). Thus, it is not suicide at all, in a religious sense. With respect to killing innocents, they have argued that the end justifies the means, however. Since the goal is the eradication of opposition to Islam (defending the faith is one meaning of jihad, a central tenet of Islam), and since opposition includes whole nations of people, everyone is to some degree culpable. While women and children are not appropriate targets in and of themselves, they may be killed incidentally, according to al Qaeda's clerics (Gunaratna 2002, 76).

This religious underpinning explains why some have argued that the best weapon against al Qaeda may be a religious one. If moderate clerics, for example, can convince the puritanical fanatics that they are interpreting the holy writ incorrectly, they can undermine recruitment efforts (Miles 2002). Likewise, since the struggle is ideological and cultural, Western actors must convey the desirability of liberal democratic principles and the market (Berman 2001).

To help clarify the relative uniqueness of al Qaeda, consider other terrorist organizations, such as the Palestine Liberation Organization (PLO), the Provision Irish Republican Army (IRA), and Euskadi Ta Askatasuna (ETA). Each has carried out hundreds of killings of both military personnel and civilians through shootings and bombings in order to alter the policies of states. But each is territorially based. And each has been willing to engage in negotiations with the target state.

Consider the story of ETA, for example. Formed in the 1950s by Basque separatists in Spain and France, ETA fought against the repression of Basque identity and culture by Spanish dictator Francisco Franco, who targeted Basques in part because they had fought against him during the Spanish Civil War prior to World War II. In the early years, their demand for an independent Basque homeland and their limited acts of violence in the 1950s and 1960s were not entirely repudiated by the rest of the world, and France apparently provided sanctuary to ETA militants (Martinez-Herrera 2002, 11). Many in Spain's pro-democracy community secretly applauded ETA's assassination of Franco's heir-apparent in 1973. ETA has also enjoyed the support of roughly one in six residents of the Basque region—particularly from those who identified themselves as ethnically Basque—and its various allied political parties have consistently received enough votes to win seats in the local parliament and mayorships (Martinez-Herrera 2002, 6). After Franco died in 1975, ETA stepped up its attacks, killing nearly one hundred each year in the late-1970s, even as the new leader, King Juan Carlos, instituted constitutional rule and agreed to considerable autonomy for the Basque region (Woodworth 2001, 6). ETA argued (with considerable support from Basque parties) that the constitutional reforms were mere window-dressing and that Basque rights were still limited and Spanish police were still brutal (points that were supported by outside investigators; AI 2002).

But in the late-1990s, the mood shifted. An increasing number of Basques were split on the issue of independence and thousands rallied to call for a peaceful settlement of the dispute with Spain. ETA's support dwindled to five percent in the region and the government of Spain estimated its full-time military force at just thirty (BBC 2006). On March 22, 2006, ETA announced a permanent cease-fire and a willingness to support constitutional means to secure Basque independence.

A similar pattern was followed by the IRA and PLO, although the situation in Palestine is far more volatile (see case 6 on the Camp David Accords).

Al Qaeda's Organization

Al Qaeda differs from most terrorist organizations in that it is not territorially based but rather has a consciously global presence (Table 9.1). Its essential elements consist of a governing council (*shura majlis*) consisting of roughly one dozen bin Laden loyalists who help staff four policy committees (military, religious, financial, and public relations). These bodies behave in ways that resemble a philanthropic foundation by issuing overall purposes and guidelines, reviewing proposals for terrorist

Table 9.1 Al Qaeda's Global Network

Countries with Islamic Militant Organizations Linked to al Qaeda	Countries with al Qaeda Terrorist Cells (Working Alone)	Countries with Sources of al Qaeda Funding	Countries Where al Qaeda Attacks Have Occurred
Yemen	United States	United Kingdom	Yemen
Egypt	United Kingdom	Germany	Somalia
Algeria	Germany	Saudi Arabia	Egypt
Malaysia	France	United Arab Emirates	Saudi Arabia
Chechnya (Russia)	Netherlands	Sudan	United States
Somalia	Belgium	Sweden	Philippines
Philippines	Canada	Denmark	Indonesia
Lebanon	Spain	Norway	Spain
Iran		Algeria	
Tajikistan		Germany	
Uganda		United States	
Indonesia		Philippines	
China		Pakistan	
Eritrea			
Bosnia			
United Kingdom			
Palestine			
Uzbekistan			
Kashmir (India)			
Sudan*			
Pakistan*			
Afghanistan*			

*Former al Qaeda headquarters.
Sources: Gunaratna 2002; Alexander and Swetnam 2002.

actions, and approving, funding, and sometimes organizing those actions. The proposals usually come from individual terrorist cells and regional offices.

Roughly 5,000 militants make up the rank-and-file of al Qaeda. They work in small, largely disconnected cells (called *anqud*—grape cluster) made up of between two and fifteen individuals. The cells are relatively autonomous in their operations and are expected to be self-sustaining financially to a large extent (many cells rely on credit card fraud and theft). They are only vaguely aware of what other cells are planning and can organize their own operations with al Qaeda's blessing. Abu Zubaydah was responsible for coordinating their performance until his capture in March 2002 in Pakistan. The 055 Brigade, formed in Afghanistan, is organized along more traditional military lines and was the group encountered by coalition forces fighting in that country in October and November 2001.

Election to al Qaeda is a very high honor for an Islamic militant. Al Qaeda officials generally select only one out of every ten men who pass through their training camps. They are looking for "young Muslim men who are pure, believing and fighting for the cause of Allah" (Gunaratna 2002, 72). The key factors seem to be absolute loyalty and the willingness to sacrifice everything, including one's life, in the cause. In addition, al Qaeda fighters must be among the most highly skilled of those trained in the camps.

Terrorist attacks are generally carefully planned and executed, although they are not always successful. An attack was attempted against the USS *Sullivan*, but failed when the boat loaded with explosives sank (it was overloaded). Likewise, assassination attempts against Hosni Mubarak, Bill Clinton, and Fidel Ramos (then president of the Philippines) were foiled for various reasons. Numerous terrorist attacks have also been detected and prevented, including a series of attacks planned on New York City landmarks (such as the UN and Holland Tunnel) in 1999. Detecting and linking attacks to al Qaeda is especially difficult because, unlike most terrorist organizations, the group rarely claims responsibility. In fact, it goes to great lengths to sow doubt about its role in the attacks, in part to add to the organization's mystique.

In the case of the September 11 attacks, planning began in the spring of 2000 under the direction of Mohammed Atta. Twenty militants were selected from several different cells, organized into four five-man teams, and allowed to secret themselves into the United States on student visas or across the Canadian border. This activity was followed by training at several flight schools around the country, the purchase of one-way business-class tickets, and other preparations.

Training covers the gamut of information that would-be terrorists might need to know, including religious indoctrination. A ten-volume (later eleven) "encyclopedia" of terrorism was written and published by al Qaeda in the mid-1990s (discovered by American intelligence agencies in 1999). It explains how to build explosives, how to use various weapons, how to organize paramilitary attacks, and how to build weapons of mass destruction. [Bin Laden is believed to have purchased some fissile materials in his quest for an atomic weapon. He may already have the capability to launch an attack with a "dirty" bomb that would scatter radioactive material (Gunaratna 2002, 70).] The encyclopedia also provides training on how militants should blend into the host society, even if it means violating Islamic lifestyle codes (Gunaratna 2002, 70).

The geographic spread of al Qaeda is remarkable. Although its headquarters has moved between Pakistan, Sudan, and Afghanistan, its cells can be found in more than fifty countries. The countries with the largest number of militants are Algeria (where al Qaeda supports the Islamic Salvation Front), Egypt (where it has ties to the Muslim Brotherhood), and Yemen (where the USS Cole was attacked). There are still militants scattered across Pakistan, the Middle East, and Central Asia (al Qaeda left Bosnia in 1995 to the relief of local militants, who considered them too brutal). Al Qaeda has close ties with Islamic militants in Chechnya, Tajikistan, Iran, Pakistan, Palestine, Lebanon, western China, the Philippines, Saudi Arabia, and, increasingly, in Southeast Asia and Africa—notably Indonesia, Malaysia, Uganda, and Somalia, where al Qaeda–trained militants killed 18 American soldiers in 1992 (Gunaratna 2002, Ch. 3 and 4). Interestingly, Iraq and Libya are not known to have supported al Qaeda, although they have supported other terrorist organizations.

More troubling to Western audiences is the fact that al Qaeda has active cells and regional nodes in the United Kingdom, France, Germany, the United States, and other developed states. Ramsi Yousef and Sheik Omar Abdul Rahman, who were loosely linked to al Qaeda, were based in a Brooklyn community center when they orchestrated the first World Trade Center bombing. In September and October 2002, the U.S. Justice Department arrested several individuals living in Buffalo, Portland, and Detroit on charges of conspiring with al Qaeda. Previously, cells had been identified in Washington, D.C., Chicago, New Jersey, and elsewhere in the United States. London has long been a principal hub of al Qaeda planning and financing, as are France and Germany, which has four known cells (Gunaratna 2001, 111–131). The subway and bus bombings in London in July 2005 were reportedly carried out by Islamic militants with sympathies—but not direct ties—to al Qaeda.

The cells and regional offices maintain frequent contact by means of the most modern communications channels. In the past, they have used cellular telephones, satellite phones, encrypted e-mail, and secret Web sites to maintain contact with their worldwide membership. This fact enabled the FBI to eavesdrop on communication between al Qaeda headquarters and militants, thereby enabling agents to anticipate and break up several planned attacks in the late 1990s. In response, al Qaeda has switched to more traditional (and slower) methods of face-to-face communication. Given the lack of infiltrators, spies, and defectors, this trend may mean that future al Qaeda operations will be more difficult to detect.

Of considerable urgency to the United States is the high level of activity of al Qaeda–affiliated operatives under the leadership of Abu Masab al-Zarqawi in Iraq who have been apparently responsible for the deaths of dozens of Americans and thousands of Iraqis (especially Shiites) since 2003. He is alleged to have masterminded the Madrid train bombings (see below) as well as several spectacular attacks on mosques and kidnappings. In October, he formally linked his organization to al Qaeda's. That said, his status is mysterious. Some have claimed that he died in 2004, others that he was captured and then released by the United States in 2005. Still others that his activities are in fact quite limited (some believe bin Laden "fired" him) and that it is the United States that has amplified his role through astute propaganda (Ricks 2006). He was confirmed killed by an American air strike in July 2006.

Al Qaeda's Finances

Al Qaeda has a reputation for being very well financed, thanks to Osama bin Laden's fortune. However, it is estimated that the entire operation of al Qaeda costs only about $40 million per year and that bin Laden's fortune plays almost no part in its day-to-day funding. On the one hand, al Qaeda operations are generally very inexpensive. The September 11 attacks, the organization's most expensive by far, cost only $500,000 by most estimates. Local cells are expected to take care of their own finances to a large extent (the attackers in the first World Trade Center bombing had to get the deposit back on the truck that exploded to pay for their airfare home!). On the other hand, bin Laden has made several shrewd business decisions that have allowed al Qaeda to prosper from excellent returns on the investments. While in Sudan, in particular, he began several enterprises, including a bank, a large farming operation, a tannery, and a construction company, and he signed contracts to build a major highway and several buildings for the Sudanese government (Wright 2001, 251).

Al Qaeda also receives much of its funding from Islamic clerics and wealthy Muslim sympathizers in the Middle East. Saudi Arabia, for example, has uncovered a donation of $50 million from a group of fundamentalist clerics in 1999. Khalid bin Mahfouz, a wealthy Saudi banker, has transferred funds and facilitated other transactions over the years. The Dubai Islamic Bank in the United Arab Emirates has also been directly implicated (Alexander & Swetnam 2001, 29). Numerous nonprofit organizations, as well as banks, have been identified by law enforcement authorities in dozens of countries as front operations through which millions are transferred to al Qaeda. In reality, many of those who have handled al Qaeda funds were unaware of it because the monies typically pass through several legitimate businesses or organizations on their journey between source and destination (Wright 2001, 252).

In more recent years, al Qaeda has been forced to become more creative and resourceful as much of its funding has been cut off by Western governments. Those who carried out the Madrid bombings (see below) were partly financed by the sale of hashish (*Los Angeles Times* May 23, 2004, A1). It reportedly flowed through Morocco and on to Madrid and other European capitals. Dramatic increases in the sale of opium in Afghanistan, in spite of the government's efforts, could in turn provide resources for al Qaeda bases located near the poppy fields.

AL QAEDA AFTER SEPTEMBER 11

As of September 10th, 2001, bin Laden felt extremely sure of himself, it would seem. He had brought about the defeat and collapse of the Soviet Union in a mere five years. He had expelled the Americans from Somalia with a single attack. He had survived a full-scale cruise missile attack after the Africa attacks. He was beginning to feel powerful in the extreme. He had reached the conclusion that the United States was weak, tentative, and easily intimidated. He expected to remove them from Saudi Arabia in the future. It seems reasonable, given this view of his own importance, that bin Laden believed the September 11 attacks might bring down American democracy and capitalism once and for all.

The purpose of terrorism is outlined in terrorist manuals:

> [T]hey build a reserve of fighters by preparing and training new members for future tasks; they serve as a form of necessary punishment, mocking the regime's admiration among the population; they remove the personalities that stand in the way of the Islamic da'wa (call); they publicize issues; they help to reject compliance and submission to the regime and its practices; they provide legitimacy to the Islamist groups; they spread fear and terror through the regime's ranks; and they attract new members to the organization. (Gunaratna 2002, 75)

To this we could add that terrorism is also intended to provoke repression and over-reaction on the part of the target government, as this response breeds resentment, which in turns swells the ranks of militants. The abuses committed by American troops at Abu Ghraib and (allegedly) in Guantánamo Bay, Cuba have become effective rallying cries for al Qaeda operatives and Iraqi militants across the Middle East. Recruitment has become so easy that several militant groups—including al Qaeda—have created application forms to facilitate processing (Darling 2004). They have been found in Baghdad, Fallujah, Tehran, and elsewhere.

It is unlikely, therefore, that the Bush administration surprised bin Laden with the forceful response provided by the United States, its allies, and the United Nations. In a matter of hours after the September 11 attacks, the UN General Assembly, the UN Security Council, and NATO had voted unanimously to approve war against al Qaeda. Thousands of Western troops were deployed to support the tens of thousands of Northern Alliance forces. Within a few weeks, in spite of stiff opposition, they broke through and seized control of Kabul and Kandahar, taking hundreds of prisoners.

In addition, the international community agreed to impose harsh penalties against al Qaeda, Afghanistan, and any private or public organizations affiliated with the terrorist group. To illustrate the degree of international commitment to the war against al Qaeda, even Cuba, which has had extremely poor relations with American governments over the years, agreed to help the United States by capturing and returning any prisoners who might escape from the various detention centers in Guantánamo Bay on Cuba's eastern coast. Al Qaeda's repudiation among Middle Eastern governments has been unequivocal and unanimous (with the exception of kind words from Iraq). In Pakistan, President Pervez Musharraf has purged Islamic fundamentalists from ISA and other government agencies, although the government has yet to establish clear control over the pro–al Qaeda regions in the north. The fight against Islamic militancy has become a defining feature of the post–September 11 international system, to the point that it has evolved into, to a large extent, the new "cold war." Al Qaeda attacks in Madrid, Spain in March 2004 (on the anniversary of the U.S.–UK invasion of Iraq) resulted in nearly 200 deaths and thousands of casualties. The goal seems to have been to influence the upcoming elections in Spain—and perhaps they did, in that the anti-war opposition party was swept to power and Spain began plans to withdraw its troop from Iraq (*Los Angeles Times* March 12, 2004, A1).

Al Qaeda's position at this point is far weaker than before the World Trade Center attacks. It has lost in the neighborhood of 1,000 militants in Afghanistan, Pakistan, the Philippines, and elsewhere. Tens of millions in assets have been frozen. The organization has no headquarters and many of its most closely guarded secrets are now in the hands of Western governments. Although Osama bin Laden is still alive as of this writing (July 2006. He continues to issue messages from time to time from undisclosed locations), many of his top lieutenants have been killed or captured, including Ahmed Khalfan Ghailani who was captured in Pakistan and provided a wealth of intelligence information to interrogators (*Los Angeles Times* August 16, 2004, A1). However, this is not to say that al Qaeda has been defeated.

The organization has proved to be quite resilient in the past, having survived expulsion from two states during the 1990s. Given the cell structure of the organization, it is able to reconstitute itself rather quickly. Bin Laden has also made arrangements for his succession (although the loss of his second-in-command, Abu Zubaydah, in March 2002 was a serious blow (Gunaratna 2002, 228). Thus, there is reason to believe that the organization will continue to carry out attacks against Western targets. Attacks against a French tanker near Yemen and against American military personnel training in Kuwait and the Philippines, along with a massive attack against foreigners in Indonesia in the fall of 2002, signaled a renewed capacity to commit acts of terror (*Chicago Tribune* October 15, 2002, 1).

In at least one area, the situation may be to al Qaeda's advantage. The destruction of the World Trade Center was greeted with celebration in many circles in the Arab world. It established al Qaeda as the most daring and single-minded challenger to the Western world. This sort of recognition will likely enhance the organization's recruitment efforts, because it adds to the prestige of those who share al Qaeda's goals. It is also likely that as governments move against al Qaeda militants and fundamentalist organizations, they will overreact and provoke a backlash that will further bolster the organization's recruitment.

CONCLUSION

What does the al Qaeda story teach us about terrorism generally? First and foremost, it is wrong to think that terrorists are always unorganized, unfocused, or undisciplined. The al Qaeda example illustrates that they can be highly focused (even though the goals may border on the irrational), highly organized, and extremely disciplined (to the point of fanaticism). The degree of focus eliminates any possibility of self-doubt—a prerequisite of fanaticism. As a consequence, there may be no possibility of reasoning or negotiating with its members. This contrasts sharply with most terrorist organizations, which have at least a few reasonable objectives generally seek only greater political power. Al Qaeda's quest to rid the Arab and Muslim world of Western influence is a political nonstarter, leaving no room for compromise.

Second, al Qaeda demonstrates that terrorist groups with disparate objectives can find common cause and collaborate with one another. This is not the first time this has happened: During the 1970s the Irish Republican Army, the Basque ETA, and other radical groups worked together. Never before has a global structure like al Qaeda's existed, however. Its defeat will, therefore, require a global response.

Al Qaeda demonstrates the destructive potential of terrorist organizations and raises the stakes. Although more people have been the victims of terrorist attacks over the history of the conflicts in Palestine, Northern Ireland, Kashmir, and other areas, never before has a terrorist organization carried out a single, massive attack that killed thousands in an instant. Potential victims must now take the terrorist threat as seriously as if they were defending against a state-sponsored military attack. Unfortunately, terrorists do not play by the same rules as states: They do not reside in one country, they do not wear uniforms, they do not march in columns and ranks, and they do not comply with the Geneva Conventions. Thus states may be faced with dilemmas with regard to appropriate and effective tactics and strategies. A military solution will likely go only so far, but a criminal approach may give the terrorists too many opportunities for escape.

This said, it would be prudent for Western states to consider seriously what types of actions might exacerbate the situation. Repression or over-reaction, for example, might increase recruitment, while half-measures might leave the organization too strong. The invasion of Iraq in March 2003 has been paradoxical, in that it is fairly clear now that the purported ties between Saddam Hussein and al Qaeda, trumpeted by the Bush administration prior to the attack, were minimal. On the other hand, the presence of American troops in Baghdad has served as a magnet for insurgents and terrorist guerrillas who have flooded into the country across ill-guarded borders. All of this was predicted in advance (Lemann 2002).

Perhaps the most profound implication of al Qaeda's actions is the loss of the sense of security felt by most Americans before September 11. Although the nation has perfected the art of denial, the gnawing realization persists in the back of people's minds that there is nowhere to hide. Such is life in the twenty-first century.

 DEBATE TOPIC

Should the priority for the West be the arrest and imprisonment of existing al Qaeda leaders rather than a political settlement of the disputes that spur young men to join the organization?

PRO

Those pressing for arrest or military defeat of al Qaeda stress three points: (1) Al Qaeda presents a clear and present danger and must be stopped. (2) Many of al Qaeda's political demands are not feasible or not genuine and should not be addressed. (3) It would take too long to solve all of the world's injustices at any rate.

CON
Those arguing for addressing fundamental problems argue as follows: (1) Some grievances are legitimate, including the Palestinians' lack of a state. (2) U.S. interventionism has gone too far and should be pulled back. (3) The West's influence is too great, since it encompasses political, economic, and cultural areas.

THINKING THEORETICALLY

An older—somewhat discredited—approach to international relations is idealism. We will contrast it to constructivism with respect to the role of norms.

Idealists argue that international life is manageable through the creation and enforcement of international law. This, in turn, is sustained by a commitment on the part of leaders of nations to certain overarching goals: creating global stability, permitting state autonomy, and perhaps peace and freedom. Idealists are not naïve about the existence of evil and violence—on the contrary, they emphasize order precisely because it will require such effort and focus. The story of al Qaeda may seem at first to show how fragile global order really is, but again, as the idealist might have predicted (if anyone had asked them!), the attacks on September 11 have brought out the best in the governments of the world. They have engaged in numerous cooperative ventures that have resulted in successfully coordinated strikes at al Qaeda bases as well as hundreds of arrests and numerous convictions. Even the United Nations—widely disparaged as ineffective—appears to have found new energy.

Constructivists would point to the importance of norms—including norms articulated by idealists—to explain the passions that animate al Qaeda and the difficulty the Western world faces in combating them. Al Qaeda, simply put, is a rejectionist force, constructivists would argue, that has developed such intense anti-Western feeling that negotiation is out of the question. While there might have been legitimate grievances in the past, for some, these no longer matter. What is required is a wholesale change of thinking—something that has almost no chance of occurring.

QUESTIONS TO CONSIDER

1. Are there other terrorist groups that make use of other systems of religious teachings to justify their violence?

2. How does al Qaeda compare to the Nazis?

3. How much should the West curtail its civil liberties in its struggle against al Qaeda?

4. How do al Qaeda's structure and operation compare to those of other transnational organizations, such as NGOs or multinational firms?

WEBSITES

Al Qaeda on U.S. Government Web sites

www.fbi.gov/terrorinfo/counterrorism/waronterrorhome.htm
www.cia.gov/terrorism/index.html
State Department: www.usinfo.state.gov/topical/pol/terror/homepage.htm

Competing Opinions on al Qaeda

Azzam: www.azzam.com
Anti-Defamation League: www.adl.org/terrorism_america/bin_l.asp
Institute for the Secularization of Islamic Society: www.secularislam.org
Federation of American Scientists: www.fas.org/irp/world/para/ladin.htm

REFERENCES

Alexander, Yonah, and Michael S. Swetnam. *Usama bin Laden's al Qaida: Profile of a Terrorist Network* (Ardsley, NY: Transnational Pubs., 2001).

Al-Turabi, Hasan. "Principles of Governance, Freedom and Responsibility in Islam." *American Journal of Islamic Social Science* 4 #1 (1987): 1–11.

Amnesty International (AI). "Amnesty International Report 2002 – Spain." 2002. Accessed on May 8, 2006 at: http://web.amnesty.org/web/ar2002.nsf/eur/spain!Open.

BBC. "Who are ETA?" published on-line on March 22, 2006. Accessed May 8, 2006 at: http://newvote.bbc.co.uk.

Beres, Rene Louis. "The Meaning of Terrorism: Jurisprudential and Definitional Clarifications." *Vanderbilt Journal of Transnational Law* 28 (March 1995): 239–256.

Berman, Paul. "Terror and Liberalism." *American Prospect* 12 #18 (October 22, 2001): 18–27.

Bush, George. "The President's State of the Union Address." Washington, D.C., January 29, 2002.

Chicago Tribune, October 15, 2002, 1.

Christian Science Monitor, September 9, 2002, 1.

Darling, Dan. "Want an al Qaeda Job? Apply now – with references, please." *The American Enterprise* 15 #6 (September 2004): 1.

Davidson, Lawrence. *Islamic Fundamentalism* (Westport, CT: Greenwood Press, 1998).

Gunaratna, Rohan. *Inside Al Qaeda: Global Network of Terror* (New York: Columbia University Press, 2002).

Herf, Jeffrey. "What Is Old and What Is New in the Terrorism of Islamic Fundamentalism?" *Partisan Review* 69 #1 (Winter 2002): 25–33.

Huband, Mark. *Warriors of the Prophet: The Struggle for Islam* (Boulder, CO: Westview Press, 1998).

Lemann, Nicholas. "The War on What?" *The New Yorker* (September 16, 2002): 36–44.

Los Angeles Times, August 16, 2004, A1.

Martinez-Herrara, Enric. "Nationalist Extremism and Outcomes of State Policies in the Basque Country, 1979-2001." *International Journal on Multicultueral Societies* 4 #1 (January 2001): 1–22.

Miles, Jack. "Theology and the Clash of Civilizations." *Cross Currents* 51 #4 (Winter 2002): 451–460.

O'Ballance, Edgar. *Islamic Fundamentalist Terrorism, 1979–95: The Iranian Connection* (New York: NYU Press, 1997).

Ricks, Thomas. "Military Plays Up Role of Zarqawi." *Washington Post* April 10, 2005, A01.

Schafer, David. "Islam and Terrorism: A Humanist View." *The Humanist* 62 #3 (May–June 2002): 16–21.

Tucker, David. *Skirmishes at the Edge of Empire: The United States and International Terrorism* (Westport, CT: Praeger, 1997).

Woodworth, Paddy. "Why Do They Kill?" *World Policy Journal* 18 #1 (Spring 2001): 1–12.

Wright, Robin. *Sacred Rage: The Wrath of Militant Islam* (New York: Touchstone Book, 2001).

CASE 10

Excerpts From the 9/11 Commission Report: Intelligence

INTRODUCTION: INTELLIGENCE

Intelligence is a word pregnant with intrigue and mystery. In fact, intelligence, as used in government circles, simply means the gathering and analysis of information on foreign policy problems. The vast majority of intelligence is gathered and analyzed the same way research papers are written—by informed observers using public documents. It is common knowledge in Washington that the *New York Times* routinely provides better information about unfolding events than the Central Intelligence Agency (whose job it is to know what is going on). Some more unusual sources of intelligence include spying, electronic surveillance, and satellite reconnaissance. As technology has advanced, the significance of electronic information gathering has increased, typically at the expense of traditional spying.

Today, analysts rely increasingly on electronic intelligence, including telephone intercepts (both cellular and ground-based), e-mail and Internet traffic monitoring, and other electronic communications. The National Security Agency, along with the CIA and various defense and diplomatic intelligence-gathering organizations, monitor and catalogue millions of conversations and e-mails each day in dozens of languages. Such intercepts have allowed U.S. federal agencies to discover various terrorist plots in advance. However, the flow of information is often overwhelming and takes days—even weeks—to translate and interpret. Such delays may have prevented the U.S. government from identifying pre–September 11 communications that could have prompted a heightened state of alert.

What follows is an excerpted passage from the 9/11 Commission Report, issued in September 2004. The material follows a chronological sequence, although it does not follow the order of the Report itself. As you read the material, consider the following: Were the institutional arrangements for gathering, analyzing, and disseminating intelligence information adequate to the task? Did the public officials fulfill their responsibilities to carry out this analysis and give proper advice to policymakers? What responsibility do policymakers have with respect to the final decisions and response?

KEY FIGURES
(THE 9/11 COMMISSION REPORT HAS AN EXTENSIVE LIST OF NAMES ON PAGES 431–438.)

George Tenet   Director of Central Intelligence, 1997–2004.

Osama bin Laden   Leader of the al Qaeda terror network.

John Ashcroft   Attorney General, 2001–2005.

Robert Mueller   FBI Director, 2001–

George W. Bush   President of the United States, 2001–

Richard Clarke   National Security Council (NSC) counterterrorism coordinator, 1997–2001.

Dick Cheney   Vice President of the United States, 2001–

Stephen Hadley   Deputy National Security Advisor, 2001–2005.

Condoleezza Rice   National Security Advisor, 2001–2005.

Zacarias Moussaoui   Frenchman convicted in connection with the 9/11 plot.

Colin Powell   Secretary of State, 2001–2005.

Donald Rumsfeld   Secretary of Defense, 2001–2006.

Abu Zubaydah   Alias for Zein al Abideen Mohaned Hussein—Palestinian al Qaeda operative.

Mohammed Atta   Egyptian who led the 9/11 plot, he hijacked American Airlines flight 11.

Abdul Aziz al Omari   Saudi hijacker of American Airlines flight 11.

Satam al Suqami   Saudi hijacker of American Airlines flight 11.

Wail al Shehri   Saudi hijacker of American Airlines flight 11.

Waleed al Shehri   Saudi hijacker of American Airlines flight 11.

Thomas Pickard   Acting FBI Director, June 25–September 4, 2001

Betty Ong   Flight attendant on American Airlines flight 11.

Madeline "Amy" Sweeney   Flight attendant on American Airlines flight 11.

CHRONOLOGY

2001

April 13   FBI issues alert to all its field offices to gather information on pending al Qaeda attacks.

April 20   Richard Clarke gives a briefing to top officials, reporting that "Bin Ladin [is] planning multiple operations."

May 29   Clarke warns NSA Condoleezza Rice to press CIA and FBI on planning against al Qaeda attack.

June 30   Multiple sources indicated bin Ladin is planning a "spectacular" attack, although most indications point to overseas targets.

July 2   Expecting an attack over the Fourth of July holiday, the FBI warns its field offices to "exercise extreme vigilance."

July 5   Richard Clarke briefs a gathering of federal security agencies on the al Qaeda threat, although the emphasis is placed on foreign targets.

July   The "Phoenix memo" is transmitted to FBI headquarters warning of Middle Eastern men taking flight training.

July 31   The FAA issues a warning against possible attacks in the Middle East.

August 23   The CIA is briefed on the case of Zacarias Moussaoui, who has been taking flight training in Minnesota.

SEPTEMBER 11, 2001

6:00am   Mohammed Atta and Abdul Aziz al Omari begin the attack by boarding a flight from Portland, Maine to Boston, Massachusetts.

7:40am   All the hijackers have made their way on board American Airlines flight 11 in Boston. Others are boarding United flights 175 and 93 and American flight 77 in Boston, Newark, and Dulles.

8:14am   American flight 11 is hijacked. By 9:28, all four flights will have been hijacked by the al Qaeda terrorists.

8:25am   The FAA first learns of the hijacking of American flight 11. It alerts the military at 8:38 and jets are scrambled by 8:46.

8:46:40am   AA11 strikes the north tower of the World Trade Center. It will be followed at 9:03:11 by flight UA175 striking the south tower.

8:54am   AA77 is hijacked and flown toward the Pentagon, which it will strike at 9:37:46.

9:25am   The FAA center at Dulles International Airport orders a nationwide ground stop.

9:57am   Roughly 30 minutes after it is hijacked, the passengers on board UA flight 93 revolt. The plane crashes in a wood near Shanksville, Pennsylvania at 10:03:11.

2002
January 29   Under pressure from Democrats who control the Senate, President Bush begins negotiations on the make-up of an official inquiry into the intelligence failures leading up to 9/11.

March 23   President Bush formally opposes the formation of an independent commission to study the matter, preferring to leave it to Senate intelligence committees.

November 27   President Bush appoints Henry Kissinger to head the 9/11 Commission, although Kissinger withdraws when he learns he must reveal the names of all of the clients of Kissinger Associates. Former New Jersey Governor Thomas Kean is appointed in December in his place.

2003
March 31–June 17   The 9/11 Commission holds numerous hearings at multiple locations. Throughout the process, the Bush administration raises objections and concerns.

2004
September 23   The Final Report is issued to broad praise. President Bush pledges to implement the vast majority of its recommendations.

November 23   Legislation to implement the Final Report's recommendations is blocked in a key vote in Congress. President Bush promises to re-introduce new legislation in January.

2006
May 3   Zacarias Moussaoui receives a life sentence without parole for his role in the 9/11 plot.

"THE SYSTEM WAS BLINKING RED"

The Summer of Threat—pp. 254–260

As 2001 began, officials were receiving frequent but fragmentary reports about threats. Indeed, there appeared to be possible threats almost everywhere the United States had interests—including at home.

To understand how the escalation in threat reporting was handled in the summer of 2001, it is useful to understand how threat information in general is collected and conveyed. Information is collected through several methods, including signals intelligence and interviews of human sources, and gathered into intelligence reports. Depending on the source and nature of the reporting, these reports may be highly classified—and therefore tightly held—or less sensitive and widely disseminated to state and local law enforcement agencies. Threat reporting must be disseminated, either through individual reports or through threat advisories. Such advisories, intended to alert their recipients, may address a specific threat or be a general warning.

Because the amount of reporting is so voluminous, only a select fraction can be chosen for briefing the president and senior officials. During 2001, Director of Central Intelligence George Tenet was briefed regularly regarding threats and other operational information relating to Osama bin Ladin. He in turn met daily with President Bush, who was briefed by the CIA through what is known as the President's Daily Brief (PDB). Each PDB consists of a series of six to eight relatively short articles or briefs covering a broad array of topics; CIA staff decides which subjects are the most important on any given day. There were more than 40 intelligence articles in the PDBs from January 20 to September 10, 2001, that related to bin Ladin. The PDB is considered highly sensitive and is distributed to only a handful of high-level officials.

The Senior Executive Intelligence Brief (SEIB), distributed to a broader group of officials, has a similar format and generally covers the same subjects as the PDB. It usually contains less information so as to protect sources and methods. Like their predecessors, the attorney general, the FBI director, and Richard Clarke, the National Security Council (NSC) counterterrorism coordinator, all received the SEIB, not the PDB. Clarke and his staff had extensive access to terrorism reporting, but they did not have access to internal, nondisseminated information at the National Security Agency (NSA), CIA, or FBI.

The Drumbeat Begins

In the spring of 2001, the level of reporting on terrorist threats and planned attacks increased dramatically to its highest level since the millennium alert. At the end of March, the intelligence community disseminated a terrorist threat advisory, indicating a heightened threat of Sunni extremist terrorist attacks against U.S. facilities, personnel, and other interests.

On March 23, in connection with discussions about possibly reopening Pennsylvania Avenue in front of the White House, Clarke warned National Security Advisor Condoleezza Rice that domestic or foreign terrorists might use a truck bomb—their "weapon of choice"—on Pennsylvania Avenue. That would result, he said, in the destruction of the West Wing and parts of the residence. He also told her that he thought there were terrorist cells within the United States, including al Qaeda.

In response to these threats, the FBI sent a message to all its field offices on April 13, summarizing reporting to date. It asked the offices to task all resources, including human sources and electronic databases, for any information pertaining to "current operational activities relating to Sunni extremism." It did not suggest that there was a domestic threat.

On April 20, a briefing to top officials reported "Bin Ladin planning multiple operations." When the deputies discussed al Qaeda policy on April 30, they began with a briefing on the threat.

In May 2001, the drumbeat of reporting grew louder with reports to top officials that "Bin Ladin public profile may presage attack" and "Bin Ladin network's plans advancing." In early May, a walk-in to the FBI claimed there was a plan to launch attacks on London, Boston, and New York. Attorney General John Ashcroft was briefed by the CIA on May 15 regarding al Qaeda generally and the current threat reporting specifically. The next day brought a report that a phone call to a U.S. embassy had warned that bin Ladin supporters were planning an attack in the United States using "high explosives." On May 17, based on the previous day's report, the first item on the CSG's agenda was "UBL: Operation Planned in U.S." The anonymous caller's tip could not be corroborated.

Late May brought reports of a possible hostage plot against Americans abroad to force the release of prisoners, including Sheikh Omar Abdel Rahman, the "Blind Sheikh," who was serving a life sentence for his role in the 1993 plot to blow up sites in New York City. The reporting noted that operatives might opt to hijack an aircraft or storm a U.S. embassy. This report led to a Federal Aviation Administration (FAA) information circular to airlines noting the potential for "an airline hijacking to free terrorists incarcerated in the United States." Other reporting mentioned that Abu Zubaydah was planning an attack, possibly against Israel, and expected to carry out several more if things went well. On May 24 alone, counterterrorism officials grappled with reports alleging plots in Yemen and Italy, as well as a report about a cell in Canada that an anonymous caller had claimed might be planning an attack against the United States.

Reports similar to many of these were made available to President Bush in morning intelligence briefings with DCI Tenet, usually attended by Vice President Dick Cheney and National Security Advisor Rice. While these briefings discussed general threats to attack America and American interests, the specific threats mentioned in these briefings were all overseas.

On May 29, Clarke suggested that Rice ask DCI Tenet what more the United States could do to stop Abu Zubaydah from launching "a series of major terrorist attacks," probably on Israeli targets, but possibly on U.S. facilities. Clarke wrote to Rice and her deputy, Stephen Hadley, "When these attacks occur, as they likely will, we will wonder what more we could have done to stop them." In May, CIA Counterterrorist Center (CTC) Chief Cofer Black Rice that the current threat level was a 7 on a scale of 1 to 10, as compared to an 8 during the millennium."

High Probability of Near-Term "Spectacular" Attacks

Threat reports surged in June and July, reaching an even higher peak of urgency. The summer threats seemed to be focused on Saudi Arabia, Israel, Bahrain, Kuwait, Yemen, and possibly Rome, but the danger could be anywhere—including a possible attack on the G-8 summit in Genoa. A June 12 CIA report passing along biographical background information on several terrorists mentioned, in commenting on Khalid Skeikh Mohammed, that he was recruiting people to travel to the United States to meet with colleagues already there so that they might conduct terrorist attacks on bin Ladin's behalf. On June 22, the CIS notified all its station chiefs about intelligence suggesting a possible al Qaeda suicide attack on a U.S. target over the next few days. DCI Tenet asked that all U.S. ambassadors be briefed.

That same day, the State Department notified all embassies of the terrorist threat and updated its worldwide public warning. In June, the State Department initiated the Visa Express program in Saudi Arabia as a security measure, in order to keep long lines of foreigners away from vulnerable embassy spaces. The program permitted visa applications to be made through travel agencies, instead of directly at the embassy or consulate.

A terrorist threat advisory distributed in late June indicated a high probability of near-term "spectacular" terrorist attacks resulting in numerous casualties. Other reports' titles warned, "Bin Ladin Attacks May be Imminent" and "Bin Ladin and Associates Making Near-Term Threats." The latter reported multiple attacks planned over the coming days, including a "severe blow" against U.S. and Israeli "interests" during the next two weeks.

On June 21, near the height of the threat reporting, U.S. Central Command raised the force protection condition level for troops in six countries to the highest possible level, Delta. The U.S. Fifth Fleet moved out of its port in Bahrain, and a U.S. Marine Corps exercise in Jordan was halted. U.S. embassies in the Persian Gulf conducted an emergency security review, and the embassy in Yemen was closed. The CSG had foreign response teams, known as FESTs, ready to move on four hours' notice and kept up the terrorism alert posture on a "rolling 24 hour basis."

On June 25, Clarke warned Rice and Hadley that six separate intelligence reports showed al Qaeda personnel warning of a pending attack. An Arabic television station reported bin Ladin's pleasure with al Qaeda leaders who were saying that the next weeks "will witness important surprises" and that the U.S. and Israeli interests will be targeted. Al Qaeda also released a new recruitment and fundraising tape. Clarke wrote that this was all too sophisticated to be merely a psychological operation to keep the United States on edge, and the CIA agreed. The intelligence reporting consistently described the upcoming attacks as occurring on a calamitous level, indicating that they would cause the world to be in turmoil and that they would consist of multiple—but not necessarily simultaneous—attacks.

On June 28, Clarke wrote Rice that the pattern of al Qaeda activity indicating attack planning over the past six weeks "had reached a crescendo." "A series of new reports continue to convince me and analysts at State, CIA, DIA [Defense Intelligence Agency], and NSA that a major terrorist attack or series of attacks is likely in July," he noted. One al Qaeda intelligence report warned that something "very, very, very, very" big was about to happen, and most of bin Ladin's network was reportedly anticipating the attack. In late June, the CIA ordered all of its station chiefs to share information on al Qaeda with their host governments and to push for immediate disruption of cells.

The headline of a June 30 brief to top officials was stark: "Bin Ladin Planning High-Profile Attacks." The report stated that bin Ladin operatives expected near-term attacks to have dramatic consequences of catastrophic proportions. That same day, Saudi Arabia declared its highest level of terror alert. Despite evidence of delays possibly caused by heightened U.S. security, the planning for attacks was continuing.

On July 2, the FBI Counterterrorism Division sent a message to federal agencies and state and local law enforcement agencies summarizing information regarding threats from bin Ladin. It warned that there was as increased volume of threat reporting, indicating a potential for attacks against U.S. targets abroad from groups "aligned with or sympathetic to Usama Bin Ladin." Despite the general warnings, the message further stated, "The FBI has no information indicating a credible threat of terrorist attack in the United States." However, it went on to emphasize that the possibility of attack in the United States could not be discounted. It also noted that the July 4 holiday might heighten the threats. The report asked recipients to "exercise extreme vigilance" and "report suspicious activities" to the FBI. It did not suggest specific actions that they should take to prevent attacks.

Disruption operations against al Qaeda–affiliated cells were launched involving 20 countries. Several terrorist operatives were detained by foreign governments, possibly disrupting operations in the Gulf and Italy and perhaps averting attacks against two or three U.S. embassies. Clarke and others told us of a particular concern about the possible attacks on the Fourth of July. After it passed uneventfully, the CSG decided to maintain the alert.

The CSG arranged for the CIA to brief intelligence and security officials from several domestic agencies. On July 5, representatives from the Immigration and Naturalization Service (INS), the FAA, the Coast Guard, the Secret Service, Customs, the CIA, and the FBI met with Clarke to discuss the current threat. Attendees report that they were told not to disseminate the threat information they received at the meeting. They interpreted this direction to mean that although they could brief their superiors, they could not send out advisories to the field. An NSC official recalls a somewhat different emphasis, saying that attendees were asked to take the information back to their home agencies and "do what you can" with it, subject to classification and distribution restrictions. A representative from the IND asked for a summary of the information that she could share with field offices. She never received one.

That same day, the CIA briefed Attorney General Ashcroft on the al Qaeda threat, warning that a significant terrorist attack was imminent. Ashcroft was told that preparations for multiple attacks were in late stages or already complete and that little additional warning could be expected. The briefing addressed only threats outside the United States.

The next day, the CIA representative told the CSG that al Qaeda members believed the upcoming attack would be "spectacular," qualitatively different from anything they had done to date.

Apparently as a result of the July 5 meeting with Clarke, the interagency committee on federal building security was tasked to examine security measures. This committee met on July 9, when 37 officials from 27 agencies and organizations were briefed on the "current threat level" in the United States. They were told that not only the threat reports from abroad but also the recent convictions in the East Africa bombings trial, the conviction of Ahmed Ressam, and the just-returned Khobar Towers indictments reinforced the need to "exercise extreme vigilance." Attendees were expected to determine whether their respective agencies needed enhanced security measures.

In mid-July, reporting started to indicate that bin Ladin's plans had been delayed, maybe for as long as two months, but not abandoned. On July 23, the lead item for CSG discussion was still the al Qaeda threat, and it included mention of suspected terrorist travel to the United States.

On July 31, an FAA circular appeared alerting the aviation community to "reports of possible near-term terrorist operations . . . particularly on the Arabian Peninsula and/or Israel." It stated that the FAA had no credible evidence of specific plans to attack U.S. civil aviation, though it noted that some of the "currently active" terrorist groups were known to "plan and train for hijackings" and were able to build and conceal sophisticated explosive devices in luggage and consumer products.

Tenet told us that in his world "the system was blinking red." By late July, Tenet said, it could not "get any worse." Not everyone was convinced. Some asked whether all these threats might just be deception. On June 30, the SEIB contained an article titled "Bin Ladin Threats Are Real." Yet Hadley told Tenet in July that bin Ladin was trying to study U.S. reactions. Tenet replied that he had already addressed the Defense Department's questions on this point; the reporting was convincing. To give a sense of his anxiety at the time, one senior official in the Counterterrorist Center told us that he and a colleague were considering resigning in order to go public with their concern. . . .

Government Response to the Threats—pp. 263–265

National Security Advisor Rice told us that the CSG was the "nerve center" for running the crisis, although other senior officials were involved over the course of the summer. In addition to his daily meetings with President Bush, and weekly meetings to go over other issues with Rice, Tenet was speaking regularly with Secretary of State Colin Powell and Secretary of Defense Donald Rumsfeld. The foreign policy principals routinely talked on the telephone every day on a variety of topics.

Hadley told us that before 9/11, he and Rice did not feel they had the job of coordinating domestic agencies. They felt that Clarke and the CSG (part of the NSC) were the NSC's bridge between foreign and domestic threats.

There was a clear disparity in the levels of response to foreign versus domestic threats. Numerous actions were taken overseas to disrupt possible attacks—enlisting foreign partners to upset terrorist plans, closing embassies, moving military assets out of the way of possible harm. Far less was done domestically—in part, surely, because to the extent that specifics did exist, they pertained to threats overseas. As noted earlier, a threat against the embassy in Yemen quickly resulted in its closing. Possible domestic threats were more vague. When reports did not specify where the attacks were to take place, officials presumed that they would again be overseas, though they did not rule out a target in the United States. Each of the FBI threat advisories made this point.

Clarke mentioned to National Security Advisor Rice at least twice that al Qaeda sleeper cells were likely in the United States. In January 2001, Clarke forwarded a strategy paper to Rice warning that al Qaeda had a presence in the United States. He noted that two key al Qaeda members in the Jordanian cell involved in the millennium plot were naturalized U.S. citizens and that one jihadist suspected in the East Africa bombings had "informed the FBI that an extensive network of al Qaeda 'sleeper agents' currently exists in the US." He added that Ressam's abortive December 1999 attack revealed al Qaeda supporters in the United States. His analysis, however, was based not on new threat reporting but on past experience.

The September 11 attacks fell into the void between the foreign and domestic threats. The foreign intelligence agencies were watching overseas, alert to foreign threats to U.S. interests there. The domestic agencies were waiting for evidence of a domestic threat from sleeper cells within the United States. No one was looking for a foreign threat to domestic targets. The threat that was coming was not from sleeper cells. It was foreign—but from foreigners who had infiltrated into the United States.

A second cause of this disparity in response is that domestic agencies did not know what to do, and no one gave them direction. Cressy told us that the CSG did not tell the agencies how to respond to the threats. He noted that the agencies that were operating overseas did not need direction on how to respond; they had experience with such threats and had a "playbook." In contrast, the domestic agencies did not have a game plan. Neither the NSC (including the CSG) nor anyone else instructed them to create one.

This lack of direction was evident in the July 5 meeting with representatives from the domestic agencies. The briefing focused on overseas threats. The domestic agencies were not questioned about how they planned to address the threat and were not told what was expected of them. Indeed, as noted earlier, they were specifically told they could not issue advisories based on the briefing. The domestic agencies' limited response indicates that they did not perceive a call to action.

Clarke reflected a different perspective in an e-mail to Rice on September 15, 2001. He summarized the steps taken by the CSG to alert domestic agencies to the possibility of an attack in the United States. Clarke concluded that domestic agencies, including the FAA, knew that the CSG believed a major al Qaeda attack was coming and could be in the United States.

Although the FAA had authority to issue security directives mandating new security procedures, none of the few that were released during the summer of 2001 increased security at checkpoints or onboard aircraft. The presentation mentioned the possibility of suicide hijackings but said that "fortunately, we have no indication that any group is currently thinking in that direction." The FAA conducted 27 special security briefings for specific air carriers between May 1, 2001, and September 11, 2001. Two of these briefings discussed the hijacking threat overseas. None discussed the possibility of suicide hijackings or the use of aircraft as weapons. No new security measures were instituted.

Rice told us she understood that the FBI had tasked its 56 U.S. field offices to increase surveillance of suspected terrorist plots. An NSC staff document at the time describes such a tasking as having occurred in late June but does not indicate whether it was generated by the NSC or the FBI. Other than the previously described April 13 communication sent to all FBI field offices, however, the FBI could not find any record of having received such a directive. The document asking field offices to gather information on Sunni extremism did not mention any possible threat within the United States and what the FBI's directives should contain and did not review what had been issued earlier.

Acting FBI Director Pickard told us that in addition to his July 19 conference call, he mentioned the heightened terrorist threat to individual calls with the special agents in charge of field offices during their annual performance review discussions. In speaking with agents around the country, we found little evidence that any such concerns had reached FBI personnel beyond the New York Field Office.

The head of counterterrorism at the FBI, Dale Watson, said he had many discussions about possible attacks with Cofer Black at the CIA. They had expected an attack on July 4. Watson said he felt deeply that something was going to happen. But he told us the threat information was "nebulous." He wished he had known more. He wished he had had "500 analysts looking at Usama Bin Ladin threat information instead of two."

Attorney General Ashcroft was briefed by the CIA in May and by Pickard in early July about the danger. Pickard said he met with Ashcroft once a week in late June, through July, and twice in August. There is a dispute regarding Ashcroft's interest in Pickard's briefings about the terrorist threat situation. Pickard told us that after two such briefings Ashcroft told him he did not want to hear about the threats anymore. Ashcroft denies Pickard's charge. Pickard says he continued to present terrorism information during further briefings that summer, but nothing further on the "chatter" the U.S. government was receiving.

The attorney general told us he asked Pickard whether there was intelligence about attacks in the United States and that Pickard said no. Pickard said he replied that he could not assure Ashcroft that there would be no attacks in the United States, although the reports of threats were related to overseas targets. Ashcroft said he therefore assumed the FBI was doing what it needed to do. He acknowledged that in retrospect, this was a dangerous assumption. He did not ask the FBI what it was doing in response to the threats and did not task it to take any specific action. He also did not direct the INS, then still part of the Department of Justice, to take any specific action.

In sum, the domestic agencies never mobilized in response to the threat. They did not have direction, and did not have a plan to institute. The borders were not hardened. Transportation systems were not fortified. Electronic surveillance was not targeted against a domestic threat. State and local law enforcement were not marshaled to augment the FBI's efforts. The public was not warned. . . .

Phoenix Memo—pp. 272–277

. . . In July 2001, an FBI agent in the Phoenix field office sent a memo to FBI headquarters and to two agents on international terrorism squads in the New York Field Office, advising of the "possibility of a coordinated effort by Usama Bin Ladin" to send students to the United States to attend civil aviation schools. The agent based his theory on the "inordinate number of individuals of investigative interest" attending such schools in Arizona.

The agent made four recommendations to FBI headquarters: to compile a list of civil aviation schools, establish liaison with those schools, discuss his theories about bin Ladin with the intelligence community, and seek authority to obtain visa information on persons applying to flight schools. His recommendations were not acted on. His memo was forwarded to one field office. Managers of the Osama bin Ladin unit and the Radical Fundamentalist unit at FBI headquarters were addressees, but they did not even see the memo until after September 11. No managers at headquarters saw the memo before September 11, and the New York Field Office took no action. . . .

Zacarias Moussaoui

On August 15, 2001, the Minneapolis FBI Field Office initiated an intelligence investigation on Zacarias Moussaoui. . . . He had entered the United States in February 2001, and had begun flight lessons at Airman Flight School in Norman, Oklahoma. He resumed his training at the Pan Am International Flight Academy in Eagan, Minnesota, starting on August 13. He had none of the usual qualifications for flight training on Pan Am's Boeing 747 flight simulators. He said he did not intend to become a commercial pilot but wanted the training as an "ego boosting thing." Moussaoui stood out because, with little knowledge of flying, he wanted to learn how to "take off and land" a Boeing 747.

The agent in Minneapolis quickly learned that Moussaoui possessed jihadist beliefs. Moreover, Moussaoui had $32,000 in a bank account but did not provide a plausible explanation for this sum of money. He had traveled to Pakistan but became agitated when asked if he had traveled to nearby countries while in Pakistan (Pakistan was the customary route to the training camps in Afghanistan). He planned to receive martial arts training, and intended to purchase a global positioning receiver. The agent also noted that Moussaoui became extremely agitated whenever he was questioned regarding his religious beliefs. The agent concluded that Moussaoui was "an Islamic extremist preparing for some future act in furtherance of radical fundamentalist goals." He also believed Moussaoui's plan was related to his flight training. . . .

There was substantial disagreement between Minneapolis agents and FBI headquarters as to what Moussaoui was planning to do. In one conversation between a Minneapolis supervisor and a headquarters agent, the latter complained that Minneapolis's FISA request was couched in a manner intended to get people "spun up." The supervisor replied that was precisely his intent. He said he was "trying to keep someone from taking a plane and crashing into the World Trade Center." The headquarters agent replied that this was not going to happen and that they did not know if Moussaoui was a terrorist.

There is no evidence that either FBI Acting Director Pickard or Assistant Director for Counterterrorism Dale Watson was briefed on the Moussaoui case prior to 9/11. Michael Rolince, the FBI assistant director heading the Bureau's International Terrorism Operations Section (ITOS), recalled being told about Moussaoui in two passing hallway conversations but only in the context that he might be receiving telephone calls from Minneapolis complaining about how headquarters was handling the matter. He never received such a call. Although the acting special agent in charge of Minneapolis called the ITOS supervisors to discuss the Moussaoui case on August 27, he declined to go up the chain of command at FBI headquarters and call Rolince.

On August 23, DCI Tenet was briefed about the Moussaoui case in a briefing titled "Islamic Extremist Learns to Fly." Tenet was also told that Moussaoui wanted to learn to fly a 747, paid for his training in cash, was interested to learn the doors do not open in flight, and wanted to fly a simulated flight from London to New York. He was told that the FBI had arrested Moussaoui because of a visa overstay and that the CIA was working the case with the FBI. Tenet told us that no connection to al Qaeda was apparent to him at the time. Seeing it as an FBI case, he did not discuss the matter with anyone at the White House or the FBI. No connection was made between Moussaoui's presence in the United States and the threat reporting during the summer of 2001. . . .

[It is worth noting that Moussaoui was charged with conspiracy to commit terrorism, use weapons of mass destruction, and aircraft piracy, among other things. He was the only individual to be tried in the United States in connection with the events of 9/11. After lengthy delays over evidence, the formal trial took place in early 2006, resulting in a conviction and a life sentence without parole. Throughout the trial he behaved erratically—confessing and then retracting his confession, for example—and refused to cooperate with court-appointed counsel. Ultimately, the jury decided that his decision to withhold key information from authorities contributed to the success of the 9/11 attacks. At the same time, they generally believed that he was not a central figure and therefore did not deserve to be executed (*New York Times* May 4, 2006, A1, A28).]

Time Runs Out

As Tenet told us, "the system was blinking red" during the summer of 2001. Officials were alerted across the world. Many were doing everything they possibly could to respond to the threats.

Yet no one working on these late leads in the summer of 2001 connected the case in his or her inbox to the threat reports agitating senior officials and being briefed to the President. Thus, these individual cases did not become national priorities. As the CIA supervisor "John" told us, no one looked at the bigger picture; no analytic work foresaw the lightning that could connect the thundercloud to the ground. . . .

"WE HAVE SOME PLANES"—pp. 1–7

Tuesday, September 11, 2001, dawned temperate and nearly cloudless in the eastern United States. Millions of men and women readied themselves for work. Some made their way to the Twin Towers, the signature structures of the World Trade Center complex in New York City. Others went to Arlington, Virginia, to the Pentagon. Across the Potomac River, the United States Congress was back in session. At the other end of Pennsylvania Avenue, people began to line up for a White House tour. In Sarasota, Florida, President George W. Bush went for an early morning run.

For those heading to an airport, weather conditions could not have been better for a safe and pleasant journey. Among the travelers were Mohammed Atta and Abdul Aziz al Omari, who arrived at the airport in Portland, Maine.

INSIDE THE FOUR FLIGHTS

Boarding the Flights

Boston: American 11 . . . Atta and Omari boarded a 6:00 am flight from Portland to Boston's Logan International Airport.

When he checked in for his flight to Boston, Atta was selected by a computerized prescreening system known as CAPPS (Computer Assisted Passenger Prescreening System), created to identify passengers who should be subject to special security measures. Under security rules in place at the time, the only consequence of Atta's selection by CAPPS was that his checked bags were held off the plane until it was confirmed that he boarded the aircraft. This did not hinder Atta's plans.

Atta and Omari arrived in Boston at 6:45. Seven minutes later, Atta apparently took a call from Marwan al Shehhi, a longtime colleague who was at another terminal at Logan Airport. They spoke for three minutes. It would be their final conversation.

Between 6:45 and 7:40, Atta and Omari, along with Satam al Suqami, Wail al Shehri, and Waleed al Shehri, checked in and boarded American Airlines Flight 11, bound to Los Angeles. The flight was scheduled to depart at 7:45. . . .

The security checkpoints through which passengers, including Atta and his colleagues, gained access to the American 11 gate were operated by Globe Security under a contract with American Airlines. . . .

In passing through these checkpoints, each of the hijackers would have been screened by a walk-through metal detector calibrated to detect items with at least the metal content of a .22 caliber handgun. Anyone who might have set off that detector would have been screened with a hand wand—a procedure requiring the screener to identify the metal item or items that caused the alarm. In addition, an X-ray machine would have screened the hijackers' carry-on belongings. The screening was in place to identify and confiscate weapons and other items prohibited from being carried onto a commercial flight. None of the checkpoint supervisors recalled the hijackers or reported anything suspicious regarding their screening.

While Atta had been selected by CAPPS in Portland, three members of his hijacking team—Suqami, Wail al Shehri, and Waleed al Shehri—were selected in Boston. Their selection affected only the handling of their checked bags, not their screening at the checkpoint. All five men cleared the checkpoint and made their way to the gate for American 11. Atta, Omari, and Suqami took their seats in business class (seats 8D, 8G, and 10B, respectively). The Shehri brothers had adjacent seats in row 2 (Wail in 2A, Waleed in 2B), in the first class cabin. They boarded American 11 between 7:31 and 7:40. The aircraft pushed back from the gate at 7:40. . . .

The Hijacking of American 11

American Airlines Flight 11 provided nonstop service from Boston to Los Angeles. On September 11, Captain John Ogonowski and First Officer Thomas McGuiness piloted the Boeing 767. It carried its full capacity of nine flight attendants. Eighty-one passengers boarded the flight with them (including the five terrorists).

The plane took off at 7:59. Just before 8:14, it had climbed to 26,000 feet, not quite its initial assigned cruising altitude of 29,000 feet. All communications and flight profile data were normal. About this time the "Fasten Seatbelt" sign would usually have been turned off and the flight attendants would have begun preparing for cabin service.

At that same time, American 11 had its last routine communication with the ground when it acknowledged navigational instructions from the FAA's air traffic control (ATC) center in Boston. Sixteen seconds after the transmission, ATC instructed the aircraft's pilots to climb to 35,000 feet. That message and all subsequent attempts to contact the flight were not acknowledged. From this and other evidence, we believe the hijacking began at 8:14 or shortly thereafter.

Reports from two flight attendants in the coach cabin, Betty Ong and Madeline "Amy" Sweeney, tell us most of what we know about how the hijacking happened. As it began, some of the hijackers—most likely Wail al Shehri and Waleed al Shehri, who were seated in row 2 in first class—stabbed the two unarmed flight attendants who would have been preparing for cabin service.

We do not know exactly how the hijackers gained access to the cockpit; FAA rules required that the doors remain closed and locked during flight. Ong speculated that they had "jammed their way" in. Perhaps the terrorists stabbed the flight attendants to get a cockpit key, to force one of them to open the cockpit door, or to lure the captain or first officer out of the cockpit. Or the flight attendants may just have been in their way.

At the same time or shortly thereafter, Atta—the only terrorist on board trained to fly a jet—would have moved to the cockpit from his business-class seat, possibly accompanied by Omari. As this was happening, passenger Daniel Lewin, who was seated in the row just behind Atta and Omari, was stabbed by one of the hijackers—probably Satam al Suqami, who was seated directly behind Lewin. Lewin had served four years as an officer in the Israeli military. He may have made an attempt to stop the hijackers in front of him, not realizing that another was sitting behind him.

The hijackers quickly gained control and sprayed Mace, pepper spray, or some other irritant in the first-class cabin, in order to force the passengers and flight attendants toward the rear of the plane. They claimed they had a bomb.

About five minutes after the hijacking began, Betty Ong contacted the American Airlines Southeastern Reservations Office in Cary, North Carolina, via an AT&T airphone to report an emergency aboard the flight. This was the first of several occasions on 9/11 when flight attendants took action outside the scope of their training, which emphasized that in a hijacking, they were to communicate with the cockpit crew. The emergency call lasted approximately 25 minutes, as Ong calmly and professionally relayed information about events taking place aboard the airplane to authorities on the ground.

At 8:19, Ong reported: "The cockpit is not answering, somebody's stabbed in business class—and I think there's Mace—that we can't breathe—I don't know, I think we're getting hijacked." She then told of the stabbings of the two flight attendants.

At 8:21, one of the American employees receiving Ong's call in North Carolina, Nydia Gonzalez, alerted the American Airlines operations center in Fort Worth, Texas, reaching Craig Marquis, the manager on duty. Marquis soon realized this was an emergency and instructed the airline's dispatcher responsible for the flight to contact the cockpit. At 8:23, the dispatcher tried unsuccessfully to contact the aircraft. Six minutes later, the air traffic control specialist in American's operations center contacted the FAA's Boston Air Traffic Control Center about the flight. The center was already aware of the problem.

Boston Center knew of a problem on the flight in part because just before 8:25 the hijackers had attempted to communicate with the passengers. The microphone was keyed, and immediately one of the hijackers said, "Nobody move. Everything will be okay. If you try to make any moves, you'll endanger yourself and the airplane. Just stay quiet." Air traffic controllers heard the transmission; Ong did not. The hijackers probably did not know how to operate the cockpit radio communication system correctly, and thus inadvertently broadcast their message over the air traffic control channel instead of the cabin public-address channel. Also at 8:25, and again at 8:29, Amy Sweeney got through to the American Flight Services Office in Boston but was cut off after she reported someone was hurt aboard the flight. Three minutes later, Sweeney was reconnected to the office and began relaying updates to the manager, Michael Woodward.

At 8:26, Ong reported that the plane was "flying erratically." A minute later, Flight 11 turned south. American also began getting identifications of the hijackers, as Ong and Sweeney passed on some of the seat numbers of those who had gained unauthorized access to the cockpit.

Sweeney calmly reported on her line that the plane had been hijacked; a man in first class had his throat slashed; two flight attendants had been stabbed—one was seriously hurt and was on oxygen while the other's wounds seemed minor; a doctor had been requested; the flight attendants were unable to contact the cockpit; and there was a bomb in the cockpit. Sweeney told Woodward that she and Ong were trying to relay as much information as they could to people on the ground.

At 8:38, Ong told Gonzalez that the plane was flying erratically again. Around this time Sweeney told Woodward that the hijackers were Middle Easterners, naming three of their seat numbers. One spoke very little English and one spoke excellent English. The hijackers had gained entry to the cockpit, and she did not know how. The aircraft was in a rapid descent.

At 8:41, in American's operations center, a colleague told Marquis that the air traffic controllers declared Flight 11, a hijacking and "think he's [American 11] headed toward Kennedy [airport in New York City]. They're moving everybody out of the way. They seem to have him on a primary radar. They seem to think that he is descending."

At 8:44, Gonzalez reported losing phone contact with Ong. About this same time Sweeney reported to Woodward, "Something is wrong. We are in a rapid descent . . . we are all over the place." Woodward asked Sweeney to look out the window to see if she could determine where they were. Sweeney responded: "We are flying very low. We are flying very, very low. We are flying too low." Seconds later she said, "Oh my God we are way too low." The phone call ended.

At 8:46:40, American 11 crashed into the North Tower of the World Trade Center in New York City. All on board, along with an unknown number of people in the tower, were killed instantly. . . .

FAA Awareness—pp. 18–21

Although the Boston Center air traffic controller realized at an early stage that there was something wrong with American 11, he did not immediately interpret the plane's failure to respond as a sign that it had been hijacked. At 8:14, when the flight failed to heed his instruction to climb to 35,000 feet, the controller repeatedly tried to raise the flight. He reached out to the pilot on the emergency frequency. Though there was no response, he kept trying to contact the aircraft.

At 8:21, American 11 turned off its transponder, immediately degrading the information available about the aircraft. The controller told his supervisor that he thought something was seriously wrong with the plane, although neither suspected a hijacking. The supervisor instructed the controller to follow standard procedures for handling a "no radio" aircraft.

The controller checked to see if American Airlines could establish communication with American 11. He became even more concerned as its route changed, moving into another sector's airspace. Controllers immediately began to move aircraft out of its path, and asked other aircraft in the vicinity to look for American 11.

At 8:24:38, the following transmission came from American 11:

American 11: We have some planes. Just stay quiet, and you'll be okay. We are returning to the airport.

The controller only heard something unintelligible; he did not hear the specific words "we have some planes." The next transmission came seconds later:

American 11: Nobody move. Everything will be okay. If you try to make any moves, you'll endanger yourself and the airplane. Just stay quiet.

The controller told us that he knew then it was a hijacking. He alerted his supervisor, who assigned another controller to assist him. He redoubled his efforts to ascertain the flight's altitude. Because the controller didn't understand the initial transmission, the manager of Boston Center instructed his quality assurance specialist to "pull the tape" of the radio transmission, listen to it closely, and report back.

Between 8:25 and 8:32, in accordance with the FAA protocol, Boston Center managers started notifying their chain of command that American 11 had been hijacked. At 8:23, Boston Center called the Command Center in Herndon to advise that it believed American 11 had been hijacked and was heading toward New York Center's airspace.

By this time, American 11 had taken a dramatic turn to the south. At 8:32, the Command Center passed word of a possible hijacking to the Operations Center at FAA headquarters. The duty officer replied that security personnel at headquarters had just begun discussing the apparent hijack on a conference call with the New England regional office. FAA headquarters began to follow the hijack protocol but did not contact the NMCC to request a fighter escort.

The Herndon Command Center immediately established a teleconference between Boston, New York, and Cleveland Centers so that Boston Center could help the others understand what was happening.

At 8:43, the Boston Center controller received a third transmission from American 11:

American 11: Nobody move please. We are going to the airport. Don't try to make any stupid moves.

In the succeeding minutes, controllers were attempting to ascertain the altitude of the southbound flight.

Military Notification and Response. Boston Center did not follow the protocol in seeking military assistance through the prescribed chain of command. In addition to notifications within the FAA, Boston Center took the initiative, at 8:43, to contact the military through the FAA's Cape Cod facility. The center also tried to contact a former alert site in Atlantic City, unaware it had been phased out. At 8:37:52, Boston Center reached NEADS. This was the first notification received by the military—at any level—that American 11 had been hijacked:

FAA: Hi. Boston Center TMU [Traffic Management Unit], we have a problem here. We have a hijacked aircraft headed towards New York, and we need you guys to, we need someone to scramble some F-16s or something to help us out.
NEADS: Is this real-world or exercise?
FAA: No, this is not an exercise, not a test.

NEADS ordered to battle stations the two F-15 alert aircraft at Otis Air Force Base in Falmouth, Massachusetts, 153 miles away from New York City. The air defense of America began with this call.

At NEADS, the report of the hijacking was relayed immediately to Battle Commander Colonel Robert Marr. After ordering the Otis fighters to battle stations, Colonel Marr phoned Major General Larry Arnold, commanding general of the First Air Force and NORAD's Continental Region. Marr sought authorization to scramble the Otis fighters. General Arnold later recalled instructing Marr to "go ahead and scramble them, and we'll get authorities later." General Arnold called NORAD headquarters to report.

F-15 fighters were scrambled at 8:46 from Otis Air Force Base. But NEADS did not know where to send the alert fighter aircraft, and the officer directing the fighters pressed for more information: "I don't know where I'm scrambling these guys to. I need a direction, a destination." Because the hijackers had turned off the plane's transponder, NEADS personnel spent the next minutes searching their radar scopes for the primary radar return. American 11 struck the North Tower at 8:46. Shortly after 8:50, while NEADS personnel were still trying to locate the flight, word reached them that a plane had hit the World Trade Center.

Radar data show the Otis fighters were airborne at 8:53. Lacking a target, they were vectored toward military-controlled airspace off the Long Island coast. To avoid New York area air traffic and uncertain about what to do, the fighters were brought down to military airspace to "hold as needed." From 9:09 to 9:13, the Otis fighters stayed in this holding pattern.

In summary, NEADS received notice of the hijacking nine minutes before it struck the North Tower. That nine minutes' notice before impact was the most the military would receive of any of the four hijackings. . . .

Map 10.1 Flight path of American Airlines 11 on September 11, 2001

How to Do It? A Different Way of Organizing the Government—pp. 399–400

As presently configured, the national security institution of the U.S. government are still the institution constructed to win the Cold War. The United States confronts a very different world today. Instead of facing a few very dangerous adversaries, the United States confronts a number of less visible challenges that surpass the boundaries of traditional nation-states and call for quick, imaginative, and agile responses.

The men and women of the World War II generation rose to the challenges of the 1940s and 1950s. They restructured the government so that it could protect the country. That job is now the job of the generation that experienced 9/11. Those attacks showed, emphatically, that ways of doing business rooted in a different era are just not good enough. Americans should not settle for incremental, ad hoc adjustments to a system designed generations ago for a world that no longer exists.

We recommend significant changes in the organization of the government. We know that the quality of the people is more important than the quality of the wiring diagrams. Some of the saddest aspects of the 9/11 story are the outstanding efforts of so many individual officials straining, often without success, against the boundaries of the possible. Good people can overcome bad structures. They should not have to.

The United States has the resources and the people. The government should combine them more effectively, achieving unity of effort. We offer five major recommendations to do that:

unifying strategic intelligence and operational planning against Islamist terrorists across the foreign-domestic divide with a National Counterterrorism Center;

unifying the intelligence community with a new National Intelligence Director;

unifying the many participants in the counterterrorism effort and their knowledge in a network-based information-sharing system that transcends traditional governmental boundaries;

unifying and strengthening congressional oversight to improve quality and accountability; and

strengthening the FBI and homeland defenders.

EPILOGUE

On December 6, 2004, after months of wrangling by the Bush administration and members of Congress, an accord was finally reached that will lead to passage of legislation designed to implement many of the 9/11 Commission's recommendations. A key provision of the legislation is the creation of the National Counterterrorism Center, led by a single intelligence chief with authority over both civilian and military intelligence operations. To offset concerns about the powers of such an office to encroach on citizens' privacy rights, the office will include a watchdog agency on civil liberties (*New York Times* December 7, 2004, A1).

 DEBATE TOPIC

Given the resources and training of those involved in homeland defense on September 11, 2001, was the attack unavoidable?

PRO

1) The terrorists were well organized and financed, determined, secretive, and few in number, and so they could operate almost without detection. 2) In a free society, it is impossible to monitor and control the behavior of all those who threaten it. 3) The airlines, the FAA, the military, and the White House were in close contact with each other within less than an hour of the first hijacking, which demonstrates that the system worked.

CON

1) Domestic and foreign intelligence did not add to each other, such that alerts of foreign threats were largely ignored at home. 2) Airport and aircraft security made it too easy for individuals known to pose a threat to board and seize the aircraft. 3) Immigration policies were not strictly followed, making it possible for individuals known to pose a threat to enter and remain in the country.

THINKING THEORETICALLY

The events discussed in this case provide interesting insights for those in search of a more general understanding of the world. In particular, let us compare what this story has to say to those who see the world from a realist perspective versus theories of institutionalism.

The fact that the attacks on September 11 were carried out by a nonstate actor for reasons other than strategic interest would be profoundly confusing to a realist. After all, they assume that the world consists of states existing in an anarchical system competing with each other for status and resources. The emergence of al Qaeda requires them to reconsider whether states are really the key players. On the other hand, it does not surprise realists at all that the first action taken by the United States following 9/11 was to overthrow the Taliban regime. This is, after all, conventional state-to-state interaction.

Institutionalists would be far more satisfied that their theories are on the mark, however. After all, much of what we see in this account is the story of how bureaucratic organizations attempt to make sense of the world and often fail, with disastrous consequences. Institutionalists would use the 9/11 account as a cautionary tale to any who believe organizational process doesn't matter.

QUESTIONS TO CONSIDER

1. Who is most to blame for the attack? What do we mean by heroism in the context of 9/11? Who was a hero? How do rules of procedure help or hurt in an emergency? Which rules worked well? Which ones didn't?

WEBSITES

Official 9/11 Commission site: **www.9-11commission.gov**

Executive Summary of Report: **www.washingtonpost.com/wp-srv/nation/911report/ documents/911ReportExec.pdf**

Entire report: **www.gpoaccess.gov/911**

News stories about the 9/11 Commission: **www.newsmax.com/hottopics/9!11_Commission.shtml**

Debate on implications of the report: **www.brookings.edu/comm/events/20040923.pdf**

CASE 11

U.S. Interventionism: Strategic and Humanitarian Intervention

INTRODUCTION

As Americans consider their foreign policy choices in the post–Cold War era, a key question is whether the United States should play the role of global policeman. Should American troops be used to alter the domestic affairs of foreign nations? On the surface the obvious answer seems to be no, but in many instances in the past, the answer has been a resounding yes. Whether justified in terms of humanitarianism, enforcement of international law, or some strategic imperative, the United States has been rather quick to deploy its troops.

To better understand this interventionist tendency, we will look carefully at three very different cases drawn from the past thirty-five years. Before doing so, however, we will review various theories of intervention. The most obvious reason for U.S. intervention is strategic: The United States intervenes when its global interests are jeopardized (Deibel & Gaddis 1987). Given the way a great power strives for stability and preservation of the status quo, the temptation to intervene where the system is unstable can be irresistible. Some 2,500 years ago, when the small island of Melos petitioned Athens for respect of its neutrality, Athens refused, stating that it simply could not tolerate such an implicit challenge to its status as the dominant regional power. "The strong do what they can and the weak do what they must," was Athens's blunt reply.

Though not a particularly noble reason for intervention, its advocates often point to the need to preserve the balance of power and prevent enemies from encroaching on the American sphere of influence. The Monroe Doctrine of the early nineteenth century cautioned would-be imperialists in Europe from snatching colonial prizes in the Western Hemisphere. The Roosevelt Corollary to that warning had the military teeth to back it up and coincided with American intervention in Cuba, Nicaragua, Guatemala, Panama, Mexico, and across Latin America shortly after the turn of the century. Since World War II, various senior diplomats have justified U.S. intervention as simply preserving the status quo. George Ball, a former under secretary of state, pointed out that it is up to great powers—in this case the United States—to enforce international standards of peace and stability, unilaterally if necessary (Barnet 1968, 258).

Another key factor cited by many analysts to justify intervention is the desire to spread liberal values and (during the Cold War) block the encroachment of Communist ideology. Certainly the idealism of the Woodrow Wilson, Franklin Delano Roosevelt, and Harry Truman administrations, as well as the intense anti-Communist passions displayed by Secretary of State John Foster Dulles under Eisenhower, demonstrate that democracy, freedom, and the free market were all key preoccupations of U.S. policymakers. Wilson drew up his "Fourteen Points" during World War I to map out a way to make the world "safe for democracy." As he put it when trying to persuade Congress to declare war on Germany in 1917:

> We have no selfish ends to serve. We desire no conquest, no dominion. We seek no indemnities for ourselves, no material compensation for the sacrifices we shall freely make. We are but one of the champions of the right of mankind. (Wilson 1990, 15)

When Harry Truman challenged Congress in 1947 to fund the incipient Cold War offensive, he declared: "I believe that it must be the policy of the United States to support free peoples who are resisting attempted subjugation by armed minorities or by outside pressures." Presidents Lyndon Johnson, Ronald Reagan, and George W. Bush added their own doctrines, with the result that the United States gradually expanded the scope of unilateral intervention it considers justified.

Insurrections in the Third World were not unusual during the Cold War years, but only a few warranted U.S. intervention. It was those situations that combined evidence of Communist meddling with a threat to an existing U.S. alliance where intervention was most likely.

Related to this is the notion that the U.S. has an obligation to alleviate acute suffering around the world. While more limited in its application, "humanitarian intervention" has become more important since the end of the Cold War. This stems in part from the increasing number of states that have "imploded" (where the central government has ceased to function effectively)—sometimes as a result of the loss of support from one of the superpowers (see Somalia)—or where civil war has broken out (see Yugoslavia). The doctrine declares that where innocent civilians are suffering extreme abuse—especially genocide—the world in general and the U.S. in particular have a "responsibility to protect" (ICISS 2001). As put by Bill Clinton in an address to American peacekeeping troops in Macedonia:

> But never forget, if we can do this here, and if we can then say to the people of the world, whether you live in Africa, or Central Europe, or any other place, if somebody comes after innocent civilians and tries to kill them en masse because of their race, their ethnic background or their religion, and it's within our power to stop it, we will stop it. (White House OPS 1999)

It is important to point out that humanitarian intervention often looks very different from other forms of intervention, in that U.S. troops are deployed on a more limited scale and with more strict "rules of engagement" (don't fire until fired upon, don't seek out the enemy, minimize civilian casualties and physical damage). They also perform more acts of community service, such as working to build schools, providing medical treatment to civilians, and helping to train the local police force. In some cases, there is no clear "enemy" except perhaps lawless bands of marauding criminals.

A final factor that has contributed to the U.S. decision to intervene is economic interest. Marxist interpretations of U.S. intervention have long stressed the role of major capitalist actors in the shaping of U.S. foreign policy. Harry Magdoff has probably gone as far as any Marxist to explain the dynamic. He argues that, although one may not find capitalists dictating policy to their political counterparts, the two groups have an unusual harmony of interest. American foreign investments bring large profits and extraordinary monopoly control for both business and government. American firms can control access to key raw materials, such as oil, which in turn are essential to the military—hence collusion between major capitalists and the Pentagon. These sorts of factors lead to a tendency for the state to intervene aggressively when foreign economic interests are threatened—which, as it turns out, usually involves attacking anticapitalist Third World rebels (Magdoff 1969).

Rather than attempt to assess the validity of these various perceptions of U.S. intervention, we will move into the case studies. The three cases of U.S. intervention are the Dominican Republic in 1965, Chile in 1973, and Somalia in 1992. The methods, causes, and justifications of intervention were rather different. When combined with other cases of U.S. intervention discussed elsewhere in the text (Cuba, Vietnam, Iraq), they should provide a fairly balanced and general view of the issue.

KEY FIGURES
U.S. INTERVENTIONISM

Dominican Republic

Rafael Trujillo   Absolute leader of the Dominican Republic, 1930–1961, serving at times as president. He was assassinated in 1961, opening the way for civilian rule.

Joaquin Balaguer   President of the Dominican Republic, 1961, 1978. His election was made possible by the U.S. intervention in 1965.

Juan Bosch   President of the Dominican Republic, 1961–1963. His left-leaning policies alarmed the United States and helped prompt intervention in 1965.

Donald Reid Cabral   Leader of the Dominican Republic, 1963–1965. His junta overthrew Bosch, but was unable to bring stability.

(continued)

(continued)

W. Tapley Bennett   U.S. Ambassador to the Dominican Republic in 1965. He urged U.S. military intervention to prevent a radical take-over.

Hector García-Godoy   Leader of a caretaker government, 1965–1966. He sponsored elections that brought Balaguer to power.

Chile

Jorge Alessandri   President of Chile, 1958–1964.

Eduardo Frei   President of Chile, 1964–1970. His moderately progressive policies were encouraged by U.S. policymakers, but his failure at the polls made him less useful in preventing Allende's radicalization of Chilean policies.

Salvador Allende   President of Chile, 1970–1973. His radical policies prompted the United States to push for his ouster.

Edward Korrey   U.S. Ambassador to Chile during Allende's administration. He urged U.S. pressure on Chile.

Roberto Viaux   Chilean general whose failed attempts to overthrow Allende resulted in his repudiation by would-be American supporters.

Augusto Pinochet   President of Chile, 1973–1991. He led a violent coup against Allende that resulted in Allende's assassination. Pinochet's government was marked by police brutality.

Somalia

Mohammed Siad Barre   Leader of Somalia from 1969 to 1991.

Mohammed Farah Aidid   Leader of a major faction in Mogadishu.

Mohammed Ali Mahdi   Provisional leader of Somalia around 1991 and 1992.

CHRONOLOGY
U.S. INTERVENTIONISM

1844
The Dominican Republic becomes independent.

1916–1924
American forces occupy the Dominican Republic.

1960
Italy and the UK grant independence to their Somali colonies, leading to the unification and independence of Somalia in July.

1961
Rafael Trujillo is assassinated, Juan Bosch elected president in the Dominican Republic.

1963
Bosch is overthrown by the military in the Dominican Republic.

1964
Eduardo Frei is elected president in Chile.

1965
The United States deploys troops in the Dominican Republic.

1966
Joaquin Balaguer is elected president in the Dominican Republic.

1969
Somali leader is assassinated. Mohammed Siad Barre seizes power shortly thereafter.

1970
Salvador Allende is elected president in Chile.

1972
Chile struggles under American economic sanctions.

1973
Augusto Pinochet seizes power in Chile in a coup. Allende is assassinated.

1988
In Somalia, civil war erupts.

1991
As Siad Barre loses control of Mogadishu, the civil war in Somalia spreads and spawns internal fighting between clans and factions.

1992
As fighting continues and a famine spreads, the United Nations approves a U.S. plan for military intervention to ensure food aid gets to the civilians. Troops disembark in December, encountering little resistance and succeeding in restoring peace for a time.

1993
UN troops take command in March and begin to encounter organized resistance from several sectors. Twenty-four Pakistanis are killed in an ambush in June and eighteen U.S. Rangers are killed in October. The Clinton administration soon announces plans for a withdrawal in early 1994.

DOMINICAN REPUBLIC: 1965

U.S. relations with the Dominican Republic epitomized for many years the imperialist impulse in U.S. foreign policy. Although it gained its independence from Spain in 1844, this island nation bordering Haiti remained vulnerable to outside interference—including a brief attempt at colonization by the United States. It had seen a succession of dictators before the first major U.S. military intervention—an occupation force that lasted from 1916 to 1924 and resulted in the strengthening of the country's army and a more hospitable climate for U.S. investment (Gleijeses 1978, 18).

That armed intervention set the stage for the second major intervention by the United States into the Dominican Republic in 1965. Rafael Leonidas Trujillo overthrew the constitutional government left behind in 1930 and began a thirty-year reign of terror (Barnet 1968, 155). Trujillo's principal virtue, from the American perspective, was that he provided a stable anti-Communist bulwark in the Caribbean. Trujillo also did much to give his country the appearance of growth and prosperity, although the image concealed a deeply divided society where incomes were extremely unequal, the established wealthy class mistrusted the newcomers—"nouveau riche"—and the overzealous Trujillo family, and the middle class was virtually nonexistent. Nonetheless, Trujillo reigned supreme until 1960, when his acts of terror against opponents at home and abroad caused even the conservative Catholic Church in the Dominican Republic to repudiate him.

The United States, though supportive of conservative governments in the region, feared Trujillo would so oppress his people that he would precipitate Marxist revolution. Fulgencio Batista did just that in Cuba in 1959, and the United States faced an angry Castro only ninety miles from Florida. In mid-1960, the Eisenhower administration withdrew support for the Trujillo regime and endorsed economic sanctions favored by other Latin American states through the Organization of American States (OAS) (Gleijeses 1978, 21). Trujillo was assassinated on May 30, 1961, by a small group of coup plotters in the army, although their hopes of establishing a new regime were dashed as Trujillo loyalists moved quickly to preserve at least the form of power if not the content.

For the new Kennedy administration, the search was under way for a moderate democratic leader in the Dominican Republic, although the president acknowledged that failing that, a dictator would be better than a Communist (Barnet 1968, 158). The country went through a succession of quasi-military leaders, each receiving moderate U.S. support. The opportunistic Joaquin Balaguer, a former Trujillo cabinet member, held office with the support of Trujillo's family for a brief period following the assassination. Then the military, following the exile of Trujillo's son and brothers, took de facto control under General Pedro Echeverria (Gleijeses 1978, 57). Balaguer eventually resigned his post in favor of Rafael Bonelly, another former Trujillo official, who was even more eager to work with the United States (to the military's annoyance) (Yates 1988, 181). The United States and the OAS finally lifted the anti-Trujillo sanctions following the announcement of national elections scheduled for June 1, 1961. The Kennedy administration felt that it had finally found the path to what it sought, although there was intense disagreement over whether it could afford the risk of a Communist sympathizer winning the election.

The presidential elections included numerous candidates from across the political spectrum, although three parties dominated the campaign: the Revolutionary Dominican Party (PRD) under Juan Bosch; the National Civic Union (UCN), which already held sway in the transitional regime; and an assortment of leftist parties dominated by the June 14 movement. Contrary to its militant name, the PRD was a moderate left-of-center party with a reformist, anti-Trujillo agenda. In contrast to the June 14 movement, which included both armed and Castroite elements, the PRD seemed a viable alternative to the parties of the right (Gleijeses 1978, 39).

The elections were honest and fair, in spite of an atmosphere of never-ending violence and unrest that gripped the country after Trujillo's death. Juan Bosch and the PRD emerged victorious with well over half of the votes cast; Bosch received 59 percent of the vote—nearly twice that of his UCN rival (Gleijeses 1978, 86). The United States moved quickly to endorse the elections and support the Bosch administration, although U.S. ambassador John Bartlow Martin had strong reservations. He had grown accustomed to the former regimes and had become so heavily involved in Dominican policymaking that even many conservative Dominicans had challenged his interference. Martin often criticized Bosch as a "divider" and even a "destroyer" because of his willingness to openly criticize and challenge U.S. policy in the region, including the regional aid program known as the Alliance for Progress (Barnet 1968, 166). Martin suspected Bosch of Marxist sympathies.

The Bosch administration was under pressure to carry out the many reforms it had promised. After it began by introducing a new constitution, restoring some sense of integrity to the government, moving squatters and landless peasants onto their own plots, and taking steps to limit profit taking by foreign corporations, the conservatives began to organize concerted opposition to the regime. An important problem, from the perspective of affluent Dominicans and the military, was Bosch's failure to deport the known Marxists in the June 14 movement and other radical parties. Bosch argued that constitutional protection should be extended to all, regardless of their political coloration (Draper 1968, 29). This was the last straw, and in September 1963, the military took power. Bosch fled to Puerto Rico, and a three-man government was set up in his place. With the resignation of one of the "triumvirate" members in December, the new military government came under the dominance of Donald Reid Cabral and secured the support of the new Lyndon Johnson administration (Barnet 1968, 167). A feeble rebellion by the June 14 movement reduced the number of its armed guerrillas to less than one hundred. For the time being, the situation was stabilized and, from the perspective of ardent anti-Communists in Washington and Santo Domingo, more secure. In fact, the regime lasted little more than a year.

In spite of considerable support from the United States, the Reid regime was a failure from the start. Its attempts at economic development foundered amid corruption and falling sugar prices (Gleijeses 1978, 118). Its use of torture alienated the masses and spurred calls for reform and even revolution from both far-left and center-left sections (including the exiled Bosch). The wealthy elite grew weary of the stagnant economy, and the military bristled at Reid's clumsy attempts to reform its ranks. By early 1965, some factions of the military were organizing a revolt in combination with former Bosch and Balaguer supporters, with the aim of returning constitutional government (Gleijeses 1978, 132). On April 24, the rebellion (officially termed a countercoup) erupted. On April 25, loyalists to the regime responded. The nation fell into civil war and chaos, with the heart of Santo Domingo at the epicenter.

Early on, the rebels scored impressive victories, leading to the resignation of Reid and the naming of former Bosch supporter José Rafael Molina Ureña as provisional president. The victory was short-lived, however, and before the end of April, Ureña was forced into hiding. In the meantime, poorly organized rebels took control of the streets of the capital amid rumors of atrocities. Reports of Communists taking over leadership of the rebellion were accepted without hesitation by CIA and embassy officials and the new ambassador, W. Tapley Bennett, who requested U.S. military forces to begin evacuating American civilians trapped in the city. Even after an initial wave of some 500 Marines arrived, Bennett concluded on April 28 that the situation called for still more dramatic U.S. intervention. He claimed that Americans were being shot at and that some 1,500 Communists were overrunning the capital (Barnet 1968, 171). Johnson was forced to respond on the grounds that Bennett's alarm could not be ignored, although he doubted the authenticity of the reports. The administration later chose to ignore Bennett's pleas (Yates 1988, 64).

By May 17, 1965, 24,000 troops had been deployed in and around Santo Domingo. U.S. troops were originally placed around neighborhoods where Americans lived and worked to evacuate them as rapidly as possible. Once this mission was accomplished, the operation moved to contain the rebellion by virtually surrounding the inner-city area of the capital with a belt of U.S. troops (Yates 1988, 75). This move effectively eliminated any prospect for a rebel victory and assured the loyalist military government, now under the command of Generals Antonio Imbert Barrera and Elias Wessin y Wessin, a relatively free hand in mopping up opposition to the regime. All the while, the U.S. troops proclaimed a policy of "neutrality" in the conflict.

The constitutionalist rebels regrouped after the initial shock of the U.S. deployment and found leadership under rebel Colonel Francisco Caamaño Deñó. Although not a Communist himself, he allowed several Marxists to play a role in leading the rebellion. Some debate arose over the significance of these Marxists (Thomas & Thomas 1967). The consensus is that, contrary to the impression of embassy, CIA, and State Department staff at the time, the anti-U.S. rhetoric that poured out of rebel headquarters during much of the war was merely posturing. In fact, the vast majority of the rebels sought merely the return of the Bosch administration rather than some Castroite revolution (Barnet 1968, 173).

Once the situation was stabilized, the United States sought to create an effective multilateral presence in the city. The OAS organized a peacekeeping force that was deployed in mid-May and subsumed the U.S. presence. From that point onward, the emphasis of the operation was on finding a diplomatic solution to the crisis (Slater 1970). The U.S. troops played the role of genuine peacekeepers, not only containing the constitutionalist rebellion but also preventing the loyalist troops from entering their inner-city haven (Yates 1988, 145).

Ultimately, after months of effort and sporadic fighting between OAS forces and the rebels, a settlement was reached on September 3, 1965, which provided for a provisional government under the leadership of former Bosch official Hector García-Godoy. Caamaño left the island for an overseas diplomatic post in January 1966, along with Ureña. Marines were withdrawn from the island over the course of the year, with the last units departing on September 21 after a seventeen-month stay. The military was partially contained in the new regime, although it mounted several unsuccessful coup attempts later on. The García-Godoy regime sponsored elections on June 1, 1966, which returned Balaguer to power under a cloud of tainted voting.

CHILE: 1973

Chileans elected a self-proclaimed Marxist to the presidency in 1970, much to the dismay of the White House and major U.S. firms that were operating in Chile at the time. The story of what they did to change the result of that election is an example of indirect and covert intervention.

Chile, unlike the Dominican Republic, enjoyed a tradition of democratic rule that extended, at least nominally, to the pre–World War II era. When President Jorge Alessandri, leader of the conservative National Party, was defeated by Christian Democratic Party (PDC) candidate Eduardo Frei in 1964, the government moved toward the type of progressive reforms the Kennedy administration had advocated. Though he was a nationalist who did not want to serve as lackey to U.S. interests, Frei was willing to accommodate U.S. business needs. In particular, he agreed to limit government intervention in the economy to those things that had the best chance of reversing the drastic inequality of income and wealth that had developed. In his dealings with such U.S. firms as Kennecott Copper and International Telephone and Telegraph (ITT), he generally negotiated new arrangements fairly and in good faith (Kissinger 1979, 657). The principal targets of his policies were the wealthy landowners, who were forced to relinquish property that was then redistributed to peasants (Sater 1990, 151). The policies of Frei were satisfactory enough to the Johnson administration that it secretly provided hundreds of millions of dollars for his party's election campaigns (Rojas Sandford 1976, 57).

Much of the support Frei received from the United States could be explained by the opposition he faced: Salvador Allende Gossens, leader of the newly formed Unidad Popular—a coalition party of leftist movements in Chile. His party represented the greatest challenge to Christian Democrats in the 1962 and 1964 elections. The radical, anti-U.S. nature of his policies was seen as inimical to U.S. interests. In the September 1970 presidential elections, however, American observers and policymakers became convinced that he would do poorly against Alessandri and the PDC candidate Radomiro Tomic (Eduardo Frei was forbidden by the constitution to serve consecutive terms). Allende's election victory—which consisted of a 30,000-vote edge over Alessandri (out of 3 million votes cast)—came as a stunning shock in Washington (Kissinger 1979, 670). Henry Kissinger wished aloud that the United States had pumped more secret funds into the election, but he and Richard Nixon had been dissuaded by a State Department concerned about interference in domestic affairs (Kissinger 1979, 669). The ambassador, Edward Korrey, stated unequivocally that Allende's victory, though perhaps still reversible given certain provisions in the Chilean Constitution, was a serious blow.

Nixon was livid over the Allende victory and was desperate to prevent Allende from taking office in November. Nixon told CIA Director Richard Helms to ignore the State Department and do "whatever it takes" to reverse the outcome, offering up to $10 million for immediate actions (Kissinger 1979, 673). What transpired involved two "tracks" of intervention.

Track I was a fairly straightforward approach: Convince conservative members of the Chilean Congress to vote against Allende's bid—an option that seemed feasible given the narrow Allende win and Alessandri's decision to contest the election. To accomplish this, the United States warmly endorsed Alessandri's proposal to resign as soon as the Congress elected him president, thus forcing a new election six months later. The hope was that Frei, who could run for another nonconsecutive term, would be able to defeat Allende in a head-to-head race. Unfortunately, Frei was not interested in the scheme (Whelan 1981, 40; Sater 1990, 162).

At the same time, Nixon engineered an economic and financial embargo of Chile through private and government channels. He wanted the Chilean economy to "scream" (Kissinger 1979, 673). With the help of Chilean conservatives in the banking sector, rumors of Marxist excesses were spread, precipitating a run on several banks and a flight of some $50 million in private savings. All of these efforts went for naught, however, and the inevitability of an Allende presidency loomed large in Washington (LaFeber 1989, 620).

Track II intervention came into effect immediately before the late October congressional vote and involved a rather awkward attempted coup by the military with U.S. backing. Corporate executives of ITT, Pepsi-Cola, and other firms were eager to support a military takeover and lobbied the administration intensively throughout the Allende era (Sergeyev 1981, 138). At this initial stage, the coup attempt involved supporting General Roberto Viaux's attempt to kidnap the commander of the Santiago garrison, General Rene Schneider, and form a junta to replace the Congress. Weapons and funds were provided in early October but were cut off on October 15 after Viaux failed repeatedly (Kissinger 1979, 676). Viaux continued his efforts on his own and managed to capture the general, but Viaux killed him inadvertently in a skirmish. As a result, the conservative elements in Congress and the elite within the army closed ranks around Allende and the constitution and endorsed his election victory. He was sworn in as president in November.

The Allende administration was known above all for its rhetoric, which was consistently anti-American and anticapitalist. Allende made numerous contacts with Soviet Bloc countries and received modest financial support from Moscow and Eastern Europe as well as some sugar from Cuba. He moved rapidly, and often in violation of Chilean law, to nationalize not only large farms but also foreign businesses and factories (Rojas Sandford 1976, 95). Although resigned to the election's outcome at first, the Nixon administration later invoked the Gonzalez amendment and curtailed all multilateral lending to Chile pending just compensation for the seizures (LaFeber 1989, 620). Private U.S. banks dropped their lending to Chile from $219 million in 1970 to $32 million in 1971. Whereas in the 1960s Chile borrowed an average of $150 million each year from U.S. government sources, the figure slipped to $40 million in 1971 and to nothing in 1972 (Rojas Sandford 1976, 148). Many state-owned firms failed for lack of spare parts and capital due to this "invisible blockade."

In spite of his aggressive anti-U.S. stance, Allende tried to maintain a working relationship with his conservative Latin neighbors and Western financial institutions (Sater 1990, 165). After nationalizing Kennecott Copper (with the initial support of the opposition parties), Allende attempted to export copper to Europe (in contravention of international law). The executives at Kennecott tracked the shipments—allegedly with the help of the Navy—and brought lawsuits against Chile in whatever country they were delivered. With the collapse of the price of copper in 1972 and the growing reticence of Europeans to deal with Allende, the sales of copper grew perilously low. This factor, combined with a growing international debt, forced the Allende regime into an international crisis by 1972.

Allende, unable to secure adequate support from abroad, found his domestic programs were failing. His deficit spending program to stimulate consumption and reward his proletarian supporters quickly spurred inflation, which topped the 200 percent mark by 1973. Unable to satisfy workers whose purchasing power fell precipitously, Allende was in the uncomfortable position of dealing with an increasing number of strikes by his core supporters of the past. Truckers, copper miners, physicians, and others engaged in months-long walkouts to protest government policies, wreaking social chaos in the process. To preserve some semblance of stability, Allende invited military officers to his cabinet in 1972 and then again in 1973 (Whelan 1981, 6). When the generals came in the second time, they never left.

Beginning in August 1973, Allende faced pressure from an increasingly defiant military to address the civil disturbance in the country. On August 23, he accepted the resignation of his military commander, Carlos Prats Gonzalez, who declared that he could no longer contain the pressure for a coup, and appointed Augusto Pinochet as his successor (Rojas Sandford 1976, 179). By September Pinochet had joined with the navy in a plan to overthrow the regime. On September 11, beginning with the occupation of the port of Valparaiso, the military attacked and seized the presidential offices at la Modena. By late afternoon, Allende was dead and one of the most brutal military regimes in Latin American history was in power.

Although one can argue that the fall of Allende was made possible only by three years of American pressure, it appears that the U.S. government did not have any direct hand in the coup itself. Even critics of U.S. policy acknowledge that the CIA and the White House learned about the coup at the same time as the rest of the world (Whelan 1981, 40).

SOMALIA: 1992–1993

In late 1992, with the election already lost, U.S. President George H. W. Bush acted to insert several thousand U.S. troops into Somalia in the Horn of Africa with the express aim of alleviating human suffering and restoring a modicum of stability in a country suffering "implosion." Within less than a year, the Clinton administration made the decision to withdraw these forces following the bloody events on October 3, 1993 when eighteen U.S. Rangers were killed in events later immortalized in the film *Blackhawk Down*. Since then, the lessons of Somalia have been burned deeply into the minds of American policymakers, prompting them to become very selective about when and where to undertake "humanitarian intervention." The events that led up to this series of decisions warrant consideration, if only because they show how humanitarian intervention has operated in practice. The lessons learned from experience demonstrate that where there is no clear strategic imperative requiring a U.S. military presence, any commitment of military forces is likely to be indecisive and short-lived (Endless 2003).

Somalia became independent in 1960 following the decision by Italy and the United Kingdom to withdraw from their respective halves of the country. Unification was declared shortly thereafter, although one could legitimately ask whether it was ever achieved. After a fairly promising start, Somalia began to experience a long succession of civil and international wars, beginning with the assassination of its first leader, Abdi Rashid Ali Shermarke, and the ascension of Major-General Muhammed Siad Barre in 1969. In 1977, Somalia went to war with its neighbor, Ethiopia. In 1988, a civil war erupted between several powerful family groups (known as "clans").

The fighting that began in 1988 continues in various forms to this day. The hostility between clans in Somalia stems only in part from differences in ethnicity and social status. Rather, it stemmed from a deliberate strategy of "divide and rule" undertaken by Barre during the 1980s. Once it was clear that only certain clans were receiving services from the state, it made sense for rival factions to arm themselves and attack government facilities. By 1991, Barre's area of control was limited to parts of the capital city of Mogadishu. He ultimately fled the area and took up positions in the countryside from which he launched attacks against the new provisional government.

The provisional government under Mohammed Ali Mahdi had little more success than Barre at securing control of the capital, let alone the surrounding areas. This stemmed in part from attacks by an intra-clan rival—Mohammed Farah Aidid. By late 1991, war was endemic across all of Somalia. The rival armed groups devastated both the cities and the countryside, causing millions to flee into refugee camps. International relief agencies intervened to avert a growing famine, but to no avail. In fact, the food supplies themselves became military targets as soldiers sought to both control it for themselves and deny it to their rivals.

By mid-1992, Western reporters were making their way to the refugee camps to film the human tragedy that was unfolding. The United Nations Security Council was already working on the issue having imposed an arms embargo and brokered a cease-fire when images of starving Somalis began appearing on the evening news in the United States. The administration of George H. W. Bush was reticent about taking concerted action during a campaign year (candidate Bill Clinton had already made it clear he did not think the United States should intervene). There was no clear political advantage to intervention, and there was also no clear strategic necessity (Kennan 1993). Instead, it supported a UN peacekeeping operation (named UNOSOM—later renamed UNOSOM I). This said, a growing number of voices in the United States began to demand action—principal among them the Congressional Black Caucus. Ordinary citizens found the images difficult to tolerate and black representatives in Congress began to question whether the administration's inaction stemmed from racial prejudice.

As put by Bush Press Secretary Marlin Fitzwater:

> After the election, the media had the free time [to cover Somalia] and that was when the pressure started building up. We heard it from every corner that something must be done. Finally, the pressure was too great. The President said, "I just can't live with this for two months." (Seib 1997, 44 in Endless 2003, 186)

Although in the final analysis it is probably not the case that CNN caused the United States to intervene, it is clear that the images forced the Somalia situation to the top of the policymakers' agenda (Livingston 1997).

In late November 1992, as the war was intensifying and UN peacekeepers were increasingly targeted by the warring clans, the Bush administration informed the UN that it was willing to lead a multilateral force to bring stability to the country. The reasons, as put by Bush were simple: "The people of Somalia, especially the children, need our help. We're able to ease their suffering. We must help them live. We must give them hope. America must act" (Endless 2003, 188). On December 9, "Operation Restore Hope" was deployed in Somalia, consisting of 37,000 troops (almost entirely American) from 21 countries.

The operation proved remarkably successful at the outset. Within days, Mogadishu was secured and the troops began to fan out across the country. Soon the emergency food aid was flowing without impediment and the death rate (which peaked at roughly 100 a day) ebbed. By February, the new Clinton administration was working hard to carry out an orderly transfer of control to a new UN force (UNOSOM II) in order to permit the gradual withdrawal of Americans. The formal transfer took place in May 1993.

Shortly after the transfer occurred, the situation quickly deteriorated. Warring clans—especially those led by Aidid—began once again targeting peacekeepers. This stemmed not only from the desire to control territory and upset the status quo (which favored Aidid's opponents for the moment) but also because UN troops were engaging in disarmament programs in the hope of removing weapons from all factions. Naturally this meant that the UN forces were seen as a threat rather than merely a neutral presence. In June 1993, twenty-four Pakistani peacekeepers were killed in an ambush orchestrated by pro-Aidid troops. The fighters operated under cloak of civilian protection and sympathy to some extent, making it extremely difficult for the UNOSOM forces to recognize and thwart attacks. Then on October 3, 1993, eighteen Americans were killed when Aidid's forces ambushed them. The attack has been immortalized in the feature film *Blackhawk Down*.

The effect on the Clinton administration was immediate and intense. It was already clear that Clinton did not want the Somalia operation to be prolonged, and he was especially opposed to any intervention that would result in high levels of American casualties. While accepting the notion that humanitarian intervention may sometimes be warranted—even where no clear strategic imperative exists—he did not believe such operations should involve large sacrifices of troops and material. Within a week of the attack, he announced the United States' intention to withdraw all American troops within six months. He followed through on the plan, leaving Somalia to the UNOSOM II forces. The situation in Somalia has only marginally improved in the ten years since that withdrawal. It remains a "failed state."

CONCLUSION

U.S. intervention overseas has many explanations. The Cold War was a dominant preoccupation throughout the period under study—including in Panama because of its connection to Nicaragua. But the danger of Communist encroachment in the Western Hemisphere is not uniform across the cases. Clearly, in the case of Chile, the pro-Soviet connection is the most plausible—but interestingly enough, this case involved the least U.S. involvement. On the other hand, the most troops were deployed in the Panama case, where there seemed to be no Communist conspiracy.

One could argue that at issue was the extent to which tangible American interests were at stake—U.S. nationals in the Dominican Republic, American corporate assets in Chile. But here again, one finds in Chile perhaps the greatest threat to American assets but the least intervention. Only in the Dominican Republic does one find the perception of danger to both geopolitical and tangible local U.S. interests in proportion to the scale of intervention. Given the unique multilateral character of the invasion force (after OAS involvement), the Dominican Republic case challenges the notion that the United States always "goes it alone" in its own hemisphere.

The Somalia case is more confusing, since there were no clear strategic, ideological, or economic incentives to intervention. Rather, the only obvious motivation was compassion, shrouded in hopefulness and confidence. The Bush administration felt it had the means to do a good thing, and that it therefore had the duty. However, once it became clear that more means were necessary to get the job done, U.S. policymakers made a tactical retreat, leaving to others to continue the mission of mercy. George Kennan warned at the time that the country should remember that the purpose of the U.S. military might is to protect American interests, not alleviate suffering for its own sake. Only where the latter overlaps with the former is intervention warranted (Kennan 1993).

Does U.S. intervention in the Middle East over the last decade break from this pattern? In some ways the Persian Gulf War was a collective security operation that was merely led by the United States (see Case 8). U.S. involvement in Afghanistan is perhaps another matter. In late 2001, following the September 11 attacks and UN and NATO resolutions authorizing retaliatory measures, the United States deployed air and ground troops in Afghanistan to support the Northern Alliance's war against the Taliban regime. Within a few weeks, the Northern Alliance succeeded in overcoming considerable opposition (and Western skepticism) to seize the country's capital, Kabul. Eventually, organized opposition was largely eliminated and a new regime under Ahmed Karzai was installed. The United States has left behind a sizable residual force to support the new government and has been joined by other countries in providing aid and assistance to Karzai. The intervention in Iraq in 2003 is discussed at length in Case 8, so we will leave the reader to consult that material and decide whether it is consistent with past patterns or not.

Such an operation seems to break from previous patterns. First, in the case of Afghanistan, there was a clear attack against vital U.S. interests that warranted a military response. This opinion was shared unanimously by the international community. Even Cuba, Syria, Iran, and North Korea applauded U.S. efforts. Second, the Taliban regime clearly had little popular support, given the relative ease with which Northern Alliance forces were able to advance across the country once their intentions were clear and their prospects were good. One could argue, given the apparent popularity of Karzai (he handily won reelection in 2005), that the United States has promoted democracy in Afghanistan. Finally, the operation received prior approval from important multilateral agencies.

 DEBATE TOPIC

How ready should the United States be to use its military force to change the international political environment? Should military intervention be ruled out as a last resort, or should it always be a "live option"?

PRO

Points made by those who argue that the use of force should be a "live option" include: (1) Military capability and military intervention are directly related: what's the point in having it if its use is prohibited? (2) Great powers have great interests: the greater the extent of American interests around the world, the greater the need to protect them—by force if necessary. (3) American troops have demonstrated again and again their skill at remedying a wide range of international problems. It would be irresponsible not to make use of their abilities to protect the country.

CON

Points made by those who oppose military intervention include: (1) most problems the U.S. faces are political, economic, and social—none of which are easily remedied through the imposition of force. (2) Military actions more often than not create new problems which must eventually be solved through nonmilitary means. Why not start there? (3) American use of military force often undermines our relations with allies, making it more difficult to fight problems like international terrorism.

 THINKING THEORETICALLY

Intervention in general has been a topic of great interest to Marxist scholars. They are quick to point out the hypocrisy of powerful states in that at the same time as they extol the virtues of independence and the principle of nonintervention, they are quick to send in troops in

(continued)

(continued)

order to secure access to vital raw materials or simply to make life easier for multinational corporations. The case of Chile has been a favorite since it appears that U.S. decision making was heavily influenced by the needs of such American firms as ITT and Kennecott Copper. Even in the case of the Dominican Republic, the fear of a socialist in the Caribbean was enough to send in troops under the flimsiest of pretenses. Marxists would argue that the United States will do almost anything to prevent the establishment of governments that wish to nationalize foreign firms, exclude American products, and deny access to their raw materials.

Of course, Marxists have little to say about Somalia. There appears to be no material benefit to be gained from sending troops to such a place. It has no important raw materials, little foreign investment, and little trade. From a strategic point of view, it might be considered important since it sits near the mouth of the Red Sea—a key trading route (the Gulf of Suez lies on the other end). Idealists have offered a more promising explanation of the Somalia intervention: humanitarianism. They have argued that for once the world got it right, in that the international community recognized a human catastrophe and, setting aside questions of strategic or economic interest, sent in forces to protect the weakest of the earth's inhabitants. They argue that it is a case of the powerful using their capacity to help the weak. Of course, the failure of the mission casts doubt on the sincerity of the commitment to save Somalis, but at any rate the idealists may be on to something since nothing else seems to explain why the operation would have been authorized.

Questions to Consider

1. Was coercion the best approach in the three cases? Did the United States achieve its apparent objectives?

2. Were Presidents Johnson, Nixon, and Bush so eager to intervene because they were personally annoyed at the situation and felt a compulsion to vent their frustrations?

3. How was international law used by the United States to legitimize its intervention? Is this a proper role for international law? How did international organizations enter into the picture

Websites

It is perhaps needless to say that the subject of U.S. interventionism is extremely controversial. As a result, most websites on this issue are biased. The following offer a mixture of views. (Note that the Special Forces site plays the Green Beret song!)

Military Sources

Department of Defense: **www.defenselink.mil**

Special Forces: **www.socom.mil**

NATO: **www.nato.int**

CIA: **www.odci.gov**

Archives

National Security Archive: **www.gwu.edu/~nsarchive**
Resource Center of the Americas: **www.americas.org**
Library of Congress: **lcweb.loc.gov/lexico/liv/m/Military_intervention.html**
The United Nations: **www.un.org**
The History Guy: **www.historyguy.com**

Other Groups

Balkan Anti-NATO Center: **www.geocities.com/b_antinato/**
Committee Against U.S. Interventionism: **www.antiwar.com**
Anti-Intervention Network: **www.vvawai.org/ain-home.html**

REFERENCES

Barnet, Richard J. *Intervention and Revolution: The United States in the Third World* (New York: New American Library, 1968).

Commission of Inquiry. *The U.S. Invasion of Panama: The Truth Behind Operation "Just Cause"* (Boston: South End Press, 1991).

Conniff, Michael. *Panama and the United States: The Forced Alliance* (Athens, GA: University of Georgia Press, 1992).

Deibel, Terry L., and John Lewis Gaddis, eds. *Containing the Soviet Union: A Critique of U.S. Policy* (New York: Pergamon-Brassey's, 1987).

Draper, Theodore. *The Dominican Revolt: A Case Study in American Policy* (New York: Commentary, 1968).

Dulles, Allen. *The Craft of Intelligence* (New York: Harper & Row, 1963).

Endless, Brian. *International Legitimacy and the United Nations Security Council.* Loyola University Chicago Ph.D. dissertation, 2003.

Gleijeses, Piero. *The Dominican Crisis: The 1965 Constitutionalist Revolt and American Intervention.* Trans. by Lawrence Lipson (Baltimore, MD: Johns Hopkins University Press, 1978).

Hoopes, Townsend. *The Devil and John Foster Dulles* (Boston: Little, Brown, 1973).

ICISS (International Commission on Intervention and State Sovereignty). *The Responsibility to Protect.* Ottawa: International Development Research Center, 2001. Available online at: **www.dfait-maeci.gc.ca/iciss-ciise/pdf/Commission-Report.pdf.**

Kennan, George. "The Sources of Soviet Conduct." *Foreign Affairs* 25 (July 1947): 566–582.

Kennan, George. Somalia, "Through a Glass Darkly." *New York Times* September 30, 1993, A33.

Kissinger, Henry. *The White House Years* (Boston: Little, Brown, 1979).

LaFeber, Walter. *The American Age: United States Foreign Policy at Home and Abroad Since 1750* (New York: W. W. Norton, 1989).

Livingston, Steven. "Clarifying the CNN Effect: An Examination of Media Effects According to Type of Military Intervention." Harvard University Research Paper R-18, June 1997.

Magdoff, Harry. *The Age of Imperialism: The Economics of U.S. Foreign Policy* (New York: Monthly Review Press, 1969).

Rojas Sandford, Robinson. *The Murder of Allende and the End of the Chilean Way to Socialism.* Trans. by Andree Conrad (New York: Harper & Row, 1976).

Slater, William F. *Chile and the United States: Empires in Conflict* (Athens, GA: University of Georgia Press, 1990).

Seib, Philip. *Headline Diplomacy: How News Coverage Affects Foreign Policy.* London: Praeger, 1997.

Sergeyev, F. F. *Chile: CIA Big Business* (Moscow: Progress Publishers, 1981).

Slater, Jerome. *Intervention and Negotiation: The United States and the Dominican Revolution* (New York: Harper & Row, 1970).

Thomas, A. J., Jr., and Ann Van Wynen Thomas. *The Dominican Republic Crisis 1965* (Dobbs Ferry, NY: Oceana Publications, 1967).

Whelan, James R. *Allende: Death of a Marxist Dream* (Westport, CT: Arlington House, 1981).

Wilson, Woodrow. "The World Must Be Made Safe for Democracy." In John Vasquez, ed., *Classics of International Relations*, 2nd ed. (Englewood Cliffs, NJ: Prentice Hall, 1990), 12–15.

Yates, Lawrence A. *Power Pack: U.S. Intervention in the Dominican Republic, 1965–1966*, Leavenworth Papers #15 (Washington, DC: U.S. Government Printing Office, 1988).

White House, Office of the Press Secretary. "Remarks by the President to the KFOR Troops" (Skopje, Macedonia), June 22, 1999.

PART

3

INTERNATIONAL COOPERATION

CASE 12

Human Trafficking

INTRODUCTION

Norms

Why do states do what they do? Depending on your theoretical perspective, the answer may be that states use whatever means they can to achieve security. This is the realist approach. Liberals and rational choice theorists tend to focus on a similar kind of instrumental approach—meaning that the ends justify the means—although they argue that there is more than one end. Institutionalists and constructivists argue that while states seek their own advantage and will look for the means to achieve them, they may be constrained by a certain "menu" of options that are limited by international law, social convention, or appropriateness.

This "logic of appropriateness" is central to the study of norms in international life. By norms we refer to broad—sometimes vague—codes of conduct that are aimed at channeling behavior in predictable ways (Finnemore 2004). Specifically, those who focus on norms in international life have argued that under certain circumstances, they may cause a state to act in ways that appear outwardly irrational. In other words, states may opt to forego taking an action that could lead to a favorable outcome on the grounds that such an action would be "inappropriate" or "wrong."

At the personal level, it is easy to think of situations where we all choose not to steal, lie, cheat, injure, or abuse—even though doing so would give us some benefit—simply because we believe doing so would be contrary to our system of ethics—or norms. Imagine you are driving in your car late at night on an isolated country road. You encounter a stop sign. Do you stop? Instrumentalists (such as realists or rational choice theorists) would predict that you would not since it is to your advantage to keep moving and the chances of getting caught are minimal. Constructivists would ask to what extent you have internalized the norm of stopping at stop lights. If it is something you deeply believe in, you will likely stop—even if you are in a hurry.

Now imagine you encounter the stop sign in the country, but your mother is sitting in the seat next to you. Would you be more or less likely to stop?

Instrumentalists and constructivists would both want to know how strongly your mother feels about stop signs, what type of relationship you have with her, whether she is likely to call you father or bring it up at Thanksgiving dinner, or perhaps turn you in to the police. . . . Instrumentalists would expect you to make a careful calculation of the pros and cons, risks and opportunities, and then act in your self-interest, regardless of what your mother might think. Constructivists would expect you to take very seriously your relationship with your mother and the implications of her disapproval and would predict that you would likely stop even if you are running late. Note that theories of norms and theories of interests sometimes predict the same behavior. For example, if your mother, who is sitting next to you, is also a police officer, both theories would predict that you would most likely stop at the sign.

Where the question becomes interesting is where actors choose to forego promising options because they are inappropriate. Is it possible that governments might do this? Consider, for example, the historically profitable enterprise of slavery and the slave trade. For centuries—especially during the 1600s and 1700s, the major powers of the world actively captured blacks from Equatorial Africa and shipped them by the millions to the American tropics for work on sugar and cotton plantations. The trade was considered perfectly appropriate—even ingenious—and it produced tremendous material benefits for those engaged in it. Then in the late 1700s, a number of individuals—mostly British humanitarians—began to protest the practice. Within a few short decades, the United Kingdom outlawed first the slave trade and then slavery itself. Not only was the law promulgated, it was also enforced with considerable vigor as the British Royal Navy sent patrol ships along the African and American coasts to intercept slavers from many different countries. Great Britain pressured the other great powers to enter into agreements on mutual search and seizure and over the course of forty years brought the slave trade to a halt (Kaufman & Paper 1999).

Instrumentalists have a difficult time explaining this behavior. The British government could have probably ignored or even silenced the abolitionists at home. They certainly were under no pressure to abandon slavery from abroad—on the contrary, by abandoning it the UK cost itself millions of pounds in lost income. By enforcing the ban, the UK further lost hundreds of men and many fighting ships. Faced with examples like this, scholars are inclined to look to norms as the key explanatory variable. In other words, the British abandoned slavery because they came to see it as wrong.

Today, human trafficking has been compared to the slave trade. But unlike the slave trade, which essentially disappeared in the late 1800s, trafficking in human beings appears to be thriving. This seems to contradict the premise that states are guided by norms of appropriate conduct since almost all trafficking is in violation of very old rules. Or is it? As we consider this topic, we will ask several questions. Is human trafficking a violation of national or international law? If so, why are these laws not being enforced? And what does this tell us about the importance of norms in predicting state practice?

CHRONOLOGY

1803
Denmark abolishes the slave trade.

1807
Great Britain abolishes the slave trade. The Royal Navy begins to patrol the Atlantic in search of slavers after 1811.

1834
Great Britain abolishes slavery across the Empire.

1863
Abraham Lincoln issues the Emancipation Proclamation, freeing slaves in the Confederacy.

1888
Brazil frees its slaves, thereby ending slavery in the Western Hemisphere.

1910
The International Convention for the Suppression of the White Slave Trade is approved.

1926
The League of Nations approves the Slavery Convention.

1949
The UN approves the Convention on the Suppression of the Traffic in Persons and Exploitation of the Prostitution of Others.

1956
The UN approves the Supplementary Convention on the Abolition of Slavery, the Slave Trade and Institutions and Practices Similar to Slavery.

1975
The first UN Conference on Women is held. It addresses human trafficking.

1979
The UN approves the Convention on the Elimination of All Forms of Discrimination Against Women.

1990
The UN Convention on the Rights of the Child outlaws abuse and exploitation of children.

1996
The World Congress Against Commercial Sexual Exploitation of Children draws attention to this growing problem.

1999
The ILO approves the Worst Forms of Child Labor Convention.

2000
The UN Protocol to Prevent, Suppress and Punish Trafficking in Persons, Especially Women and Children comes into effect. The United States passes the Trafficking Victims Protection Act into law.

2003
The United States passes the US PROTECT Act into law.

SOME FACTS ON HUMAN TRAFFICKING

Human trafficking has been defined a number of ways, although most definitions agree that it consists in the transporting of an individual across an international boundary through deceit, manipulation, intimidation, and/or coercion for the purpose of exploitation (Buckwalter et al. 2006, 405). Specifically, most scholars and international agencies focus on the movement of women for the purposes of sexual exploitation. But other forms of trafficking include bringing children to wealthy families to serve as maids or laborers—even camel jockeys—or bringing adults for the same purpose. A key element of trafficking is trickery—and thus voluntary illegal immigration is usually not included in the definition. Even where individuals make conscious decisions to work with a trafficker, it is because they are given promises that are not kept (Hughes 2000, 636).

As far as statistics are concerned, there is considerable variation. The most widely accepted figures come from the U.S. State Department, which estimates that 900,000 people are trafficked each year, and that the business of exploiting trafficked persons is worth close to $10 billion (U.S. Department of State 2005, 6). Some estimate the number to be many times higher (Bruch 2004, 6). In the United States alone, it is thought that nearly 20,000 people are trafficked into the country, with as many as 50,000 being exploited at any given time (Miko 2003, 4). In Western Europe, it is estimated that roughly half of all prostitutes are foreigners—the vast majority of them having been trafficked from Eastern Europe (Hughes 2002). Of the 5,000 prostitutes in London, roughly 80 percent are from Eastern Europe and Russia and roughly half are under 18. Ninety percent of prostitutes in Italy are foreigners.

The two maps on the following page summarize some of the data on trafficking patterns. As you can see, Eastern Europe and Russia are important source countries, along with Thailand, China, and Nigeria. The destination for many of these trafficked persons is Western Europe and North America, with Japan, Thailand, Turkey, Israel, Australia, and Southern Asia as other destinations. Many countries experience a great deal of internal trafficking as well, with women and children being brought into cities from rural areas. And finally, much of the trafficking involves only developing countries. Nigeria and other Equatorial African countries traffic with each other and with Middle Eastern countries (UNODC 2006).

The extent of trafficking raises the question: how can so many people allow themselves to be trafficked? There are several causes of trafficking, which can be described as "macro-level" and "micro-level." At the macro-level, scholars have pointed to a number of global and national factors. To begin, there is the issue of globalization, which includes both voluntary and involuntary elements. States, by entering into trade agreements which lower barriers to international exchange, have opened the door for criminals. Drug dealers, weapons traders, and human traffickers have found it much easier to navigate international borders today than fifty years ago. Consider the fact that there are virtually no border checkpoints in the European Union, which now includes much of Eastern Europe. An individual in Poland can travel to Portugal and back without much fear of deportation. On the other hand, modern technology—especially electronic communication—has made it increasingly difficult for states to control their borders even when they try. The

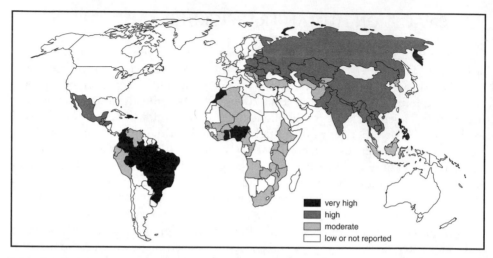

Map 12.1 Countries of Origin for Human Trafficking—2004
Source: UNODC 2006, p. 59 The United Nations is the author of the original material.

collapse of strong states across the world has left a large number of governments with little capacity to organize the type of forces necessary to control border flows (Omelaniuk 2005).

Other factors include poverty at home that drives emigration, made more difficult by stricter immigration laws. The result is increased illegal immigration (Zalewski 2005, 117). In addition, women and children lack the resources and the attention to get states to mobilize in their behalf—they are low status actors. On the other hand, the traffickers often enjoy privileged connections with the police and governmental authorities who intervene in their behalf by blocking tough laws and ensuring nonenforcement of existing ones (Robi 2005, 138).

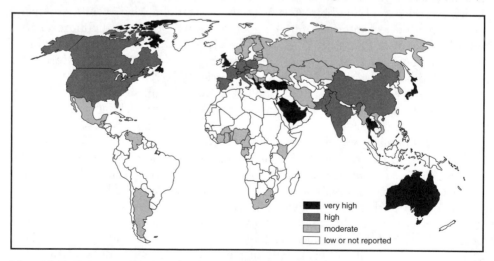

Map 12.2 Countries of Destination for Human Trafficking—2004
Source: UNODC 2006, p. 64 The United Nations is the author of the original material.

Some countries turn a blind eye to collusion in trafficking by the police (U.S. Department of State 2003, 66).

At the micro-level, the fact is that most trafficked women and children are recruited by friends or relatives or other people they trust (UNODC 2006, 61). Trafficking networks may even send "successful" prostitutes back to their home village to recruit new villagers—in some cases this is the only way for the prostitute to free herself from bondage (Miko 2003, 6). Most of those trafficked are vulnerable in one way or another. Runaways, the illiterate, those who were sexually abused, the poor, ethnic minorities, and others are particularly susceptible to promises of a better life and are willing to take considerable risks to achieve it (U.S. Department of Justice 2006).

Once the individual accepts the trafficker's proposition (or is kidnapped outright), she is often intimidated, abused, and attacked by her exploiter who typically takes away her identification and travel papers, requires a large debt be repaid from her earnings, and keeps her in isolation from those who might rescue her. Degraded and fearful, most trafficked women resign themselves to their situations, although the overwhelming majority would welcome escape (U.S. Department of State 2005, 8).

The stories of a few trafficked persons will help clarify the nature of human trafficking.

The Satias, two Cameroonian sisters and their husbands, recruited young Cameroonian girls, aged fourteen and seventeen, to work as domestics in their Washington, D.C. homes. The girls were recruited with the promise of studying in the United States in exchange for providing childcare and domestic help. Once in the United States, the domestic servants were confined to the Satias' homes, working in excess of fourteen hours a day without remuneration. The younger survivor escaped after two years of captivity. A year later the older survivor fled, after having been exploited for five years. In 2001, the Satia sisters and their husbands were charged with forced labor. Found guilty, they received criminal sentences ranging from five to nine years and were ordered to pay their victims over $100,000 in restitution. (Bales 2004, 41)

Irina, aged 18, responded to an advertisement in a Kiev, Ukraine newspaper for a training course in Berlin, Germany in 1996. With a fake passport, she traveled to Berlin where she was told that the school had closed. She was sent to Brussels, Belgium for a job. When she arrived, she was told she needed to repay a debt of $10,000 and would have to earn the money in prostitution. Her passport was confiscated, and she was threatened, beaten, and raped. When she didn't earn enough money, she was sold to a Belgium pimp who operated in Rue d'Aarschot in Brussels's red light district. When she managed to escape through the assistance of police, she was arrested because she had no legal documentation. (Paringaux 1998, cited in Hughes 2000, 631)

Karin, a mother of two, was looking for a job in Sri Lanka when a man befriended her and convinced her that she could land a better job in Singapore as a waitress. He arranged and paid for her travel. A Sri Lankan woman met Karin upon arrival in Singapore, confiscated her passport, and took her to a hotel. The woman made it clear that Karin had to submit to prostitution to pay back the money it cost for her to be flown to Singapore. Karin was taken to an open space for sale in the sex market where she joined women from Indonesia, Thailand, India, and China to be inspected and purchased by men from Pakistan, India, China, Indonesia, and Africa. The men would take the women to nearby hotels and rape them. Karin was forced to have sex with an average of 15 men a day or night. She developed a serious illness, and three months after her arrival was arrested by Singaporean police during a raid on the brothel. She was deported to Sri Lanka. (U.S. Department of State 2005, 16)

These anecdotes help clarify the nature of trafficking by shedding light on the type of people who perpetrate it. In many cases, the trafficking is like a small family business, with just a few trusted insiders—often blood relatives—involved. In other cases, trafficking is carried out by much more sophisticated networks and organizations—some of which are organized hierarchically like a corporation (UNODC 2006, 35). This said, trafficking always requires at least some level of organization. The recruitment or abduction is typically carried out by an acquaintance of the victim—often with the help of local authorities. Transit involves higher levels of funding since one must pay for an airline ticket, forged documents, temporary housing, and local transportation. Collusion with customs agents can facilitate this stage. The third phase of the operation is called the "exploitation" phase, and may last a few months or a few years. It is when the trafficker makes his or profit by pimping or working the victim. This can also be facilitated by local authorities—especially where prostitution is illegal—and some police have been known to arrest escapees and take them back to their brothels or plantations. Finally, once the money is made, it must be laundered through banks and legitimate investments—something that can also be facilitated by the help of corrupt bankers and regulators (UNODC 2006, 57).

A NORM AGAINST TRAFFICKING?

The pervasiveness of human trafficking—which likely involves in one way or another upwards of 150 countries—is puzzling. Are there not laws on the books in every country banning slavery? Is not human trafficking slavery in almost every respect? So why is it permitted to exist?

The fact is that for more than one hundred years, human trafficking has been distinguished from slavery and the slave trade in most national regulations—as well as under international law. Human trafficking was originally nicknamed the "white" slave trade since in the late 1800s and early 1900s it was thought to involve mostly white, European young women being abducted or deceived into prostitution in other European countries. Early laws, such as the Mann Act in the United States, targeted alleged gangs of urban immigrants who trafficked in white women. The racial overtones of these laws were apparent, and this carried over into international treaties which appeared aimed at protecting "pure and innocent" young women from their swarthy predators (Bruch 2004, 9).

By 1949, the international community had broadened its antitrafficking rules to cover not just white women being sold into prostitution, but all those who were forced into labor overseas—even if the individual had given verbal consent for the arrangement (Bruch 2004, 9). States were enjoined to adopt clear legislation with stiff penalties for violation. But throughout these years, trafficking was not equated with slavery, and it was generally agreed that new regulations were required to address the problem.

In the 1970s, the scale of human trafficking was on the rise and receiving special attention. At international conferences on women's issues held in 1975, 1979, and 1980, states began to take renewed interest in protecting women from exploitation. These debates culminated in the UN's Protocol to Prevent, Suppress and Punish Trafficking in Persons in 2000. The Protocol calls upon states to criminalize trafficking in their national laws and to collaborate with each other to suppress trafficking (Bruch 2004, 14). The Protocol's implementation is being overseen by the UN's Office on Drugs and Crime—which gives a clear indication of how the problem is being viewed. Trafficking is seen as an extension of other organized criminal behavior rather than a question of the rights of women as persons or workers. More will be said on this later.

At the national level, roughly three-fourths of the governments have now adopted laws specifically outlawing trafficking (Mattar 2005, 3). These laws differ considerably in both substances and penalties. The United States has adopted perhaps the most sweeping legislation in the form of the Trafficking Victims Protection Act (TVPA) of 2000 and the U.S. PROTECT Act of 2003. The TVPA, which has been renewed and tightened since its original passage, outlaws trafficking and creates a penalty of up to life in prison if the victim is under the age of 14, although twenty years (bargainable to something lower, of course) is the standard penalty (Mattar 2005). In Europe, the recommended sentence is eight years.

The TVPA also provides for protection for the victim, assuming the victim steps forward. This comes in the form of medical care and other social services, as well as a special T-visa for those who believe they would be in peril if they were deported to their home country. Thus far, well under one thousand such visas have been granted—which casts some doubt on the earlier estimate that 50,000 trafficked persons are residing in the United States (Buckwalter et al. 2006, 410).

The U.S. PROTECT Act is unusual in its effort to stamp out child sexual exploitation by criminalizing the acts of their "clients." When an American travels overseas, even if sex with a child is not the principal goal (an improvement over a 1994 law), he is subject to harsh penalties upon his return if he has had sex with a minor. Sex tourism, to put it in perspective, may account for as much as ten percent of the gross national product of some Southeast Asian nations (U.S. Department of Justice 2006). Since the mid-1990s, a number of European governments have outlawed this practice, although the penalties under U.S. law are especially tough since it considers anyone under 18 a child.

In order to discourage the exploitation of trafficked persons in their midst, Swedish legislators have taken an unusual approach. Specifically, it involves outlawing the purchase of sex acts—while the sale of sex acts is not prohibited. This means that the penalties of the law fall entirely on the "Johns" rather than the prostitutes. Adopted in 1999, the justification for the law is that the sex trade is inherently exploitative of women—particularly in male-dominated societies. Women's rights, status, and dignity are always in jeopardy under this situation, and the only way to protect them is to outlaw it (Hughes 2000, 649). Many states have adopted similar policies, including "shaming" Johns, conducting "John schools" where those who purchase sex acts are given sensitivity training by social workers and former prostitutes.

The United States' TVPA also provides for international shaming by requiring the State Department to rank every country in the world with respect to its efforts at combating trafficking. The so-called "tier system" ranks countries according to a standard laid out in the legislation. Specifically, the United States asks whether the state is 1) prohibiting and punishing trafficking, 2) ensuring that the punishments are appropriately severe, 3) ensuring punishments will be adequate to deter trafficking, and 4) working consistently to eliminate trafficking (Miko 2003, 14). In recent years, countries from every region of the world have been ranked in the third tier—failing to meet the minimum standard. In 2005, these were Bolivia, Burma, Cambodia, Cuba, Ecuador, Jamaica, Kuwait, North Korea, Qatar, Saudi Arabia, Sudan, Togo, the United Arab Emirates, and Venezuela (U.S. Department of State 2005, 42). Note that several of these countries appear on the maps presented earlier in the case. Oddly enough, Vietnam and Thailand made it to the second tier, even though there is considerable evidence that trafficking is continually growing in these countries—something which has led many observers to question the validity of the rankings (Hughes 2002).

To answer our initial questions, one could argue that most states are not generally in violation of any norms against trafficking because until quite recently these norms were not clearly articulated. States opted to view the rules against slavery very narrowly. Even in the United States, antislavery legislation has been interpreted by the Supreme Court to refer only to "chattel slavery" in which owners held legal title to a human being. It has only been recently that U.S. law has been broadened to encompass various forms of slave-like practices.

For that matter, many states would argue that by prohibiting prostitution, they were already doing enough to prevent trafficking. There was no need, so they argued, for separate rules on the subject. The same could be said for child labor laws and so forth. And of course laws against illegal immigration covered any transit issues.

But it is also clear that most of the laws that might have stopped human trafficking were not being enforced—even in countries with ample capacity to do so. Willful disregard of laws that might have halted trafficking—and in some cases active collusion between the authorities and the perpetrators—made the laws irrelevant. And so it is reasonable to argue that while trafficking itself—at least in the form it had taken in recent years—may not have been outlawed in so many words, there were plenty of laws that were being broken by almost every state almost all of the time. It is hard not to conclude that the norm against trafficking, such as it was, was not constraining state behavior in any significant way.

WHAT NEXT?

Ending human trafficking is one of highest priorities for the international community today, along with many other ills such as arms trafficking, drug trafficking, terrorism, pollution, and other cross-border ills. And just as solutions to the other problems seem hard to come by, it is perhaps unfair to expect a quick remedy to the problem of human trafficking as well.

Of special concern in this issue is the basic philosophy underpinning the measures states adopt. Scholars have identified at least three different approaches, some of which are mutually exclusive. The approaches have been described as the "law enforcement" approach, which is closely related to the "moralistic" approach, the "labor" approach, and the "human rights."

The "Law Enforcement" Approach

The law enforcement or moralistic approach adopts a "zero-tolerance" policy toward trafficking on the grounds that it violates the basic ethnical and moral systems of most societies. To begin, most states have outlawed prostitution, and so any enterprise aimed at importing women for sexual exploitation is inherently illegal. Remedies include prosecuting the prostitutes, their pimps, their Johns and any intermediaries that were involved in the trafficking. To advocates of this approach, human trafficking is tantamount to organized crime, no matter the scale of the operation (Bruch 2004, 19). As we have seen, the UN has generally taken this approach, as evidenced by the delegation of enforcement of anti-trafficking treaties to the Office on Drugs and Crime.

This approach has proven effective in Sweden and other places where those who purchase sex acts are targeted. But this is still the exception, in part because Johns are generally "high status" actors with money and position in society who can manipulate the system to their advantage. As we have seen, state authorities are often involved in exploitation directly—or at least indirectly. In 2002, for example, the communication adviser to the prime minister was arrested for buying sex from a minor. This is the exception, in that most people in this position of power enjoy impunity (Bales 2004, 8).

In addition to corruption, most states do not have the capacity to strictly enforce all the laws related to trafficking even when they have the will to do so. The United States, with the capacity to invade and conquer whole countries, cannot seem to prevent more than ten million immigrants from crossing the border each year. Illegal immigration in Europe is even greater, and once in Europe an individual can travel relatively freely within the EU. The same is true of enforcing antiprostitution laws since much of the activity takes place in concealed locations or even private residences.

But the "law enforcement" approach carries with it important dilemmas. In many European countries and a few American states, prostitution is legal. In such places, prostitution is regulated and even taxed. To separate out trafficked—and thus illegal—prostitutes from legal ones becomes remarkably difficult. There is even considerable evidence that where prostitution is legal, trafficking increases (Hughes 2002).

And finally, the law enforcement approach can heap more pain and suffering on those who have been victimized the most by trafficking: the children and women who were trafficked. As we have seen in our individual cases, many trafficked persons are treated merely as illegal aliens and subject to deportation. This sometimes leaves the trafficked person even worse off, since "they often lack the education and skills to continue supporting themselves. Having been betrayed by their own family or loved ones, these women and children often feel they have no place to go and may even form attachments to the very people who exploit them and return to prostitution as their sole means of support" (Robi 2005, 140). They are often rejected by those in their home villages as "fallen women" with no worth and no place in society.

The "Labor" Approach

Diametrically opposed to this approach is one that takes as its starting point the premise that sex workers are workers, first and foremost. Advocates of this approach adopt a libertarian view that all business can be considered legitimate if there is no exploitation. Women, they argue, may voluntarily choose to become sex workers—even in a foreign country—as a way out of poverty. They may enter into contracts to become sex workers on the understanding that these contracts are enforceable under law. The business could be regulated—with periodic health inspections, pensions, and even trade unions. The state could become actively involved in protecting sex workers just as it protects miners or musicians.

Under such a scenario, the question becomes whether the individual is being treated unfairly—not whether his or her activities are inherently immoral. Coerced exploitation would be outlawed for sex workers just as it is for miners and musicians. Sex workers would be protected under the same domestic and international regulations that currently govern child labor and other forms of exploitative work. There would no need for special legislation against trafficking since everything of significance is already covered. Note, for example, that the International Labour Organization has condemned the sex trade in Thailand—but not because it is inherently wrong. The ILO's concern was that basic laws against worker exploitation are not being enforced (Bruch 2004, 25).

The ILO and World Health Organization have openly adopted a prolabor perspective with the support of the European Parliament which argued in a resolution that "it is advisable to draw up legislation on unregulated work within the [European] Union in order to reduce the vulnerability and lack of rights of persons working in this sector, and to ensure access to health care, social services and insurance" (Wijers & van Doorninck 2002).

But is it reasonable to equate prostitution with other forms of gainful employment? It is difficult to imagine an activity that has a greater tendency to degrade the individual. Note that 75 percent of trafficked prostitutes interviewed in Ukraine in the mid-1990s had not anticipated being forced into prostitution and nearly all wanted to get out. For the other 25 percent, the image of prostitution they had was very different from the reality—borne of such Hollywood films as "Pretty Woman" (Hughes 2000, 636). One might even make the argument that a willingness to engage in prostitution is evidence that a woman has lost her self-esteem to the point of being unable to make a reasoned decision.

The "Human Rights" Approach

A third view—which something of a hybrid of the other two—has been characterized by its focus on existing international human rights conventions. In particular, the "human rights" approach endorses implementation of existing human rights treaties banning slavery and the slave trade, and advocates encourage reliance on mere expansion of these rules to cover trafficking. Kevin Bales, director of Free the Slaves, has repeatedly argued that, contrary to conventional wisdom, human trafficking really is modern slavery. "Throughout history, the core characteristic of slavery, whether it was legal or not, is violence. The slave master or slaveholder controls a slave by using or threatening violence. Slavery is about no choices at all, no control over your life, and a constant fear of violence. This is the key to slavery" (Bales 2004, 3).

To advocates of this approach, the key is to persuade states that the norm against slavery is still valid and that it should be enforced at least as vigorously now as it was in the days when the Royal Navy patrolled the Atlantic Ocean. At the same time as the slave traders should be stopped, the slaves should be assisted. They should be seen as victims, to be sure, but victims with rights. The right to live and work and be as they please—where they please.

While compelling, the human rights approach raises as many questions as it answers. For example, if the victim of trafficking has rights, does this include the right to be prostitutes? For that matter, do states have the right to ban prostitution as part of its effort to create a safe society? And what about the rights of traffickers? If women give their consent, are they not merely middlemen, helping them achieve their dreams?

In other words, while the human rights approach may have fundamental merit, at least with respect to its premise, it requires resort to one of the other two approaches to reach an outcome. And ultimately, if reliance on states' willingness to comply with a norm is the solution to the problem, then we must resign ourselves to a large number of states opting for noncompliance. This would include the fifty (or so) states that at this point do not have any specific law against trafficking and seem uninterested in drafting them (Matter 2005, 3).

Common to almost all of the recommendations for ending human trafficking is an emphasis on the demand side. And since demand ultimately involves individual choices, with or without penalties, the solution will bear on whether individuals are committed to the norm of nonexploitation. After all, if there were no men willing to purchase sex acts from trafficked women, there would be no profit in their being trafficked, and thus the activity itself would whither away.

DEBATE TOPIC

Is it realistic to hold that women may choose to place themselves in prostitution and that it should therefore be permissible for them to be transported overseas for this purpose?

PRO

Those who endorse this view argue that it is not for society to make moral judgments about the merits of one's career—so long as no one is injured by the choice. Since there is obviously a demand for commercial sex acts, it should be permissible for women to opt to fill that need and profit thereby. It is paternalistic and presumptuous to argue otherwise.

CON

Unlike any other career path, prostitution is inherently degrading. The Hollywood myth of the "happy hooker" should not be taken as evidence that prostitution has an "up side." On the contrary, to choose prostitution is evidence of a profound misunderstanding of the nature of the activity—or else is evidence of a personality that has been stripped of self worth. The state has an interest in preventing women from engaging in such self-destructive behavior, just as it works to prevent smoking, drug use, and reckless driving.

THINKING THEORETICALLY

In this case we addressed what instrumentalist thinking and normative thinking might tell us about the power of rules to govern international behavior. Two other perspectives that bear on the question are feminism and Marxism. Feminists would argue that human trafficking is inherently related to the dominance of males in global society. Female issues as well as women themselves, they argue, are denigrated and ignored by men who are far more interested in questions of military might and economic power. It should come as no surprise that most of the traffickers are men, almost all of the clients are men, and almost all of the corrupt policemen that allow the activity to continue are also men. For that matter, most of those negotiating treaties and passing national legislation are men who see women as second-class and unworthy of effective protection. The long-term solution is the replacement of men in positions of power—or at least their sensitization to the needs of women.

Marxists also see exploitation as part and parcel of how the world is structured, but to them it has less to do with gender and more to do with class and business interests. The reason human trafficking occurs, they argue, is because there's money to be made. Capitalists are blind with respect to the victims, so long as the profits are high. Thus Marxists see a continuum between the old slavery and the new trafficking, both of which are tremendously lucrative. Until a new economic order is installed that dignifies the worker over the business owner (whether that business be licit or illicit), this form of exploitation will exist.

QUESTIONS TO CONSIDER

1. To what extent is human trafficking really like the slave trade? Does it matter that prostitution is legal in many countries? Why aren't countries patrolling the oceans and airports to catch traffickers?

2. To what extent is trafficking the fault of Western countries that consume commercial sex while at the same time prohibiting much of the immigration that would naturally occur?

3. How can one intervene to halt a practice that is driven in part by the victims' families and friends? Are there government policies that could break the process at the source?

4. To what extent do you think trafficking is related to poverty—both personal and national? Is this a reflection of global inequalities?

WEBSITES

Free the Slaves: **www.freetheslaves.net**

End Child Prostitution in Asian Tourism (ECPAT): **www.epcat.net/**

Coalition Against Trafficking in Women (CATW): **www.catwinternational.org**

Protection Project: **www.protectionproject.org**

U.S. State Department's Office to Monitor and Combat Trafficking in Persons: **www.state.gov/g/tip/**

U.N. Office on Drugs and Crime: **www.unodc.org/unodc/index.html**

International Labour Organization (ILO): **www.ilo.org**

REFERENCES

Bales, Kevin. *New Slavery: A Reference Handbook.* Portugese (Brazil) (Santa Barbara, CA: ABC-CLIO, 2004).

Bruch, Elizabeth. "Models Wanted: The Search for an Effective Response to Human Trafficking." *Stanford Journal of International Law* 40 (Winter 2004): 1–45.

Buckwalter, Ellen, Maria Perinetti, Susan L. Pollet, and Meredith S. Salvaggio. "Modern Day Slavery in our Own Backyard." *William and Mary Journal of Women and the Law* 12 (Winter 2006): 403–435.

Finnemore, Martha. *The Purpose of Intervention: Changing Beliefs about the Use of Force* (Ithaca, NY: Cornell University Press; 2004).

Hughes, Donna. "The 'Natasha' Trade: The Transnational shadow market of trafficking in women." *Journal of International Affairs* 53 (Spring 2000): 625–651.

Hughes, Donna. "Foreign Government Complicity in Human Trafficking: A Review of the State Department's 2002 Trafficking in Persons report." Report given to the House Committee on International Relations, June 19, 2002.

Kaufman, Chaim D., and Robert A. Pape. "Explaining Costly International Moral Action: Britain's sixty-year campaign against the Atlantic slave trade." *International Organization* 53 #4 (Autumn, 1999): 631–668.

Matter, Mohammed. "Trafficking in Persons: The European vs. the U.S. approach." Speech delivered in Brussels, Belgium on May 11, 2005. Accessible at: **www.protectionproject.org.**

Miko, Francis. "Trafficking in Women and Children: The U.S. and International Response." In Troubnikoff, Anna, ed. *Trafficking in Women and Children: Current Issues and Developments.* (New York: Nova Science Pubs.; 2003): 1–29.

Omelaniuk, Irena. "Trafficking in Human Beings." United Nations Expert Group Meeting on International Migration and Development—UN Secretariat. July 8, 2005.

Paringaux, Roland-Pierre. "Prostitution Takes a Turn for the West." *Le Monde,* May 24, 1998.

U.N. Office on Drugs and Crime (UNODC). Trafficking in Persons: Global Patterns. (2006) Accessible at: **www.unodc.org/pdf/traffickinginpersons_report_2006.04.pdf.**

U.S. Department of Justice. "Child Sex Tourism." (2006) Accessible at: **www.usgoj.gov/criminal/ceos/sextour.html.**

U.S. Department of State "Victims of Trafficking and Violence Protection Act 2000: Trafficking in Persons Report." In Troubnikoff, Anna, ed. *Trafficking in Women and Children: Current Issues and Developments.* (New York: Nova Science Pubs.; 2003): 51–72.

U.S. Department of State. Trafficking in Persons Report. (2005) Accessible at: **www.state.gov/documents/organization/47255.pdf.**

Wijers, Marjan, and Marieke van Doorninck. "Only Rights Can Stop Wrongs: A Critical Assessment of Anti-trafficking Strategies." Presented at EU/IOM STOP European Conference on Preventing and Combating Trafficking in Human Beings—A Global Challenge for the 21st Century. Brussels, Belgium, September 18–20, 2002. Accessible at: **www.walnet.org/csis/papers/wijers-rights.html.**

Zalewski, Anna. "Migrants for Sale: The International Failure to Address Contemporary Human Trafficking." *Suffolk Transnational Law Review* 29 (Winter 2005): 113–137.

CASE 13

The International Criminal Tribunal for Rwanda

INTRODUCTION

International Law

International law is a collection of principles, rules, and procedures designed to govern international affairs—particularly relations among nation-states. It is derived from a wide variety of sources: treaties, conventions, protocols, traditions, scholarly writings, customs, habits, and so on. Although international law aims at creating the sort of order in international society that exists in domestic society, it lacks a crucial element: centralized enforcement. Because there is no world government, international law can be applied only by the consent of members of the international community. Historically, international citizens have been reluctant to take the risks required to enforce international law militarily, so wars come and go as always. An important exception to this rule was the disposition of Nazi war criminals in 1945.

States dominate the character and implementation of international law. To a large extent, it is a system of rules under which actors other than states (e.g., firms, international organizations, individuals, minority groups) have little voice or standing. For example, the premier international tribunal—the International Court of Justice—restricts its contentious proceedings to states. Only if a government chooses to promote the cause of some other actor may that figure's case be heard (this has happened very rarely). Thus crimes by and against private individuals have almost always been prosecuted in national, not international, courts.

Where the behavior of individual soldiers and officers in combat is concerned, states have been careful to prevent even national courts from exercising jurisdiction. Military justice permits officers of a nation's defense force to judge individual soldiers and sailors, granting them limited rights to defend themselves. The Hague and Geneva Conventions create international standards of conduct in wartime, but provide no automatic enforcement by way of an international tribunal. Governments have resisted creating such a permanent arrangement, as was seen recently in the United States' objections to its service men and women being brought before the newly formed International Criminal Court.

The Genocide Convention, signed in 1948, also provides for international enforcement of the most repugnant crimes imaginable—although the treaty leaves it up to states to devise the means of enforcement. The Nuremberg and Tokyo War Crimes tribunals were the first to prosecute individuals for a variety of war crimes and so-called "crimes against humanity," which at the time included genocide. But it was not until the two post–Cold War criminal tribunals established for Yugoslavia and Rwanda in 1993 and 1994, respectively, that the Genocide Convention itself was enforced.

This story of the establishment and operation of the International Criminal Tribunal for Rwanda raises as many questions as it answers. Why did states hesitate to create it in the first place? What were its aims? Why was it approved over Rwandan objections and why did it have such a negative image in that country for so long? And what has it accomplished? More importantly, will it deter future genocides?

KEY FIGURES

Jean Paul Akayesu   Former bourgmestre of Taba. He is the first individual convicted of genocide by the ICTR in 1998.

Juvenal Habyarimana   President of Rwanda from 1973 until his death in April 1994 which touched off the genocide.

Jean Kambanda   Former Prime Minister of Rwanda. He pleads guilty to genocide, crimes against humanity, and incitement to genocide and is sentenced to life in prison in 1998.

Col. Theoneste Bagosora   Senior military officer, generally considered the instigator and organizer of the genocide.

Richard Goldstone   Chief Prosecutor of both the Yugoslav and Rwandan war crimes tribunals until 1996.

Louise Arbour   Chief Prosecutor of the ICTR, 1996–1999.

Andronido Adede   Registrar of the ICTR until his resignation in disgrace in 1997.

Honore Rakotomanana   Deputy Prosecutor of the ICTR (over Kigali operations) until his resignation in disgrace in 1997.

CHRONOLOGY

1959
Hutus led by Gregoire Kayibanda rebel against Belgian rule.

1962
Kayibanda becomes Rwanda's first president upon the country's independence. Shortly thereafter he orchestrates the killing of hundreds of Tutsis.

1973
Juvenal Habyarimana seizes power in a coup, claiming to be the true heir of the revolution of 1959.

1991
Following several years of warfare, the RPF and Habyarimana's government agree to the first of several cease-fires. They engage in direct talks for national reconciliation.

1993
The government and moderate Hutus agree to a peace plan with the RPF at Arusha, Tanzania. The plan is repudiated by hard-line Hutus who denounce Habyarimana's betrayal of the Hutu cause. Even some moderate Hutus join the hard-liners as the country becomes utterly polarized by late 1993.

1994
April 6   The plane carrying President Habyarimana is shot down as it lands at Kigali airport. Radio stations begin broadcasting a previously arranged signal to begin attacks on Tutsis throughout the country under the leadership of the Army and the Interhamwe militias.

April   Throughout the month, hundreds of thousands of Tutsis are shot, raped, and cut to pieces by marauding troops, militiamen, and ordinary citizens. The UN forces are powerless and even fall victim to the violence themselves. Thousands flee to neighboring Congo where they establish refugee camps.

July   The RPF takes power in Kigali as Hutu militias and the Army are routed. The UN Security Council requests an inquiry into the genocide.

November   With the report in hand, the UN Security Council votes to create the International Criminal Tribunal for Rwanda.

1995
The Tribunal opens its doors, although it still lacks a courtroom and jail.

1996
The Tribunal issues its first indictments and begins receiving prisoners.

1997
Following a UN inquiry, the Deputy Prosecutor and Registrar resign in disgrace.

1998
The Tribunal issues its first verdict—a ruling of guilt on charges of genocide. It later convicts the former prime minister, Jean Kambanda.

2001
Observers become increasingly impatient with the slow pace of the ICTR, which undertakes reforms to accelerate the proceedings.

2003
The Tribunal has its most productive year as it issues rulings on cases involving nine defendants.

THE RWANDAN GENOCIDE

During the month of April 1994, somewhere between 500,000 and 900,000 ethnic Tutsis were systematically slaughtered by government-directed gangs of Interhamwe extremists, Hutu soldiers and police, and others. This was not the first time that Hutus—the majority ethnic group that resented the higher wealth and status the Tutsis had historically enjoyed under first German and later Belgian rule—had engaged in systematic slaughter of Tutsis. It had also happened shortly after Hutus came to power and achieved independence in 1962 and then again prior to a coup in 1973 that brought Juvinal Habyarimana to power.

But the April events were different. They came after Habyarimana signed a peace accord in Arusha, Tanzania with the RPF—the Tutsi rebel group that had fought the Hutu government for many years. The agreement, signed in August 1993, created democratic institutions where moderate Hutu parties such as the CDR could form a coalition government (Eltringham 2004, 87). It also limited his position and reduced him to the status of a figurehead. Many radical Hutus, including the Interhamwe, accused him and the moderates of a sell-out and are presumed to have been behind the downing of an aircraft he was traveling in on April 6, 1994 (Magnarella 2000, 117).

Almost immediately, the radio station RTLM began broadcasting a signal to begin the systematic slaughter of Tutsis and moderate Hutus in retaliation for the assassination—for which they were naturally blamed. Throughout the country, under the overall coordination of Col. Theoneste Bagosora, gangs of Interhamwe, accompanied by village bourgmestres (mayors), army captains, and prominent citizens, moved from house to house and refuge to refuge, pulling out Tutsis for execution—usually by machete (Power 2002, 330). The first targets were educated Tutsis—especially school teachers—and the police and others tortured and killed ordinary Tutsis to discover their whereabouts. Then the slaughter became more indiscriminant, involving children in hospitals, the elderly, the infirm, and so forth. Attacks were not limited to death by machete, as thousands of women and girls were rounded up for physical abuse and rape—often followed by mutilation and murder (for a detailed description of the genocide, see Gourevitch 1998).

The international response to the genocide was, in a word, pathetic. For several weeks, the major powers denied that atrocities were occurring. As early as April 24th, Lt.-Gen. Romeo Dallaire—the commander of the UN peacekeeping force in Rwanda—had alerted his leaders in New York that a genocide was taking place. But the major powers denied him additional troops—as they had repeatedly done in the past. The United States refused to use the term "genocide" for fear that doing so would create an obligation to send troops and the French and Belgian governments were looking for ways to withdraw what few troops they had previously sent (Dallaire 2003, 364). This was particularly true of Belgium which has lost a number of men to the Interhamwe. It was not until July 1994—long after the genocide was over and the RPF had installed a government dominated by Tutsis and moderate Hutus—that the Security Council called for an investigation of the events of April (Yacoubian 2003, 133). In October, this investigation exposed the scope of the atrocities.

ESTABLISHMENT OF THE ICTR

Once the Security Council was presented with the formal report, it acted to establish an international criminal tribunal to prosecute those individuals most responsible for the atrocities. But this decision was anything but automatic. To begin, the major powers opposed establishing a wholly autonomous court but instead chose to make it an extension of the tribunal in The Hague for Yugoslavia. They refused to base the tribunal in Rwanda itself on the grounds that it should be impartial and to protect the safety of all involved. They also limited the scope of the Tribunal to just those serious crimes committed during 1994. And finally, they limited the most serious penalty to life in prison even though many more junior suspects faced the death penalty in Rwanda itself. For these reasons, when the resolution came to a vote, Rwanda cast the only negative vote (China abstained) (Neuffer 2001, 130).

The lack of enthusiasm for a criminal tribunal in Rwanda has prompted questions about the great powers' motives. Some wonder whether the lack of interest stems from the simple fact that what happened in Rwanda is an "African" problem, and therefore cannot be solved (Moghalu "Image and Reality," 2002, 34). Many, including UN Secretary-General Boutros Boutros-Ghali noted with despair the scale of interest in and support for intervention in Yugoslavia in contrast to the relative disdain for Rwanda. Even after the Tribunal was formed, the lack of support was so deep that it appear to reveal an effort by great powers to sabotage it.

Still others wondered whether the major powers were concerned about setting a legal precedent for intervention in the internal affairs of a country—which could be considered a violation of the state's sovereignty (especially where the state was clearly complicit in perpetrating genocide). It took significant negotiation to persuade them that the Rwanda situation qualified as a "threat to international peace"—a provision in the UN Charter that must be met before the Security Council could authorize the use of force or the creation of a tribunal (Power 2002, 484).

Many of Rwanda's neighbors had their own reasons to be suspicious of an international tribunal since the collapse of the Hutu-dominated regime shifted the balance of power in the African Great Lakes region. Governments in Cameroon, the Congo, and Kenya each balked at turning over suspects to the ICTR when the time came and had to be reminded of the possibility of Security Council sanctions before they relented (Magnarella 2000, 51).

Given these circumstances, one might rightly ask whether the Tribunal was doomed from the start. Its budget in 1996 was a mere $36 million. The offices in Arusha, the Tribunal's seat, lacked secretaries, e-mail, working telephones, air conditioning, and even a courtroom and a jail at the beginning. Only thirty of the eighty positions for investigators had been filled, and many of these faced opposition when they arrived in Rwanda to do their work (Neuffer 2001, 256–265). The chief prosecutor was Richard Goldstone who operated from The Hague until Louise Arbour was appointed in late 1996. Although gifted and tenacious, she had no experience as a prosecutor. The deputy prosecutor in Kigali was Honore Rakotomana—a man with a well-earned reputation for moving slowly and without clear direction. The register, Andronido Adede, the man responsible for managing the office and protecting witnesses—was unwilling to delegate the simple task of handing out indictments and so spent 250 days in 1996 traveling to various countries around Africa (Magnarella 2000, 61–63).

The nine judges appointed by the Security Council and Secretary-General were deeply frustrated by the situation. They were eager to begin their work of issuing indictments, arresting suspects, getting suspects transferred from other countries, holding preliminary hearings, and ultimately beginning trials. Instead, they found very slow going and little support from UN headquarters. A Swedish judge resigned in protest. Still others called upon the UN to conduct an investigation into the mismanagement of the Tribunal. The investigation exposed not only the problems already mentioned, but also graft, corruption, nepotism, internal bickering, and infighting, and a general lack of accountability. To quote from the UN report:

> In the Tribunal's Registry not a single administrative area functioned effectively. Finance had no accounting system and could not produce allotment reports, so that neither the Registry nor United Nations Headquarters had budget expenditure information. . . . United Nations rules and regulations were widely disregarded. . . . The Office of the [Deputy] Prosecutor in Kigali had administrative, leadership and operational problems. Functions were hampered by lack of experienced staff as well as lack of vehicles, computers and other office equipment and supplies. (UN OIOS 1997, cited in Magnarella 2000, 60–61)

Following the dissemination of the report (which became available over the UN's Web site), Adede and Rakotomanana resigned and were replaced by far more effective individuals. The work of the Tribunal shifted into a new gear—although it continues to be plagued by a lack of resources and technical capacity to this day.

THE WORK OF THE ICTR

Any discussion of the work of the ICTR invariably tells us as much about the individual writing as it does about the agency itself. Some—especially those working closely with the Tribunal—have argued that its survival alone is something of a miracle (Moghalu "International Humanitarian Law," 2002). Others—especially the Rwandan government and Tutsi survivors, will be satisfied with nothing less than wholesale summary executions (Kamatali 2005).

A first step in understanding the work of the ICTR is to understand its powers. It was given relatively strict guidelines, as specified in its Statute—amended to Security Council resolution 955 in 1994. It is only to address serious crimes, including genocide (which also includes incitement and conspiracy to commit genocide), crimes against humanity, and certain war crimes. This means that it is only marginally interested in destruction of property, theft, and even murder—unless these were part of a systematic effort to destroy an ethnic group. In addition, it is only interested in events that occurred inside Rwanda in 1994. This means that events leading up to that year or events that have occurred since (including widespread killings in the refugee camps in the Congo) are off-limits. With respect to strategy, the prosecutor elected to focus only on the 100–150 most prominent individuals—leaving the other tens of thousands of suspects to be tried in Rwanda, Belgium, or other countries. The implication is significant since this means that no one in Arusha is concerned about having convicted only a handful of suspects—even though others would like to see a far greater number.

Of particular interest are the procedures of the Tribunal, which offer a mix of different Western systems. Each suspect is identified with an indictment that spells out the nature of his or her crimes, followed by an international arrest warrant. These must be honored by governments since the ICTR does not have its own police force. Roughly a dozen countries, including the United States, have arrested and extradited these suspects (UN 1997). Once in custody in Arusha, the suspects are arraigned and assigned a defense attorney (if they have not hired their own). Numerous pretrial motions are considered with respect to questions of admissible evidence, discovery, witnesses, and so forth. Ultimately, a trial is scheduled and witnesses are cross-examined. The three judges that sit on each trial then render a verdict, which can be appealed to a seven-member panel. The judges have discretion with respect to accepting or rejecting evidence—and can even accept as sufficient the words of a single witness. The judges also have discretion with respect to sentencing—taking into account the seriousness of the crime and various aggravating and mitigating factors (such as the suspect's status in the government or his willingness to cooperate with the Tribunal) (ICTR 1998-Kambanda Case).

The process is naturally quite slow—although the judges' willingness to entertain many pretrial motions and the complexity of the cases (and lack of telephones or translators) make the processes even slower. Rwandans in particular find the whole exercise alien. For instance, they find the cross-examination of witnesses and victims to be tantamount to abuse (Moghalu "Image and Reality," 2002, 29). They also find that waiting four years from arrest to conviction (a typical span) to be unacceptable. And finally, they wonder why in the world the accused should have so many rights.

As of mid-2006, the Tribunal could take satisfaction in a number of achievements. It had disposed of cases involving thirty different defendants (although appeals were pending on three), secured convictions on such crimes as genocide, extermination, war crimes, and various crimes against humanity, and in the process created new law. Among the convicted were several bourgmestres, three prefects, four ministers, and a prime minister. In the dock were still more senior leaders, including the notorious Col. Bagosora. Although the convictions were slow in coming at first, the pace has gradually accelerated. From 1996 through 2000, only eight cases were resolved—leading to convictions for seven defendants. But from 2001 to 2005, cases on 21 defendants were resolved, with convictions for eighteen of them. What is more, four of these defendants lodged guilty pleas, greatly accelerating their cases (ICTR 2006). Of the twenty-five defendants, eleven received the maximum sentence of life in prison (although this was reduced to 45 years by the Appeals Chamber in the case of Juvenal Kajelijeli).

THE CASE OF JEAN-PAUL AKAYESU

Akayesu was the bourgmestre in Taba. A Hutu, he had a reputation for fairness and was seen as a father-figure to much of the town (ICTR Sept. 2, 1998, paragraph 53). He was ambivalent about the Interhamwe and actually fought to keep them out of his area in the days after April 6, 1994. However, on April 18 he met with some of their leaders, at which point he changed his policy and instead provided them with assistance and encouragement. He was instrumental in bringing about the massacre of 2,000 Tutsis in his town. He specifically ordered the killing of more than a dozen unarmed Tutsis, tortured others to locate Tutsi intellectuals, and led Interhamwe thugs to their locations. He also encouraged the rape and sexual assault of dozens of Tutsi women, many of whom had sought refuge in his mayoral compound.

The prosecutor charged Akayesu with numerous crimes, including genocide, complicity in genocide, incitement of genocide, extermination, six counts of murder, and war crimes. The charges of rape and sexual assault were added later as additional evidence came to light. Genocide is defined as "any of the following acts committed with intent to destroy, in whole or in part, a national, ethnical, racial or religious group, as such: killing . . . causing serious bodily or mental harm . . ." or otherwise impairing the survival of the group (ICTR Sept. 2, 1998, paragraph 23). Extermination, on the other hand, must fulfill the following criteria:

> 1) the accused or his subordinate participated in the killing of certain named or described persons, 2) the act or omission was unlawful and intentional, 3) the unlawful act or omission must be part of a widespread or systematic attack, 4) the attack must be against the civilian population, 5) the attack must be on discriminatory grounds. (ICTR Sept. 2, 1998, paragraph 592)

The key difference between the crimes involves the degree of planning and the aim of destroying the group—extermination may not have such sweeping aims, although it may be part of a genocidal plot. Oddly enough, it is possible to be guilty of extermination but not of murder since the latter requires actually perpetrating the act rather than simply ordering it.

The judges on the Tribunal were forced to address for the first time the specific question of what constituted a "group" as defined. Tutsis, after all, did not have any distinct racial, linguistic, or religious traits that separated them from Hutus. The Statute of the Tribunal did not include the killing of political opponents (which the Tutsi were accused of being as supporters of the RPF) under the rubric of "genocide." However, "decades of discrimination—by custom of patrilineal descent and by laws, such as that requiring cards that identified each person by ethnie, or ethnic group, of Hutu or Tutsi—had led the Tutsi to be regarded as a distinct, stable, permanent group" (Amann 1999, 196). Further, the Tribunal ruled that "the identification of persons as belonging to the group of Hutu or Tutsi had . . . become embedded in Rwandan culture" and was assigned from birth (ICTR Sept. 2, 1998, paragraph 171). Thus, the Tutsi qualified as a group under the Statute. Demonstrating that the government was engaged in a systematic attempt to eradicate Tutsis was a much simpler matter since the records showed planning, incitement, calculated efforts, systematic attacks, and so forth. Thus the Tribunal was able to rule that a genocide had occurred and that Akayesu was part of it.

This was the first time that the crime of genocide had been prosecuted. The Nuremberg and Tokyo tribunals addressed only war crimes, aggression, and the vaguely defined "crimes against humanity" since the Genocide Convention was not drafted until 1948. The Yugoslav war crimes tribunal, for its part, has had a far more difficult time convicting suspects of genocide since it has been more difficult to prove intent. The ruling has been praised for showing a reasonable degree of flexibility in interpreting the definition of a "group" without allowing too broad of a scope (Amann 1999, 198).

The other significant move by the Tribunal stemmed from the persuasive argumentation of Pierre Prosper, an American prosecutor, who argued that to "destroy" a group involved far more than killing. It could include stripping the group of its dignity and integrity. "Prosper believed that a group could physically exist, or escape extermination, but be left so marginalized or so irrelevant to society that it was, in effect, destroyed" (Power 2002, 486). Given this, the systematic rape and sexual abuse of Tutsi women constituted a crime against humanity tantamount to genocide. The Tribunal agreed and convicted Akayesu of rape and sexual assault—and went so far as to define rape more broadly than traditionally done in domestic criminal courts in an effort to clarify the coercive and even political nature of the act. He was also convicted of several counts of murder and one count of extermination, although he was acquitted of war crimes on the grounds he was not a military officer. He was sentenced to life in prison, which was upheld on appeal.

THE CASE OF JEAN KAMBANDA

Jean Kambanda was the acting prime minister in Rwanda during the period of the genocide. Although not necessarily the instigator or mastermind, he was clearly in a position to put a stop to the violence and chose not to. He was arrested in Kenya under pressure from the prosecutor and extradited to the Tribunal in July 1997. Upon his arrival, Kambanda pled guilty to all of the charges brought against him, including genocide, incitement to genocide, and various crimes against humanity—including extermination (ICTR Sept. 4, 1998). He provided considerable evidence of high-level planning of the genocide by the Rwandan authorities which has helped in other cases.

He was dismayed when the Tribunal sentenced him to life in prison since he was expecting leniency as a reward for his guilty plea and willingness to cooperate, and immediately appealed the sentence. The Appeals Chamber considered his complaint that the Tribunal had exceeded its discretion. The Chamber found that it had not, since the aggravating circumstances outweighed the mitigating circumstances. In other words, the seriousness of the crimes of genocide, incitement to genocide, extermination, and murder—combined with the defendant's extremely high position in the state and his authority over both civilian and military actors—outweighed the benefits of his help to the Tribunal. The sentence was upheld (Swaak-Goldman 2001).

OTHER CASES OF NOTE

In 1998, Major Bernard Ntuyahaga surrendered to the ICTR. He was promptly arrested and charged with a number of counts, including genocide, but most were thrown out by an ICTR judge. The prosecutor's office, discouraged by the lack of significance of the remaining charge (murder) in light of its aim of only going after the most prominent suspects in the genocide, decided to drop the remaining charge in February 1999. He requested instead that he be turned over to Belgium since the crime involved the deaths of Belgian peacekeepers. In a surprise move, the ICTR instead released him to Tanzanian authorities in March on the grounds that it lacked the powers to extradite an uncharged individual to a national court. Tanzania ultimately arrested him and then refused to extradite him to Belgium, causing an international incident. He ended up returning to Rwanda (Magnarella 2000, 66–69).

Jean-Bosco Baratagwiza was a prominent diplomat and senior official of a Hutu extremist party who directed the extermination of Tutsis in Gisenyi prefecture. He also played a major role in the RTLM station that issued the orders to kill Tutsis. He was duly charged with numerous crimes, including genocide, by the prosecutor's office of the ICTR. Cameroon, which had arrested him, extradited him to the ICTR where he was convicted of genocide, incitement to genocide, and crimes against humanity including extermination. He filed an appeal prior to the beginning of the trial, however, arguing that his arrest and detention in Cameroon on the ICTR's behalf were both illegal. The Appeals Chamber was sympathetic to his arguments and ruled for a halt to the proceedings against him. In fact, the ruling, which was later reversed on the basis of "new information," was aimed more at Prosecutor Arbour than the defendant. As put by Shabas, "the tone of the decision was shrill and self-righteous . . . [resulting in the ICTR's reputation in Rwanda reaching] a new low" (Shabas 2000, 566–567).

The Appeals Chamber has reversed a number of convictions and acquittals over the years. It has reduced some sentences and increased others as well, although on balance the judgment of the Tribunals has generally been validated.

ASSESSING THE ICTR

The ICTR has eleven cases involving twenty-seven individuals going as of June 2006 with the goal of prosecuting a score of additional suspects by the end of 2008 when its third term of office (or mandate) expires. Of special interest is the case involving Col. Bagosora which should be resolved in 2006. On the other hand, four of the cases were only begun in 2005 and 2006, which means they will probably not be resolved until 2007.

At the current pace, it seems likely that the ICTR will have ruled on cases involving a total of 70 cases by the end of 2008, although appeals will likely taken until 2009. This represents roughly half of the target. The Security Council will be forced to consider whether to offer the Tribunal a fourth mandate beyond 2008, which may or may not happen. Much depends on the verdict of the Tribunal itself.

Overall, in spite of frustration with the pace of proceedings, which stems from both the poor start in 1996 and the nature of the cases and procedures themselves, the fact remains that the Tribunal has convicted a fairly large number of the most prominent perpetrators of genocide. Its work pace is comparable to that of the International Criminal Tribunal for Yugoslavia and even that of many national criminal courts. Furthermore, the ICTR has been able to function without the more flamboyant and distracting performances seen in Nuremberg, The Hague, or in Baghdad where famous defendants such as Hermann Goering, Slobodan Milosevic, and Saddam Hussein, who used their respective situations to proclaim their innocence, rally the faithful and condemn the court itself. On the contrary, ICTR proceedings have been remarkably dull—a prosecutor's preferred scenario.

In addition, as previously noted, the ICTR has made law, advancing international agreement on the definition of genocide, rape, and so forth. Other tribunals, including the Yugoslav tribunal, have referred to the ICTR's reasoning in their own judgments.

But even if the verdict on the ICTR is generally positive, what of the general approach? Has the ICTR solved the problems Rwanda is facing? Some have pointed out that no RPF fighters have been indicted as of yet, even though it is well known that in the midst of the fighting in April–July 1994 they also committed atrocities against the Hutus (Kamatali 2005, 101). Unlike the Yugoslav tribunal which has prosecuted Croats, Serbs, and Muslims, the ICTR has opened itself up to the criticism of providing "victor's justice" —meaning that only those who lost the overall conflict are being held accountable for their misdeeds. This does little to mend fences between the parties in Rwanda.

For that matter, the Tribunal, by taking a punitive approach, does little to contribute to reconciliation—even if its justice were perfect. Punitive justice is likely to satisfy only one party. Any even at that, an alternative approach might be compensation rather than vengeance. In other words, require the guilty to pay some form of damages to the victims and their families, either with deeds or money, in order to restore the status quo (Kamatali 2005, 99). Finally, another approach to justice involve reconciliation—a remote possibility when it comes to genocide to be sure, but one which has been used to good effect at the South African Truth and Reconciliation Commission where perpetrators and victims confront each other in a quest for knowledge and mutual understanding. It could even lead to rehabilitation in the case of minor offenders.

Ultimately, the decision to prosecute involves a judgment about whether justice, peace, reconciliation, or some other objective should take precedence. And this is a question where philosophy and politics intersect.

DEBATE TOPIC

In cases of civil war, should the international community insist on prosecuting those who may have committed atrocities?

PRO

Those who favor justice in such situations generally argue the following: first, the international community has an interest in punishing the most egregious crimes, regardless of the political context. Second, punishing criminals can resolve some political issues by resolving some of the hostile feelings of the victims and their families. Third, the pursuit of justice usually brings important facts to light, so that future relations between the warring factions can be rooted in truth rather than myth or propaganda.

CON

Justice and peace are often irreconcilable by their very nature. In most places in the world where there is peace, it is because victims of past injustice have either forgiven the perpetrators or resigned themselves to the status quo. Justice does not bring about reconciliation and peace in and of itself, and can exacerbate tensions where those convicted believe there was a miscarriage of justice. Justice can produce martyrs that are used by the next generation of militants.

THINKING THEORETICALLY

Realists are generally skeptical of the value of international law, arguing that all justice is always victor's justice. They argue that not only are the rules interpreted and enforced by those who win the wars, but they are usually written and re-written by them to their own advantage. Law is simply a way to persuade weak states that the powerful are acting fairly. As we consider the case of the ICTR, we can see evidence that law operates partially in that no RPF suspects have been charged even though it is well known that they committed serious war crimes. For that matter, even the crime of genocide itself was defined by those states that prevailed in World War II, and was carefully crafted to condemn the Nazi Holocaust but not Stalin's purges.

Idealists are just as convinced that states can craft laws that are fair to all states and are enforced even-handedly. They see law as a place where power matters little (although they are not naïve as to its potential). They are quick to point out that even the great powers have often submitted to law, as we saw in the case of the United States voluntarily surrendering a suspect to the ICTR. To idealists, the problem is one of political will, coupled with good procedures and carefully worded agreements. They would be quick to hold up the ICTR as a model of law in service of justice and peace.

Questions to Consider

1. What might the international community do to make postconflict justice more fair and immediate? How would you organize a trial of someone charged with genocide?

2. Why is it so difficult to define and prosecute certain crimes under international law? What can the ICTR learn from national criminal legal systems?

3. Should the international community even be in the business of prosecuting war criminals? Isn't this best left to states that have sovereign rights over their citizens and territories?

Websites

The ICTR: http://69.94.11.53/default.htm
The ICTY: www.un.org/icty/
The ICC: www.icc-cpi.int
Analysis of the ICTR: www.globalpolicy.org/intIjustice/rwandaindx.htm
The United Nations: www.un.org

References

Amann, Diane Marie. "Prosecutor v. Akayesu. Case ICTR-96-4-T." *The American Journal of International Law* 93 #1 (January 1999): 195–199.

Dallaire, Romeo. *Shake Hands with the Devil: The Failure of Humanity in Rwanda* (New York: Carroll & Graf; 2003).

Eltringham, Nigel. *Accounting for Horror: Post-Genocide Debates in Rwanda.* (London: Pluto Press; 2004).

Gourevitch, Philip. *We Would Like to Inform You that Tomorrow We Will Be Killed with Our Families: Stories from Rwanda* (New York: Farrar Straus & Giroux; 1998).

ICTR. "The Prosecutor v. Jean-Paul Akayesu. Case No ICTR-96-4-T – Judgement," September 2, 1998.

ICTR. "The Prosecutor v. Jean Kambanda. Case No ICTR 97-23-S – Judgment and Sentence," September 4, 1998.

ICTR. "Achievements of the ICTR," 2006. Available at: http://69.96.11.53/ENGLISH/factsheets/achievements.htm.

Kamatali, Jean-Marie. "From the ICTR to ICC: Lessons from the ICTR Experience in Bringing Justice to Rwandans." *New England Journal of International and Comparative Law* 12 (Fall 2005): 89–103.

Magnarella, Paul J. *Justice in Africa: Rwanda's Genocide, Its Courts, and the UN Criminal Tribunal* (Aldershot, UK: Ashgate; 2000).

Moghalu, Kingsley Chiedu. "Image and Reality of War Crimes Justice: External Perception of the International Criminal Tribunal for Rwanda." *Fletcher Foreign of World Affairs* 26 (Fall 2002): 21–43.

Moghalu, Kingsley Chiedu. "International Humanitarian Law from Nuremberg to Rome: The Weighty Precedents of the International Criminal Tribunal for Rwanda." *Pace International Law Review* 14 (Fall 2002): 273–305.

Neuffer, Elizabeth. *The Key to My Neighbor's House: Seeking Justice in Bosnia and Rwanda* (New York: Picador; 2001).

Power, Samantha. *A Problem from Hell: America and the Age of Genocide* (New York: Perennial; 2002).

Shabas, William. "Baraygqiza v. Prosecutor (Decision, and Decision (Prosecutor's Request for Review or Reconsideration)) Case No. ICTR-97–19-AR72." *The American Journal of International Law* 94 #3 (July 2000): 563–571.

Swaak-Goldman, Olivia. "Kamdanda v. Prosecutor. No ICTR 97–23-A." *The American Journal of International Law* 95 #3 (July 2001): 656–661.

UN OIOS. "Audit and Investigation of the International Criminal Tribunal for Rwanda." UN Doc. A/51/789, February 6, 1997.

Yacoubian, George S., Jr. "Evaluating the Efficacy of the International Criminal Tribunals for Rwanda and the Former Yugoslavia: Implications for Criminology and International Criminal Law." *World Affairs* 165 #3 (Winter 2003): 133–151.

CASE 14

Apartheid in South Africa

INTRODUCTION

Human Rights

"Inalienable rights," a notion fundamental to the American system, means that people enjoy certain privileges simply by virtue of being human, and no government has the right to take those privileges away. Where the rights originated matters little; "inalienable" means that they came before governments were ever established. When we speak of "human rights" in international affairs, we are generally referring to those inalienable rights. They include not only the familiar freedom of speech, freedom from slavery and discrimination, and the right to participate in public life, but also rights with unique importance on the global level: self-determination, prohibition against genocide, and the right to peace. Over time, a consensus has developed on these and still other economic and social rights, such that countries that routinely and wantonly violate them are frequently the object of international censure.

This consensus has been expressed in the form of several important documents, the most celebrated of which is the Universal Declaration of Human Rights. This statement (not a binding law) was drafted shortly after World War II by representatives of more than fifty countries under the leadership of Eleanor Roosevelt, Franklin Roosevelt's widow. In it, governments agree that such fundamental civil rights as freedom of speech, thought, and assembly are paramount and that no government should restrict them without a strong public purpose. The document also declares that democracy and all its ancillary characteristics (elections, a free press, due process in the courtroom, and so forth) are the ideal form of government. The document further urges states to attend to the economic, social, and physical needs of their citizens, and it declares that all people have a right to such things as an education, housing, food, and employment.

Over the years, the rights enumerated in the Universal Declaration have been expanded upon and made more binding, such that today governments have gone so far as to intervene militarily to overthrow regimes that have repeatedly violated fundamental human rights in egregious ways (see Case 10). At the very least, many governments that have violated basic human rights have been subjected to diplomatic and economic penalties and sanctions. South Africans understand this relationship better than most.

> Either the white man dominates or the black man takes over. I say that the non-European will not accept leadership—if he has a choice. The only way the Europeans can maintain supremacy is by domination. . . . And the only way they can maintain domination is by withholding the vote from the non-Europeans. (Dr. Daniel F. Malan, South African Prime Minister, 1948–1954)
>
> We, the people of South Africa, declare for all our country and the world to know that South Africa belongs to all who live in it, black and white, and that no government can justly claim authority unless it is based on the will of all the people . . . that only a democratic state based on the will of all the people can secure their birthright without distinction of colour, race, sex or belief. . . . (Freedom Charter of the African National Congress, 1955)

These two quotes present the essence of the struggle in South Africa. Unlike the civil rights movement in the United States, South Africa pitted a minority in power against an overwhelming but largely powerless majority. That minority controlled most of the wealth, schools, businesses, and property of the country against the will of the majority. Moreover, that minority became more and more determined, during the middle part of this century, to maintain not only its power but also its exclusive right to citizenship in an ever more narrowly defined state.

Many misconceptions exist about the nature of apartheid, the policy of separation of the races in South Africa. Furthermore, there is much ignorance about the origins and basis for this national policy. Although the history that follows is extremely brief, we hope it will shed some light on this vital and burning issue of international politics.

KEY FIGURES
APARTHEID IN SOUTH AFRICA

Hendrik Verwoerd   Prime Minister of South Africa, 1958–1966. An avowed white supremacist, he was the principal architect of the apartheid laws.

P. W. Botha   Prime Minister of South Africa, 1979–1989. He began the process of dismantling the apartheid laws after imposing martial law.

F. W. de Klerk   Prime Minister of South Africa, 1989–1994. He ended apartheid.

Daniel Malan   Prime Minister of South Africa, 1948–1954, and former Dutch Reformed Church minister.

Sol Plaatje   Founder of the African National Congress in 1912.

Nelson Mandela   Leader of the African National Congress, he was imprisoned for 27 years under apartheid. He became the first president of postapartheid South Africa, 1994–1999.

Steve Biko   Black Consciousness activist and founder of SASO. He was arrested and died in prison in 1976.

Mangasuthu Buthelezi   Ruler of the KwaZulu nation and leader of the Inkatha Party.

Walter Sisulu   A leader of the ANC.

Allan Boesak   Founder of the United Democratic Front in 1983.

Jan Smuts   Afrikaner general in the Boer War, and later political leader and Prime Minister of the Union (later Republic) of South Africa, 1919–1924.

Desmond Tutu   Roman Catholic Archbishop in South Africa. He fought apartheid and led the Truth and Reconciliation Commission under Mandela.

CHRONOLOGY
APARTHEID IN SOUTH AFRICA

1652
South African area is claimed and settled by Dutch.

1815
The British purchase the Cape Colony and establish a governmental presence. They begin discriminating against native African tribes and Dutch-born Boer settlers. A dispute leads to the killing of British troops and the hanging of their Boer attackers at Slachter's Nek.

1837
Thousands of Boers migrate inland in the beginning of the Great Trek.

1838
Piet Retief's Boers defeat a large Zulu army. Afrikaners see it as a sign of God's protection.

1867
Diamonds and other minerals are discovered in Kimberly.

1875
The first apartheid laws exclude blacks from diamond mine ownership. Later, they would exclude blacks from gold-mining profits in Johannesburg in the 1880s.

1899
British settlers under Alfred Milner begin a war to displace Afrikaners. The Boer War lasts until 1902, when Afrikaners surrender.

1910
The Union of South Africa under British dominance is formed.

1912
The African National Congress is formed to protect fast-eroding rights for nonwhites.

(continued)

(*continued*)

1918
Black workers strike and are arrested en masse.

1922
Two hundred Afrikaner miners were killed in government attempts to quell labor unrest.

1924
Afrikaner politicians gain significant electoral victories, speeding up passage of antiblack legislation.

1936
Blacks are no longer allowed to vote.

1948
Afrikaners control the South African government for the first time. They issue a Declaration of Grand Apartheid.

1950s
The government of Prime Minister Daniel Malan passes a series of apartheid laws, including the Population Registration Act, the Separate Amenities Act, the Bantu Authorities Act, and the Prohibition of Mixed Marriages Act.

1952
The ANC leads a series of antiapartheid demonstrations that turn violent.

1955
The Freedom Charter is passed at the Congress of the People. Many ANC leaders are imprisoned.

1960
The ANC is outlawed. A Pan-African Congress demonstration is suppressed in what is known as the Sharpeville Massacre.

1968
The South African Student Organization is founded by Steve Biko.

1973
The UN General Assembly passes the International Convention on the Suppression and Punishment of the Crime of Apartheid.

1976
Soweto riots result in 600 deaths. Steve Biko is killed while in police custody.

1977
The Sullivan principles are articulated, urging multinational corporations operating in South Africa to promote racial justice in the workplace.

1983
Outdoor meetings of blacks are banned.

1984
Two nonwhite national assemblies are created under a new constitution. Unrest in Sharpeville prompts the government to declare a state of emergency in 1985.

1985
Struggling under international economic sanctions, South African business leaders openly support the black franchise.

1987
Liberal whites form the National Democratic Movement in response to the increasingly hard-line attitude of the Afrikaner Conservative Party.

1989
P. W. Botha resigns the prime minister's post. F. W. de Klerk becomes prime minister and begins dismantling the apartheid laws.

1990
Nelson Mandela is released from prison after 27 years.

1992
The ANC is fully legalized. CODESA begins planning a new constitution.

1993
CODESA produces a draft constitution that is accepted by the Parliament. Mandela and de Klerk win the Nobel Peace Prize.

1994
Nelson Mandela is elected president of South Africa.

1996
The New South African Constitution is formally signed into law by Nelson Mandela in Sharpeville.

1998
The Truth and Reconciliation Commission issues its final report.

1999
Thabo Mbeki is elected to succeed Mandela.

2002
South Africa hosts the United Nations Conference on Racism.

ORIGINS OF SOUTH AFRICA: 1652–1910

Beginning in the days of Magellan, the Cape of Good Hope was recognized as a useful waystation for travelers between Europe and India. The Dutch first decided in 1652 to establish a permanent claim and settlement under the leadership of Jan van Riebeeck. He almost immediately set about establishing a viable farming colony populated by "freeburghers" (pioneer farmers), which extended into the neighboring territory. Native black tribes opposed this encroachment, which prompted van Riebeeck to assert white superiority by force. Within fifty years, black slaves from other African territories were imported to expand the farming capacity of the colony. "Thus he persuaded the company to take the four decisions that shaped

South Africa: to found the colony, to settle freeburghers, to establish superiority over the local tribes and to import slaves" (Lapping 1986, 4).

By the end of the eighteenth century, the Dutch were unable to control overseas territories because they were under attack by Napoleon's France. The British first protected and then purchased the Cape Colony in 1815, dispatching a colonial administration to govern the settlement. They introduced "pass laws" for the first time, which obliged the nomadic African Khoikhoi to carry a written "pass" proving their association with a particular Dutch settler. The British presence was resented from the start by the now-independent Dutch settlers, or Boers ("farmers"). In 1815, while carrying out an arrest order against several Boers, a British detachment was attacked. The offending Boers were arrested and later hanged at Slachter's Nek—an event that served as a symbol of British authoritarianism (Lapping 1986, 10).

British officialdom became ever more ubiquitous as English-speaking missionaries attempted to establish schools for both Afrikaner (descendants of Dutch settlers) and black children. Ultimately, the Boers decided that they could no longer tolerate the imposition of British culture and power, and they embarked on one of the great migrations of people in history: the Great Trek. In 1837, some 6,000 Afrikaners began moving both eastward along the coast and some 800 miles northward into largely unpopulated wilderness to found a new homeland for themselves. The principal concentrations were in the area south of the current city of Johannesburg in the Orange Free State and along the coast near modern-day Durban in Natal province. By 1854, some 10,000 Afrikaners and an equal number of colored and black servants had migrated from Cape Colony toward what would become the heart of South Africa.

White South African propaganda maintains that the Boers arrived in an unpopulated territory where blacks later migrated (in part drawn by the prosperity of the whites) (Republic of South Africa 1973, 10). In fact, not only does ample archaeological evidence reveal a substantial African presence before the Great Trek, but the Zulu nation under Shaka Zulu had already advanced far into the same territory and engaged in several bloody skirmishes with the advancing Boers. The most famous skirmish involved trekker Piet Retief who, after being tricked by a Zulu interpreter, was cornered along with his pioneers by several thousand Zulu warriors on December 15, 1838. By virtue of their position against a mountain pass, the Boers were able to protect their rear and face the Zulus with overwhelming firepower. While 3,000 Zulus were killed, not a single Boer perished. Many Afrikaners attribute the Boers' success to a covenant with God entered into the day before, offering Afrikaner devotion and piety in exchange for victory (Lapping 1986, 16). (They also promised to build a church, which was later converted to a stable.)

The Boers eked out a living during the first years after their trek, but in 1867 mineral discoveries began to rapidly alter the character of their nation. Rapid population growth following the discovery of diamonds in Kimberly, in the western Orange Free State, overwhelmed the underequipped British authorities, who quickly moved en masse to administer the territory. Famous explorers, financiers, and speculators from across the empire converged on the area and made easy fortunes. Cecil Rhodes became one of the richest men in the world by purchasing numerous apparently dry wells from impatient excavators—the holes actually contained billions of dollars worth of diamonds.

Within ten years, the British government, with Afrikaner urging, established race-based laws to govern the ownership of diamond mines. As put by Brown: "The momentous step in the development of apartheid occurred in 1867 when diamonds were discovered along the Orange and Vaal rivers. . . . [I]n 1875 the right to own and operate a diamond concession was permitted only to whites" (Brown 1981, 59). From 1875 on, the blacks of South Africa were effectively excluded from profiting from the most promising opportunity to come to the African continent until the oil strikes in Libya. Instead, they were relegated to the status of mere laborers. The same was true for gold mining after it started around Johannesburg in 1880.

A radical interpretation does not seem out of place:

Whenever superior races settle on lands where lower races can be profitably used for manual labour in agriculture, mining and domestic work, the latter do not tend to die out, but to form a servile class. This is the case, not only in tropical countries where white men cannot form real colonies, working and rearing families with safety and efficiency, and where hard manual work, if done at all, must be done by "coloured men," but even in countries where white men can settle, as in part of South Africa and of the southern portion of the United States. (Hobson 1965, 258, in Magubane 1979, 8)

As further explained by Magubane:

South Africa is not a plural society; it is a society with a dual labor market: a primary (white) market of relatively secure, well-paid jobs, and a secondary (black) market of insecure, filthy, low-paid jobs. African workers are confined to a marginal, yet indispensable, role by fraud, violence, and a system of institutionalized racism that protects "the white masters of the world." (Magubane 1979, 17)

As the end of the century neared, the struggle for control of gold and diamonds in the heart of South Africa continued to intensify. Although the British were able to establish clear control in the Kimberly area, Afrikaners held out in the Orange Free State and farther to the north in the Transvaal, where the plucky Boer Paul Kruger retained control in 1899 after three abortive British seizures. In 1899, a new British governor, Alfred Milner, embarked on a systematic, all-out effort to dislodge the independent Afrikaners from the Transvaal and elsewhere in the north by deploying a large British army into the region. The Boer War that ensued lasted nearly three years and caused tens of thousands of casualties. In particular, the British introduced "concentration camps" by capturing thousands of women and children and interring them in tent cities across the region, where disease and malnutrition took some 26,000 civilian lives. In the countryside, the British practiced a "scorched earth" policy to deprive the Boer guerrillas of finding sustenance from the land (Lapping 1986, 31).

After the Boers finally surrendered in 1902, the British moved to consolidate their gains by inviting more British settlers into the country and establishing a united federal state with the consent of the Afrikaners in the Transvaal and the

Orange Free State (a form of expansive home rule tantamount to independence was offered as an inducement). A new generation of Afrikaner politicians, led by Jan Smuts and Louis Botha, embraced the British offers. In 1910, the Union of South Africa was proclaimed a part of the British Empire.

ESTABLISHMENT AND CONSOLIDATION OF APARTHEID: 1910–1965

Part of the deal made with the Afrikaners involved British concessions on social policy. A series of race-related laws guaranteeing Afrikaner superiority was implemented in the 1910s. Before discussing the details of these and other laws, we will look at the philosophy and social norms that undergird apartheid.

The Afrikaners held that their presence in South Africa was more than merely a coincidence of human migration—rather it was the product of divine intervention on behalf of the white race. Dr. Daniel Malan, prime minister in 1948–1954 and former Dutch Reformed Church minister, declared:

> We hold this nationhood as our due, for it was given us by the architect of the universe. His aim was the formation of a new nation. The last hundred years have witnessed a miracle behind which must lie a divine plan. Afrikanerdom is not the work of men but the creation of God. . . . Not because we Afrikaners are tremendously good people, but because God, the Disposer of the lot of the nations, has a future task for our People. (Lapping 1986, 66)

Malan "made the attempt with as ambitious—or ridiculous—a claim as any politician has ever made: that God's destiny for the Afrikaner people, the reason he had chosen them, punished them, saved them, was to preserve the white race" (Lapping 1986, 71).

Shortly after the consolidation of the republic, the Transvaal and Orange Free State enacted a number of restrictive racial policies. In particular, new pass laws forced blacks, "coloreds" (blacks originally imported from other parts of Africa), and a growing Indian immigrant population to carry identification cards at all times. Failure to produce the pass when confronted by a police officer typically resulted in incarceration. Controls on physical movement were combined with continued restrictions on property ownership, and severe limitations on nonwhite suffrage prompted protests and petitions by certain educated blacks, four of whom formed the African National Congress (ANC) in 1912. These Africans asked little more than a retention of certain rights they had been granted prior to 1910 as British subjects. They failed to get a hearing with the king in 1913 under the leadership of Sol Plaatje. In the meantime, the Native Lands Act was passed in London, thereby creating a system of reservations for blacks—some 7.3 percent of South Africa's poorest land was designated for the more than 60 percent of the population that was black. Rather than alienate the newly pacified Afrikaners, the monarchy and Parliament in London refused to reverse the policy.

An important parallel development occurred in the Indian community, where Mohandes Gandhi, the advocate of nonviolent resistance and future leader of India, organized a series of demonstrations against pass laws and property restrictions. Although for a time he was successful in securing a softening of pass law enforcement, the effort was fairly short-lived (Lapping 1986, 49).

In the 1920s and 1930s, relations among Africans, Afrikaners, and the English deteriorated. Black worker strikes in 1918, born of frustration with the failure of the ANC accommodation, led to massive arrests. Meanwhile, the Afrikaner workers protested and struck over the limited promotions some black mine workers received (some whites were passed over by British managers), and in 1922 Prime Minister Jan Smuts ordered troops to quell the disturbance. Some 200 Afrikaner miners were killed in the ensuing action. The event led to an electoral victory for pro-Afrikaner militants in 1924, which in turn led to strengthened white worker rights and eventual removal of the limited black electoral franchise by 1936.

Black workers began to adopt an increasingly militant style in the 1940s. By 1944, Anton Lembede had organized the Youth League, loosely affiliated with the ANC, and began training what would become the next generation of ANC leadership: Nelson Mandela, Walter Sisulu, and Oliver Tambo (Lapping 1986, 82). They adopted a more consciously pro-black, anticapitalist philosophy and urged violence and widespread action against the white government.

Conservative Afrikaner politicians latched onto the misery of the Depression with its attendant anti-British and anti-Jew fearfulness and the symbolism surrounding the centennial of the Great Trek to catapult themselves into power in the 1948 elections—the first to produce an all-Afrikaner cabinet. The importance of the 1948 election cannot be exaggerated. At the same time the United States was working to desegregate the military, schools, and all public facilities, the Afrikaner government in South Africa embarked on a program to introduce and intensify racial separation. In 1950, Prime Minister Malan appointed Dr. Hendrik F. Verwoerd minister of native affairs. Verwoerd, in this position and later as prime minister until his assassination in 1966, was the single most important architect of apartheid (Lapping 1986, 106).

Verwoerd's legislative strategy took a systematic approach to separating the races. The Population Registration Act set out to classify every resident of South Africa by race. It then "empowered the government to mark off areas for residence, occupation and trade by the different races and then to move each race into its own area, by force if necessary" (Lapping 1986, 105). This basic classification was refined and clarified over the years, although as recently as 1985, nearly 800 people had their racial classifications legally changed. The Prohibition of Mixed Marriages Act ensured racial purity in mainstream family relations, while the Immorality Amendment Act of 1957 outlawed any intercourse whatever between individuals of different races.

Verwoerd was famous for his promotion of the status and symbolic powers of black tribal leaders across South Africa. He promoted himself as the great "Bantu" (Native African) chief of chiefs and joined the tribal leaders in elaborate

ceremonies reaffirming their legitimacy as rulers of black nations. The South
African government began to emphasize differences among the various black tribes:

> In a nutshell, the inescapable feature of the South African situation is that South
> Africa is a country of many nations: Four million whites of European origin, four
> million Xhosa, four million Zulu, two million Tswana, two million Sotho and so on.
> Each group is a minority—there is in fact no single majority group. (Republic of
> South Africa 1973, 29)

Verwoerd hoped to accomplish the dual goal of undermining black solidarity and
creating a vast network of black supporters of the white Pretoria regime. In this
context, the Bantu Authorities Act of 1951 designated specific homelands for each
of ten major African tribes that resided in South Africa (see Map 14.1). Regardless of

Map 14.1 The Homelands

where members of these various tribes happened to be living at the time, the government expected that they would migrate to their areas and away from white cities. In these territories, the black leaders were permitted control of certain governmental functions (subsidized often to the tune of 75 percent of their budgets by Pretoria) and "tribal citizens" could exercise their right to vote. South African citizenship was denied, however. In the late 1960s, a few of these homelands were granted independence by the Pretoria government (Transkei in 1976, Bophuthatswana in 1977, Venda in 1979, and Ciskei in 1981), although this move did little to change their government other than reinforce the separate legal status of homelands residents. As put by one of Verwoerd's successors in a speech before Parliament:

> If our policy is taken to its logical conclusion as far as the black people are concerned, there will not be one black man with South African citizenship. . . . Every black man in South Africa will eventually be accommodated in some independent new state in this honourable way and there will no longer be a moral obligation on this parliament to accommodate these people politically. (Omond 1985, 102)

In this context, Verwoerd argued that education was to be strictly controlled and segregated:

> Native education should be controlled in such a way that it should be in accord with the policy of the state. . . . If the native in South Africa today in any kind of school in existence is being taught to expect that he will live his adult life under a policy of equal rights, he is making a big mistake. . . . There is no place for him in the European community above the level of certain forms of labor. (Omond 1985, 80)

Lemon has pointed out that South Africa is one of the only countries where the educational system for a majority of its citizens is specifically designed to restrict, rather than create opportunities by limiting them to a homeland-specific training (Lemon 1987, 52). This policy was later extended to the university level.

In general terms, living conditions for blacks were deplorable, so the government had to adopt very aggressive measures to force as many Africans as possible to relocate to their respective homelands. Over a five-year period, many thousands of blacks were moved out of white neighborhoods. The elderly and infirm were specifically targeted for removal. As put by one of Verwoerd's successors in 1967:

> It is accepted government policy that the Bantu are only temporarily resident in the European areas of the Republic for as long as they offer their labour there. As soon as they become, for one reason or another, no longer fit to work or superfluous in the labour market, they are expected to return to their country of origin or the territory of the national unit where they fit ethnically. (Lapping 1986, 154)

By 1980, roughly half of black Africans were residing in the Bantustans—the end result of thirty years of government effort (Lemon 1987, 199). Estimates indicated that as many as 3.5 million people were relocated in connection with the Native Lands Act during the 1980s, with another 1.8 million being vulnerable to future expulsion (Omond 1985, 114).

A variety of laws, including restricted property rights, intensified pass laws, and the Separate Amenities Act of 1953, which prohibited multiracial use of public facilities, were passed and enforced with great vigor.

These actions created a large migrant worker population in South Africa. The mere relocation of workers did little to spur the relocation of the workplace. In 1970, some 1 million blacks were forced to migrate to work. That figure had increased to 1.4 million by 1982 (Lemon 1987, 199). Such an imposed lifestyle wreaked havoc on the black family:

> From the standpoint of the homelands and their people, the economic and social disadvantages of the migrant labour system are overwhelming. Socially, the break-up of family life and impediments to normal sexual relationships affect some of the most basic human needs . . . illegitimacy, bigamy, prostitution, homosexuality, drunkenness, violence and the breakdown of parental authority [are] direct effects of the system, whilst venereal disease, tuberculosis, malnutrition and beriberi are some of the indirect results of the lifestyle of migrant laborers. Men are degraded by a system which deprives them of a family role, whilst women are left behind feeling lonely and helpless, anxiously waiting for letters and money from their husbands. (Lemon 1987, 200)

Not all blacks accepted the new order. The ANC attracted an increasingly diverse assortment of followers—coloreds, Indians, Communists, academics—with a leadership under growing pressure to radicalize the movement. Albert Luthuli, ANC leader in the 1950s, was cautious about radical demands and worked to keep the ANC legal and able to work with the government. In 1952, the ANC initiated what was expected to be a series of peaceful demonstrations and civil disobedience gestures as part of this moderate approach. The campaign degenerated into a series of melees between police and passersby untrained in nonviolent techniques. The government cracked down on ANC leaders, restricting their travel to their own neighborhoods. Although the ANC consequently lost stature with the government, its membership grew from a mere 7,000 to some 100,000 (Lapping 1986, 119).

In 1955, the organization held a momentous Congress of the People to protest apartheid laws and draft a plan of action. The Freedom Charter was the result of the Congress's desire for a democratic, multiracial South Africa. In addition to civil rights, the Freedom Charter called for land reform, labor rights, and redistribution of wealth to "the people as a whole." It represented the most radical and united statement by blacks in South Africa's history and became a rallying cry for all opponents of apartheid.

The South African government, dismayed at the apparent power of the ANC as an alternative political order, responded ferociously. The leaders of the ANC were declared traitors to the state and were imprisoned. As a direct consequence, the world's attention was drawn even more sharply to the plight of blacks in South Africa. A lengthy and bitter trial ensued under the glaring eye of international public opinion. The government's prosecutor bungled the charges of treason and Communist sympathies, instead creating ideal opportunities for the ANC leaders to make their own case publicly, clearly, and eloquently. Nelson Mandela presented himself as the indignant lawyer and future leader of the ANC with this scathing attack on the legitimacy of the proceedings:

> Firstly, I challenge it because I fear that I will not be given a fair and proper trial. Secondly, I consider myself neither legally nor morally bound to obey laws made by a parliament in which I have no representation. In a political trial such as this one, which involves a clash of the aspirations of the African people and those of whites, the country's courts, as presently constituted, cannot be impartial and fair. In such cases, whites are interested parties. To have a white judicial officer presiding, however high his esteem, and however strong his sense of fairness and justice, is to make whites judges in their own case. . . . The white man makes all the laws, he drags us before his courts and accuses us, and he sits in judgment over us. . . . I feel oppressed by the atmosphere of white domination that lurks all around in this courtroom. Somehow this atmosphere calls to mind the inhuman injustices caused to my people outside this courtroom by this same white domination. (Mandela 1990, 134)

In the end, all of the accused were acquitted, primarily because of prosecutorial incompetence.

Having failed to achieve its goal through the use of laws then on the books, the government, now under Verwoerd himself, adopted new laws. The ANC was included among outlaw organizations under the 1960 Unlawful Organization Act. By 1963, such prominent ANC leaders as Walter Sisulu, Nelson Mandela, Robert Sobukwe, and Oliver Tambo were imprisoned or forced into exile.

The 1960 Sharpeville Massacre was a case of police impatience. The Pan-African Congress, a black organization with more radical objectives than the ANC, organized a demonstration of 5,000 people in what was thought to be a model township. However, unemployment, dissatisfaction with the pass laws, and forced migration had created intense hostility with the white government. The marchers surrounded a police station, where they waited for most of the day. Then a scuffle broke out, the crowd surged forward, and the police began shooting into the throng. Nearly 100 blacks were killed—most of them in the back—in the ensuing chaos. Luthuli called for a day of work stoppage and peaceful protest, which the government in turn repressed by arresting 18,000 strikers across the country. New laws permitted the government to detain suspects indefinitely with a judge's approval and to detain for interrogation anyone the police wanted. The Public Safety Act allowed the government to declare a state of emergency and thereby suspend most of the few remaining civil rights in specific areas for limited but renewable periods of time (Omond 1985, 158). By 1963, South Africa was reviled in international circles as the worst human rights violator on the planet.

STALEMATE: 1965–1988

The period from 1965 to 1988 can be described as a stalemate between a galvanized but largely leaderless black community and an increasingly ambivalent white government unable to maintain both social domination and economic prosperity. The inflexible apartheid of the Verwoerd era was inherently unstable. While it protected the white population from association with blacks, it deprived the nation of its most important asset: black labor and intellect. At best, black Africans were learning to manipulate the system for their own ends—hardly the basis for legitimate government (Lambley 1980, 125). Even more serious was the impact of increasingly strict international economic and diplomatic sanctions on the vitality of the South African economy. These objective conditions would ultimately force the white government to reverse most of apartheid's structures during the 1980s and begin the process of democratizing the country in the 1990s.

A leaderless black community drifted for much of the 1960s, when new philosophies and organizational structures began to emerge. Steve Biko, a black medical student in Natal province worked to form an all-black student group known as the South African Student Organization in 1968. Steve Biko put it eloquently:

> Black Consciousness is an attitude of mind and a way of life. . . . Its essence is the realization by the black man of the need to rally together with his brothers around the cause of their oppression—the blackness of their skin—and to operate as a group to rid themselves of the shackles that bind them to perpetual servitude. It is based on a self-examination which has ultimately led them to believe that by seeking to run away from themselves and emulate the white man, they are insulting the intelligence of whoever created them black. This philosophy of Black Consciousness therefore expresses group pride and the determination of the black to rise and attain the envisaged self. . . . (Fatton 1986, 78)

In the context of the spread of this Black Consciousness movement, black students across South Africa protested their forced education in Afrikaans in the 1970s. In Soweto, an overcrowded township near Johannesburg where many black intellectuals resided, feelings were particularly strong and spilled over into large demonstrations. In June 1976, protests swelled to tens of thousands. On one occasion, the police fired into the crowd, which then went on a rampage through neighboring black and white areas for several days. In the end, nearly 600 black protesters were killed and some 3,000 wounded. The police incarcerated and beat numerous individuals, not the least of whom was Steve Biko himself, who died following police beatings.

Government repression intensified even as leaders of the Nationalist Party, which ruled South Africa for most of the century, began to reconsider the long-term viability of apartheid. Executions of blacks increased from roughly 50 each year in the mid-1970s to 125 per year in 1977–1980 (Omond 1985, 144). Outdoor meetings were banned selectively at first and then outright in 1983. Declarations of states of emergency became more common and travel restrictions intensified.

On the other hand, the new prime minister, P. W. Botha, began to seriously consider relaxing apartheid laws as early as 1979 in the face of growing opposition in the South African business community. Business leaders pointed out that the economy would thrive best if the work force—largely black—was stable and content and if blacks could become affluent enough to provide a market for goods made in South Africa (St. Jorre 1986, 63). Foreign firms operating in compliance with the voluntary pro–civil rights standard known as the "Sullivan principles" were proving that a policy of racial equality in the workplace could increase both productivity and profitability.

In the early 1980s, several regulations were passed that loosened some of the more "purely irritating" aspects of apartheid, including the laws against interracial marriage. The number of blacks admitted to white universities increased, restrictions on black job advancement relaxed, and pass laws became more permissive (Omond 1985, 47, 85). In 1984, a new constitution provided for the election of two new nonwhite assemblies. Reverend Allan Boesak of the newly formed United Democratic Front (UDF), a loose coalition of moderate antiapartheid organizations, warned prospective Indian voters in 1983:

> Working within the system for whatever reason contaminates you. It wears down your defenses. It whets your appetite for power. . . . And what you call "compromise" for the sake of politics is in fact selling out your principles, your ideals and the future of your children. . . . (Lapping 1986, 171)

Other moves toward relaxation of apartheid did little to satisfy blacks. The ANC continued to grow in popularity and strength, subsuming the Black Consciousness movement in 1984 and attracting the endorsement of even the United Democratic Front moderates (Brewer 1986, 274).

In Sharpeville in 1984, black residents protested proposed rent and bus fare increases by targeting black administrators in the area. Violence spread rapidly as many collaborators were subjected to the "necklace" (a tire, doused in gasoline, placed around the victim's neck and set on fire). Unable to control the unrest, the government declared a state of emergency (particularly around Port Elizabeth) in July 1985 (Lemon 1987, 339). Eight thousand people were arrested in the first year and more than 750 killed by police and army forces. The army quickly gained a reputation for brutality by beating and electrocuting detainees on their way to prison. Children were specifically targeted during this period—many of them shot in the back while fleeing the soldiers. Children incarcerated under the state of emergency were, like their adult counterparts, subjected to torture, beating, terror, and often death (Lawyers 1986, 6–8). Efforts to have children receive medical treatment at hospitals were frustrated by the police practice of arresting any injured patients—thus many died without treatment after being shot during a demonstration. Likewise, attempts by physicians to reveal the extent of prison violence were halted by official cover-ups. The state of emergency was extended several times until it began to be lifted piecemeal in 1989 and 1990. Thirty more antiapartheid groups were banned, including the UDF, and some 50,000 individuals were detained from 1985 to 1988.

White South Africans were divided to the breaking point over the pace and direction of reform. Racist Afrikaners broke with the National Party to form the Conservative Party, which soon became the major opposition in Parliament and activated a latent vigilante organization—the Afrikaner Resistance Movement. Conservative Party leader Andries Treurnicht defiantly declared:

> People who think that Mr. Botha's "crossing of the Rubicon" and his abdication of white government mean the end of the Afrikaner and broader white nationalism are making a big mistake. We will not allow the Oppenheimers and American pressure groups to create a potpourri of people or to establish a nonracial economic empire upon the ruins of a white Christian culture and civilization. A people is only conquered when it has destroyed its own spirit. We are not prepared to consider national suicide . . . no one will silence the awakening white nation. The battle for the return of our political self-determination has only just begun. (Treurnicht 1986, 100)

Liberal white politicians increasingly joined antiapartheid parties—particularly after the state of emergency began in 1985. This culminated in the formation of the National Democratic movement in 1987. Botha's political support was thus threatened from both the left and the right until in 1989 he felt compelled to resign his post.

International sanctions intensified during the mid-1980s, including disinvestment by numerous foreign firms operating in the country. By the end of the decade, some $12 billion in foreign investment had been withdrawn or sold to local investors (in soft local currency that was of no use in repaying mounting foreign debts). International banks, bending to pressure from institutional depositors and shareholders and universities, city governments, and pensions, began to impose conditions of political reform on debt rescheduling. By 1989, the net effect of these sanctions was that the South African economy, according to local independent estimates, was 15 percent smaller than it should have otherwise been.

To express their dismay in 1985, 91 South African business leaders took out an ad in the country's largest newspaper, calling for "the granting of full South African citizenship to all our people." Still others met with Walter Sisulu, leader-in-exile of the banned ANC, at his headquarters in Zambia to discuss dismantling apartheid (Mann 1988, 81).

DISMANTLING APARTHEID: 1989–1994

Following Botha's resignation in 1989, the new government of F.W. de Klerk moved aggressively to dismantle the most disturbing and fundamental aspects of apartheid, in spite of growing white violence and continuing black violence.

Between 1989 and 1991, the legislative keystones of apartheid were removed one by one: the Group Areas Act, the Separate Amenities Act, the Population Registration Act, and various provisions barring peaceful political assembly and organization. The state of emergency was lifted throughout much of the country (although continuing unrest may well have justified retaining the provision in certain areas), and police powers were circumscribed. Perhaps most dramatic of all, Nelson Mandela was released from prison in February 1990, shortly after Walter Sisulu was released and less than a year before Oliver Tambo, president of the ANC, returned to South Africa after a thirty-year exile.

As put by Payne:

> By removing most of apartheid's legal underpinnings by June 1991, with the notable exception of black voting rights, South Africa had made a major and largely unanticipated first step toward creating a relatively egalitarian and nonracial society. The overwhelming white support in the March 1992 referendum for de Klerk's reforms underscored the commitment to change. Dismantling the more intractable social and economic components of a legal system of racial domination into which all South Africans had been socialized for almost half a century was clearly a more Herculean endeavor. Nonetheless, the vast majority of South Africans had embraced a hopeful but uncertain future. (Payne 1992, 149)

The political processes at work in South Africa centered on the Convention for a Democratic South Africa (CODESA), a constitutional convention that brought together nearly all black and most white parties and the homelands governments. Although some parties rejected the legitimacy of the exercise, it had the full backing of the government, the Inkatha Party, and the ANC. A referendum of white voters in February 1992 revealed that an overwhelming majority supported the CODESA efforts to establish a fully democratic government in South Africa. The result went far to marginalize white conservatives, who felt compelled to join the process. The funerals of Afrikaner nationalist Andries Treurnicht and black Communist leader Chris Hani in April 1993 were a study in contrasts, with tens of thousands mourning Hani and only a few hundred turning out for Treurnicht.

Events in September and October of 1993 dramatically changed the prospects for a peaceful transition to democracy for South Africa. The CODESA process reached its conclusion with the drafting of a federal-style constitution, which was expected to be ratified by the white-controlled Parliament. Prior to that, a "supercabinet" consisting of representatives from each party involved in the CODESA had been proposed, accepted by Parliament, and organized to control the National Party's cabinet during the transition (*New York Times* September 24, 1993, A1). The "transitional executive council" (TEC) had the power to override de Klerk's government to assure fairness in the national elections set for April 27, 1994. These remarkable steps forward resulted in an end to the sweeping economic and diplomatic boycotts imposed on South Africa by the United Nations, the Organization for African Unity, the Commonwealth, and the European Community, not to mention the United States. Loans and investments were expected to flow freely into South Africa to take advantage of the end of sanctions (*Christian Science Monitor* 1993). As recognition for their achievement, Nelson Mandela and Frederick de Klerk were awarded the Nobel Peace Prize in mid-October.

These historic achievements were not just the beginning of South Africa's healing, but also marked an intensified and broader conflict. The ANC–Inkatha rivalry intensified as black-on-black violence resulted in an average of ten deaths each day. A short-lived show of solidarity by Mandela and Buthelezi collapsed into mutual recriminations as Buthelezi pulled his Inkatha Freedom Party out of CODESA. He demanded virtual autonomy for the KwaZulu region he governed— something Mandela was unwilling to grant. Blacks in Buthelezi's native Natal province were split in their support of the ANC and Inkatha, and many saw Buthelezi's efforts as a last-ditch attempt to retain some degree of power.

In April 1994, black, white, and colored South Africans voted in what was universally described as a peaceful, fair, and open election. The ANC won 63 percent of the vote. On May 10, 1994, Nelson Mandela was sworn in as South Africa's president.

POSTAPARTHEID SOUTH AFRICA

The inauguration ceremony of Nelson Mandela was a mixture of pomp and party. He declared:

> We enter into a covenant that we shall build a society in which all South Africans, both black and white, will be able to walk tall, without any fear in their hearts, assured of their inalienable right to human dignity—a rainbow nation at peace with itself and the world. . . . Never, never, never again shall it be that this beautiful land will again experience the oppression of one by another. . . . (Sparks 1999, 66)

Following Mandela's speech, jets and helicopters flew over the crowd, trailing the colors of the new flag to the tune of a new national anthem. Emotions ran high as the world witnessed a rare peaceful transition from authoritarian to democratic regime.

Ten years have passed since that momentous event, and many report cards have been written about the Mandela period. First and foremost, he is given high marks for carrying out a peaceful and orderly change of government, particularly given the risks involved. He bent over backward to accommodate white concerns, particularly by using a consensus approach to decision making during the two-year period of Government of National Unity, when all major parties had a seat in the cabinet. He introduced a moderate budget, limited social welfare programs (which required considerable fine-tuning) to alleviate black poverty, and worked to open South Africa's economy to the world along liberal principles (Brent 1996). Gone were the threats of large-scale nationalization and Marxist policies. Political violence came to a virtual standstill. With his introduction of a Truth and Reconciliation Commission under the leadership of Desmond Tutu, Mandela also moved to resolve long-standing grievances of blacks and whites alike. The commission's report, issued in late 1998, offered a mountain of evidence from those who confessed to human rights abuses in exchange for amnesty that the National Party was guilty of systematic atrocities and abuses. But the black parties also came under attack—which prompted ANC and Inkatha Freedom Party leaders to condemn the report. Perhaps the greatest victory came on June 16, 1999, when Mandela's appointed ANC successor, Thabo Mbeki, won the presidency with 66 percent of the vote—a margin even greater than Mandela's. Although he experienced a period of public disapproval in 2002, his popularity is strong once again. Pik Botha, a former apartheid enforcer, even announced his intent to join the ANC in early 2000. He was reelected overwhelmingly in 2004 and was in a strong enough position politically to remove Buthelezi from the cabinet and later sack his deputy Jacob Zuma for corruption.

Although the political achievements of Mandela and the ANC are breathtaking, serious problems persist and new ones have emerged. South Africa's economy, slated to grow at 6 percent by 2000, has slipped into the doldrums, in part because of the global repercussions of the Asian financial crisis. Unemployment of blacks approaches 50 percent in some communities, and there is a growing feeling of despair as the gap between wealthy whites and poor blacks continues to widen. In the transition to a postapartheid regime, little attention was paid to structural problems in South African society, and it is likely that this weakness will catch up to the new Mbeki government (Statman 1997).

Visitors to South African black townships still see poverty, illiteracy, and poor living conditions, all compounded by dramatically increasing crime rates and the spread of the AIDS virus. In spite of broad efforts to combat the spread of HIV/AIDS, its prevalence has increased from 24.8 percent in 2001 to 29.5 percent in 2004—or 5.6 million people. In 2003, after years of ambivalence, the government announced a new initiative to bring generic versions of HIV-fighting drugs to far more patients. The policy is ambitious, and has been delayed by a lack of trained physicians, but given the scale of the problem an ambitious program is doubtless called for (AVERT 2004). By 2005, the government could announce that it had established an AIDS clinic in all 53 districts in the country.

Crime is in some ways a result of a combination of new freedom (drugs and guns now flow almost freely into South Africa thanks to reopened borders), poverty, and frustration, as well as a legacy of an apartheid-era police force that was trained to persecute rather than protect blacks (Gordon 1998). Murder rates in South Africa reached a peak in 1995 with nearly 27,000 cases reported countrywide. The figure has gradually receded since then, and came in at under 20,000 for 2005. "While crime rates are among the highest in the world, the conviction rate, estimated at eight percent, is among the lowest. The high level of crime is a disincentive for much-needed foreign investment. It also contributes to disillusionment with democracy among South Africans" (USAID 2004). As a result, solving crime and other similar problems will require a multipronged policy strategy, and it is even possible that some tactics will be mutually contradictory. For example, rapid growth probably requires opening the market more, which will result in weak companies going bankrupt and laying off their workers, most of whom are likely to be black.

CONCLUSION

For all their troubles, the vast majority of South Africans are willing to support Mbeki and wait for better times (his popularity ratings are very high). For the moment, at least, they can clearly remember the pains of oppression, so the taste of freedom is deliciously sweet. It is doubtful, however, whether this situation will continue much longer.

Perhaps even more serious is the AIDS epidemic, which has swelled in significance in recent years. Nearly five million South Africans are HIV-positive (one in nine), and most victims are ostracized and even attacked by their neighbors. Mbeki's reaction has been somewhat puzzling, as he casts blame on multinational drug companies that refuse to offer low-cost AIDS drugs while simultaneously questioning the link between HIV and AIDS. The government, meanwhile, did not make antiretroviral drugs available to rape victims until mid-2002. As of 2005, Mbeki's policies seemed to be growing more coherent and promised a more effective program (BBC News April 24, 2002).

Overall, life is still filled with violence, poverty, and despair for the vast majority of South Africans. Children growing up in the townships are increasingly turning to gang culture for validation and survival. As put by Virginia Gamba of the Institute of Security Studies, "In twelve years time [2014] you'll have at least a quarter of a million orphans, with no role models to guide them. They won't care less, because they themselves are infected with HIV. . . . The escalation of violence could be so great that it becomes the only determinant of whether life is worth living. Such a future threatens democracy itself" (BBC News April 10, 2002).

Who is to blame? Have the political and social freedoms that have been achieved by average South Africans been abused in some way? Are South Africans to blame for the increase in crime and disease, or are these merely normal social ills that afflict every advanced, liberal democracy? Is it possible that the white minority government would be facing the same challenges if it were still in office? Most South Africans seem to think so, because there is no talk of returning to the political "Stone Age" of apartheid.

This point leads us back to the original concept for this case—human rights. South Africa is posing an increasingly troubling question for observers: Are political freedom and social order somehow contradictory? The Universal Declaration provides for both civil and economic rights, after all. Most world leaders and human rights activists would find it disturbing to think that civil rights must necessarily bring social breakdown, although the precedent has already been set in Russia. Fascists have always claimed that freedom was antithetical to social order and economic progress, while liberals have pointed out repeatedly that liberty and the good society can coexist—and that they are mutually reinforcing.

At this point, South African leaders are working hard to achieve both social and economic progress and to consolidate democracy and civil rights. One can hope that they will soon turn a corner and be able to guarantee both for the average South African.

DEBATE TOPIC

Many African states continue to struggle with the status of minority groups in government. Is South Africa a model for other African states, such as Zimbabwe, Rwanda, and Namibia?

PRO

Supporters of the South African model point out: (1) The remarkable freedom for whites, blacks, and coloreds in the country allows free speech and free political activity for all. (2) Strong constitutional guarantees allowed a peaceful transition of government after Mandela's term of office ended. (3) South Africa now has a leadership role in international life and enjoys high regard at the United Nations and elsewhere.

CON

South Africa is not to be imitated, according to some: (1) South Africa is unique in many ways and enjoys special economic and resource advantages not shared by other African states. (2) The leadership in South Africa has not demonstrated the capacity to deal with serious social issues any more effectively than many other African governments. (3) South Africa has yet to fully empower the millions of poor and unemployed, with the result that the freedom is one-dimensional to a large extent.

THINKING THEORETICALLY

Why do countries internalize international human rights norms? There are essentially two schools of thought. One says that countries learn that international norms have inherent merit and seek to imitate each other over time. This enhances their reputations and makes life easier overall. The more attractive the norm, the more quickly and fully it will be embraced. The other says that internalization is mostly the product of almost coercive pressure and inducements that come close to bribes. The more powerful the international agents, the more likely they will bring about change. The first theory is constructivist, the second is institutionalist.

What does the South Africa story teach us? First of all, it clear that international pressure affected the timing and scope of the reforms. The sanctions were impressive for their specificity in that they targeted only those who stood to gain the most from the existing order of things. Note that it was the business community in South Africa that first caved in to the pressure—even though it had been able to ignore (mostly) the widespread protests of blacks within the country.

On the other hand, it is also clear that the reforms were closely tied to the norms themselves. Both blacks and white wanted a constitutional, democratic system—not some other alternative that might have produced a different form of fairness (socialism, communalism, communism, etc.). Also, it is interesting to see how profoundly the ideology and beliefs of the conservative Afrikaners changed once the end of apartheid was in sight. While this may have stemmed from an instinct for political survival, it is also apparent that at least some individuals experienced a change of heart similar to a religious conversion. The Truth and Reconciliation Commission made this change all the more intense for many.

The bottom line is that both of these theories seem to explain an important part of the story—although neither does it alone.

Questions to Consider

1. To what extent has nonviolence succeeded where violence has not? Have Mahatma Gandhi's theories been validated by the South Africa experience?

2. How have human rights been perceived by various groups in South Africa? How have South Africans responded to international standards of human rights? To what extent did the international community succeed in changing the human rights policies of the South African government? Does the South African situation strengthen the case for economic sanctions?

Websites

The South African government's official web site: **www.gov.za**
The ANC home page: **www.anc.org.za**
COSATU's home page: **www.cosatu.org.za**
South African politics Web site: **www.polity.org.za/default.htm**
The Universal Declaration of Human Rights: **www.un.org/Overview/rights.html**

References

AVERT. "South Africa Statistics." October 2004. Available at: **www.avert.org/aidssouthafrica.htm**.

BBC News, April 24, 2002.

Brent, R. Stephen. "Tough Road to Prosperity." *Foreign Affairs* 75 #2 (March/April 1996): 113–126.

Brewer, John D. *After Soweto: An Unfinished Journey* (Oxford: Clarendon Press, 1986).

Brown, Godfrey N. *Apartheid: A Teacher's Guide* (New York: UNESCO, 1981).

Christian Science Monitor, October 1, 1993, 8.

Fatton, Robert, Jr. *Black Consciousness in South Africa: The Dialectics of Ideological Resistance to White Supremacy* (Albany: SUNY Press, 1986).

Gordon, Diana R. "Crime in the New South Africa." *The Nation* 267 #15 (November 9, 1998): 17–21.

Hobson, J. A. *Imperialism* (Ann Arbor: University of Michigan Press, 1965).

International Labor Organization. *Special Report of the Director-General on the Application of the Declaration Concerning Action Against Apartheid in South Africa and Namibia* (Geneva: ILO, 1990).

Lambley, Peter. *The Psychology of Apartheid* (Athens: University of Georgia Press, 1980).

Lapping, Brian. *Apartheid: A History* (New York: George Braziller, 1986).

Lawyers Committee for Human Rights. *The War Against Children: South Africa's Youngest Victims* (New York: Lawyers Committee, 1986).

Lemon, Anthony. *Apartheid in Transition* (Boulder, CO: Westview Press, 1987).

Magubane, Bernard Makhosezwe. *The Political Economy of Race and Class in South Africa* (New York: Monthly Review Press, 1979).

Mandela, Nelson. *The Struggle Is My Life* (New York: Pathfinder, 1990).

Mann, Michael. "The Giant Stirs: South African Business in the Age of Reform" in Philip Krankel, Noam Pines, and Mark Swilling, eds., *State Resistance and Change in South Africa* (London: Croom Helm, 1988): 52–86.

New York Times, September 24, 1993, A1.

Omond, Roger. *The Apartheid Handbook* (London: Penguin, 1985).

Payne, Richard J. *The Third World and South Africa: Post-Apartheid Challenges* (Westport, CT: Greenwood Press, 1992).

Republic of South Africa. *Progress Through Separate Development: South Africa in Peaceful Transition* (New York: Information Service of South Africa, 1973).

Sparks, Alision. "The Status of the Dream." *The Wilson Quarterly* 23 #12 (Spring 1999): 66–67.

St. Jorre, John de. "White South Africa Circles the Wagons" in Mark A. Uhlig, ed., *Apartheid in Crisis* (New York: Vintage Books, 1986): 61–84.

Statman, James M. "No More Miracle?" *ReVision* 20 #2 (Fall 1997): 32–38.

Treurnicht, Andries P. "Conservative Party Congress Speech" in Mark A. Uhlig, ed., *Apartheid in Crisis* (New York: Vintage Books, 1986): 100–102.

USAID. "USAID's strategy in South Africa." 2004. Available at: **http://www.usaid.gov/ locations/sub-saharan_africa/countries/southafrica/**.

CASE 15

The Kyoto Protocol: Collective Goods

INTRODUCTION

As a result of increasing human activity and economic growth, a growing number of issues cross national boundaries. Refugees, ocean pollution, space exploration, pandemics, ozone depletion, and global warming are but a few examples. These problems, while the product of specific actions in specific states in most cases, affect much of the planet. Once in place, they are not easily solved by just one or two countries, but require collective action from numerous players.

A "pure" collective good is one that does not belong to any one player, nor could it. Once in place, it cannot be withheld from any one player, but is available to all (in practice, very few things fit this description, but many come close). This is not to say that a collective good is free, however. Typically, collective goods require considerable sacrifice and expense, and the story of the creation of collective goods comes down to the fight over who will pay for it. A simple example would be how a group of four roommates divides up the bill for a pizza. One simple solution would be to split the bill equally. But suppose one person goes to pick up the pizza and feels that his time and gas are worth something—and makes the argument that his share of the bill should be lower. What if one person is carbo-loading for a marathon and plans to eat more than one-fourth of the pie—should he pay more? What if one person is short of cash that day—can he pay less and work it off by doing everyone's dishes? Perhaps you've had this experience. Because we're dealing with roommates, where no one has ultimate authority, the solution will probably be negotiated (unless one is a weight-lifter and simply knocks a few heads to get his way . . .).

This situation emerges in international affairs where sovereign states have problems that are inherently trans-boundary in nature. Sometimes, governments agree on the need for a collective good, such as rules to govern chlorofluorocarbon (CFC) emissions to prevent depletion of the ozone layer (which protects living things on earth from some of the sun's harmful ultraviolet rays). Acknowledging the need for a collective good is merely the first step, however. Questions may arise regarding the source of the CFCs, for example, and states may insist that those who have caused the most damage historically should be expected to pay the most for the repair now. If these states are willing to make the contribution, then all will be well—but such is often not the case. It is more likely that, unless some actors emerge as leaders who are willing to shoulder the bulk of the costs of the collective good, no solution will emerge (Olson 1965). A widely held belief is that the creation of a collective good requires a single player able and willing to absorb most of the costs of its creation and maintenance. Such an actor is called a *hegemon* (Kindelberger 1986).

Once the collective good is in place, how does one maintain it? Because it isn't possible to deny the good to anyone, one cannot simply "charge admission" (although, as mentioned earlier, this idea rarely holds in practice and so states are, in fact, "charged admission"). Suppose governments agree to strict guidelines on CFC emissions, for example, and a few states are willing to make deep cuts. What if other countries decide to renege on their commitments and revert back to CFC production? The benefits of the program will probably still occur, and the "free-riders" will enjoy the same benefits as the burden-carriers. Only if a major player refuses to go along is the collective good jeopardized (such an actor is called a "spoiler"). The incentive to cheat is clearly high. But if there are enough free-riders, problems could arise. If nothing else, those carrying the burden will grow to resent their sacrifice and the unfairness of the arrangement. There will probably need to be some penalties for noncompliance, but these may be difficult to design and enforce given the inability to deny benefits to cheaters.

The story of the creation of the rules on global-warming gases is illustrative of the problems inherent in collective goods.

KEY FIGURES
THE KYOTO PROTOCOL

Bill Clinton   U.S. President, 1993–2001. He supported the basic framework of the Kyoto Protocol, although his administration sought ways to give the United States separate rules.

George W. Bush   U.S. President, 2001–present. His administration rejected the Kyoto Protocol.

Al Gore   U.S. Vice President, 1993–2001. The author of *Earth in the Balance*, he was a strong supporter of stricter pollution controls.

John Prescott   British Deputy Prime Minister, 1997–present. As the country's senior environmental policy official, he has been instrumental in pressing for the Kyoto Protocol's conclusion.

Mikhail Kasyanov   Russian Federation Prime Minister. He announced the country's plans to ratify the Kyoto Protocol in 2002.

Raul Estrada   Chairman of the FCCC meetings leading to the Kyoto Protocol.

Timothy Wirth   Under U.S. Secretary of State for Global Affairs, 1993–1997. He was the principal U.S. negotiator at the Kyoto meetings.

CHRONOLOGY
THE KYOTO PROTOCOL

1988
The Intergovernmental Panel on Climate Change (IPCC) is formed by UNEP and WMO. Officials in Toronto recommend a reduction of CO_2 emissions by 20 percent by 2005.

1990
IPCC issues a report declaring its certainty that human activity is resulting in pollutants that will intensify the greenhouse effect. The panel predicts that the earth's temperature will increase by one degree Celsius by 2025.

1992
The UN Conference on the Environment and Development is held in Rio de Janeiro. It results in the Framework Convention on Climate Change (FCCC), among other agreements.

1995
Signatories to the FCCC meet in Berlin to outline specific targets on emissions.

1997
Signatories agree to the broad outlines of emissions targets in Kyoto, Japan. The United States dissents.

2000
Efforts to accommodate American and Australian objections to the Kyoto draft agreement fail at a meeting of signatories in The Hague.

2001
George W. Bush withdraws U.S. endorsement of the Kyoto Protocol and goes back on a campaign promise to reduce reliance on coal-burning power plants. Following important breakthroughs in Bonn in June, participants in the November Marrakesh meetings finalize the provisions of the Kyoto Protocol without U.S. support.

2002
Russia and Canada ratify the Kyoto Protocol to the FCCC, bringing the treaty into effect officially on February 16, 2005.

GLOBAL WARMING

As we all know from the tremendous precautions taken by astronauts to protect themselves against the cold of space, the earth would become a frigid wasteland without a capacity to trap solar energy as it bounces off its surface. Misnamed the "greenhouse effect" (actual greenhouses operate on a different principle of physics), this is accomplished by the thin layer of atmosphere that covers the globe. A few substances, including carbon dioxide and methane, are able to absorb and trap ultraviolet rays from the sun and thereby assist in preventing heat from escaping into space (Sparber & O'Rourke 1998, 2).

Another well-known fact is that the planet's average surface temperature has gone through rather dramatic swings over its long history. Most recently, it was

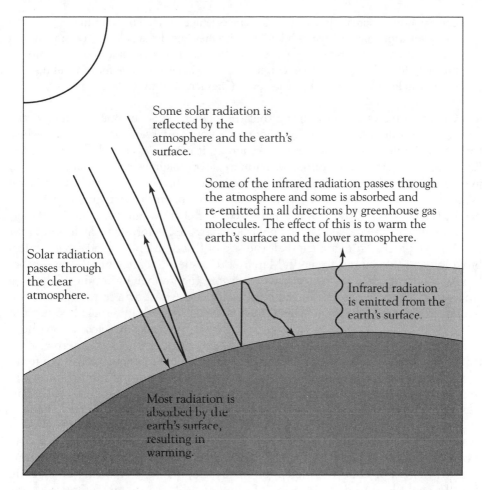

Figure 15.1 Solar radiation

nearly ten degrees cooler during the great Ice Age that resulted in the spread of Northern Hemisphere glaciers well south of the current Canada–U.S. border.

Two more facts are known as well. First, since the Industrial Revolution at the end of the eighteenth century, humanity—especially the peoples of the West—has been burning fossil fuels at a tremendous rate, in contrast to the entirety of human experience to that point. Second, earth's surface temperature has been moving inexorably higher over the past one hundred years.

Noting these facts, observers—both scientists and amateurs—began expressing concern in the early 1980s over the possibility that human activity was intensifying the greenhouse effect to the point that the earth was experiencing human-induced global warming. As put by Breidenich and her coauthors:

> most scientists believe that anthropogenic [human-generated] emissions of green-
> house gases increase the heat-absorbing capacity of the atmosphere and will result in a

corresponding increase in the global average temperature. This warning is predicted to have various global impacts, including the melting of the polar ice caps; rising sea levels; increased intensity and frequency of storms; changes in amounts and timing of precipitation; changes in ocean currents; and an enlarged range for tropical diseases such as malaria, cholera and dengue fever. (Breidenich et al. 1998, 316)

Conservative estimates indicate that the planet may continue warming at the rate of three or four degrees per century unless some intervention occurs to reverse the trend. While this may not sound like much, it is useful to recall that during the Ice Age, the earth's temperature was a mere seven degrees cooler than today on average. One group of environmental organizations has created a website (Global Warming: Early Warning Signs, www. climatehotmap. org) that maps specific, local events (updated regularly) that are harbingers of global warming around the planet.

Among the specific alerts: The polar ice caps are beginning to melt and break up. A piece of the Antarctic ice shelf the size of Rhode Island (1,260 square miles) broke off and floated out to sea in March 2002. Scientists attribute this and other breakups of Antarctic ice to a nearly five-degree (Fahrenheit) warming of the area since 1945. Watery patches have appeared in the Arctic where the ice has not melted in the past. The area covered by sea ice has declined by roughly 6 percent since 1980. Glaciers in the Himalayas have shrunk dramatically (close to one hundred feet per year), leading some to predict the loss of all central and eastern glaciers by 2035. In Spain, half of the glaciers present in 1980 are now gone. Partly as a result of ice melting, sea levels are rising at three times the normal rate, resulting in increased flooding in low-lying areas from Bangladesh to the Chesapeake Bay. Mangrove forests in Bermuda's coasts are dying off due to rising sea water levels.

In addition, global weather patterns are likely to change significantly. For example, the temperate zones of the planet will shift northward, resulting in longer growing seasons in Scandinavia and Canada, and more tropical climates in China and Missouri. For countries that are already tropical, the resulting changes in rainfall, could lead to desertification of some areas. Ocean temperatures will rise, contributing to intensification of tropical storm and hurricane activity, along with unusual phenomena such as El Niño. To illustrate, high temperatures in Great Britain are increasingly rising above sixty-eight degrees Fahrenheit (more than twenty-five days per year in the 1990s versus fewer than five days per year in the 1770s). Severe heat waves were common in 1998 and 1999, resulting in hundreds of fatalities in cities such as Chicago. Changes in Indonesia's temperatures have contributed to a spreading of malaria into higher elevations (Telesetsky 1999).

These changes will, in turn, bring about important socioeconomic changes, including a redistribution of the world's agricultural centers, and increased food scarcity in some areas, both of which will contribute to large-scale movements of populations in search of food security. This migration could contribute to shifts in global power distributions and an increase in local conflicts. It is probably enough to offer this list of potential problems (and a few opportunities).

Global warming remains an extremely controversial issue. One reason is the continuing disagreement among scientists about it. Although an overwhelming majority of climatologists are on record stating that human activity is contributing to global warming, a small minority rejects this conclusion as premature. The existence of the merest dispute has been seized upon by politicians and firms that are predisposed to resist the standard remedies for global warming. The George W. Bush administration, for example, has explained its resistance to cuts in carbon dioxide emissions in terms of continuing doubts among scientists. According to Lindsay, "uncertainty also explains why global warming has not yet emerged as a burning issue in the United States. . . . Few Americans list global warming as a top environmental concern . . . and by a two-to-one margin they say it will not pose a serious threat during their lifetime" (Lindsay 2001, 27).

CREATING RULES ON GLOBAL WARMING GASES

Global warming is controversial largely because of the types of solutions that exist. When it comes to reducing the biggest culprit—carbon dioxide—what is required is a reduction in the burning of fossil fuels and an increase in carbon-absorbing forests. At this point, however, considerable resistance emerges in seeking alternatives to fossil fuels. Two important factors are coal-burning power plants and the internal combustion engine. They are the predominant contributors to the 30 percent increase in CO_2 concentrations in the atmosphere since 1750 (Telesetsky 1999, 781). Dramatic changes would require auto manufacturers, utility companies, highway contractors, and most mining companies to either drastically curtail production or undertake considerable research to develop new products. Some, including former Vice President Al Gore, have suggested that nothing less than the replacement of the internal combustion engine will be enough to begin to solve the problem (Gore 1993).

While these emissions occur mostly in the developed West, the developing South is industrializing at a rapid rate and is expected to emit a large share of global-warming gases (the name for all gases that contribute to the phenomenon, including carbon dioxide and methane). In addition, developing countries are guilty of removing one of the key natural defenses against carbon dioxide concentrations by cutting large portions of the planet's forests. Young trees are especially effective recyclers of CO_2 because they absorb it through their leaves and convert it to oxygen. Deforestation has cost the earth a large fraction of its forests in recent years, and relatively little of it has grown back. The forests are being eliminated in part to provide farmland to the growing populations of the developing world, which also increases demand for fossil fuels. The problem is thus exacerbated doubly.

Getting to Kyoto

In the late 1980s, governments around the world began debating whether and how the problem of global warming could be tackled. In 1988, a panel of scientists and government officials proposed reducing carbon dioxide levels by 20 percent by 2005 as a starting point (Barrett 1998). That same year, the UN General Assembly invited the UN Environmental Programme and the World Meteorological Organization to form the Intergovernmental Panel on Climate Change—a collection of

2,000 climatologists from more than one hundred countries—to study the facts regarding global warming. They reported in 1990 that human-induced emissions were, in fact, contributing to the earth's gradual warming.

The issue was placed on the agenda of the United Nations Conference on the Environment and Development, scheduled for June 1992 in Rio de Janeiro, Brazil. The meetings were intended to be a dramatic, high-level event where the world's leaders would address and develop answers for a wide range of environmental problems, from desertification to ocean pollution. What emerged from the meetings was a series of broad agreements—mostly on principles—and a laundry list of policy goals. Buried in the mix was the UN Framework Convention on Climate Change that called upon sponsoring states to keep emissions of global-warming gases to 1990 levels to prevent acceleration of temperature increases in the years to come. But little more was spelled out at that time, and the signatories agreed to meet again to hammer out the details in the form of a "protocol" of legally binding measures (Breidenich et al. 1998, 318).

As put by Lindsay:

> global warming poses a collective goods dilemma. Countries know that pursuing virtuous global warming policies makes little sense if no one else follows suit. Any individual reduction on their part will be swamped by emissions from others. Indeed, going first could be economically lethal . . . Fairness issues exacerbate the collective goods problem. (Lindsay 2001, 27)

Four groups of states emerged early on, and most of the negotiations involved trade-offs between them. First and foremost was the European bloc, led by Germany and France, which called for the deepest cuts in emissions. These countries were driven by both ideological and practical considerations. On the one hand, pollution in Europe had prompted the emergence of a strong and active environmental movement that considered global warming a "clear and present danger," the substance of which was beyond debate (Gelbspan 2002). These states also were in a position to explore alternatives to fossil fuels by virtue of the fact that most countries were concerned about their dependence on foreign oil and had already begun efforts to wean themselves off it. France had begun a massive nuclear power program in the 1960s and had significantly reduced its reliance on coal-burning plants, for example. It also introduced numerous energy-saving initiatives and fuel taxes to encourage efficiency. By 2000, per capita energy use in Europe was half that of the United States—a fact that has bred deep resentment of the United States' efforts to give itself exceptions from the Kyoto Protocol (Mathews 2001). The European states were consistently the most forceful advocates for deep cuts and strong legal commitments.

The second group consisted of mature, developed economies that, for a variety of reasons, were not yet ready to make the deep cuts Europe proposed. This group, labeled "industrialized laggards" by European analysts, consisted of Canada, Japan, and Australia, and was led by the United States (Oberthur & Ott 1999, 17). The U.S. position remained consistently skeptical throughout the 1990s. Even at Rio de Janeiro, the George H. W. Bush administration refused to endorse the full array of agreements reached, preferring to adopt a "wait-and-see" approach. The Clinton administration, prodded by Vice President Gore, warmly welcomed the Rio agreements on principle, although it found its hands were tied when it came to making specific, legal commitments. Members of the U.S. Senate, in particular, expressed their deep concern with any treaty that might result in economic stagnation or unemployment. They also opposed any agreement that would treat developing countries more leniently than Western countries. In 1997, the Senate unanimously passed a resolution prohibiting the White House from signing any global warming agreement that did not remedy these issues (Barrett 1998, 22).

The nations in this group worked to minimize mandatory cuts in emissions. Australia managed to negotiate an increase for itself, for example. The United States sought permission for moderate reductions in emissions by offsetting them with increases in the size of its carbon dioxide-absorbing forests ("carbon sinks"). This group also promoted various emissions-trading schemes that would allow high polluters to reduce their exposure by exchanging credits with low-polluting countries in a variety of ways.

The third group was the Eastern European states in economic transition. Although they were known to be very heavy polluters, their difficult economic transitions created a pollution windfall. High failure rates for their heavy industries meant that many smokestacks were idled, and pollution levels plummeted even as unemployment lines swelled.

Finally, the developing countries sought special protections during the negotiation of the Kyoto Protocol. They argued that, given their dependence on industrialization for economic growth, it was unfair to ask them to set aside poverty-alleviating development for the sake of the environment. Besides, they pointed out, global warming was almost entirely the fault of Western industrialization in the past—hence the need for Western states to carry the bulk of the cost of emissions controls. They pointed out that, on a per capita basis, developing countries produced very little pollution (for example, China emits one-tenth the carbon dioxide emitted by the United States per capita—Oberthur & Ott 1999, 21). Oil-exporting countries pleaded for rules that would not jeopardize their export levels, lest they collapse economically and politically. Only the small island states in the developing world felt strongly that global warming should be halted (given their special vulnerability to rising ocean levels).

Pollution Trading at Kyoto

One of the first steps undertaken at Kyoto was the establishment of an emissions baseline against which future rules would be measured. This goal was achieved with relative ease, because it is possible to measure carbon dioxide emissions with considerable precision, and thereby estimate the total volume of global-warming gases coming from each country. The negotiators developed a table that listed the total amount of emissions and each country's share (see Table 15.1). Special attention was given to the so-called Annex I countries that were responsible for the overwhelming majority of pollution—namely, the industrialized West.

Once the baselines were established, the pollution trading began in earnest. Almost every participant in the Kyoto negotiations entered the discussion with the

Table 15.1   1990 Emissions Baseline for Kyoto Protocol Signatories

	Total CO_2 Emissions for 1990 (thousands of gigagrams)	Share of Annex I Country Totals
United States	4,957	36.00
European Union	3,289	24.05
France	367	2.68
Germany	1,014	7.24
Italy	429	3.14
United Kingdom	577	4.22
Australia	289	2.11
Canada	463	3.38
Japan	1,155	8.45
Economies in Transition	3,364	24.60
Russia	2,389	17.47
Poland*	415	3.03

*Poland and a few other economies in transition were allowed to utilize 1988 or 1989 levels as the baseline (slightly higher than 1990).
Source: UN Framework Convention on Climate Change, www.unfccc.int.

goal of minimizing costly reforms. Even the Europeans sought ways to permit some European Union members to have small reductions, or even increases, in CO_2 emissions. The three principal ways of reducing the emissions reduction targets were to (1) plead "special circumstances," (2) exchange emissions with lower-polluting countries, and (3) devise offsetting mechanisms involving improvements to the environment. The first strategy was taken up by many developing countries and most of the U.S.-led bloc. Australia was perhaps the most successful, negotiating for itself the right to increase its carbon dioxide emissions to 8 percent above its 1990 baseline (see Table 15.2).

The second strategy was also promoted by the U.S. delegation against the resistance of the Europeans. The Americans argued that, since the goal of the Kyoto meeting was reduction of global levels of global-warming gas levels, so long as one country's increase was offset by another country's decrease, the total objective could be met. They proposed to create a "market for emissions," whereby countries would be allowed to convert some of their emissions into a "budget" that they could sell to countries that were well ahead of global emissions averages. In particular, the United States was interested in taking advantage of the collapse of East European emissions resulting from economic depression and deindustrialization, which created "hot air" opportunities (Barrett 1998). At the end of the day, this arrangement was approved by the signatories, although it was not enough to satisfy the U.S. negotiators. Even the Europeans negotiated a special arrangement whereby their

Table 15.2   Kyoto Targets for 2002–2012, Relative to 1990 Base Year*

United States	93%
European Union	92%
France	92%
Germany	92%
Italy	92%
United Kingdom	92%
Australia	108%
Canada	94%
Japan	94%
Economies in Transition	103%
Russia	100%
Poland*	108%

*Poland and a few other economies in transition were allowed to utilize 1988 or 1989 levels as the baseline (slightly higher than 1990).
Source: UN Framework Convention on Climate Change, www.unfccc.int.

emissions were counted as a whole. As a consequence, Germany and France's deep emissions cuts would allow increases in emissions in Spain and Greece ("joint implementation").

The third strategy was promoted by the United States and some developing countries. The U.S. delegation pressed especially hard for a more generous treatment of so-called carbon sinks. Given the carbon-absorbing character of forests, and given the United States' commitment to reforestation, the government believed it should get credit for reductions in emissions as a result of forest absorption (Barrett 2001). Some have estimated that approval of this strategy could allow the United States to cut in half the reductions it must make against the 1990 baseline (Teleset-sky 1999, 805).

Developing countries pressed for arrangements that, like the World Bank's Global Environmental Facility, would give developed countries credit for helping a developing country lower its global-warming gas emissions. Special projects and initiatives under the so-called Clean Development Mechanism would be graded according to the degree of emissions reduction they produced, and the donor country would have its emissions for the year cut by a similar amount (Coghlan 2002, 168–171). This tactic is intended to use market incentives to cause states to do good (Breidenich et al. 1998, 325).

As these provisions were negotiated and (mostly) adopted at Kyoto, more general issues were debated as well. The United States pressed for a more flexible deadline for reducing emissions than the drop-dead deadline proposed by the Europeans. Ultimately, compromise was reached on the establishment of a five-year period rather than a single date for achievement of the targets. The average emissions per year for the period 2008–2012 would be the ultimate test of compliance with Kyoto—meaning that the final day of reckoning would not come until 2012. So long as targets were reached, on average, during this period, countries would be considered compliant. Further, the United States insisted on lax enforcement mechanisms with respect to noncompliance. Other than regular reporting to the FCCC Secretariat, no specific set of enforcement mechanisms was created, although the parties to the Kyoto have agreed to consider this question in the future (Breidenich et al. 1998, 330). With the United States' ultimate rejection of the treaty, it is possible that the Europeans will insist on tougher enforcement measures (Gelbspan 2002).

As a way to prevent adoption of a meaningless treaty, the negotiators agreed that it would not come into force until it was ratified by at least 55 states responsible for at least 55 percent of the world's global warming gasses. This meant that almost all of the world's major polluters would have to come on board before the Kyoto Protocol would take legal effect.

IMPASSE AT THE HAGUE

The Kyoto meetings ended in passage of the Kyoto Protocol, signed by the United States, European states, and more than one hundred other participants, albeit not without the dramatic and personal intervention of Al Gore, the Japanese prime minster, and other high-ranking diplomats. The meetings also benefited from the able chairmanship of Raul Estrada of Argentina, who had led previous FCCC meetings and knew the participants well (Reiner 2001, 38).

The meetings were declared a victory by environmentalists, but it was a hollow victory at best. The agreement, after all, faced almost unanimous Senate opposition and left many contentious issues unresolved. As put by Reiner, "The Kyoto Protocol, prepared in December 1997, had masked irreconcilable differences among participants by papering over many fundamental disagreements among and within the negotiating parties" (Reiner 2001, 36).

History was not working in favor of resolving global warming. Most countries, including the United States, continued to expand carbon dioxide emissions during the 1990s. In the United States, the proliferation of sport-utility vehicles, which emit up to five times more global-warming gases than their passenger-car counterparts, made achieving reductions difficult. Even in the Netherlands, where the government implemented tough emission-reducing policies, emission levels did not fall. Those countries that had reduced emissions had done so largely because of reasons beyond their control. Germany benefited from the collapse of heavy industry in the East after reunification, and the United Kingdom was able to reach its targets by using its newly discovered North Sea oil to convert coal-burning power plants to less-polluting oil-burning ones (Reiner 2001, 37).

The signatories gathered again at The Hague in November 2000 with the goal of eliminating ambiguities and "agreements in principle" left over from Kyoto. Since little had changed in the U.S. position and the Senate's attitude, there was little expectation of success. The practicalities of the negotiations were also hampered by the U.S. presidential election and its notorious "Florida fiasco" that kept Al Gore and other Clinton administration officials away from the meetings at critical times. The apparent opposition of candidate George W. Bush did nothing to improve the mood at the meetings.

Even as American negotiators felt compelled to be cautious, newly elected Green politicians in the German (and French) delegations felt emboldened to press for deeper concessions, including cutting back the emissions trading schemes. The result was an agreement to disagree. While the United States did not block approval of the agreements by other states, it refused to endorse the result. As put by the chief U.S. negotiator at The Hague:

> [European countries] ignored environmental and economic realities, insisting on provisions that would shackle the very tools that offer us the best hope of achieving our ambitious target at an affordable cost. . . . Some seem to have forgotten that [emissions trading] is a fundamental feature of the Kyoto Protocol—accepted by all parties as a legitimate means of meeting our targets. . . . Some of our negotiating partners also chose to ignore physical realities of our climate system, depriving parties of another important [tool] by refusing them credit for carbon [sinks]. . . . And finally, they ignored the political reality that nations can only negotiate abroad what they believe they can ratify at home. (Frank E. Loy, Department of State press release, November 25, 2000, in AJIL 2001, 648)

Decisions on outstanding issues were postponed until meetings to be held in Bonn and Marrakech over the next year.

THE CURRENT SITUATION

The new Bush administration, which was led by two former oil men, had an ideological and political antipathy toward the Kyoto Protocol. It mistrusted the scientific basis for the sacrifices being required of the United States, was strongly wedded to market schemes that would permit the country to reduce its exposure, and was antagonistic toward any enforcement mechanisms that would punish noncompliance. This said, candidate Bush had promised to shrink the role of coal-burning power plants in the United States during his tenure, but was forced to backpedal shortly upon taking office under pressure from utility companies.

Seeing no way to accommodate both the demands of the European and developing countries and the interests of conservatives and industry in the United States, the Bush administration formally rejected the Kyoto Protocol in March 2001. Environmental Protection Agency chief Christine Todd Whitman was charged with making the announcement that the Kyoto treaty was "dead" as far as the United States was concerned.

Nevertheless, the United States sent representatives to the Bonn and Marrakech meetings later in the year, and even succeeded in winning considerable concessions from chastened Europeans eager to bring the United States back into the process. Negotiators in Bonn agreed to most of the U.S. demands regarding carbon sinks and emissions trading, for example (AJIL 2001, 649). The United States also watched from the sidelines as the negotiators reached final agreement on the provisions of the Kyoto Protocol in Marrakech in November 2001.

The latest position of the Bush administration is that it will not interfere with efforts by other countries to implement the Kyoto Protocol, and will work toward reducing what it calls "greenhouse gas intensity"—emissions per unit of economic activity (total emissions divided by GDP). The target of 18 percent reduction by 2011 will result, admittedly, in an overall increase in emissions (AJIL 2002, 487). And with each new scientific report confirming the scientific evidence that global warming is induced by human activity, the Bush administration's skepticism about the urgency of the problem grows increasingly anachronistic. Even Bush's own climate change experts have finally given its support to this scientific conclusion (CCSP 2006).

Meanwhile, countries have ratified the Kyoto Protocol. The Framework Convention on Climate Change maintains a running tally of ratifications by number of countries and the proportion of total emissions they represent (see its website, www. fccc. int). At the 2002 Johannesburg Summit on Sustainable Development, the governments of Russia and Canada announced that they were moving ahead with ratification, meaning that the 55 percent target would be exceeded. The Kyoto Protocol officially came into effect in February 2005. As of May 2006, that chart showed 163 ratifications by countries that, together, were responsible for 61.6 percent of global emissions of greenhouse gases.

The Russian and Canadian ratifications present the United States with an odd situation. As with the cases of the International Criminal Court, the Convention on the Rights of the Child, and the Landmine Ban, new international rules and institutions are being created without direct U.S. involvement (Stiles 2004). In fact, many American firms wonder why they do not have the opportunity to participate in emissions trading and other schemes like the Europeans and Japanese. As far as whether this means the problem of global warming is now under control, we should recall that it was a watered-down version of Kyoto that was adopted, and that even the original Kyoto Protocol was not particularly robust. The treaty provides numerous exceptions, exemptions, and exclusions that may well make it a less-than-effective tool for solving the original problem.

CONCLUSION

The Kyoto Protocol to the United Nations Framework Convention on Climate Change became international law in 2002, in spite of U.S. opposition. This case helps to demonstrate several important aspects of collective goods that might come as a bit of a surprise. First, this process calls into question the widely held assumption that a "hegemon" is needed to create a collective good (Kindelberger 1986). U.S. leadership was clearly beside the point after a critical mass of countries had reached agreement on Kyoto. Furthermore, even if all the signatories work hard to implement the agreement (an unlikely scenario given the temptation to cheat), little change in global warming trends will probably occur. So long as Americans continue to produce more than one-third of the world's total global-warming gas emissions, other states' efforts may be negligible. Ultimately, the collective good of maintaining (or lowering) the earth's temperature will likely not be achieved in spite of the treaty.

Second, the story of the Kyoto Protocol illustrates the way in which economics and international law intersect. The schemes to trade emissions, in particular, were clever ways of using the market to achieve socially beneficial results. While innovative, the schemes were seen by some as merely a shell game that would ultimately allow heavy polluters to delay needed reforms.

Finally, the Kyoto Protocol story illustrates the difficulty of achieving agreements on economic sacrifices in the face of even slightly ambiguous science. In contrast to the Montreal Protocol, which brought about strict, binding limits on CFC emissions in the face of unanimous scientific agreement on their deleterious effects on the ozone layer, the Kyoto Protocol failed in part because a few scientists were unwilling to endorse the majority view concerning global warming (Lindsay 2001). From another perspective, this case shows how science can be manipulated by self-interested politicians and industrialists (one is reminded of how cigarette manufacturers misrepresented scientific findings on the links between smoking and cancer).

 DEBATE TOPIC

Should the United States ratify the Kyoto Protocol?

PRO
The United States should ratify the agreement for the following reasons: (1) It is the best mechanism available for solving the problem of global warming. (2) The United States needs to be engaged in the process of implementation to protect its interests in the future. (3) The United States is expected to take a leadership role and appears shortsighted by not ratifying the treaty.

CON
The United States need not ratify the agreement for these reasons: (1) The Kyoto Protocol would cost American jobs and cause bankruptcies. (2) The agreement gives China and India carte blanche to pollute for years to come. (3) Current American laws are doing an adequate job of limiting carbon dioxide emissions while giving the government maximum flexibility.

THINKING THEORETICALLY

The case of creating a collective good around the climate change issue pits two prominent theories against each other: realism and liberalism. Realists would have predicted that few countries would be interested in addressing global warming since the costs of remedying it are so great. Only those that truly stand to lose, such as island states or countries with low coastlines (Bangladesh), would be determined to fight it. Some countries, such as Canada, might actually come out ahead as their cold climates warmed and more of their lands could be cultivated. In general, no rich country would want to hamper its ability to expand economically by burning as much fossil fuel as needed. And no poor country would fail to cut down more forest to bring more land into cultivation. And so, realists would probably have a difficult time explaining why Kyoto happened at all—although they would not be surprised to note that it was a watered-down version (without U.S. endorsement) that emerged.

Liberals come in many forms. Some of them advocate the creation of such public goods as Kyoto and acknowledge the importance of state intervention in areas where markets produce negative externalities. In essence, they argue that where the market would cause the depletion of a vital resource, or where the market gives no incentives to create a public good (national defense, highways, a functioning legal system, etc. . . .), the state must intervene. Kyoto presents something of an exception, however, since there is no global state that can collect taxes by force and spend them on public goods. Instead, states must work things out on their own. This usually requires leadership on the part of the most powerful state. Here again, the result has been unexpected since the world's leader took a pass on this one.

QUESTIONS TO CONSIDER

1. Can financial incentives be used to induce reductions in carbon dioxide emissions? If so, how?

2. To what extent do ethical values govern the decision to pollute?

3. On the basis of what principles should the cost of pollution abatement be distributed?

4. What part are you playing in global warming?

WEBSITES

Governmental Sites

U.S. Environmental Protection Agency: **yosemite.epa.org/ globalwarming.nsf/content/index.html**

NOAA: **www.ngdc.noaa.gov/paleo/globalwarming/home.html**

Climate Change Science Program: **www.climatescience.gov**

United Nations Framework Convention on Climate Change: **www.unfccc.int**

Other Organizations

The Cooler Heads Coalition: **www.globalwarming.org**

Global Warming: Early Warning Signs: **www.climatehotmap.org**

Sierra Club: **www.sierraclub.org/globalwarming**

Union of Concerned Scientists: **www.ucsusa.org/warming/env-home.html**

A Skeptical View

Still Waiting for Greenhouse: **www.vision.net.au/~daly**

REFERENCES

AJIL. "U.S. Rejection of Kyoto Protocol Process." *American Journal of International Law* 95 #3 (July 2001): 647–650.

AJIL. "Bush Administration Proposal for Reducing Greenhouse Gases." *American Journal of International Law* 96 #2 (April 2002): 487–488.

Barrett, Scott, "Political Economy of the Kyoto Protocol." *Oxford Review of Economic Policy* 14 #4 (Winter 1998): 20–43.

Breidenich, Clare, Daniel Magraw, Anne Rowley, and James W. Rubin. "The Kyoto Protocol to the United Nations Framework Convention on Climate Change." *American Journal of International Law* 92 #2 (April 1998): 315–331.

CCSP (Climate Change Science Program) "Report Reconciles Atmospheric Temperature Trends." Press release. May 2, 2006.

Coghlan, Matthew. "Prospects and Pitfalls of the Kyoto Protocol to the United Nations Framework Convention on Climate Change." *Melbourne Journal of International Law* #1 (May 2002): 165–184.

Gelbspan, Ross. "Beyond Kyoto Lite: The Bush Administration's Absence from the Global-Warming Talks Could Actually Lead Other Nations to Pursue a Bolder Approach." *The American Prospect* (February 25, 2002): 26–29.

Gore, Al. *Earth in the Balance: Ecology and the Human Spirit* (New York: Plume, 1993).

Kindelberger, Charles. *The World in Depression, 1929–1939* (Berkeley: University of California Press, 1986).

Lean, Geoffrey. "Russia and Canada Shock Summit with Plans to Ratify Kyoto Treaty." *New Zealand Herald*, April 9, 2002.

Lindsay, James M. "Global Warming Heats Up: Uncertainties, Both Scientific and Political, Lie Ahead." *Brookings Review* 19 #4 (Fall 2001): 26–30.

Mathews, Jessica T. "Estranged Partners." *Foreign Policy Magazine* (November/ December 2001): 48–53.

Oberthur, Sebastian, and Hermann E. Ott. *The Kyoto Protocol: International Climate Policy for the 21st Century* (Berlin: Springer, 1999).

Olson, Mancur. *The Logic of Collective Action* (Cambridge, MA: Harvard University Press, 1965).

Reiner, David. "Climate Impasse: How the Hague Negotiation Failed." *Environment* 43 #2 (March 2001): 36–43.

Sparber, Peter, and Peter E. O'Rourke. "Understanding the Kyoto Protocol." *Briefly: Perspectives on Legislation, Regulation, and Litigation* 2 #4 (April 1998).

Stiles, Kendall. "Theories of Non-hegemonic Cooperation." Paper presented at the annual meetings of the American Political Science Association, Chicago, September 2–5, 2004.

Telesetsky, Anastasia. "The Kyoto Protocol." *Ecology Law Quarterly* 26 #4 (November 1999): 797–814.

CASE 16

Sweatshops, Outsourcing, and Global Production

INTRODUCTION

Globalization

In the summer of 1996, Sydney Schanberg related the following account in a *Life* magazine story:

> As I traveled [in Pakistan], I witnessed conditions more appalling than [the last]— children as young as six bought from their parents for as little as $15, sold and resold like furniture, branded, beaten, blinded as punishment for wanting to go home, rendered speechless by the trauma of their enslavement. One 12-year-old Pakistani, Kramat, who had been making bricks since he was sold by his achingly poor father six years ago, his teeth now rotting, his hair tinged with red streaks, a sign of malnutrition, said morosely: "I cannot go anywhere. I am a prisoner." (Schanberg & Dorigny 1996, 39)

Also in 1996, Charles Kernaghan of the National Labor Committee, a watchdog group that monitors corporate labor practices, testified before a congressional committee that many American apparel companies knowingly used suppliers in developing countries that practiced indentured servitude, used child labor, and repressed and failed to pay their workers (Kernaghan 1999). One such company manufactured the Kathie Lee clothing line, which was sold nationwide by Wal-Mart (in 1995 it earned $9 million for the line's namesake, talk-show host Kathie Lee Gifford). When it was revealed that the Kathie Lee clothing company subcontracted to factories that employed girls as young as 13 to work for 31 cents per hour for fifteen-hour shifts, Gifford was indignant. As the reports were confirmed to her through company sources, she pledged to improve working conditions and offered to open up all of the company's factories to independent inspection (Press 1996, 6). Finally, the American public took notice of an international problem that linked Wal-Mart shoppers with children in developing countries more directly than anyone had ever understood before.

Thus began the full-blown campaign known as the anti-sweatshop movement. Many students became activists in the United Students Against Sweatshops campaign and succeeded in persuading their colleges to stop using sweatshops to manufacture their apparel. Beyond understanding that children are being made to work in horrible conditions, however, few really understand the sources of this situation and the implications of the efforts to stop it.

During the 2004 presidential campaign, Senator John Kerry railed against "Benedict Arnold CEOs" who plotted to take jobs away from Americans and hand them to Indians and Chinese on the other side of the world (Mankiw & Swagel 2006, 11). While this "outsourcing" had similarities to the type of corporate decisions that led to sweatshops, it had a distinctly middle-class dimension. Hundreds of thousands of layoffs had occurred in the technology and service sectors during the 1990s and 2000s, with many of those jobs being picked up by Indian and Chinese firms where highly-trained technicians and engineers could do the same work for a small fraction of the cost of their American counterparts (Ghausi 2002; Kasbekar 1999). Some have predicted that by 2015, roughly 3.3 million jobs will be lost (Drezner 2004). Anyone who has spoken to a tech support person from India has experienced this white-collar outsourcing.

In this case, we will explore the phenomenon known as the "global factory" (Rothstein & Blim 1992), which is an important aspect of globalization (Mittelman 2000). Today, the production of manufactured goods as well as services is dispersed throughout the world and thereby links corporate units, warehouses, middlemen, workers, and consumers across many nations as never before in the history of capitalist production. In addition, corporations extend their brand names and products into every corner of the world in the hope of establishing new markets for their goods. Although the notion of an international division of labor is nothing new (the concept dates back to the eighteenth century), what is different now is the degree to which the linkages are dense and close, leading to a transformation of social structures around the world (Gill 1995, 76). This idea helps to explain everything from sweatshops in Indonesia, to downsizing in Seattle, to merger mania in New York, to the emergence of a global culture and the withering away of differences between states and nations.

The global factory arose from modern innovations such as the assembly line process, faster communication and transportation—particularly the Internet where high-tech jobs are concerned—and the opening of national markets through the World Trade Organization. What is unique about this new structure, however, is how ancient, traditional social arrangements interact with the Western capitalist system. What might have been a tolerable situation, such as the work of young daughters on a family farm, becomes exploitative and dangerous when transferred to a garment factory or a plantation. The contrast between these situations and the lofty language of workers' rights articulated by Western investors, middlemen, and consumers makes the situation all the more bizarre.

What is clear is that everyone on the planet is increasingly linked, and that what happens in one spot on the globe almost invariably affects others on the opposite side. This adage applies not only to global production but also to international finance, travel, and even politics. Just as globalization has brought everyone closer together, so has it created considerable tension. An imbalanced currency in Thailand exposes financial weaknesses in Brazil. A sick cow in England causes panic in Spain. A mosquito carrying a disease that originated in Egypt bites and kills an old man in Chicago.

In the most extreme example, the World Trade Center and Pentagon bombers claimed they were aiming to cripple the United States economically and psychologically as part of their fight against Western culture (however hypocritical or cynical the claim). Ironically, they took advantage of globalization to carry out the attack. The funding came from Osama bin Laden, who inherited considerable sums from his family's international construction businesses. The terrorists were generally successful for their own part, and some had spent their formative years studying in Western colleges, thanks to modern travel and liberal immigration policies. That they would select modern aircraft as their weapon, rather than, say, a crude homemade bomb, adds to the paradox. One could argue that globalization contributed to providing both the ends and the means of the attack.

As we consider sweatshops and outsourcing, we will find numerous interpretations of the effects of globalization. Given its controversial character, the material is presented here almost as a debate, with the reader being left to do most of the interpretation.

THE SWEATSHOP PHENOMENON

Sweatshops are nothing new. Workers—especially women—have been required to labor in cramped, dangerous conditions since the Industrial Revolution in the 1750s. In the eighteenth century, the French government actually created sweatshops as a way of rescuing destitute women and children from a life on the street (DiCaprio 1999, 519). The sweatshop was commonly instituted in the textile industry by garment manufacturers in Great Britain and the United States who felt squeezed by middlemen and suppliers demanding ever-lower manufacturing costs in spite of high clothing costs. The difference was "sweated" out of labor through low wages and a form of indentured servitude, which were easier to arrange with children and women, who were particularly vulnerable in the workplace.

Sweatshops became a target of labor and humanitarian activists by the early 1900s, spurred in the United States by a series of catastrophes (including fires) in which hundreds of workers lost their lives in the early part of the twentieth century. Gradually, worker safety regulations, child labor laws, and legislation that protected workers' rights to organize were passed by federal and state agencies. By the 1940s, sweatshops were thought to be a thing of the past.

In the 1980s, however, sweatshop garment factories were discovered in New York and Los Angeles, giving rise to another outcry. Sweatshops and debt bondage (where a loan is provided to cover a working fee that is paid off over a period of time, during which the worker is forced to stay on) were particularly prevalent in the textile industry and in agriculture, where new downward price pressures were becoming particularly intense, in part because of the international market forces mentioned earlier. During 1981–1984, the federal government successfully prosecuted twenty cases of slavery (*U.S. News & World Report* January 16, 1984, 68). Sweatshops in Queens were hidden behind storefronts to prevent detection by the 800 federal work inspectors (down from more than 1,000 in the 1970s). During the 1990s, the trend continued, to the point that by 1993, as many as half of all women's garments were made by factories that violated minimum wage and other labor laws (*U.S. News & World Report* November 22, 1993, 48).

Overseas, an estimated 200 million children under age 14 (the lowest legal working age in any country) work full-time (although for many, working a mere forty hours per week would be a relief). The problem is particularly acute in South Asia. It is estimated that in Pakistan, 11 million children work six days per week for nine or ten hours per day (Schanberg & Dorigny 1996). Their employers are in violation of international labor codes drafted by the International Labour Organization, including the Minimum Age Convention of 1973 and conventions against forced and bonded labor (*UN Chronicle* 1986).

Sweatshops do not operate in a vacuum, to be sure. Although many market to local and regional outlets, others are linked to well-known Western brands. Some of the most famous offenders were Nike, Reebok, the Gap, Mattel, and Disney. The White House quickly became involved in setting up a national task force to investigate and regulate the issue. In August 1996, eight apparel firms, a half-dozen human rights organizations, and several trade union representatives were organized into the Apparel Industry Partnership with the aim of establishing a workplace code of conduct (Appelbaum & Dreier 1999, 77). In spite of pressure by the Labor Department and activists, the result was a relatively weak set of standards guaranteeing only that corporations will work to abide by local labor standards in whatever country they operate. Since then, the activists (joined by a few companies) have come up with the Social Accountability 8000 code, a laundry list of basic workplace standards that grant firms SA8000 certification and the right to affix a "no sweat" label to their products. Avon and Toys 'R' Us expressed an early interest in certification (Spar 1998, 9).

A number of U.S. legislators have taken up the sweatshop issue as well. Donald Pease (D-Ohio) and Tom Harkin (D-Iowa) introduced bills to ban the importation of products manufactured by child labor during the George Bush administration (Senser 1994, 13). It was in part because of threats of harsher regulations that the voluntary codes of conduct were agreed upon.

THE OUTSOURCING PHENOMENON

For most Americans, the question of sweatshops is a relatively distant and abstract one, involving poor children in Asia producing goods that cost less in American stores. Only those working in the manufacturing sector, a gradually shrinking population, were directly affected. This changed when the advent of high-speed Internet connections, coupled with better education levels, legal structures, and growth in the Third World made the exportation of certain high-tech activities feasible and profitable. Many activities in today's economy require neither face-to-face interaction nor the shipment of heavy goods. A telephone line is all that is needed to set up a tech support office, telemarketing agency, or even business consulting service. Add an Internet connection and it is possible to transmit a bank's depositor data, manuscripts in need of copy-editing, and so forth. One can even find firms overseas that diagnose X-rays and CAT scans overnight in Bangalore, India—just in time for a 7 AM surgery in New York (Leonhardt 2006).

The result has been the loss of many jobs held by people with advanced degrees and high salaries. While analysts disagree on the scale of the phenomenon, a widely cited estimate point to an average of roughly 200,000 white collar jobs lost to Indian and other firms as a result of outsourcing in the United States (Drezner 2004). As we will see below, firms have found that they only recoup a fraction of the wage differential between Third World and American workers, often encounter great difficulties in managing information flows, and sometimes encounter such high levels of consumer complaint that they reconsider the arrangement (Weidenbaum 2005). The lack of highly skilled workers is pushing wages up in the technology sector in India, sometimes at the rate of 15 percent per year (Schieber 2004). Not that outsourcing is entirely problematic. Some have estimated that the U.S. economy gains twelve to fourteen cents for every dollar it spends on overseas outsourcing (Drezner 2004). In some cases, firms have been able to hire more workers in the U.S. with the savings it gains from outsourcing. Overall, the benefits are diffused across the national economy in the form of cost and price savings (Mankiw 2004).

COMPETING PERSPECTIVES

Globalization is a concept that has generated more "heat" than "light." Although the meaning and significance of globalization are still unclear, people have developed strong and contrary positions on its worth. Much of the debate on globalization (and, by implications, on sweatshops) focuses on the values, philosophies, and personal backgrounds of the debaters.

Robert Gilpin identifies three principal points of view on globalization: the free market perspective, the populist (or nationalist) perspective, and the communitarian perspective. Free market advocates ascribe to globalization, the power to bring in "an era of unprecedented prosperity as more and more nations participate in the global economy, and as financial and technology flows from developed to less developed countries lead to equalization of wealth and development around the world" (Gilpin 2000, 297). Populists, such as Ross Perot and Patrick Buchanan, "blame globalization for most of the social, economic and political ills afflicting the United States and other industrial societies" (Gilpin 2000, 297). They accuse globalization of weakening the independence and inherent vitality of the economies and societies of the major powers. Communitarians, in contrast, criticize globalization on the grounds that it foists "a brutal capitalist tyranny, imperialist exploitation and environmental degradation upon the peoples of the world. They fear a world dominated by huge multinational corporations that will remove all obstacles limiting economic growth . . ." (Gilpin 2000, 298).

We will separate out two facets of the free market perspective: the overall growth of the global economy and the economic development in the Third World per se. Many worry that attacks against sweatshops may ultimately undermine growth in developing countries—which is a very different argument than saying that the search for ever-lower wages will help the global economy as a whole. Also, we will separate out the structural Marxist approach from the humanitarian view under the umbrella of the communitarian perspective. The first focus is on the arguments against sweatshops and outsourcing made by labor unions.

Labor Perspective

Perhaps the most familiar commentary on globalization in the United States comes from the defenders of working-class people. The trade union movement and other populist organizations have built a strong case against free trade and global investment. They point to the tendency since the early 1970s for the wealthy to get an ever-increasing share of national wealth relative to the working class and middle class. For example, in early 2000, the Economic Policy Institute and the Center of Budget and Policy Priorities reported that during the 1990s, the average income of the wealthiest one-fifth of Americans grew by 15 percent, while the income of the middle class grew by only 2 percent and that of the poorest one-fifth stayed the same. In 1999, household income for the wealthiest one-fifth of the population was ten times greater than the income for the poorest one-fifth (AFL-CIO 2000). By 2003, following two years of recession, average household incomes had fallen by $1,500 per year and poverty had increased steadily since 2000 (U.S. Census Bureau 2004). One-fifth of all jobs in the United States provide wages that are too low to support a family of four above poverty, let alone provide insurance or other benefits (AFL-CIO 2004).

Even some economists have acknowledged that worker insecurity increased during the 1990s during the era of "downsizing." Aaronson and Sullivan analyzed trends in employment longevity and noted that the number of workers who choose to stay with a company for more than ten years has dropped substantially over the last twenty years. In the mid-1980s, the average man aged 45 to 54 had been at his place of employment thirteen years. By 1995, that figure had dropped to less than ten years (Aaronson & Sullivan 1998, 21). The overall rate of "displacement" (all forms of involuntary change of workplace) doubled between 1988 and 1995 for workers with five years of tenure on the job. This trend in turn contributed to much higher levels of anxiety about job security during the 1990s and may have contributed to relatively low wage increases throughout the decade. As put by Labor Secretary Robert Reich, "Wages are stuck because people are afraid to ask for a raise. They are afraid they may lose their job" (Reich 1997, in Aaronson & Sullivan 1998, 17). This whole problem is attributed to globalization, where wage competition has spread internationally. Once the recession began to spread in 2000 and 2001, pressure to keep low-wage jobs intensified for labor, but so did pressure to find new sources of cheap labor in order to lower prices still further. The result was the dramatic expansion of outsourcing to new types of activity including service sector jobs such as tech support and customer service which was increasingly performed by middle-class Indians in Mumbai and Bangalore. Even the most sanguine economists acknowledge that trade causes localized pain in any national economy in the form of job losses (Mankiw 2006).

Wage competition is most intense for low-skilled work, according to this perspective (Freeman 1995). People who work in a company that manufactures textiles or footwear in the United States and receive wages of, say, ten dollars per hour (including benefits) are directly threatened by overseas workers who are willing to do the same job for ten cents per hour and no benefits. Nike CEO Phil Knight, while still a business school student, made plans to build an entire company based on outsourcing manufacturing to low-wage countries, making none of the product in the United States or other countries where the consumers were located. He was not alone. More and more firms relocated relatively low-tech industrial production to developing countries after 1975. During the 1980s, hundreds of U.S. firms moved to Mexico to establish "maquiladoras"—manufacturing plants located just across the border that could use cheap Mexican labor, pay lower corporate taxes, and be freed from American health, safety, and environmental regulations, while retaining easy access to the U.S. market. During the 1990s, even more companies relocated to China for the same reasons, except that strict antiunion laws and an authoritarian government made Chinese workers even more placid than those in Mexico. Anecdotal evidence points to a direct zero-sum relationship between the relocation of these jobs and higher unemployment among unskilled workers in the United States (Korten 1995, 229–237).

For labor unions, then, the sweatshop issue primarily involves protecting American jobs and wages in the face of the globalization of the assembly line. The alliance that has formed between student activists and trade unionists is seen by many as a healthy and even exciting new type of activism. It closes the rift that goes back to the Vietnam War, when trade union leaders condemned antiwar protesters (Appelbaum & Dreier 1999, 77). Others fear that unions may be manipulating students to support protectionist measures that may ultimately hurt overseas workers (Olson 2000).

Global Free Market Perspective

It can be said that liberals (in the eighteenth-century sense of the term) invented globalization. They have consistently been skeptical of the prominence attached to the state by populists and instead have imagined and designed an international structure that minimizes territorial and political boundaries. Their vision of the world is the Internet, where countries simply do not matter anymore (Hudson 1999). Liberals first thrilled at what they called "interdependence" in the 1970s, and they were among the first to identify "globalization" (Ruggie 1995). Although some liberals fear such a world order might grow out of control, most believe it is government interference in the marketplace of goods and ideas that has brought misery to humanity.

Bryan and Ferrell wrote that when the spread of multinational corporate investment and the lowering of trade and investment barriers through the World Trade Organization open up global markets, the potential exists for creative and entrepreneurial activity to flourish worldwide (Bryan & Ferrell 1996). Economists point to the dramatic increase in average incomes worldwide as a direct result of fewer economic barriers, lower transportation costs, and new technologies. Micklethwait and Wooldridge point out that globalization simply has not contributed to a dramatic rise in overall incomes but has done so by creating new jobs, contrary to the forecasts of populists. The North American Free Trade Agreement, which populists expected to eliminate U.S. jobs, has instead generated 14 million new job openings since 1994 (Micklethwait & Wooldridge 2000, 109). Their biggest fear is that trade unions may hijack globalization for narrow, short-sighted reasons: "[T]he goal of eradicating child labor is a noble one, but when it has been linked to trade, it has nearly always been for protectionist reasons and has often had disastrous consequences for those it has tried to help" (Micklethwait & Wooldridge 2000, 113). If wages seem to decline, the cause is primarily a mismanaged economic transition from local to global production (Richardson 1995).

Some analysts stress that wage differentials are not as serious a concern as labor defenders claim because they are directly related to productivity. As Golub points out, if one takes into account the cost of output per worker-hour, then wages are virtually the same worldwide (Golub 1999, 22). In the Philippines, for example, although wages are roughly one-tenth the wages of American workers, worker productivity is even less, with the result that work done in the Philippines is actually 8 percent more expensive than work done in the United States. Similar figures apply to Malaysia and India (although the same is not true in Mexico and South Korea, where relative productivity outpaces relative wages; Golub 1999, 23). When the relative purchasing power of these low wages is factored in, the developing country workers are actually better off than their Western counterparts because they can buy far more per unit of output (i.e., a Bangladeshi who is paid fifty cents to produce one shirt each hour can buy more local goods at the end of a ten-hour day with five dollars than can her counterpart in New York who is paid five dollars to produce ten shirts per hour and thereby earns fifty dollars).

Sweatshops, though deplored in principle, are accepted as part of the process of globalization, as is outsourcing. As put by Greg Mankiw, one-time chairman of George Bush's Council of Economic Advisors, "When we talk about outsourcing, outsourcing is just a new way of going international trade. . . . Outsourcing is the latest manifestation of the gains from trade that economists have talked about at least since Adam Smith" (Mankiw 2006, 8). Corporations have pointed out that consumers benefit tremendously when producers take advantage of wage differentials, and this pressure from consumers forces producers to seek ever-lower wage rates. In the 1980s, Levi Strauss tried to keep its production in the United States and maintain high relative wage rates in developing country factories, but it could not sustain those practices. It had to close fifty-eight U.S. plants and lay off more than 10,000 workers to stay competitive (Korten 1995, 233). As put by Reebok's Indonesia representative: "Cutting costs is part of our business" (Brecher & Costello 1994, 20). "Costs of running a factory are about 16 percent more if you comply with the new labor laws" in China, according to one exporter. Since customers don't seem to care much about the treatment of workers, compliance guarantees you will lose sales (*South China Morning Post* October 27, 2003, 2). All these problems are blamed on pressures to get prices ever lower in a Wal-Mart-dominated retail environment. In the high-tech sphere, products must now hit the market quickly as they will likely be eclipsed by some new innovation within eight months (Ghausi 2002).

Developmental Perspective

Still other liberals question whether Western criticism of sweatshops misses the point that those in sweatshops are, after all, working. In countries where unemployment is higher than 50 percent and low-paying farm labor accounts for most of the jobs, many see employment in factories as the way out of perpetual poverty. Consider, for example, that in 1990 a typical Chinese farmer earned $1,130 per year, while an unskilled Chinese factory worker made roughly $2,000 and a skilled factory worker earned $5,800. During a recent visit to Bangladesh, the author met dozens of adult men with children to raise who earned only enough for one or two servings of rice per day (less than ten cents) working as hired farm help in depressed villages. In comparison, the young women who eagerly went to the garment factory each morning in the city and earned two dollars per day were in the upper middle class.

From this point of view, the anti-sweatshop campaign and the anti-outsourcing backlash are seen with skepticism in Third World capitals. Molly Ivins has argued that they actually made development more difficult for many of these countries, although it may help those who are already working in the factories (Ivins & Smith 1999). Particularly when linked to trade unions, the sweatshop movement seems to be aimed at curtailing exports of garments and other basic manufactured goods, which could lead to severe depression in many countries. Already most developing countries are working hard to improve the climate for international business, and they are finding it difficult to keep the factories that have relocated there. International capital always has other opportunities to reduce wages by relocating to another developing country (in Bangladesh, wages are kept low to prevent companies from moving to China, for example). Even worse, the alternative to sweatshop jobs going to developing countries is the possibility that the manufacturing process will simply be mechanized, thereby eliminating the jobs entirely (Kristof 2002). The flow of contracts to Indian firms will likely create four million new well-paying jobs and contribute directly to the lifting of the nation out of poverty in a generation (Mehta 2005).

Structural Marxist Perspective

In response to the developmental perspective, numerous scholars have developed a structural analysis of the world economy, based loosely on the work of Marx, Lenin, Fernand Braudel, and Immanuel Wallerstein. This structural Marxist perspective argues that the development that occurs as a result of globalization is not the sort of development any country should want. Rather, it is better understood as taking a subordinate place in the global economy, where countries must surrender control over their national destinies to provide the raw material of capitalist production. As early as the 1700s, economists began to note that capitalist production tended to concentrate relatively high-tech activities in advanced, industrialized nations, whereas low-tech activities were sloughed off to remote, inhospitable regions (Mittelman 2000, 54). Later, Lenin pointed out that not only was high-tech manufacturing concentrated in the powerful countries, but so were banking and corporate decision making, which led to a global structure that transcended traditional imperialism in search of both raw materials and labor and new consumer markets. Gradually, more and more regions were brought into this "world economy," such that national boundaries became increasingly insignificant in the pursuit of efficiency and profit (Wallerstein 1991; Korten 1995, 239). As put by Ernst Mandel, "Capital by its very nature tolerates no geographical limit to its expansion" (Mandel 1975, 310). It was on these Marxist ideas that the concepts of the global factory and the global assembly line were based in more recent years (Gereffi 1994).

In this context, sweatshops are viewed as merely part of the inexorable expansion of capital production on a global scale. A product moves in steps from raw material to finished good, going from factory to factory in a "commodity chain" in which profits gradually increase as one gets closer to the point of final sale. Sweatshops are driven to a large extent by pressures from brand-name companies seeking lower production costs. They put pressure directly on international traders and overseas buyers and indirectly on the factories themselves. As put by Gereffi:

> The main job of the core company in buyer-driven commodity chains is to manage these production and trade networks and make sure all the pieces of the business come together as an integrated whole. Profits in buyer-driven chains thus derive not from scale economies and technological advances as in producer-driven chains, but rather from unique combinations of high-value research, design, sales, marketing, and financial services that allow the buyers and branded merchandisers to act as strategic brokers. . . . (Gereffi 1994, 99)

Factory managers constantly complain of being required to reduce costs so as to maintain contracts with foreign companies. They are in an extremely vulnerable position because the company can change suppliers with the stroke of a pen.

In spite of these relatively new mechanisms of exploitation, structural Marxists see very little new in the contemporary debate about globalization (Germain 2000). While this might give some hope that we need not fear that some horrific new problem has emerged, it also offers a pessimistic prediction that there is no reason to expect anything to change much, no matter how many well-intentioned campaigns are mounted. Although antislavery campaigns in the 1800s ended the more blatant forms of slavery in the West, these activities simply shifted to the Third World. And although it may be possible to end formal slavery, child labor, and indentured servitude in time, there is no reason, based on this perspective, to expect that conditions will markedly improve for the workers of the world. By implication, the only solution is global revolution.

Humanitarian Perspective

Those who are squeamish about a violent overthrow of the global capitalist system focus instead on piecemeal reform and attempts to improve the living conditions of those most injured by global capitalism. The effort at humanitarian reform is as old as capitalism itself. Although it does not repudiate such age-old institutions as wage labor, private ownership of land, the assembly line, or outsourcing, it strives to create minimum standards of human treatment. National labor standards, as mentioned earlier, have been set up since the turn of the twentieth century, although their enforcement has often been spotty.

In the post–World War II era, the International Labour Organization became a forum for countries to institute new standards of conduct in their treatment of wage labor. Slavery, indentured servitude, child labor, and other practices were banned, and countries were urged to establish minimum worker safety standards, reasonable wages, vacation and overtime practices, and so forth. These treaties were endorsed by almost every country, although compliance was not consistent. While most developed countries already complied with these rules when they were established, few developing countries did. Even socialist countries (which were touted as a "worker's paradise") did not allow such basic worker freedoms as the right of workers to independently organize and strike.

When the sweatshop issue emerged in the 1980s and exploded in the 1990s, the treatment of most workers violated principles enshrined in treaties that not only had been accepted as a worthwhile aspiration but had also been explicitly accepted by the countries in question and had become the law of the land. Thus the sweatshop campaign can be seen as an effort to enforce international standards rather than set new ones. It may be unrealistic to expect that the movement can accomplish much more than this.

In this respect, the sweatshop campaign is having a measurable impact. Global corporations such as Nike and Reebok are often little more than a brand name, as we have seen. As a result, their image and reputation are all-important. In addition to joining the Apparel Industry Partnership and endorsing the Social Accountability 8000 code of conduct, many textile firms have hired independent auditors to carry out on-site inspections of garment factories overseas. Some have allowed human rights activists to tour factories, although they have generally done so under close corporate supervision (UNITE! 2000). Some apparel manufacturers have even engaged in political protests of their own, as evidenced by the nearly industry-wide boycott of Myanmar's military dictatorship. Some clothing businesses are finding it easier to take principled positions now that the entire industry is under scrutiny (Spar 1998). Still others are fighting back, arguing that poor countries are better off with sweatshops than nothing (Sowell 2002). They criticize the "self-righteous" campaigners who protest WTO meetings (as they did again in Cancun in 2002) for making life more difficult for the poor.

CONCLUSION

How do these issues relate to the broader question of globalization? It is clear that the anti-sweatshop campaign and outsourcing skepticism have brought to the attention of Western audiences the links between disparate social groups across the planet. It is hard not to think of Pakistani child workers when purchasing a soccer ball in Memphis, or of young Malaysian factory workers when buying a pair of pants in London. But recognizing the links and even understanding them is not the same as understanding whether they are good or bad or how to change them. Globalization can be seen as merely a fact of human existence. It may be up to us to determine what values are jeopardized by it.

 # DEBATE TOPIC

Should the anti-sweatshop campaign be supported on college campuses?

PRO
The anti-sweatshop campaign has many supporters, who point out the following: (1) Sweatshops are inherently unfair to their workers, given the overall profits the firms are making and the paltry wages they pay. (2) Sweatshops are unethical, in that the working conditions and wages are so low they violate minimum international human rights standards. (3) Buying goods made in sweatshops or owning stock in the parent companies makes one complicitous in the social ills that are taking place.

CON
Opponents of the campaign point out the following: (1) Sweatshops are an improvement for most developing country workers, who might otherwise be forced to beg or prostitute themselves. (2) The wages are set based on productivity and skill; workers need only improve these to obtain higher wages. (3) A boycott of sweatshop goods may simply increase mechanization, which will eliminate even the undesirable jobs.

QUESTIONS TO CONSIDER

1. How strong is the corporate claim that sweatshops and the job losses from outsourcing are a necessary evil brought about by consumer demand and a tough competitive environment? What contrary evidence can be brought to bear?

2. To what extent are sweatshops and outsourcing merely the extension of the global spread of laissez-faire capitalism? Is it possible to solve the problem in one factory or corporation without changing the global system?

3. What are the dangers of the anti-sweatshop campaign and outsourcing skepticism? What are the alternatives for achieving the same objective of improving living conditions for workers in developing countries?

WEBSITES

Social Accountability 8000 code: **www.cepaa.org/sa8000.htm**
Apparel Industry Partnership: **www.lchr/sweatshop/aipfull.htm#WORKPLACE**
Council on Economic Priorities: **www.cepnyc.org**
NAASCOM (India's outsourcing advocacy organization): **www.discountansweringservice.com/Answering-Service/naascom-call-centers.html**

Sweatshop Watch: **www.sweatshopwatch.org**
National Labor Committee: **www.nlcnet.org**
Greg Mankiw's blog: **gregmankiw.blogspot.com**
United Students Against Sweatshops: **home.sprintmail.com/~jeffnkari/USAS/**
UNITE! trade union: **www.uniteunion.org**

REFERENCES

Aaronson, Daniel, and Daniel Sullivan. "The Decline of Job Security in the 1990s: Displacement, Anxiety, and Their Effect on Wage Growth." *Economic Perspectives* 22 #1 (1998): 17–43.

AFL-CIO. "Income Equality Nosedives: The Rich vs. Everyone Else." Available at: **www.aflcio.org/articles/gap/index.html,** Accessed on January 18, 2000.

Appelbaum, Richard, and Peter Dreier. "The Campus Anti-Sweatshop Movement." *The American Prospect* (September 1999): 71–83.

Brecher, Jeremy, and Tim Costello. *Global Village or Global Pillage: Economic Reconstruction from the Bottom Up* (Boston: South End Press, 1994).

Bryan, Lowell, and Diana Ferrell. *Market Unbound: Unleashing Global Capitalism* (New York: John Wiley & Sons, 1996).

DiCaprio, Lisa. "Women Workers, State-Sponsored Work, and the Right to Subsistence During the French Revolution." *Journal of Modern History* 71 #3 (September 1999): 519–545.

Drezner, Daniel. "The Outsourcing Bogeyman." *Foreign Affairs* (May/June 2004): 22–34

Freeman, Richard. "Are Your Wages Set in Beijing?" *Journal of Economic Perspectives* 9 #3 (Summer 1995): 15–32.

Gereffi, Gary. "The Organization of Buyer-Driven Chains: How U.S. Retailers Shape Overseas Production Networks." In Gary Gereffi and Miguel Korzeniewicz, eds., *Commodity Chains and Global Capitalism* (Westport, CT: Greenwood Press, 1994).

Germain, Randall, ed. *Globalization and Its Critics: Perspectives from Political Economy* (New York: St. Martin's Press, 2000).

Ghausi, Nadjya. "Trends in Outsourced Manufacturing — Reduced Risk and Maintaining Flexibility when Moving to an Outsourced Model." *Assembly Automoation* 22 #1 (2002): 21–26.

Gill, Stephen. "Theorizing the Interregnum: The Double Movement and Global Politics in the 1990s." In Bjorn Hettne, ed., *International Political Economy*, 1995, 65–99.

Gilpin, Robert. *The Challenge of Global Capitalism: The World Economy in the 21st Century* (Princeton, NJ: Princeton University Press, 2000).

Golub, Stephen. *Labor Costs and International Trade* (Washington, DC: AEI Press, 1999).

Hudson, Yaeger, ed. *Globalism and the Obsolescence of the State* (Lewiston, NY: Edwin Mellon Press, 1999).

Ivins, Molly, and Fred Smith. "Opposing Views on Sweatshops." *Insight on the News* 15 #44 (November 29, 1999): 40–47.

Kasbekar, Vijay. "I.T. Outsourcing: India Leads." *Asian Review of Business and Technology* October 1, 1999, 1.

Kernaghan, Charles. "Sweatshop Blues: Companies Love Misery." *Dollars & Sense* 222 (March–April 1999): 18–22.

Korten, David. *When Corporations Rule the World* (New York: Kumarian Press, 1995).

Kristof, Nicholas. "Let Them Sweat," *New York Times* June 25, 2002.

Leonhardt, David. "Political Clout in the Age of Outsourcing." *New York Times* April 19, 2006.

Mandel, Ernst. *Late Capitalism* (London: NLB, 1975).

Mankiw, N. Gregory. "Outsourcing Redux." Unpublished op.ed. Available at:
    gregmankiw.blogspot.com/2006/05/outsourcing-redux.html. Accessed on May 7, 2006.

Mankiw, N. Gregory, and Phillip Swagel. "The Politics and Economics of Offshore Outsourcing."
    Unpublished manuscript. March 2004.

Mehta, Neil Singhvi. "Future of Outsourcing: India Is Seeing Giant Strides in Practices."
    Advocate February 22, 2005, 19.

Micklethwait, John, and Adrian Wooldridge. *A Future Perfect: The Essentials of Globalization*
    (New York: Crown Business, 2000).

Mittelman, James. *The Globalization Syndrome: Transformation and Resistance* (Princeton,
    NJ: Princeton University Press, 2000).

Olson, Walter. "Look for the Kiwi Label." *Reason* 32 #3 (July 2000): 52–57.

Press, Eyal. "Kathie Lee's Slip." *The Nation* 262 #24 (July 17, 1996): 6–8.

Reich, Robert. *Locked in the Cabinet* (New York: Alfred Knopf, 1997).

Richardson, J. David. "Income Inequality and Trade: How to Think, What to Conclude." *Journal
    of Economic Perspectives* 9 #3 (Summer 1995): 33–55.

Rothstein, Frances Abrahamer, and Michael Blim, eds. *Anthropology and the Global Factory: Studies
    of the New Industrialization in the Late Twentieth Century* (New York: Bergin & Garvey, 1992).

Ruggie, John Gerard. "At Home Abroad, Abroad at Home: International Liberalization and
    Domestic Stability in the New World Economy." *Millennium* 24 #3 (1995): 3–27.

Schanberg, Sydney, and Marie Dorigny. "Six Cents an Hour." *Life* 19 #7 (June 1996): 38–47.

Scheiber, Noam. "As a Center for Outsourcing, India Could Be Losing Its Edge." *New York Times*
    May 9, 2004, C3.

Senser, Robert. "Danger! Children at Work." *Commonweal* 121 #14 (August 19, 1994): 12–15.

South China Morning Post October 27, 2003, 2.

Sowell, Thomas. "Truth About Third World 'Exploitation'." *Human Events* 58 #36 (September
    2002): 21.

Spar, Debora. "The Spotlight on the Bottom Line: How Multinationals Export Human Rights."
    Foreign Affairs 77 #2 (March–April 1998): 7–13.

UN Chronicle. "50 to 200 Million Children Under 15 Are in World's Work Force, ILO Says."
    UN Chronicle 23 (November 1986): 116.

UNITE! "Sweatshops Behind the Swoosh," April 25, 2000 report. **www.uniteunion.org/
    pressbox/nike-report.html.**

U.S. Census Bureau, "Income, Poverty, and Health Insurance coverage in the United States:
    2003," by Carmen DeNavas-Walt, Bernadette D. Proctor and Robert J. Mills. (General
    Printing Office, Washington, D. C. 2004).

U. S. News & World Report January 16, 1984, 68.

U. S. News & World Report November 22, 1993, 48.

Wallerstein, Immanuel. *Geopolitics and Geoculture: Essays on the Changing World-System*
    (New York: Cambridge, 1991).

Weidenbaum, Murray. "Outsourcing: Pros and Cons." *Business Horizons* (July/August 2005): 311.

CASE 17

Regionalism in the Developing World

INTRODUCTION

Regionalism

A global order based on respect for law and tolerance of differences seems beyond our grasp, but many hope that spheres of peace can be established at the regional level. A region is whatever its members choose; it typically involves contiguous territory, common culture, and interdependent economies and societies. Although regional organizations have tended to fall flat (the Organization of African Unity is a case in point), there are indications that in Europe and perhaps elsewhere regionalism is healthy and offers a real opportunity for improving people's living conditions. Economic integration is one type of regionalism, involving reduced obstacles to trade, investment, and migration. Political integration leads to some form of federal or unitary state. The United States represents political integration well, and the European Union illustrates what is meant by economic integration.

Regional economic organizations can generally be categorized in terms of their objectives and methods. The least painful or controversial steps typically involve standardization of industrial or technical designs, such as agreeing on the gauge of railroads. This makes it somewhat easier to market goods beyond a company's local customer base. More difficult and painful are efforts to increase regional trade directly through mutual reductions in tariffs and quotas (a free trade zone). These efforts are often combined with the establishment of a common regional tariff to be placed on imports from outside the region (customs union). The tariff serves as an inducement to help soften the blow of opening domestic markets to goods from other regional players—at least goods from outside the region will still be more expensive for a time. The next most difficult level of integration involves removal of non-tariff barriers that interfere with the flow of goods and services. For example, one country in the region may have an especially high corporate tax rate, which means products from that state are necessarily more expensive. Harmonization involves making as many government policies as possible uniform across the region so that no business or consumer is penalized. Tax rates, banking interest rates, retirement benefits, teaching certification requirements, and so forth, must be made as uniform as possible.

The most difficult—and therefore rare—is outright federalization of a region, whereby the entire area is brought under a single political authority. Although some allowances may be made for local autonomy, major national policies would fall under a single jurisdiction. This would include economic, social, legal, and security policies traditionally managed at the local level. Federalization has taken place in only a few instances, such as the formation of the United States in the 1780s and of Germany in the 1870s, although some believe Europe is now pointed in this direction.

In the developing world, regionalism seems to have greater obstacles than in other areas in large part because even the achievement of economic integration is unlikely to bear fruit. Most developing countries do not trade to any great extent with each other but rely instead on access to the markets of industrialized countries. In addition, many firms and even whole sectors are teetering on bankruptcy and opening markets to more efficient foreign competitors—even those from neighboring countries—could cause economic catastrophe.

The close economic links between most developed countries and industrialized countries sometimes comes with political strings attached as well. Almost all developing countries were under colonial control in the past fifty years and the former Mother Countries usually retain considerable influence. In many cases, postcolonial institutions have been established—such as the British Commonwealth or the Zone Franc—that directly tie the old Empire together on new terms. Sometimes former colonies permit the troops of the former colonizer to remain in place after independence. But even without that, most countries' school systems, transportation networks, and linguistic heritage link them inexorably with a former colonizer.

One would expect, overall, that there would be relatively few instances of integration among developing countries. And this is largely the case. But three very interesting examples of regionalism are presented here and offer a range of possibilities for would-be region-builders.

KEY FIGURES

Julius Nyerere   President of Tanzania, 1964–1985. He advocated a more loose association for the OAU.

Haile Selassi   Emperor of Ethiopia, 1930–1974. He advocated a more loose association for the OAU.

Mohamad Mahathir   Prime Minister of Malaysia, 1981–2002. He was a strong advocate of the "ASEAN Way" and resisted foreign interference in the region.

Muammar Qaddafi   President of Libya since 1969. He played a key role in the creation of the African Union.

Carlos Menem   President of Argentina, 1989–1999. He played a key role in negotiating Mercosur.

Kwame Nkrumah   President of Ghana, 1957–1966. He called for the creation of an African federation instead of the looser OAU.

Thabo Mbeki   First President of the African Union's Assembly.

Fernando Collor de Mello   President of Brazil, 1990–1992. He played a key role in negotiating Mercosur.

Fernando Henrique Cardoso   President of Brazil, 1995–2003. Advocate of more open markets.

Luiz Ignacio Lula da Silva   President of Brazil, since 2003. His left-leaning policies have dominated Mercosur in recent years.

Hugo Chavez   President of Venezuela, since 1998. He has adopted a distinctly anti-American posture that is being imitated in a few Latin American states.

CHRONOLOGY

1963
Conference of Independent African States and Governments held at which the Organization of African Unity was formed.

1967
ASEAN is founded by five nations in Southeast Asia.

1981
The African Charter is signed. It is the first continent-wide human rights treaty.

1984
Morocco quits the OAU in protest over its admission of Western Sahara.

1991
ASEAN negotiators participate in the drafting of the Cambodian peace agreement.
Argentina, Brazil, Uruguay, and Paraguay negotiate a commitment to create a customs union by 1994.

1994
The African Economic Community agreement is signed. It aims at promoting free trade across the continent and later gave rise to the African Union.

(*continued*)

(continued)

1995
Vietnam joins ASEAN.

The Mercosur customs union comes into being.

1996
The ASEAN Regional Forum is initiated with the aim of providing a place where ASEAN states could negotiate trade and investment agreements with neighboring states such as China and South Korea.

1997
Myanmar joins ASEAN. The organization now has ten members—twice its original size.

Mercosur effectively blocks negotiations on the creation of the Free Trade Area of the Americas.

1998
The Asian financial crisis which began in late-1997 has spread across the globe, threatening international financial stability and leading to deep recessions in numerous countries.

2002
The OAU is replaced by the African Union. Shortly thereafter the AU's Peace and Security Council is created.

2006
Venezuela becomes a full member of Mercosur.

THREE CASES OF REGIONALISM: ASEAN, THE AFRICAN UNION, AND MERCOSUR

Asean

In 1967, following a harrowing confrontation between Indonesia and Malaysia which threatened to engulf the region in violence, the leaders of five Southeast Asian states (Thailand, Malaysia, Indonesia, the Philippines, and Singapore) formed the Association of Southeast Asian Nations (ASEAN). They pledged themselves to principles of mutual respect and nonviolent dispute settlement. This commitment was renewed at the first meeting of ASEAN heads of state in Bali in 1976 where the founding principles were clearly articulated:

> 1) Mutual respect for the independence, sovereignty, equality, territorial integrity and national identity of all nations; 2) The right of every state to lead its national existence free from external interference, subversion or coercion; 3) Noninterference in the internal affairs of one another; 4) Settlement of differences or disputes by peaceful means; 5) Renunciation of the threat or use of force; and 6) Effective cooperation among themselves. (ASEAN Secretariat 2006)

ASEAN's relative success has been attributed to a carefully calculated program of "agreeing to disagree" (Denoon & Colbert 1998–1999, 506). Various proposals to make ASEAN a regional military alliance have been repeatedly rejected by ASEAN members on the grounds that bilateral arrangements provide more flexibility and fewer risks (Acharya 1991, 161, 163). The organization has avoided heavy institutionalization and preferred instead to keep important decision-making informal and consensus-based. Some have argued that this approach—known as the "ASEAN Way"—is consistent with local cultural norms. As put by Kivimaki:

> The so-called Southeast Asian culture of consultation and consensus means conflict avoidance principles that include a preference for a) lengthy negotiations and b) quiet, c) non-legalistic, d) personalized e) confidence-building, aimed at f) gradual downplaying and prevention of disputes g) by means that can be accepted unanimously, h) using the principle of lowest common denominator. (Kivimaki 2001, 16)

Naturally, this approach can be maddeningly long at times. The ASEAN-brokered peace agreement in Cambodia, for example, began shortly after Vietnam's invasion of the country in 1978 and ended in 1991 with the signing of the Comprehensive Political Settlement. In the mean-time, ASEAN consensus was severely stretched as Thailand adopted a hard-line against Vietnam at the outset even though Indonesia was inclined to improve ties with what it hoped would be an ally against China (which it considered the greater threat). ASEAN states deferred to Thailand since the Vietnamese threat was more immediate (given the common border), but was taken aback when Thailand did an about-face in 1988 and decided that it would try to improve relations with Vietnam in the hope of establishing trade ties (Narine 1998, 206). In the long run, both Indonesia and Thailand got what they wanted when Vietnam joined ASEAN in 1995 (Denoon & Colbert 1998–1999, 510). By 1997, Myanmar joined Laos and Cambodia as new members. The organization now has a combined annual production worth just over $700 billion.

> While nonviolence, consensus, and noninterference may make for a uniquely tentative organization, the fact remains that ASEAN has a solid record of achievement and a promising future. As put by Kivimaki, ASEAN has demonstrated that it is possible to create a relatively peaceful and even cooperative regional association without democracy or political liberalism. It is noteworthy that, contrary to the "democratic peace" theory of international relations, that even the relatively autocratic states we find in Southeast Asia have carved out a zone of relative stability (Kivimaki 2001, 7).

Two factors may account for this success, beside the "ASEAN Way" of decision making: the withdrawal of major powers from the region and the general prosperity of the region's economy—especially in the wake of the Asian financial crisis of 1997–1998. With regard to the role of the major powers, as of 1967, Great Britain, the United States, and the Soviet Union each had a considerable interest and presence in the region—especially when one considers the Vietnam War (see case 7). But by 1971, the British had decided to withdraw from Malaysia and Singapore and the Americans had announced, via the "Nixon doctrine" that Thailand and the Philippines would need to rely on their own resources to defend themselves in the future (Acharya 1992, 16). The Malaysian government began proposing the "neutralization" of Southeast Asia—both for pragmatic and nationalist reasons (Garofano 2002, 514). While initially rebuffed, the idea was ultimately drawn up at a 1971 statement creating a Zone of Peace, Freedom and Neutrality which called for external powers to withdraw in time. The statement was codified as a treaty at the 1976 Bali Summit mentioned earlier, although it was softened considerably (Narine 1998, 200).

The relative quietude of the region owes much to the relative lack of interest on the part of great powers. But this does not mean that ASEAN members are not interested in them. In the past, ASEAN was able to influence trade policy in Australia and Japan as well as push certain initiatives through the United Nations (Kurus 1993). Since the mid-1990s, ASEAN has reached out to Australia, New Zealand, Russia, China, India, China, and South Korea with the goal of establishing some form of special relationship, whether in trade or security. Of particular importance is the ASEAN Regional Forum whereby members hope to spread the "ASEAN Way" to all the countries of eastern Asia and beyond. Initiated in 1996, members include more than a dozen countries in the region, including China, India, Russia, and both Koreas. The countries have held a number of meetings to discuss issues of mutual interest, such as the status of the South China Sea which is claimed by China even though countries in the region have long occupied and operated there as sovereigns. The group has also discussed nuclear weapons in Korea, the status of East Timor, and globalization (ASEAN Secretariat 2006).

On the economic front, the key thing ASEAN has assisted is the stabilization of the region, which has permitted each state to adopt and profit from pro-trade policies. That said, ASEAN members are attempting to forge a regional free trade area whereby governments are lowering tariffs on a number of goods beyond expectations set by the World Trade Organization. ASEAN has also promoted regional industrial projects (not all have done well) and local development projects (Hussey 1991). The result has been a significant expansion of trade in the region, although intraregional trade (among ASEAN countries themselves) remains relatively limited at only about twenty percent of the total (see Figure 17.1).

ASEAN is actively engaged in crafting regional agreements with India, Russia, and China as well, in the hope of cooperating on a wide range of activities and eventually lowering tariffs and other obstacles (Banda & Whalley 2005).

Several obstacles may prevent ASEAN from becoming a trade union or anything more than it is. For one thing, it is clear that most ASEAN members prefer a "live and let live" policy and opt not to act even when they could. The organization has been largely silent, for example, on the human rights crisis in Myanmar. It is also clear that members prefer the flexibility of bilateral arrangements, with the result that there is considerable variation in the types of economic and political agreements that have been entered into. Trade agreements between Singapore and numerous other states, for instance, threaten to undermine whatever gains ASEAN's free trade agreement might achieve (Stubbs 2002, 452). Likewise, some members have closer military ties than others. There is no indication that this will change soon.

Exports from ASEAN Countries 1996-2004

Figure 17.1 Exports from ASEAN countries

This means that many of the disputes that have plagued the region historically have yet to be resolved. There are still numerous territorial disputes and questions of compensation for past wrongs outstanding. It is conceivable—especially if a great power becomes involved—that these disputes could one day lead to violence. This would be particularly problematic if China decided to use force to assert its claims in the South China Sea—a move the United States would be unlikely to ignore.

Overall, then, it is premature to say that ASEAN is either economically integrated or a "security community" (Garofano 2002, 520). On the other hand, the conditions are clearly far better than before 1967, and ASEAN can take substantial credit (Kivimaki 2001, 21). If the ambitious goals ASEAN has set for itself materialize, it is possible that it could serve as the fulcrum for a strengthened East Asian zone of cooperation.

African Union

In 1963, heads of state from a wide range of newly independent African states met at Addis Ababa to found the Organization of African Unity (OAU) with the express purpose of promoting unity among African states, defend their sovereignty, eradicate colonialism, and promote cooperation. This would be done on the basis of strict respect for each other's legal equality, territorial integrity, commitment to noninterference, and renunciation of the use of force in settling disputes (van Walraven

1999, 138, 145). By the mid-1980s, every African nation except Morocco was a member. The association has a combined annual product of just over $500 billion.

In July 2002, the OAU closed its doors and was replaced by the African Union—a new organization modeled on the European Union that was designed to achieve many of the same goals as the OAU, but with greater effectiveness. While it is too early to assess the achievement of this goal, it is worth asking what measures the leaders of African states took to fix what they saw as the weakness of the OAU.

The OAU had an ambitious agenda that gradually expanded over its history. Born at a time of turmoil and uncertainty, the founders of the organization were inspired both by a hope of forging unity—perhaps even political unification—as well as a fear of continued interference by Western states that in the previous century had conquered and colonized almost the entire continent (Packer & Rukare 2002, 366). By the time of its demise, the organization had programs and agencies to address international conflict, civil strife, refugees, environmental degradation, human rights, economic integration, mutual development assistance, common foreign policies, and so forth. It had even begun the establishment of a regional court of human rights and the rudiments of a peace-keeping force (Zweifel 2006, 148).

But due to conflicting views on the OAU's purposes, competition among African states for power and status, and fear of interference in domestic affairs by outsiders, the organization was given relatively few resources—legal or financial—to implement these ideas. Much of the founding documents of the OAU stress the principle of sovereign equality and noninterference. As a result, the institution was never empowered to intrude directly in the numerous human rights disasters—including genocide—that afflicted the continent from the beginning (Packer & Rukare 2002, 367). The court provided for in the Charter of the OAU to resolve disputes between states by an appeal to legal principles never functioned—presumably because no state wants to be bound by its decisions (Naldi 1999, 24). The human rights convention, known as the African Charter, drafted in 1981, specifically allows states to violate their citizens' human rights "for reasons and conditions previously laid down by law" —a massive escape clause (Welch 1994, 56).

In the area of peacekeeping, the OAU Charter avoided the subject entirely, focusing instead on ad-hoc arrangements and conciliation. There was no body in OAU empowered to draft sanctions against lawless states, nor was there any established mechanism for the deployment of peacekeepers—even by invitation (Jonah 1994, 5). Rather, the chairman of the OAU's Assembly of states would from time to time weigh in on a conflict and offer mediation services. Gradually, this role also came to be filled by the senior civil servant of the OAU—the secretary-general. But since such functions were not spelled out in their job descriptions, their involvement was ad-hoc and unpredictable.

The OAU, more often than not, stayed aloof from African crises. It had little to say about the wars in the Congo in the 1960s which nearly split the country in three and prompted massive interventions by Belgian and UN forces, although it took a stand against Biafra's secession from Nigeria in 1981 (Naldi 1999, 12). Likewise, more recently, it took an ambivalent position on the question of Eritrean independence. Part of the reason for this ambivalence is the OAU's early commitment to preserving all territorial boundaries across the continent—regardless of their usefulness or wisdom (Ford 2001, 14). While this has probably discouraged a large number of border wars, it has left the organization in an awkward position where legitimate demands for self-determination arise.

In some cases, the OAU was forced to act. During the 1980s, a rebel movement in Western Sahara fighting for independence from Morocco secured the OAU's support and became a member of the organization in 1984—at which point Morocco left (Layachi 1994, 38). The event nearly destroyed the institution in the process. When Libya invaded Chad in 1980, the OAU joined the UN in demanding its withdrawal. Once Libyan troops were gone in 1981, a few thousand troops from across Africa were deployed to supervise the cease-fire in traditional peacekeeping fashion. But the numbers deployed were only half of what were committed, and the lack of resources was so severe that the OAU was forced to ask the UN for logistical support. Once the Chadian government withdrew its support for the deployment, the troops were removed after only a year (Naldi 1999, 31; Jonah 1994, 8).

This said, recent efforts by the OAU to strengthen its capacity in the areas of conflict and human rights were pointed in the right direction. In spite of its weaknesses, the African Charter on human rights promised results because it created an independent supervisory body known as the African Commission on Human and Peoples' Rights in 1987. The OAU members also issued numerous statements—some in treaty form—condemning subversion, mercenarism, foreign intervention, apartheid, and colonialism (Naldi 1999, 12). Many of these have formed the basis for new understandings of states' duties and rights—especially with respect to decolonization and the eradication of apartheid in South Africa, both of which have been essentially accomplished.

On the economic front, the OAU's achievements are even more modest, although again there are intriguing plans on paper for a common market and mutual development program. The OAU was hampered by an unwillingness and incapacity on the part of most countries to pay annual dues, and the organization routinely was forced to operate with only half of its budget paid up (Packer & Rukare 2002, 377). The fundamental economic realities of the region also operate against economic integration since there is relatively little intraregional trade and most states are more deeply linked to their former mother countries. France, Britain, and the EU generally have a strong network of economic ties covering trade, monetary policy, and development assistance that mitigate against a regional package (Packer & Rukare 2002, 367).

The creation of the African Union was prompted by a determination to strengthen African institutions. It began almost imperceptibly with a clause in a new trade agreement—the African Economic Community—drawn up in 1994. The package aimed at creating EU-like institutions in Africa, starting with a new African Union with much stronger enforcement powers. In a relatively short period of time, and largely out of the public eye, states reached consensus on the outlines of the new body (Versi 2002, 9). The overall structure would resemble the OAU in that it would have a general body composed of heads of state (the Assembly), a smaller Executive Council which would forward proposals to the Assembly, and a Permanent Representatives Committee of lower-level officials who would prepare proposals for the Executive Council. These bodies each have an unlimited agenda, although a number of technical committees would work on specific issues separately (Packer & Rukare 2002, 376).

Three new institutions promise to make the AU more effective. One is the Pan-African Parliament that includes over 200 directly-elected representatives with the power to recommend actions to the Assembly and can become an important source of legitimacy (or friction). Also new to the AU is the African Court of Justice—heir to the still-born court of the OAU. It can hear cases involving both states and individuals and could—if used—give the AU more capacity to sanction rule-breakers.

The most important new institution is not provided for in the AU's Constitutive Act: the Peace and Security Council (PSC). It was created by a separate protocol that came into effect in December 2003. Made up of 15 members, the PSC will function much like the UN's Security Council in that states can identify breaches of the peace, identify rule-breakers, and authorize sanctions and even military intervention. This in turn grows from wording in the Constitutive Act that authorizes the AU to intervene directly into the internal affairs of states under special circumstances. As put by Packer and Rukare:

> [T]he Constitutive Act does not preclude intervention by the Union, as a body concerned with peace, security, and stability in the region, in the event of internal conflict. Article 4(h) expressly provides for the 'right of the Union to intervene in a Member State pursuant to a decision of the Assembly in respect of grave circumstances, namely: war crimes, genocide and crimes against humanity. (Packer & Rukare 2002, 372)

Already, the AU has proved capable of taking forceful—if selective—action in favor of democracy and peace. When the son of the president of Madagascar took over his office in 2001, they declared the move an unconstitutional transfer of power and demanded that an election be held under penalty of expulsion and sanctions. The government thereupon held a ballot—in parliament rather than in the country as a whole—that sustained the son's office—a partial victory at best (Zweifel 2006, 156). On the other hand, the seizure of increased power by the leader of Zimbabwe has not prompted a similar outcry. And the AU deployment of peacekeepers in the Darfur region of Sudan has been beset by a lack of resources, manpower, legal authority, and cooperation by the Khartoum government (Morrison 2006, 31).

On the economic front, the African Economic Community appears to promise a far more effective attempt at integration than previously. It includes not only measures to lower trade barriers and expand aid, but also financial institutions that might one day lead to a common currency across the continent. The fact that the economic institutions are being folded into the AU means that enforcement will likely be tougher than ever before at the very least (Packer & Rukare 2002, 372).

On balance, the attempt at strengthening African integration has exposed fundamental problems in African politics generally. States have consciously avoided granting certain powers to the regional bodies and have preferred informal, ad-hoc remedies which preserve autonomy and unpredictability. The establishment of new institutions will likely not change this political reality. On the other hand, one can hope that it was a new set of attitudes that gave rise to the stronger institutions of the AU, in which case we may be on the verge of a dramatic shift in African politics.

Mercosur

The Common Market of the South, known by its Spanish acronym Mercosur, is the smallest of the three bodies we discuss in this case with only five members. But those five members have a combined gross product of more than $800 billion—more than either ASEAN or the AU. Led by Brazil, the organization is working to create a common market that links not only its members but all the states of South America. As such, Mercosur has the potential to serve as an opponent of the United States' efforts to create a hemispheric free trade pact of its own.

Mercosur was the brain-child of two Latin American leaders—Fernando Collor de Mello of Brazil and Carlos Menem of Argentina (Guerrero 2005, 21). Following on efforts during the 1980s to open their respective markets to foreign trade and investment as a way of dealing with the debt crisis (and under pressure from foreign lending agencies), the two countries began in the mid-1980s to make plans to lower tariffs and nontariff barriers between them. They also began negotiating a common external tariff that other countries would have to address when trading with them.

The logic of the free trade area and customs union was simple. By lowering barriers, firms in both countries could expand production to target both markets, which would allow them to take advantage of economies of scale by reducing costs per unit of production. Secondly, by erecting a barrier around their lucrative markets, foreign firms would have a strong incentive to relocate to their countries in order to sell locally—and duty-free. The result would be the expansion of both domestic and foreign investment—a rare feat in Latin American history (Nicoletti 1999, 36). This move would also make it easier for Latin America to compete on a global scale against an increasingly integrated Europe and North America (Cason 2000, 27).

In addition to forging an economic bloc, Brazil and Argentina saw the move as a means of consolidating their newly formed democracies (Richards 1997, 133). Both countries feared that if their economies continued to stall amid hyperinflation (Brazil's inflation in 1993 was near 2,500%!) that the people would bring back military regimes. This is one reason why Brazil in particular has been reluctant to lower tariff barriers to the outside world since doing so naturally exposes inefficient local firms to foreign competition—which would likely lead to their closure. In addition, the larger Mercosur members keep a close watch on the smaller two to ensure no political backsliding. In 1996, they warned coup-plotters in Paraguay that the restoration of military rule might result in the country's expulsion from Mercosur. No coup took place (Parish & Peceny 2002, 246).

Finally, Brazil in particular sees Mercosur as a means of expanding its political influence across the continent, hemisphere, and the world generally (Weintraub 2000, 7, 12). It aspires to expand Mercosur's membership and trade ties across the continent and around the world—especially with the European Union (Bulmer-Thomas 2000). It has put pressure on other Mercosur members to speak with one voice—something that was accomplished for the first time at a meeting with the

United States and other hemispheric leaders in 1997. At that meeting, all Mercosur members raised common objections to the American proposal for a Free Trade Area of the Americas and effectively blocked the initiative as many Latin American governments tilted their positions in Mercosur's favor (Cason 2000, 36; Richards 1997, 147). Note, however, that Mercosur is not yet designed as an alliance (in fact, Argentina is affiliated with NATO while Brazil is not) and has generally not moved into issues beyond trade and investment (Weintraub 2000, 28).

The establishment of Mercosur was relatively quick in that after some preliminary bilateral agreements in the late-1980s, Argentina and Brazil invited Uruguay and Paraguay (two smaller states located between them) to Asunción (Paraguay's capital) to sign a commitment in 1991 to form a customs union by 1995 and a free trade area by 2001 (Weintraub 2000, 8). What set these agreements apart was their specificity (Cason 2000, 28). When the customs union was formed, roughly 90% of trade among Mercosur members became duty-free and talks were begun to dramatically reduce tariffs on automobiles and other key sectors.

The operation of Mercosur is quite different than the other two bodies discussed in the case because of Brazil's overwhelming presence. Its gross national product is more than twice that of the other members combined and it has a tendency to forget its obligations to the other members when faced with economic crises. Since there is no institutionalized dispute settlement mechanism, disagreements are simply negotiated—a situation that plays into the hands of the more powerful Brazil.

Two cases in the 1990s help to illustrate this point. In 1995, to deal with pressure on its domestic automobile manufacturers, Brazil suddenly announced a quota on all car imports—the number to be imported in the second half of the year would be half that imported in the first half—a 25% reduction for the year as a whole. This was done without any consultation of Mercosur partners—including Argentina which accounted for roughly 5% of Brazil's auto imports and depended heavily on access to its market. Concerned about the anxiety and frustration this move provoked in Argentina, and also concerned that foreign investors might opt to build in Argentina in the hope of exporting to Brazil later, the government backed down and gave Argentina a partial exemption. Brazil also moved to forge agreement on a relatively high common external tariff of 35% to prevent any pro-Argentine foreign investment (Cason 2000, 31).

In 1997, Brazil again acted unilaterally to address a local crisis. Imports spiked during the previous year, encouraged by easy access to dollar-denominated credit. The government banned the use of these credits for the purchase of imports, requiring instead that all imports be paid for with cash. Mercosur members naturally protested the discriminatory policy that was sure to hurt them and Brazil granted a partial exemption. These and other experiences taught Mercosur members—and especially Argentina—that they were at best subordinate members of the organization and that this status was the price to pay for being closely linked to Brazil's economy.

The price seems reasonable overall, as evidenced by the willingness of other Latina American countries to work with Mercosur. Venezuela signed membership papers in late 2005 and became a full member in late 2006—the first outright expansion of the organization. Previously, Bolivia, Chile, and Mexico signed association agreements, along with all the members of the Andean Community

Map of Regions Discussed in the Chapter

African Union

ASEAN

Mercosur

Map 17.1 Map of regions discussed in the case

(Chile, Peru, and other countries on the Pacific coast). Invitations to join Mercosur are on the table for all Latin American countries and it appears likely that the organization will expand again in coming years—perhaps becoming the South American free trade area and a potent rival to NAFTA in the north.

Such a development would likely strengthen the members' economies in the short run, but their tentative commitment to free trade may create obstacles to long-term growth. And with Venezuela's membership, the organization's philosophy will likely tilt further to the left. Presidents Lula da Silva of Brazil and Hugo Chavez of Venezuela have taken a relatively hard line against American influence in the region and led a resurgence of populist and left-leaning parties across the continent. The situation certainly merits close scrutiny by American policymakers as it may spell a significant adjustment in hemispheric relations and power.

 DEBATE TOPIC

Should the United States encourage regional integration in the developing world?

PRO

The United States will benefit directly from increased prosperity and growth in the developing world, and since regional integration can help countries grow, the United States should encourage it. Prosperous countries will be better trading partners, will have more financial stability, and experience less social turmoil in general. So long as the regional

(continued)

(continued)

agreements do not exclude American goods or investment, they should be seen as a win-win proposition.

CON

The United States should be skeptical of efforts by developing countries to integrate unless the associations that result include the United States as a member. The pattern has been that developing countries often erect defensive trade barriers around their regional organizations in order to protect weak and uncompetitive firms. These have the effect not only of preventing local consumers from being able to choose the best products the world has to offer, but they also encourage inefficiency and waste and firms that should reform opt to stick with old methods and products.

 # THINKING THEORETICALLY

As we consider regional integration and regionalism in general, two theories might help explain what is occurring. Liberals are naturally pleased with regionalism, so long as it is not incompatible with global free trade efforts. They will point to the desire of all states to enhance the living standards of the citizens and the productivity and growth of their national firms. Integration removes artificial government controls to business and allows resources to be used most efficiently. The invisible hand is allowed to guide economic activity.

Realists, on the other hand, are skeptical of states' motives. They point out that almost every attempt at integration has been spurred by a threat from the outside. It becomes clear, especially as most of the associations erect common barriers against nonmembers, that they are designed as much to hamper economic growth in competing regions as to enhance growth in their own. Realists stress that there is no such thing as a win-win game—someone always wins a little more. The trick is to make sure it's you.

QUESTIONS TO CONSIDER

1. What seem to be the secrets to successful integration in the developing world? What explains the high number of failures in the past?

2. To what extent is regionalism driven by cultural factors? Are you aware of, or can you imagine, a regional trade pact that involves very diverse societies?

3. To what extent does regional integration undermine global free trade? Do ASEAN, Mercosur, and the African Economic Community undermine the World Trade Organization's free trade rules?

WEBSITES

ASEAN: www.aseansec.org
African Union: www.african-union.org
Mercosur: www.mercosur.org.uy

REFERENCES

Acharya, Amitav. "The Association of Southeast Asian Nations: 'Security Community' of 'Defence Community'?" *Pacific Affairs* 64 #2 (Summer 1991): 159–178.

ASEAN Secretariat. "Overview." Available at: http://www.aseansec.org/328.htm. Accessed on June 7, 2006.

Banda, O. G. Dayaratna, and John Whalley. "Beyond Goods and Services: Competition Policy, Investment, Mutual Recognition, Movement of Persons, and Broader Cooperation Provisions of Recent FTAs Involving ASEAN Countries." *National Bureau of Economic Research* 1995Working Paper 11232 (1995).

Bulmer-Thomas, Victor. "The European Union and MERCOSUR: Prospects for a Free Trade Agreement." *Journal of Interamerican Studies and World Affairs* 42 #1 (Spring 2000): 1–22.

Cason, Jeffrey. "On the Road to Southern Cone Economic Integration." *Journal of Interamerican Studies and World Affairs* 1 (Spring 2000): 23–42.

Denoon, David B. H., and Evelyn Colbert. "Challenges for the Association of Southeast Asian Nations." *Pacific Affairs* 71 #4 (Winter 1998–1999): 505–523.

Ford, Neil. "A Question of Boundaries." *African Business* September 2001, 14.

Garofano, John. "Power, Institutions, and the ASEAN Regional Forum: A Security Community for Asia?" *Asian Survey* 42 (May 2002): 502–21.

Guerrero, Modesto Emilio. *El Mercosur: Origen, Evolución, Perspectiva* (Caracas: Vadell Hermanos Editores, 2005).

Hussey, Antonia. "Regional Devlopment and Cooperation through ASEAN." *Geographical Review* 81 (January 1991): 87–98.

Jonah, James O. C. "The OAU: Peace Keeping and Conflict Resolution." In Yassin El-Ayouty, ed. *The Organization of African Unity after Thirty Years* (Westport, CT: Praeger, 1994): 3–14.

Kivimaki, Timo. "The Long Peace of ASEAN." *Journal of Peace Research* 38 #1 (January 2001): 5–25.

Kurus, Bilson. "Understanding ASEAN: Benefits and Raison d'Etre." *Asian Survey* 33 #8 (August 1993): 819–831.

Layachi, Azzedine. "The OAU and Western Sahara: A Case Study." In Yassin El-Ayouty, ed. *The Organization of African Unity after Thirty Years* (Westport, CT: Praeger, 1994): 27–42.

Morrison, Dan. "Desperation in Darfur." *U.S. News & World Report* February 20, 2006, 31–35.

Naldi, Gino J. *The Organization of African Unity: An Analysis of Its Role*, 2nd ed. (London: Mansell, 1999).

Narine, Shaun. "ASEAN and the Management of Regional Security." *Pacific Affairs* 71 #2 (Summer 1998): 195–214.

Nicoletti, René. *Identidad y Futuro del Mercosur: Por una Integración Fundada en Valores* (Buenos Aires: Lugar Editorial, 1999).

Packer, Corinne A. A., and Donald Rukare. "The New African Union and Its Constitutive Act." *The American Journal of International Law* 96 #2 (April 2002): 365–379.

Parish, Randall, and Mark Peceny. "Kantian Liberalism and the Collective Defense of Democracy in Latin America." *Journal of Peace Research* 38 #2 (March 2002): 229–250.

Richards, Donald D. "Dependent Development and Regional Integration: A Critical Examination of the Southern Cone Common Market." *Latin American Perspectives* 24 #6 (November 1997): 133–155.

Stubbs, Richard. "ASEAN Plus Three: Emerging East Asian Regionalism?" *Asian Survey* 42 #3 (May-June 2002): 440–455.

Van Walraven, Klaas. *Dreams of Power: The Role of the Organization of African Unity in the Politics of Africa, 1963–1993* (Aldershot, UK: Ashgate, 1999).

Versi, Anver. "OAU, AU Histrionics." *African Business* June 2002, 9.

Weintraub, Sidney. *Development and Democracy in the Southern Cone: Imperative for U.S. Policy in South America* (Washington: CSIS, 2000).

Welch, Claude E., Jr. "The OAU and Human Rights: Regional Promotion of Human Rights." In Yassin El-Ayouty, ed. *The Organization of African Unity after Thirty Years* (Westport, CT: Praeger, 1994): 53–76.

Zweifel, Thomas D. *International Organizations & Democracy: Accountability, Politics, and Power* (London: Lynne Rienner, 2006).

CASE 18

Europe Uniting: Supranationalism

INTRODUCTION

Over the course of human history, people have organized themselves at many levels. From tiny self-sufficient villages in jungles and on mountainsides to the encompassing empires of Antiquity and the nineteenth century, political structures have varied tremendously over time. Since roughly the seventeenth century, the dominant political unit was the sovereign state. Such units displaced both larger and smaller alternatives, such as the city-state (Venice, Florence) and empire (especially the Holy Roman Empire) (Tilly 1992; Spruyt 1996). In time, these units promised not to interfere with each other's domestic affairs, and they came to jealously protect their autonomy.

Since the end of World War II, however, the preferred institution is the nation-state which combines (at least in its ideal form) one nationality with one state. Iceland represents perhaps the best illustration of this concept, where 96% of the population is descended from ancient Norse and Celtic tribes and there are very few Icelanders outside of the island state. In time, nations of people received the right to organize such states where they did not exist—hence the approval of declarations of independence by scores of former colonies in Africa and Asia in the past fifty years.

Finally, as the state system became increasingly settled, the world's economic actors sought to break down barriers between these states in order to maximize efficiency and profits. Many governments joined these economic actors and worked to open their markets to goods and capital from abroad. The hope was not only to bring increased prosperity to their peoples but also to so closely link their societies to those of potential rival states that war would become unthinkable (since it would be just as damaging to the aggressor as to the victim).

As these plans unfolded in Europe and elsewhere, a new movement emerged: supranationalism. Advocates saw the benefits that could come from forming ever-larger political units through the creation of federations of states. Not only would money be saved through "economies of scale" (larger-scale production can save money for each new unit produced), but also by joining together, smaller states can better protect themselves from larger ones. Thus both liberal and realist thinkers saw good reasons for supranationalism. At the same time, of course, supranational-ism presented risks. Opening the market of a weak state could result in widespread business failure and even foreign takeovers. Joining larger federations would result in a loss of autonomy with the implication that a state might be forced to change its policies—perhaps even its identity—to accommodate the views of the majority of states in the federation. Ironically, it would seem there are both good liberal and realist reasons not to join federations.

Plans for European unity began out of disgust with war and carnage—not World War II, but the Thirty Years' War. After the end of the devastating war in 1648, French royal advisor de Sully developed a "Grand Design" for European unity based on religious tolerance. Though stillborn, de Sully's proposal was the first of a string of concepts calling for European unity. Following the nearly successful attempt of Louis XIV to secure French domination over Europe in the early 1700s, William Penn and the Quakers in Britain, along with the Abbe de Saint-Pierre in France, developed complex and elaborate schemes for a form of collective security for Europe (Heater 1992, 54, 58). During the nineteenth century, while idealists con-tinued to work on a global organization, which culminated in the League of Nations, the great powers experimented for a time with the Concert of Europe—an informal arrangement among the dominant European powers to keep minor conflicts in check through collaborative intervention.

The period of planning and scheming for Europe demonstrated a tension between the goals of preserving sovereignty and creating genuine supranational institutions that could coordinate state action. To a large extent, this tension has yet to be resolved.

KEY FIGURES
EUROPE UNITING

Jean Monnet   Deputy-general, League of Nations, 1919–1923; President and founder, ECSC, 1952–1955.

Jacques Delors   President, European Commission, 1985–1995. He spearheaded the Single European Act and the creation of the euro.

Paul-Henri Spaak   Prime Minister of Belgium at various times between 1938 and 1949. He led the European coordination of Marshall Plan aid and served as Secretary General of NATO, 1957–1961. He is known affectionately as the "Father of Europe."

Margaret Thatcher   British Prime Minister, 1979–1990. She worked against a number of EEC programs and proposals during her tenure.

Robert Schuman   French Foreign Minister, 1948–1952. He crafted the ECSC with Jean Monnet.

Helmut Kohl   Chancellor of Germany, 1982–1998. He promoted deeper European integration.

CHRONOLOGY
EUROPE UNITING

1922
Belgium, Luxembourg, and the Netherlands agree to form a free trade zone.

1948
The European Movement is founded in the Netherlands. The Marshall Plan is promulgated and the OEEC, predecessor to the OECD and EEC, is founded.

1949
The Council of Europe is formed.

1954
The ECSC is formed to regulate steel production.

1957
The Treaty of Rome is signed, creating the European Economic Community.

1962
The Common Agricultural Program is instituted to support farm prices.

1963
Charles de Gaulle of France blocks British membership to the EEC.

1971
The Luxembourg Compromise provides a veto to each member-state on certain issues.

1973
Great Britain, Denmark, and Ireland join the EEC in the first "enlargement."

1978
The EMS replaces previous currency stabilization schemes.

1981
Greece is admitted to the EEC.

1982
British Prime Minister Margaret Thatcher demands changes in regional funding arrangements.

1985
The Single European Act is approved.

1986
Spain and France are admitted to the ECC.

1989
The Delors Plan for a regional monetary union is approved.

1990
European states impose restrictions on British beef amid fears of "mad cow" disease.

(*continued*)

(continued)

1991
The Maastricht Treaty is approved, pending ratification by each EEC member.

1992
Almost all of the trade barriers outlined in 1985 (as part of the SEA) are removed. A currency crisis in the United Kingdom and Italy leads to the dismantling of the European Monetary System.

1994
The Maastricht Treaty comes into effect, resulting in the creation of the European Union.

1995
Sweden, Finland, and Austria are admitted to the EU.

2000
Fifteen European Union member-states agree in Nice, France, to admit twelve new members, pending approval by citizens of all fifteen states.

2002
The euro is adopted region-wide as national currencies are eliminated. Ireland becomes the last country to ratify the Nice Agreement, paving the way for the admission of most Eastern European states by 2005.

2004
Ten new countries are added to the EU, bringing the total to twenty-five. The new members are the Czech Republic, Estonia, Hungary, Latvia, Lithuania, Poland, Slovakia, Slovenia, Cyprus, and Malta.

THE EMERGENCE OF THE COMMON MARKET: 1945–1957

The Common Market originated from both external and internal forces. The post–World War II environment was utter devastation and called for urgent and dramatic steps. In addition, the growing and clear threat of Soviet Communist encroachment on Western European democracy prompted an acceleration of reconstruction and stabilization efforts. Administrative efficiency and capital utilization required a regional rather than a national approach. The result was American enthusiasm for the Marshall Plan and the regional cooperation it entailed.

In Europe, the disastrous experience with fascism and German expansionism led many to adopt a "never again" attitude. Plans were developed to solidify democratic regimes, punish fascists, and channel German war-making capacity into a broader European network. Germans sought a means to legitimize their new democratic state and put Nazism behind them. These factors, combined with the strength of Christian Democratic parties across Europe, along with their pro-Europe policies, paved the way for Jean Monnet and Paul-Henri Spaak to have great influence.

In 1948, European leaders organized a conference at the Hague, in the Netherlands, where the European Movement was founded to act as a sort of continental lobbying group to press for more integration and unity. Winston Churchill promoted European unity in a series of speeches in the late 1940s, and he served as president of the Hague conference. Here again, a conflict emerged between the "federalists"— mainly the French and Germans—who envisioned a powerful European federal government, and the "unionists," who sought merely ad hoc agreements to deal with particular problems piecemeal (Gerbet 1987, 39).

A series of events in 1948–1950 brought the conflict between federalist and unionist conceptions of Europe to a head. Europe suffered an extreme economic and social crisis following the disastrous harvest of 1948. Soviet expansion in Eastern Europe seemed relentless and foreboding. The rise of Communist parties in France, Italy, and other Western European states seemed to mirror the threat to the East. The United States thus had reason to intervene in dramatic fashion to rescue Europe from what appeared an inevitable World War III, fought this time over German industry. Jean Monnet wrote of his feelings at the time:

> [I recall] the anxiety that weighed on Europe five years after the war: the fear that if we did nothing we should soon face war again. Germany would not be its instigator this time, but its prize. So Germany must cease to be a potential prize, and instead become a link. At that moment, only France could take the initiative. What could be done to link France and Germany . . . ? (Monnet 1979, 289)

The Marshall Plan (formally known as the European Recovery Program) was an essential stopgap measure for the United States to provide necessary capital and materials for European reconstruction; the Bretton Woods institutions [World Bank and International Monetary Fund (IMF)] had proved inadequate to the task. In conjunction with the Marshall Plan, the Organization for European Economic Cooperation (OEEC) was quickly founded in 1948 to give Europeans a role in distributing the resources that flowed from the United States. The OEEC did not have authority to force nations to coordinate their plans, but "thanks to the part played by the Secretariat, the member states became used to cooperating and comparing their economic policies" (Gerbet 1987, 36).

The OEEC was not the first regional organization devoted to economic coordination in Europe. In fact, the Benelux countries (Belgium, the Netherlands, and Luxembourg) had already gone far to create a common market and customs union among themselves. Beginning in 1922, Belgium and Luxembourg pledged to eliminate tariff barriers with each other (thus creating a common market) and to coordinate their trade policies toward the rest of the world (thus creating a customs union). They also promoted the free movement of labor and capital, thereby increasing labor migration and foreign investment. When the Netherlands joined in 1947, the group became a genuinely multilateral arrangement, complete with regional institutional structures and governing authority. This Benelux arrangement served as a model for what was later to become the European Economic Community (Hurwitz 1987, 11).

The economic cooperation forged in the 1940s coincided with efforts at military and political cooperation, although the two efforts soon diverged. Northern Europe organized a peacetime military alliance shortly after the war, culminating in the

Brussels Treaty Organization in 1948, to which the United States was almost immediately invited. The North Atlantic Treaty Organization (NATO), founded in 1949, pledged mutual assistance in the event of an attack against any member and grew to include Germany, Italy, and European countries both to the north and to the south. NATO also provided significant American military support for Europe, including hundreds of thousands of U.S. troops and substantial stockpiles of nuclear weapons. Efforts to forge a truly European military pact failed in the 1950s, which may have led to greater attention to the economic sphere.

Economics and politics were never separate as far as European integration was concerned. An important illustration is the emergence of the European Coal and Steel Community (ECSC). By 1950, German industry was on the road to rapid recovery. In fact, Germany was consuming so much coal and coke from the Ruhr valley near the Rhine that France and other Europeans were experiencing shortages. Jean Monnet, the leader of France's industrial plan, saw this crisis as an opportunity to introduce the plans for integration he had developed as early as 1941. As he saw it, integrating German coal and French iron ore production would solve not only France's immediate shortage problem but a much wider problem as well:

> All successive attempts to keep Germany in check, mainly at French instigation, had come to nothing, because they had been based on the rights of conquest and temporary superiority—notions from the past which happily were no longer taken for granted. But if the problem of sovereignty were approached with no desire to dominate or take revenge—if on the contrary the victors and the vanquished agreed to exercise joint sovereignty over part of their joint resources—then, a solid link would be forged between them, the way would be wide open for further collective action, and a great example would be given to the other nations of Europe. (Monnet 1979, 293)

Thus the ECSC was a way both to keep Germany's military capacity in check and to support French economic goals. As put by Robert Schuman, the French premier who formally proposed Monnet's concept, "The community of production, which will in this manner be created, will clearly show that any war between France and Germany becomes not only unthinkable but in actual fact impossible" (Hurwitz 1987, 20).

The ECSC was created in 1951 with the signing of the Treaty of Paris on April 18 by France, Germany, Italy, and the Benelux countries. It provided for a High Authority, an international panel with powers to organize production levels, map out distribution, and promote equity across the member states. Article 9 of the treaty specified that "in the performance of these duties, [the High Authority] shall neither seek nor take instructions from any Government or any body. . . . Each member state undertakes to respect this supranational character" (Heater 1992, 162). The federalists carried the day insofar as the ECSC is concerned. The treaty also provided for a parliament made up of delegations from member countries based on population, a council with advisory powers where each state had one vote, and a court to review actions of states relative to the High Authority's decisions.

The ECSC quickly demonstrated its effectiveness and provided the impetus for the creation of yet more regional institutions. Monnet was instrumental in establishing Euratom—a European organization to facilitate cooperative development of nuclear technology.

Efforts by France and Great Britain to exert influence overseas in the mid-1950s failed. Both countries then sought refuge in a regional home where their influence could be strong. The British emphasized their Atlantic ties to the United States, whereas the French looked to Europe.

The Soviet intervention in Hungary convinced Europeans that the time had come to create what unity they could, a decision given form at a conference in Messina, Italy, in 1955 (Kusters 1987, 81). Although the French government fell in solidly behind the integration plans (partly out of fear that other Europeans would proceed without France), the British distanced themselves from what they considered a continental question.

Paul-Henri Spaak was the principal author of the 1957 Treaty of Rome, the formal agreement that created the Common Market (officially called the European Economic Community—EEC). He had served as the first head of the OEEC in 1948 and head of the Council of Europe in 1949, and was known as "Mr. Europe" (Heater 1992, 165). Spaak supported the ECSC but was eager for greater integration. He became chair of the team charged at the 1955 Messina conference with drafting a treaty for a customs union and common market. The EEC was constituted with the objective of promoting

> throughout the Community a harmonious development of economic activities, a continuous and balanced expansion, an increased stability, an accelerated raising of the standard of living and closer relations between its member states (Article 2).

Countries joined the EEC for a variety of reasons. Germany saw membership as a vehicle for international acceptance, a way to regain its sovereignty (an ironic goal, because other Europeans saw it as a way to lose theirs! (Urwin & Paterson 1990, 188). France hoped to use the EEC to dominate European politics diplomatically and to placate the strong political pressure of French farmers. Italy hoped the EEC could provide economic and diplomatic rehabilitation as well as development funding for its southern half. The Benelux countries were eager to lower continental trade barriers, which they felt discriminated against their own, more efficient industries. As time went on, these different motivations created interesting and often complex political alliances and antagonisms.

THE EEC AT WORK: 1957–1973

The first task of the EEC was to promote free trade within the community. This goal was to be achieved through the creation of a common market in which barriers to trade are dropped, a customs union through which each country's trade with other nations is uniform, free movement of labor and capital, and harmonization of social policy. The formation of a common market took less time than expected

(Williams 1991, 51). As early as 1968, all internal tariffs on industrial products were eliminated—almost two years ahead of schedule (Wistrich 1990, 33).

The ease with which the common market was created was due largely to nondiplomatic factors. The 1960s saw extraordinary growth in Europe. Average annual growth rates for the EEC-Six ranged from 4.4 percent for West Germany to 5.7 percent for France. It was relatively easy for the EEC-Six to lower trade barriers without fear of unemployment rising from more intense competition. If a firm was not competitive in one sector, another opportunity soon presented itself. Not only did the economies of the EEC-Six grow during this period, but trade was also diverted from non-EEC to intra-EEC partners. In 1958, EEC countries imported only 29 percent of all goods from the other EEC-Six; by 1972, that figure had risen to 52 percent (Williams 1991, 33).

The other principal activity of the EEC during the 1960s was to establish the Common Agricultural Program (CAP). Considered a crucial element of the Treaty of Rome (Article 38) by France, the CAP provided for a common market and customs union in all foodstuffs, price guarantees, and structural reforms. In addition, the CAP aimed at ensuring "a fair standard of living for the agricultural community." Although such an approach seems excessive by today's standards, Marsh points out that in the 1950s, Europe was a net food importer and had recently imposed food rationing. Farmers were able to argue that the only way to ensure that Europe would have sufficient food was by producing it at home. Success in agriculture was considered essential for national security (Marsh 1989, 148).

The key element in this equation was price guarantees, which placated the highly politicized and powerful farm lobbies in France, Italy, and Germany. Although several options existed, the EEC-Six decided in 1962 to proceed with a price support mechanism involving the purchase by the community of surplus production to be stored until it could be sold without lowering the price. To appease German farmers, the price levels agreed upon were the high, heavily subsidized German prices. This decision made the CAP far and away the most significant EEC expense. The Council of Ministers had hoped at the time that the high price supports would be temporary, that the common market would force inefficient producers out of business. This was not the case. Instead, the price supports became a permanent element in the EEC (Taylor 1983, 237). As pointed out by Lodge, the CAP is neither capitalist nor effective, but it has become such a vital ingredient in the political and even physical landscape of Europe that any attempt at reform risks consequences that could easily outweigh the benefits (Lodge 1990, 212). It is interesting that revisions to the Treaty of Rome in the late 1980s included significant downsizing of the CAP and experimentation with alternative policies to maintain prices.

With de Gaulle out of office in 1969, the EEC proceeded with the accession of Great Britain, Denmark, Ireland, and Norway (where the proposal was rejected in a referendum). Given Britain's heavy reliance on imports of food from New Zealand and Australia and the relatively small size of its agricultural sector, it was disadvantaged by the EEC's emphasis on the CAP. Differences of opinion were left largely unresolved, and the accession was completed in 1973. This "first enlargement" came amid optimism for the future of the EEC. A 1972 summit meeting that included three "members in waiting" committed the community to deeper integration, including "completion of the internal market, common tariffs, a common currency, and a central bank" (Williams 1991, 50). Few anticipated the trying years that were soon to come.

THE EUROPEAN COMMUNITY UNDER STRESS: 1973–1985

The quadrupling of the price of oil in 1973 had devastating effects on European economies. A decade of stagflation set in, and Britain's economic life was in constant jeopardy. The linchpin of stable currencies was gone, and demands by the Organization of Petroleum Exporting Countries (OPEC) for oil importers to end their support of Israel went far to undermine the political unity that contributed to economic cooperation. France and Germany abandoned Israel, while the Netherlands endured the oil embargo. The British pound collapsed in the mid-1970s, and labor unrest in France and Italy derailed those countries' economic growth. Germany struggled with terrorism, and Ireland and Italy pleaded for additional development financing from the EEC. None of the Europeans knew how to respond to the growing trade threat from Japan and the Far East. As put by British Prime Minister Edward Heath:

> After the oil crisis of 1973–74 the Community lost its momentum and, what was worse, lost the philosophy of Jean Monnet: that the Community exists to find common solutions to common problems. (Williams 1991, 50)

Amid this unraveling came a crisis of identity over Britain's role in the community. As a major industrial power, the United Kingdom expected to play a leading role in the EEC, but it had been "absent at the creation" and therefore was forced to deal with a set of rules and procedures that were not of its making. The most significant contention was about the budget. Britain continually found itself in conflict with the Franco-German "axis" during the 1970s (Urwin & Paterson 1990, 187).

Before going too far, we will discuss the EEC budget. Originally, the budget was simply based on a national quota calculated loosely in terms of gross national product (GNP) and renegotiated each year by the members. In 1970, this system was replaced with the "own resources" concept: The EEC would claim certain revenues on the grounds that they belonged by right to Europe as a whole. For a variety of reasons, Great Britain in the late 1970s was consistently sending Brussels some $3 billion more than it was getting back; at the same time, France was netting some $800 billion (Taylor 1983, 238).

The inequity of the situation was exacerbated by Britain's political ambivalence about European federalism generally. In 1979, Margaret Thatcher was elected prime minister on an anti-EEC platform. Her government exaggerated the United Kingdom's disadvantage by focusing on absolute rather than per capita revenues. Considering the EEC process seriously flawed and even illegitimate, the Thatcher government took an aggressive position that alienated the other EEC members. She told the EEC members bluntly, "I want my money back."

In 1982, Britain began to press the EEC for some form of financial relief. It demanded a rebate of 1.5 billion European Currency Units (ECU) to be paid by CAP beneficiaries (France and Italy in particular). When agreement was slow in coming, it threatened to use its veto to block further action by the community. Great Britain came close to precipitating a profound split in the community by 1984. Helmut Kohl of Germany left a meeting in protest. In essence, Germany called Britain's bluff. This is not to say that the United Kingdom failed. On the contrary, the EEC provided a 1 billion ECU rebate in 1984 and promised additional rebates of roughly two-thirds of the difference between Britain's tax-generated payments to the EEC and its receipts from Brussels (Urwin & Paterson 1990, 193). However, as part of this arrangement, Germany was permitted to increase substantially its share of EEC expenses—and power.

Apart from the budgetary and philosophical tensions in the community, a serious problem arose from the growing disparity of development among the members of the EU. Moving from the EEC-Six to the EC-Nine had not been particularly painful, in and of itself, except for the budget question described earlier. However, the additions of Greece in 1981 and of Spain and Portugal in 1986 created unexpected stress.

Greece was permitted to enter the EEC prematurely, EEC officials today acknowledge. Greek industry is still not competitive with that in the rest of Europe. Greek agriculture is far too tropical and labor-intensive to survive full integration (for example, the average size of a Greek farm is only one-fifth that of a Luxembourg farm). The Greek government in power in the early 1980s proved to be one of the few pro-EC governments that the Greek people would elect. Successive Greek regimes have challenged the membership decision (Williams 1991, 65).

Spain and Portugal applied for membership in 1977 and were admitted in 1986, despite serious reservations. Spain's size and the three Mediterranean countries' poverty placed heavy burdens on the rest of Europe. Spain and Portugal hoped their accession would guarantee newfound democracy and preserve their strong links to Europe. The EEC nations feared the imbalance of prices, wages, and wealth between Spain and Portugal and the rest of the community. The accession was permitted only with seven- to ten-year transitional provisions in fishing, semitropical foods, external industrial tariffs, and budget obligations (Williams 1991, 69). Efforts to rectify the discrepancies have come primarily through regional development programs administered by the European Regional Development Fund (ERDF). Never more than 10 percent of the total EEC budget, the funds funneled through the ERDF were aimed primarily at rural Mediterranean regions (not countries), although a program set in place in the mid-1980s provided funds for certain depressed industrial areas (Williams 1991, 130).

The last significant policy issue tackled during the 1970s was monetary reform. The notion of a European Monetary System (EMS) had been discussed early after the Treaty of Rome was signed, but it did not take shape until the collapse of the dollar-centered Bretton Woods system in 1971 forced Europeans to take more responsibility for their own monetary stability. The Werner Report calling for fixed exchange rates that would fluctuate in parallel was implemented in 1971. This system proved untenable after the oil crisis, however. Because inflationary pressures hit different countries unequally, and because each nation decided to adopt a different monetary strategy to deal with the crisis, currency values began to separate dramatically. Maintaining fixed exchange rates required intervention by the governments (for example, buying and selling currency, increasing interest rates), so in 1978 the "snake" system, as it was called, was abandoned in favor of the EMS, known as the "snake in the tunnel" approach (Wistrich 1990, 35).

The EMS allowed European currencies to fluctuate freely in relation to one another within a 4.5 percent band around the deutsche mark. Governments accepted the responsibility to unilaterally adopt policies that would either raise or lower the value of their currencies relative to the mark whenever they approached the limits of this range. The agreement was actually drawn up and signed by the central bankers of the EEC and was to be implemented by them rather than by political leaders. The bankers agreed not only to conservative monetary principles but also to consultation, coordination, and convergence of money policy. The members also agreed to the creation of a new accounting unit, the ECU, a forerunner of today's euro.

The Exchange Rate Mechanism (ERM) was also included in the EMS. It provided for warnings to be issued to the banks of countries whose currencies fell outside a narrower 3.5 percent band around the deutsche mark, although strong currencies used heavily in the European banking system were permitted a slightly wider range of tolerance. The effect was to impose particularly strict discipline on smaller countries (Lehment 1983, 187).

The end of this period of relative turmoil came with an epiphany—a deep recognition that the EEC was at a crossroads. The community could either continue the unionist approach advanced by Thatcher or adopt the federalist approach, which was embraced by Germany, France, and the Netherlands.

RENEWAL: 1986–2006

European countries were in position to respond to the dramatic changes that took place on the world stage in the late 1980s and early 1990s because they were undergoing far-reaching changes of their own. Beginning as early as 1984, EEC leaders launched a series of dramatic reforms of their institutions. Specifically, they strengthened the free trade regime of Europe, undertook initiatives into new economic and social policy arenas, added new members, and began to coordinate and strengthen communitywide security and foreign policy positions.

Single European Act

In 1984, the European Parliament approved a draft treaty of European union that committed countries to eventually merge their foreign and defense policies. By 1985, talk had begun to shift to the need for genuine unification of economic policies across the EEC, and committees were formed to study the question of a single market. British official Lord Cockfield developed a plan of action with a list of 282 directives to be adopted by the end of 1992 (Goldstein 1991–1992, 130). At the December 1985 Luxembourg summit, the Single European Act (SEA) was approved; it was ratified in 1986. The treaty represented a major modification of the Treaty of Rome and called for implementation of the "four freedoms": 1. Free movement of goods. This involved dismantling the many nontariff barriers that were not specifically listed in the Treaty of Rome and were still impeding trade in the community, including the establishment of a minimum sales tax (value added tax—VAT) rate with numerous exclusions. 2. A free market in services. This included banking, insurance, transportation, airlines, telecommunications, and so on. 3. Free movement of people—in other words, unrestricted immigration within the community. 4. A free market in capital—specifically, a pledge to eliminate government intervention in currency exchange and the eventual establishment of a common currency (the Delors Plan gave this movement its impetus; see the next section).

Beyond the important symbolism of the SEA, the concrete changes were substantial. By the end of 1992, virtually all government-made barriers to trade were eliminated, and efforts were set in motion to create united markets in fields that had none. For example, trucks may now travel across the EU without stopping at border crossings. This, in and of itself, cuts costs and improves efficiency substantially. Banking is liberalized to the point that any stable European bank can establish subsidiaries anywhere in the EU. Commercial insurance is liberalized, and plans are under way to do the same in the airline industry. By the end of 1992, some 95 percent of the SEA proposals had been implemented.

At the institutional level, although the SEA modifies the Treaty of Rome, it does so by simply changing the powers of existing bodies. The European Parliament is given greater voice in such matters as admitting new members (Lodge 1990, 216). The commission is strengthened and its scope of operation is broadened, which increases the likelihood that Europe-wide policies will be developed. Perhaps most important, the prospects for further progress have been strengthened by the adoption of majority rule on the Council of Ministers, thus eliminating the debilitating use of the veto (Pinder 1986, 73).

The Euro

In 1988, the European Council (or summit meeting) commissioned the new president of the European Commission, Jacques Delors, to devise a plan for monetary and currency union. In 1989, the Delors Plan was accepted. It called for a three-phase process to begin with the establishment of a European System of Central Banks (ESCB) centered on a European Central Bank and each of the twelve nations' central banks—to be governed with little political interference. This network would be the vehicle through which the European Commission and Council of Ministers would set monetary and currency policy, including the gradual harmonization of fiscal policy (government spending and taxation), currency valuation (exchange rates), monetary policy (interest rates, money supply), and bank powers (political independence of central bank leaders). After the nations of Europe completed this transition phase and satisfied the requirements of prudent monetary policy (defined flexibly by the Council of Ministers and European Council), the members of the community pledged to abandon their own currencies and central bank controls and hand over monetary policy to a single European entity (Habermeier & Ungerer 1992, 27–29).

Beginning in 1989, via the Delors Plan, European leaders moved toward establishing a single regional currency. Two key ingredients to such a venture are harmonizing and strengthening domestic fiscal and monetary policies and establishing and accepting powerful new central organs capable of setting regional monetary policy. In both cases, governments are required to adopt major changes to their way of running their national economies, which runs counter to prevailing ideology and political strategy. Many Europeans resisted EEC encroachment on monetary policy, including especially Margaret Thatcher, whose Conservative colleagues voted her out in early 1992 over her opposition to deeper integration. Likewise, more radical regimes objected to the need to subordinate their own developmental and redistributive policies to the demands of Brussels bureaucrats. The collapse of the value of the British pound and the Italian lira in 1992 provoked considerable debate in the United Kingdom and Italy, leading to a withdrawal from European monetary plans in the former and a redoubled effort to implement fiscal discipline in the latter (Gilpin 2001, 37–38).

Although politicians had considerable trepidation and hesitation, the euro was introduced in 1998 (as part of the Maastricht Treaty discussed later) and began to appear not only in government-to-government transactions but also in the prices of ordinary products sold in stores across Europe. After suffering an initial dip on the international exchange markets, the euro stabilized at a level slightly higher than the U.S. dollar and continues to gain credibility. On January 1, 2002, national currencies were officially eliminated and the euro became legal tender Europe-wide. Although there have been some complaints that merchants concealed price hikes in the currency conversion to euros, most Europeans welcomed the stability and strength of the new currency—even in Germany.

Not all EU members have joined the euro scheme, with the United Kingdom being a notable holdout. The main reason is the difficulties involved in meeting fiscal and monetary policy constraints. In the early 1990s, a serious recession gripped the region, and very few countries were able to reach the target of keeping budgetary deficits to less than 3 percent of gross domestic product (GDP). But by the late 1990s, the situation had changed substantially. From a high of 5.5 percent in 1993, overall budget deficits relative to GDP had fallen to less than 1 percent for Europe as a whole. Several countries even projected budget surpluses for the year 2000 (EC 2000, 5).

Maastricht Treaty

With the end of the Cold War in 1989 and the reunification of Germany in 1990, Europe faced a very different political context. As put by *The Economist*, "This is the decade the European Community was invented for" (Colchester 1992, S1). Amid the turmoil of political upheaval, Germany and France pressed for the rapid and full adoption of the spirit of Monnet and Spaak: European union. Rather than wait for a united Germany to assert its own identity, both Helmut Kohl and François Mitterand moved to incorporate it into the EEC network and subordinate German expansion to European imperatives. The withdrawal of Margaret Thatcher from British political life accelerated the process. These forces, along with the growing threat from Japan and questions about the future American role in Europe, were key to the pell-mell pace of the negotiation of the Maastricht agreements in December 1991. The Maastricht agreement was finalized in relative secrecy but with the strong support of the negotiators. Once the treaty was signed, it required the ratification of each member state before it went into force. In June 1992, the Danish electorate rejected the treaty by a slim margin; in September 1992, the French approved it by an equally slim margin. Leaders became concerned that they had failed to communicate the advantages of the EU clearly enough to their electorates. Ultimately, the Danes took another vote and approved the treaty, as did other European nations by large margins. The British Parliament finally approved the action without resort to a formal referendum. On January 1, 1994, the Maastricht Treaty went into effect.

The first element of the Maastricht Treaty was the strengthening of the EU-led integration itself, to be accomplished by 2000. The EU's authority was extended into such areas as education, health policy, consumer protection, law enforcement, immigration, and even culture. The Council of Ministers now act on the basis of a qualified majority vote (taking into account the size of the countries in tabulating their vote, but eliminating the veto altogether), but it must obtain the European Parliament's approval on many questions. The commission, though somewhat weaker in relation to the council, retains the initiative as the only organ authorized to propose new programs. The principle of "subsidiarity" limits the EU's authority to those programs where collective action is clearly preferable to national unilateralism—but the specific parameters of this concept have to be determined in the pro-integration European Court of Justice.

In practice, the commission continues to exert considerable authority over EU policy. An important episode illustrates the limits of council and governmental authority. In the late 1980s, the practice of feeding cows meat and bone meal was outlawed in Great Britain when it was discovered that cows were contracting bovine spongiform encephalopathy, better known as "mad cow disease." The epidemic ultimately affected more than 175,000 cows during the 1990s. In 1990, several European countries imposed unilateral bans on British beef. Under pressure from the commission, these countries lifted the ban a few weeks later. In 1995, however, Stephen Churchill died of Creutzfeld-Jakob disease, which was linked in a March 1996 study by the British health ministry to mad cow disease. Within days of the announcement, the commission issued a ban on the importation of all British beef products (Decision 94/239/EC of March 27, 1996). To protest the action, which it considered overly drastic and hasty, the UK government decided to use its political and institutional clout to obstruct other actions by the commission in other areas of EU policy. A month later, the United Kingdom agreed to end its virtual boycott of

EU activities in exchange for a pledge by the commission to gradually lift the ban. In fact, the ban remained in effect for nearly three years. The United Kingdom tried to persuade the European Parliament to pass a motion of censure against the commission, which would have resulted in its dissolution, but failed.

EU Enlargement

Following a lengthy application process that ended in each country conducting a national referendum, Sweden, Finland, and Austria were admitted into the European Union in January 1995. Norway and Switzerland, though approved for admission, opted against it in the face of popular opposition.

The accession of these three nations proceeded without major difficulty and prompted European leaders to press for further enlargement by reaching out to long-time applicants Turkey, Malta, and Cyprus as well as the Central European nations of Slovenia, Hungary, Poland, and the Czech Republic. The EU members laid out more precise membership criteria in 1993, which now include (1) stable democracy and protection of fundamental human rights, (2) a functioning market economy, and (3) the ability to "take on the obligations of membership" (EC 2000).

The EU's experience with democratization has become a model for the world. Many scholars have noted that the EU has just the right combination of sticks and carrots to induce would-be members to strengthen democratic institutions quickly (Hafner-Burton 2005). The EU was directly involved in Greek politics when it suspended its Association Agreement (intended as a sort of "probationary membership" following the military's overthrow of the government in 1967. The economic pain Greece suffered appears to have contributed directly to the restoration of democracy in 1973 (Pevehouse 2002, 524). In 1989, the EU set aside funds for Eastern European countries that were interested in eventual EU membership but that would have to first go through considerable economic and political reforms. The so-called PHARE program targeted ten Eastern European countries. In an internal performance evaluation, analysts concluded that the program was particularly instrumental in helping states draft new legislation in the area of justice and home affairs (primarily by nurturing pro–civil-rights community organizations). The general conclusion was that these new states would not have been capable of carrying out most of the projects due to a lack of funds and expertise (EU 2003). Not only does the EU provide inducements, but it is quite willing to bar membership to states that have not yet consolidated the democratic transition, as the leaders of Slovakia and Turkey have learned (Smith 2003, 135).

In the French city of Nice in late 2000, EU members agreed to extend membership to ten Eastern European countries, pending approval by the citizens of each EU member-state. In October 2002, after a second attempt, the citizens of Ireland approved the plan—the last country to do so. This resulted in memberships in 2004 for Hungary, Poland, the Czech Republic, Slovenia, Slovakia, Estonia, Latvia, and Lithuania, as well as Malta and Cyprus. Membership for Cyprus was complicated by the division of the island between Turkish and Greek government structures. Last-minute efforts to

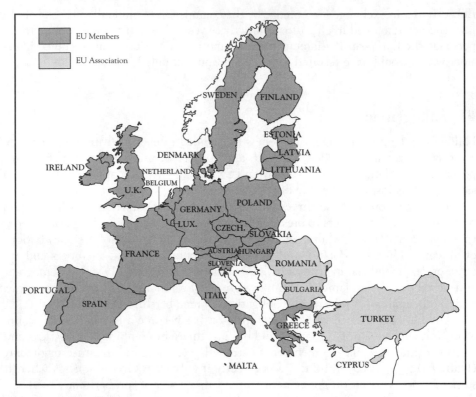

EU Members

EU Association

SWEDEN FINLAND

ESTONIA
LATVIA
DENMARK LITHUANIA
IRELAND NETHERLANDS
BELGIUM
U.K.
POLAND
GERMANY
LUX. CZECH. SLOVAKIA
FRANCE AUSTRIA HUNGARY
SLOVENIA ROMANIA
PORTUGAL BULGARIA
SPAIN ITALY
TURKEY
GREECE
MALTA CYPRUS

Map 18.1 European Union membership

resolve the dispute in order to allow inclusion of the entire island came to naught, and so only the Greek-controlled areas were formally incorporated (see Map 18.1). Membership for Turkey continues to run up against Greek opposition and a checkered human rights and economic record for the Ankara government, although Turkey is working hard to improve its laws and image (*Los Angeles Times* August 3, 2002, A7).

European Constitution

The question that will doubtless dominate EU news over the next few years is the adoption of a draft constitution. After negotiating for roughly a year, members of a constitutional convention put forward a draft document for member states to approve. This was done in June 2004, at which point the constitution is being passed along to each of the twenty-five member-states for their ratification. Should any state fail to ratify (either because the legislature rejects or a referendum fails), then the constitution will remain a proposal. What would most likely happen is the "no" countries would be given a chance to try again, as was the case for the Maastricht agreement.

The constitution is an intriguing document since on the surface it appears to constitute little more than institutional housecleaning, while many believe it is in fact a revolutionary step. The principal goal of the framers was to streamline and clarify the structures of the EU, bringing all the various bodies under a single government. But the Commission, Council, and Parliament of Europe would all remain—essentially unchanged. A new post of Foreign Minister would be created along with the post of EU President—but the functions these two would fill are already being performed by existing actors (EC 2004). Unlike Maastricht, then, the EU does not seem to extend the powers of EU institutions in any dramatic way (Federal Union 2004).

This said, the constitution provides for a new Charter of Fundamental Rights, analogous to the American Bill of Rights or the European Convention on Human Rights. While the list of rights is not especially controversial in itself, it is the fact that the European Court of Justice would be expected to enforce them that worries some. Opponents of the proposal see the constitution as "federalism by stealth" in that it appears to give a veto to the EU over a broader range of policies than before. Euroskeptics in Britain, for example, argue that such an agreement could mean that Britain will be forced to adopt the euro, accept the European Court of Justice as a court of final appeal for all British legal questions, and essentially result in loss of British sovereignty (EUFAQ 2004). Every EU member must ratify for Convention before it can take effect. In mid-2005, the voters in France and the Netherlands soundly defeated it, prompting several states to cancel their own votes. The European Council, fearful that further votes could doom the Convention, opted to set aside the timetable and instead begin renegotiating the treaty.

Security Cooperation

European governments have long been heavily involved in European security arrangements, although the arrangements have tended to be disconnected and relatively weak. The Western European Union, though still on the books, is nothing like the "non-North American NATO" it was originally envisioned to be. Efforts to reinvigorate it through Title V of the Maastricht Treaty have faltered. The European actions of failing to take a unified position on Bosnia in the early 1990s and allowing the United States to take the lead in Kosovo a few years later have led many to believe that much work is necessary on European security initiatives.

The EU provides for a High Representative for the Common Foreign and Security Policy of the Union, who will help form a consensus on foreign policy positions, but as yet this representative has not become a significant voice. The EU has also established an intelligence and policy planning unit. In 1997, the European Council signed the Treaty of Amsterdam, which is designed to give more weight and urgency to common union policies, in the hope that states will choose to "constructively abstain" rather than block union policies (EC 2000). There are currently plans in place for a new rapid-reaction force, but this effort probably will not progress very far until Turkey drops its opposition. Europeans are more likely to continue to support and strengthen the Organization for Security and Cooperation in Europe, which has played a key role in enhancing democracy and peace in southern Europe (Department of State 1995).

CONCLUSION

There is no question that the European Union is the most dramatic, far-reaching, and successful example of supranationalism today. In the 1970s, skeptics predicted the withering away of the EEC in the face of French and British sovereign demands. Today, however, most international scholars see the EU as a new standard for international cooperation. This result has been achieved in spite of a difficult decade that dealt with the reintegration of East Germany, high unemployment, and austerity in the quest for admission to the euro system.

Serious obstacles must be overcome before the experiment can be declared a success. Europe does not yet speak with one voice on all matters of security, and the United States has a heavy presence in European military matters through NATO. The Constitution has been blocked by several states, with the result that it may never be implemented. And in Italy and other states, anti-EU and anti-immigrant parties are performing increasingly well at the polls. Even in Eastern Europe, democracy seems not to be spreading as hoped. Romania, Bulgaria, Belarus, and Ukraine may even be backsliding toward authoritarianism. Nevertheless, the European states do coordinate their foreign policies on everything from trade to the environment. At the World Trade Organization, the United Nations, and other international organizations, to hear one European country's positions is generally to hear all their positions.

 DEBATE TOPIC

Will Turkey be better off joining the EU?

PRO

Turkey is already benefiting from its application to the EU in that it has been forced to carry out political reforms that increase religious tolerance, promote due process under law, and restrain the powers of the police and the state security apparatus. In addition, the economy has been liberalized, institutions consolidated, and economic growth encouraged. Joining the EU will only accelerate these trends.

CON

It will be difficult for Turkey not to feel outnumbered in an EU dominated by Christian countries. Its unique approach to Islam will be repeatedly challenged, with the result that it will gradually lose its identity, if there isn't a conservative backlash before then. Turkey's economy will also suffer since its industry is relatively uncompetitive. This will likely lead to lay-offs and increases in poverty in the short run. Both the political and economic troubles will likely lead to strong anti-EU sentiment and a major headache for whatever government is in power.

THINKING THEORETICALLY

For many years, the case of the EU has been seen as a challenge to realism since it appears that states are willingly giving up their most prized possession—sovereignty—for the sake of improving the lives of their citizens. Realists would have predicted a far different scenario—especially given Europe's well-established record for starting global wars. But some realists, setting aside the basic question of why the EU was created, point out that the internal workings of the organization still reflect the states' interest in status and security. They point to the struggle over voting rights between France and Britain, the careful allocation of votes in the Parliament to assure Germany, France, and Britain the lion's share of power, and they also look at how the most powerful states have carved out exceptions from EU rules for themselves (note that France long ago violated the EU's monetary rules but has yet to be penalized). In other words—different instruments—same tune.

But constructivists who emphasize socialization (the process by which neighbors and friends come to imitate and resemble each other) point to the considerable influence the EU has had on newcomers. Consider that of the 19 states that have joined the EU since the original 6, almost all had either been ruled by dictators, Communist despots, or royal autocrats at some point in the last fifty years. At this point, all are solidly democratic, and the states that are seeking EU membership are clearly on that same path. One could make the argument that the EU has become the world's strongest force for democracy. In addition, EU members have learned from each other how to create rules and enforce them, how to cope with the ups and downs of economic trends, and how to provide for both social welfare and corporate flexibility. The record of success, while not unblemished, is clearly remarkable—especially considering what Europe was doing prior to conclusion of the Treaty of Rome.

QUESTIONS TO CONSIDER

1. What key factors are reviving European unity? Are these forces relatively constant, or will they wax and wane?

2. Who wants European unity? The masses? The "Eurocrats"? The politicians? What does each expect to get from European unity?

3. Why is it so difficult to move from negative integration to positive integration to political unity? Will these obstacles persist in the future?

WEBSITES

Index to the European Union site: **www.eur-op.eu.int/general/en/index.htm**

EU search engine: **europe.eu.int/search.htm**

"Future of Europe" debate: **http://europa.eu.int/futurum/**

Center for European Integration link page: **www.zei.de**

REFERENCES

Colchester, Nico. "The European Community—A Survey." *The Economist* (July 11, 1992): S1–S30.

Department of State. "Fact Sheets: NATO, Partnership for Peace, OSCE, and NATO Enlargement." U.S. Department of State Dispatch, June 5, 1995.

European Commission (EX). "Public Finances in EMU—2000: Report of the Directorate General for Economic and Financial Affairs." May 24, 2000.

European Commission (EC). "Summary of the Agreement on the Constitutional Treaty." A provisional document of the European Commission. June 28, 2004. Available at: **http://europa.eu.int/futurum/documents/other/oth250604_2_en.pdf.**

European Union FAQ. "What is the EU Constitution?" Working paper of the European Union FAQ. Available at: **http://www.eurofaq.freeuk.com/eurofaq1b.html.** Accessed on October 10, 2004.

European Union (EC). *Phare ex post evaluation of country support implemented from 1997–1998 to 2000–2001: Consolidated summary report.* Brussels: EU, 2003.

Federal Union. "What is the Draft European Constitution?" Working paper of the Federal Union, 2004. Available at: **http://www.federalunion.org.uk/europe/ constitutioncampaign1.shtml.**

Gerbet, Pierre. "The Origins: Early Attempts and the Emergence of the Six (1945–52)." In Pryce, ed., *The Dynamics of European Union* : 35–48, 1987.

Gilpin, Robert. *International Economic Stuff!!!* (Princeton, NJ: Princeton University Press, 2001).

Goldstein, Walter. "EC: Euro-stalling." *Foreign Policy* 85 (Winter 1991–1992): 129–147.

Habermeier, Karl, and Horst Ungerer. "A Single Currency for the European Community." *Finance and Development* (September 1992): 26–29.

Hafner-Burton, Emelie M. "Trading Human Rights: How Preferential Trade Agreements Influence Government Repression." *International Organization* 59 #3 (Summer 2005): 593–629.

Heater, Derek. *The Idea of European Unity* (New York: St. Martin's Press, 1992).

Hurwitz, Leon. *The European Community and the Management of International Cooperation* (New York: Greenwood Press, 1987).

Hurwitz, Leon, ed. *The Harmonization of European Public Policy: Regional Responses to Transnational Challenges* (Westport, CT: Greenwood Press, 1983).

Kusters, Hanns Jurgen. "The Treaties of Rome (1955–57)." In Pryce, ed., *The Dynamics of European Union* (1987): 78–104.

Los Angeles Times August 3, 2002, A7

Lehment, Harmen. "The European Monetary System." In Hurwitz, ed., *The Harmonization of European Public Policy* (1987): 183–196.

Lodge, Juliet. "European Community Decision-Making: Toward the Single European Market." In Urwin and Paterson, eds., *Politics in Western Europe Today* (1990): 206–226.

Lodge, Juliet, ed. *The European Community and the Challenge of the Future* (New York: St. Martin's Press, 1989).

Lodge, Juliet, ed. *European Union: The European Community in Search of a Future* (New York: St. Martin's Press, 1986).

Marsh, John. "The Common Agricultural Policy." In Lodge, ed., *The European Community and the Challenge of the Future* (1989): 148–166.

Monnet, Jean. *Memoirs* (New York: Doubleday, 1979).

Pevehouse, Jon. "Democracy from the Outside-In? International Organizations and Democratization." *International Organization* 56 #3 (Summer 2002): 515–549.

Pinder, John. "Economic Union and the Draft Treaty." In Lodge, ed., *European Union* (1989): 70–87.

Pryce, Roy, ed. *The Dynamics of European Union* (New York: Croom Helm, 1987).

Smith, Karen E. *European Union Foreign Policy in a Changing World* (London: Polity, 2003).

Spruyt, Hendrick. *The Sovereign State and Its Competitors* (Princeton, NJ: Princeton University Press, 1996).

Taylor, Paul. *The Limits of European Integration* (New York: Columbia University Press, 1983).

Tilly, Charles. *Coercion, Capital, and European States, 1990–1992* (London: Blackwell, 1992).

Urwin, Derek, and William Paterson, eds. *Politics in Western Europe Today: Perspectives, Policies and Problems Since 1980* (New York: Longman, 1990).

Williams, Allan M. *The European Community: The Contradictions of Integration* (Cambridge: Blackwell, 1991).

Wistrich, Ernest. *After 1992: The United States of Europe* (New York: Routledge, 1990).

World Bank. *World Development Report* (New York: Oxford University Press, 1999).

CASE 19

Pandemics: NGOs

INTRODUCTION

For centuries, international diplomacy has been the domain of highly skilled professionals, trained by their respective governments in the art of negotiation, the niceties of protocol, and the complexities of international law. Until the twentieth century, diplomats spoke the same language—figuratively and literally (French was the traditional language of diplomacy). Then came the nationalist movement and along with it the "democratization" of diplomacy. National representatives were expected to reflect the culture and traditions of their own country and not just some amorphous international culture. The result was revolutionary.

We may well be witnessing another revolution in diplomacy at the turn of the twenty-first century. In ways not seen before, citizen-diplomats are becoming involved directly in drafting the international codes of conduct and treaties that are then signed by governments. The sight of diplomats and international civil servants negotiating side by side with human rights activists and international relief workers has become increasingly common.

This is particularly true when the issue before them is so technical or complex that only scientists or other highly-trained experts can grasp it. Consider the depletion of the ozone layer—until climatologists had developed the sophisticated satellite-based measuring instruments, and could detect a significant shift in concentrations of ozone in the upper atmosphere, no diplomat or politician had any idea there was a problem. Even once it was discovered, those setting policy were entirely dependent on the experts for advice on how to solve it.

This same is true to a large extent when it comes to pandemics. Diseases are only identifiable by highly trained experts who can not only recognize symptoms, but can also isolate the virus or bacterium under a microscope of with other sophisticated instruments. Likewise, scientists are needed to explain patterns of transmission and possible therapies or remedies. There is little government officials can do without this information. This naturally gives these non-state actors considerable latitude to inject their own opinions and values into the debate—with mixed success.

CHRONOLOGY

1918
20 million die from influenza.

1948
World Health Organization is founded.

1959
First suspected case of AIDS in Africa—identified in 1998.

1967
WHO launches smallpox eradication program.

1977
Smallpox is eradicated.

1981
HIV virus is first identified.

1987
AZT approved for general use by the US Food and Drug Administration.

1990
CIA briefs White House on AIDS pandemic. It was largely ignored.

1994
UNAIDS program is founded.

2000
Brazil begins producing and distributing generic AZT in defiance of patent laws.

At U.S. urging, the UN Security Council Resolution 1308 declaring AIDS a major security threat is adopted.

2001
UN General Assembly approves the Declaration of Commitment on HIV/AIDS.

2003
George W. Bush announces $15 billion, five-year initiative on AIDS in Africa.

2005
AZT patent expires.

HISTORY OF RECENT PANDEMICS

Epidemics are nothing new—in fact they are among the oldest things in human existence. They have contributed to the decimation of whole civilizations in the past. The bubonic plague (also known as the Black Death) is thought to have killed roughly half of Europe's population in the mid-1300s. Diseases brought by Columbus and other explorers to the New World wiped out as many as ninety million people, eradicating entire races (more than 90% of the population of Hispaniola—modern Haiti and Dominican Republic—were killed by smallpox) (Pratt 1999, 178). The influenza epidemic of 1918 killed roughly twenty million—far more than died in World War I (Gostin 2004, 565). Smallpox killed roughly 50 million in the 1700s and has been blamed for 300 million in the twentieth century. Total deaths from HIV/AIDS have been estimated at twenty million worldwide (with 70% of these in Africa).

Thanks to breakthroughs in scientific research by Pasteur, Jenner, and others, vaccines and therapies have been identified for many of the world's worst diseases. In addition, medical training, sanitation, communication, and transportation have dramatically improved in almost every corner of the planet which has made this knowledge more accessible. In theory at least, one might think that pandemics should be controllable. But other factors seem to undermine many of these advances.

In terms of immediate causes, illnesses are spreading due to urbanization and urban sprawl which puts people in closer contact with diseased animals and with each other. Unsafe practices on the part of individuals—especially with respect to sanitation, food preparation, sexual practices, and seeking medical attention and vaccines—have allowed diseases to spread much faster than otherwise. But these immediate causes are explained by broader trends that include poverty and ignorance which make expensive treatments inaccessible, undermine education efforts with respect to safe practices, and limit what services states can provide. Poor nutrition undermines the immune system, making all more vulnerable to infection. Civil unrest and warfare invariably impede access to health care and undermine safe practices. Social discrimination may cause parts of the population to be exploited and thus become vulnerable to the spread of disease—particularly in the case of rape or prostitution. Finally, the entire global system may be at fault at some level. The capitalist market pushes firms to pursue more lucrative drugs (such as cold remedies or cures for indigestion) over vaccines for Third World diseases (such as malaria). Powerful states may see no reason to spend tax monies on tropical diseases that do not affect them directly and prefer instead to invest in national defense (Spectar 2001). And technical innovations and lowered trade barriers make it far easier for people and products to move rapidly over international boundaries, making it nearly impossible for anyone to be entirely safe.

Consider the recent SARS epidemic (SARS is the acronym for Severe, Acute Respiratory Syndrome). It was first diagnosed in Guangdong province in south-eastern China in November 2002. By May 2003, the number of cases climbed from a handful to over 7,000 and climbing. Within the first six months of the disease's appearance, over five hundred people had died in ten countries; cases of infection appeared in over thirty countries, from Hong Kong to Sweden, from Kuwait to Brazil (WHO 2003). The problem caused a political crisis in China where government officials who concealed the extent of the outbreak were fired and public confidence in the regime fell.

Given the urgency of these epidemics, governments have become increasingly involved in finding solutions—but in so doing they must interact with scientists, activists, pharmaceutical firms, and health care workers on a daily basis. Consider the eradication of smallpox—one of the singular achievements of the twentieth century. As deaths from smallpox climbed to the hundreds of millions, governments were eager to devote state funds to the problem. But politicians could do nothing more than encourage scientists and take their advice. Ultimately, governments applied the insights of Edward Jenner, whose study of cowpox had led to a rudimentary vaccine in the 1790s, to buy up vast quantities of the improved vaccines. They engaged the help of doctors and nurses, school principals and teachers, and even neighborhood leaders to disseminate the vaccine as widely as possible. By the 1930s, smallpox had been contained in most industrialized countries. In 1948, the World Health Organization was created by governments and staffed by doctors and researchers. Smallpox was naturally one of its greatest concerns. But it was as yet impossible to produce the vaccine in enough areas to bring the perishable product to the people. But in the 1950s, as a result of research in private firms, as well as universities and government-funded clinics, the vaccine was freeze-dried and could then be transported around the world.

With this new product in hand, WHO staff members, supported by physician associations and major governments, were able to overcome the skepticism of several states (including the Soviet Union) and reached agreement in 1967 to eradicate smallpox by 1977. Governments provided funding, access, and encouragement as thousands of experts fanned out across the world. Reaching urban areas and coastal regions was easy. The drama of smallpox eradication came in the efforts to travel into the hinterland of poor countries, where "roads had to be cut through jungle by hand, rivers bridged, and floodwaters crossed by boat" (Pratt 1999, 184). Stories are told of Western and local physicians performing outreach, wading through snake-infested waters to get the vaccines to remote villages and thousands of local health officers being trained to use the simple, two-pronged needle that injected just the right amount of vaccine—sometimes over 1,000 times a day. By 1977, the last case of natural smallpox was identified (and cured) in Somalia.

In the remainder of the chapter, we will review the international effort to combat HIV/AIDS, with special emphasis on the role of NGOs and nonstate actors. We will consider general patterns in the spread of HIV/AIDS since the 1980s and the contrasting responses of medical experts and government policymakers. In particular, we will consider the priorities and philosophical orientations of each and ask whether these can be reconciled.

HIV/AIDS

The Human Immunodeficiency Virus and the Acquired Immunodeficiency Syndrome it produces has infected roughly thirty-five million people and will soon reach a death toll of twenty million, making it the most deadly disease in the history of humanity, surpassing both the 1918 influenza and the bubonic plague of the Middle Ages (Spectar 2001, 254). AIDS patients are dying at the rate of roughly three million per year. Roughly three-fourths of those infected are in Sub-Saharan Africa (see Figure 19.1). Only about one out of six affected reside in developed countries where infection rates peaked in the mid-1990s and survival rates have increased dramatically thanks in large part to costly antiretroviral drugs. At this point, it is clear that HIV/AIDS is primarily a developing phenomenon, especially since India and China are likely to be its next major targets.

Manifestations of the disease were first noted in America in the late 1970s, and in Africa in 1983, although the virus has been discovered in frozen blood samples dating back to the late-1950s (Okigbo et al. 2002, 619). The virus has mutated and now manifests itself in about at least ten different strains as well as several recombinations, each of which is responsive and resistant to different treatments. The disease is transmitted primarily by certain body fluids—mostly blood and semen—and early educational programs in the West focused on safe sexual practices—particularly in the male homosexual community—and the use of clean needles by intravenous drug users. Government agencies and hospitals also monitored and cleaned up the blood supply. Sex workers were also monitored more closely and given treatment to prevent the spread by heterosexual sex.

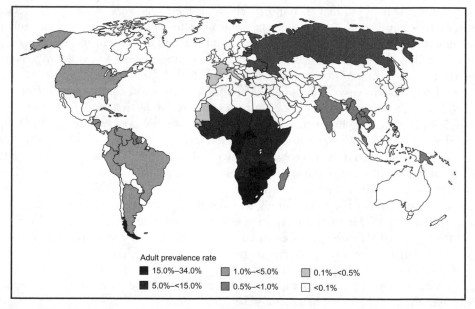

Figure 19.1 A global view of HIV infection—2005
Source: UNAIDS 2006, 14 The United Nations is the author of the original material.

In Africa, however, HIV/AIDS has spread primarily via heterosexual intercourse and transmission to children during pregnancy by infected mothers. This stems from a combination of poverty, illiteracy, unsafe sexual practices, and social mores (Okigbo 2002). The infection rate in adults in some Sub-Saharan African cities is well over half, although there are indications that in some countries the infection rate may have peaked in the mid-2000s—although the total number of infections continues to rise, albeit at a somewhat slower pace (UNAIDS 2006, 11). Pregnant women still have rising rates of infection in Southern Africa, rising from twenty to thirty percent in South Africa from 1997 to 2004, for example. Meanwhile in the rest of Africa, infection rates among pregnant women are declining slightly (from 14% in 1997 to 7% in 2004 in Kenya, for example).

The result of the high number of young adults contracting AIDS, Africa has experienced dramatic social and economic dislocations. Agricultural output fell by fifty percent from 1995 to 2000 in Zimbabwe as a result of the deaths of thousands of farmers (Spectar 2001, 261). Industrial output in other countries in the region has fallen as a result of "absenteeism, lower productivity, higher overtime costs, higher levels of health/treatment spending, more outlays for death benefits, additional staff recruitment and training expenses" (Spectar 2001, 261). It is estimated that economic growth on the continent will decline by more than one percent each year for two decades as a result of HIV/AIDS. Furthermore, the large number of children left orphaned is placing significant burdens on the survivors, some of whom have been forced to bring up to ten children into their homes.

Of particular concern has been the relatively recent emergence of HIV/AIDS in Asia where although the rate of infection is still quite low, given the enormous population size and density it is feared that the absolute number of infections could eclipse other regions. Here the virus appears to be spreading primarily in the sex worker and IV drug using populations with the result that urban areas have been hit the hardest—although there are early indications that it is spreading to rural areas as well (UNAIDS 2006, 25). In New Delhi, for example, the infection rate among drug users rose from 5% in 2000 to 14% in 2003. The infection rate among all adults in central Bangladesh rose from 1.5% in 1999 to 5% in 2004 and in Karachi, Pakistan it rose from almost nothing in 2003 to 22% in 2004.

Such is the state of affairs with respect to the HIV/AIDS pandemic. The picture is still dismal, although there are is evidence that new infections may soon begin to decline. Of course, even if there were no new infections beginning today, the burden of treating (and burying) those already infected will be crippling for many countries.

NGOs AND THE INTERNATIONAL RESPONSE TO HIV/AIDS

International actors can be classified in many ways, and a relatively simple typology distinguishes three types. Government agencies are distinguished by their accountability to political leaders. They are typically fully-funded from tax revenues and are staffed by employees whose careers will be entirely within government. There are also international organizations that are similarly structured, with professional staffs that are paid by governments via the institution. The next category is NGOs, described above. Their key characteristic is their private, non-profit status. They may spend their time on scholarly research, advocacy, public outreach, or public service provision—or some combination of these. Universities are a sub-set of NGOs. Finally, there are private agencies that operate for profit—corporations.

But the fact is that these different categories of institutions are often more similar than not. They almost all have divisions or bureaus where experts can carry out studies in a quasi-academic environment. Most corporations have extensive research and development units, some of which are essentially left alone to think (IBM is famous for having created such an office). Governments have set up similar think-tanks within larger departments. Governments have also funded research institutes that are essentially left alone. And finally, private researchers and independent NGOs routinely receive government funding. Thus, one particular individual scientist might find herself working at a private university on a government grant that produces a discovery that a private corporation brings to market. It is difficult in such situations to say exactly where government ends and the private sphere begins.

The international community has mounted a relatively aggressive campaign to halt HIV/AIDS, combining scientific research supported by government funding with aid-sponsored outreach and educational programs. In each facet, nonstate actors have played the key role. After all, were it not for physicians and researchers, the AIDS epidemic would merely be a mysterious string of deaths and illness without a name or a source. Likewise, governments are not equipped to cure diseases or provide therapies on their own, but must rely on experts.

To begin, the diagnosis of the virus was carried out by private researchers, some of whom had no direct connection to governments or international organizations. David Serwadda, a pulmonary specialist working in Uganda, was the first to identify HIV in Africa in 1983 (Okigbo et al. 2002, 619). Governments and international organizations still depend on ordinary physicians and technicians to identify cases. In Africa, one of the most important gateways is the nurses at the pre-natal clinics where pregnant mothers are screened, often for the first time. The search for a cure is primarily a private endeavor, carried out by researchers at universities, laboratories such as the Pasteur Institute in France and the Centers for Disease Control and Prevention in Atlanta, and at pharmaceutical firms such as GlaxoSmithKline where the antiretroviral "cocktail" is being mass-produced.

The story of AZT illustrates the blending of public, private, and non-profit agencies. AZT, formally known as zidovudine, was first developed by Jerome Horwitz in 1964 under a grant from the American National Institutes of Health. Although it did not work well on cancer as originally hoped, the drug was later refined in the mid-1980s by Samuel Broder, Hiroaki Mitsuya, and Robert Yarchoan (all of the National Cancer Institute) who worked with Janet Rideout and others at Burroghs Wellcome Company—now known as GlaxoSmithKline. They obtained a patent in 1986 and the Food and Drug Administration approved it for general use in 1987 (Wikipedia 2006). Thus we can see the involvement of all three players.

At the international level, the organization that has taken "point" is the World Health Organization (WHO). This international organization is a hybrid, in that since its founding it has brought together both diplomats and physicians to deal with international health. Based in Geneva, Switzerland, the organization has a universal membership of states and a professional staff of physicians and medical researchers. The staff carries out policy discussions and makes recommendations to the representatives of states who then approve or reject them and set the funding levels. The staff also interfaces with the local medical professionals and relevant government health agencies through face-to-face contact and expert consultations.

WHO also links with numerous NGOs through an established consultation system. A total of 182 NGOs have formal relations with the WHO as of January 2006. It is the focal point for reporting by hundreds of institutes and individual researchers in cases of epidemic outbreaks and carries out on going consultations to improve reporting and cataloging the data (WHO 2000). Some of these networks are disease-specific, such as FluNet that links laboratories in 89 countries. Others are supported by WHO but run by governments, such as the Global Public Health Intelligence Network in Canada. At any rate, WHO works to communicate new information to local practitioners through its Web site and weekly newsletters, as well as through large-scale conferences (a conference in 2000 brought together representatives of more than fifty private research institutes as well as numerous government agencies and state-run laboratories; WHO 2000). The WHO also uses its financial resources to purchase HIV-related medications and therapies (WHO 2006).

WHO was instrumental in creating UNAIDS—a collaborative endeavor created in 1994 by various United Nations organizations to pool resources and talent and coordinate anti-AIDS programs. WHO is the lead agency in the collaborative, which includes the High Commissioner for Refugees, UNICEF, the World Food Program, the United Nations Development Program, the UN Population Fund, the UN Office on Drugs and Crime, the International Labor Organization, UNESCO, and the World Bank. The HIV/AIDS phenomenon has so many dimensions, it seemed reasonable to attack the problem from different angles. UNICEF naturally focuses on women and children—especially pregnant women whom it tries to educate and support. The World Bank, as a relatively well-endowed development bank, has been a principal funding agency, having provided roughly two billion dollars to other international and local agencies.

ALTERNATIVE STRATEGIES

HIV/AIDS has always been controversial. When it was first identified in the United States, it was found primarily in the male homosexual community and among intravenous drug users. This brought considerable ambivalence in the public at large as many saw the illness as divorced from their own lives. Social conservatives even went so far as to dismiss the disease as self-inflicted (or perhaps divinely-inflicted) and therefore unworthy of investigation with tax-payer dollars. Even today, many governments, including the Bush administration, emphasize the moral dimension of HIV/AIDS. The United States insisted that a major UN statement in 2001 list abstinence and fidelity in marriage be first in the list of preventive measures that should be taken (DeYoung 2001, 72).

We will consider the views of several groups in turn, beginning with the U.S. government to provide a reference point. We will then turn to the human rights approach, followed by the North–South approach. The challenges faced by NGOs that advocate the latter two approaches helps illustrate the limits to NGO influence.

U.S. Government. The CDC has been the lead agency on the issue, which has allowed the political elites to skirt the question of blame. By focusing on the technical dimensions of the illness, the scientists at the CDC have been able to present their findings dispassionately with minimal resistance. On the other hand, when it has come to taking positions in international fora, the United States has been more ambivalent. The Clinton administration addressed the AIDS crisis in part as a trade issue since many governments and NGOs were demanding exemptions to the patent for AZT. AZT could be manufactured for well under a dollar a dose, but was sold for over six dollars due to GlaxoSmithKline's exclusive rights to the drug. Clinton was concerned about the implications of abandoning intellectual property rights for American firms and therefore supported the firm's position (Fidler 2004, 120).

The Bush administration, for its part, also supported the patent issue. In addition, it was more unwilling to spend much on international AIDS programs. It provided only one billion dollars to the Global Fund for AIDS in 2001 and 2002 combined—far below the level that could be expected of the country that produces nearly one-quarter of world economic output. As put by Paul Zeitz, director of the Global AIDS Alliance, "It's outrageous that the president gives such short shrift to the Global Fund. It is the best hope yet for the fight against AIDS; yet the president has let the Fund down" (Lobe 2003). But in early 2003, the Bush administration announced plans to donate $15 billion for UNAIDS over five years (2004–2008) in concentrated effort on the Sub-Saharan African and Caribbean nations most affected.

Part of the motivation for this increase came not from humanitarian concerns but rather from fears that political instability could result from the effects of the disease. The 2002 National Security Strategy document argued that AIDS was threatening the administration's goals of fighting terrorism in Africa. In particular, AIDS threatens the administration's goals of promoting stable democracy and liberal economic and political values generally (Fidler 2004, 126). As explained by Secretary of State Colin Powell: "AIDS is not just a humanitarian or health issue. It not only kills. It also destroys communities. It decimates countries. It destabilizes regions. It can consume continents. No war on the face of the earth is more destructive than the AIDS pandemic" (Spectar 2003, 538).

Both governments were concerned about the security implications of AIDS, and in 2000 the United States helped orchestrate a special session of the UN Security Council to focus on AIDS as a security issue, for example. This was the first time the Security Council addressed a public health issue, since its mandate is to deal with violent crises and threats to security. In the resulting resolution, member-states acknowledged several particularly dangerous aspects of AIDS:

> The Security Council,
> *Deeply concerned* by the extent of the HIV/AIDS pandemic worldwide, and by the severity of the crisis in Africa in particular, . . .
> *Recognizing* that the spread of HIV/AIDS can have a uniquely devastating impact on all sectors and levels of society, . . .
> *Further recognizing* that the HIV/AIDS pandemic is also exacerbated by conditions of violence and instability, which increase the risk of exposure to the disease through large movements of people, widespread uncertainty over conditions, and reduced access to medical care,
> *Stressing* that the HIV/AIDS pandemic, if unchecked, may pose a risk to stability and security, . . .
> 6. *Expresses* keen interest in additional discussion among relevant United Nations bodies, Member States, industry and other relevant organizations to make progress, *inter alia*, on the question of access to treatment and care, and on prevention. UNSC Resolution 1308 (2000)

This statement was further expanded in 2001 at an international UN conference was held in New York to discuss HIV/AIDS. The meetings resembled the UNCED gathering in that nearly all states sent very senior representatives, including heads of state and government, and were joined by thousands of NGO representatives and international organization spokesmen. The result, much like at UNCED, was a broad statement of principles (the Declaration of Commitment on HIV/AIDS) and a more specific and measurable Action Guide. While none of these are treaties and have no legally binding effect (meaning that it is not likely any country will be sanctioned for failing to achieve the goals), the high visibility and priority given to the topic seemed to have finally lifted HIV/AIDS to the forefront of the many international issues states are actively addressing. Among other things, states committed to increase funding to developing countries struggling with AIDS to between seven and ten billion per year by 2005, starting with a major fund-raising campaign in 2002. The conferees also agreed to support the work of the UNAIDS joint task force, both financially and politically.

Human Rights Advocates. Moral issues continue to influence national positions. The Vatican, for example, repeatedly opposes references to condom use in international statements, and Islamic countries block specific references to male homosexual intercourse and sex with prostitutes because these are contrary to Sharia law (DeYoung 2001, 73). This has prompted many human rights activists to advocate a different emphasis: the right to health. As explained by Fidler,

> Although human rights treaties have long recognized infectious disease control as a legitimate reason for restricting enjoyment of civil and political rights, the relationship between public health and these rights was not prominent until after WHO's creation. Various responses to HIV/AIDS, including quarantine and isolation, and widespread stigma and discrimination against people living with HIV or AIDS,

brought renewed public health attention to civil and political rights. . . . Human rights advocates argued that access to [antiretroviral] treatments formed part of the right to health under international law. The global HIV/AIDS campaign embodied the inter-dependence and indivisibility of civil and political, economic, and cultural rights claimed in international human rights discourse. (Fidler 2004, 113)

Amnesty International has issued the following demands to government to achieve a human rights–centered approach:

1. Fulfill the international commitment to the right to health.
2. Remove funding conditions that inhibit the prevention of HIV/AIDS.
3. Ensure equal access to treatment.
4. Ensure equal access to information.
5. Guarantee sexual and reproductive rights.
6. Safeguard women's rights and stop violence against women.
7. Ensure participation of people living with HIV/AIDS.
8. Share equally the benefits of scientific progress.
9. Affirm the right to privacy and confidentiality.
10. Ensure monitoring and evaluation for human rights and evidence-based solutions. (AI 2006)

This approach, which has been prompted not only by human rights activists such as the organization ACT UP, but also by most in the scientific community (narrowly defined), has advantages and disadvantages, which might explain some governments' resistance to it. For one, it urges states to provide resources and remedies, not just out of humanitarian concern, but as a matter of legal obligation. The implication is that when states refuse to provide these resources, or refuse to participate in international coordination efforts (which happens routinely—especially with respect to reporting obligations), they can be held accountable as law-breakers rather than merely chided as misers. Naturally, no government wants its actions to be obligatory in this sense—they want freedom of operation. That said, the approach also constrains states in their selection of strategies. As pointed out in the Fidler quote, they must respect basic human rights in every respect of their strategies, taking care not to discriminate on the basis of sexual orientation or gender, ensuring the empowerment of women in societies where they are routinely abused, and setting aside some patent and copyright protections in the name of health. Again, states see difficulties in some of these demands and therefore resist them.

NGOs have consistently pressed this agenda in multiple arenas. Of particular interest is their engagement with the international institutions. NGOs have provided hard facts, policy recommendations, and specific encouragement to the WHO and leaders of UNAIDS over the years. This takes place informally through face-to-face (or e-mail-to-e-mail) contact, through speech-making and literature distribution at international conferences (the 2001 meeting referred to earlier was attended by thousand of AIDS activists and experts), and by inclusion on various blue-ribbon commissions and working groups. As technical experts, NGOs are uniquely qualified to generate, disseminate, and interpret scientific data. As mentioned earlier, it would be impossible for more government agencies to address the topic without this material. Therefore they have been remarkably successful in pressing their particular approach to the issue.

NGOs have been assisted by the endorsement of numerous governments as well. Consider the issue of patents. Many governments—especially Brazil and South Africa—have been making the case for patent exemptions with the support of these NGOs. African governments hope to turn the crisis into a genuinely transnational issue that Western governments will be forced to reckon with. In particular, they have demanded access to medicines that have been on the market in the West for years—such as AZT and its successors. The drug companies naturally balk at the notion of giving away drugs that cost them hundreds of millions to design and produce. The African governments are therefore asking Western governments to buy up the drug, or at least remove their patent protections so cheaper generic versions can be produced. Part of the reason for South Africa's position was the pressure exerted upon by local activists in the Treatment Action Campaign which was able to shame the government (beginning in 1998) to acknowledging its failure to secure antiretroviral drugs—especially for pregnant women (TAC 2006).

Brazil, for example, launched a nationwide initiative to produce AZT and other drug therapies locally and distribute them free of charge in 2000. In the first three years of the program, the government spent nearly a half-billion dollars to provide drugs to all of Brazil's 85,000 AIDS patients, with the result that AIDS mortality dropped by half in São Paulo alone. Even more important, the state saved almost the same amount as it spent on avoided hospitalizations and other expenses (MAP Symposium 2002, 8). When the patent expired in 2005, the issue became moot.

North–South Perspective—This brings up the last issue that has been taken up by various NGOs–again with the support of multiple states. That is the approach that views the AIDS issue primarily as an element in the North–South debate. During the 1960s and 1970s, newly independent states in the developing world argued that their poverty was not so much the product of their own failings but rather the result of an unjust international system. In particular, they pointed out, the free market had a tendency to punish societies that were already poor and technologically backward and that there was little they could do to reverse the situation. Western powers discriminated against developing countries in trade, investment, and finance and tended to be miserly when it came to foreign aid—showing clear preferences to assist only those states that were strategically important.

While this language has generally subsided as more and more developing countries adopt pro-Western free-trade policies, the AIDS issue helped bring it back. It has been combined with general skepticism about globalization and the benefits of free-trade programs promoted by Western governments. The argument is that the West has invested huge amounts of money to suppress AIDS at home, but has largely ignored the problem in the developing world. This is reflected in foreign aid flows, drug patent rules, and overall attitudes of indifference. As put by

Peter Piot, director of the UNAIDS program: "The world stood by while AIDS overwhelmed sub-Saharan Africa." And Stephen Lewis, UN Special Envoy on AIDS in Africa stated:

> How can this be happening, in the year 2003, when we can find over $200 billion to fight a war on terrorism, but we can't find the money to prevent children from living in terror? And when we can't find the money to provide the antiretroviral treatment for all of those who need such treatment in Africa? This double standard is the grotesque obscenity of the modern world. (Fidler 2004, 107)

Critics of Western policy point out that it was not until the 1990s that they took the problem seriously. In the United States, a CIA-sponsored study that predicted dramatic increases in AIDS-related deaths (accurately, as it happened), was met with indifference by senior U.S. officials in 1990 (Spectar 2001, 273). Once the AIDS crisis peaked in the West, aid to Africa began to slump—a trend that was exacerbated by the end of the Cold War when Africa's strategic importance dropped. AIDS-related WHO spending fell from $130 million to $20 million during the first half of the 1990s while UNICEF spending dropped from $45 to $20 million. While the West was willing to spend close to $200 billion to remedy the Y2K computer glitch (which wound up not being a problem), it is unwilling to spend the same to provide antiretroviral drugs to all the world's AIDS patients (Spectar 2001, 275).

For those who take this approach, the remedy to the problem must involve a dramatic shift in structures and goals. This is similar to the arguments made by other antiglobalization activists who have protested at World Bank meetings and economic summit meetings. While it is difficult to get a clear sense of what the outcome of such dramatic reforms would be, the short-term goal is a dramatic increase in foreign aid aimed at provided drugs and other treatments to those most in need.

CONCLUSION

As this case has demonstrated, NGOs are to international policy what nails are to a building. While they may not always be conspicuous or individually powerful, they are one of the elements that holds the structure together. As with the case of the environment or humanitarian disasters in remote areas, NGOs provide the basic facts which governments cannot generate on their own. They also naturally provide an interpretation of those facts in order for states to make sense of them. Also naturally, they provide recommendations on which policy will likely be most effective—advice which governments are often ill-equipped to dispute and therefore adopt (at least in part). And finally, NGOs are often involved in implementing the policies on the ground.

NGOs sometimes are able to generate enough resources to bypass governments entirely and are able to come up with the diagnosis, remedy, and therapy on their own. Governments, aware of the skills and energy of many NGOs, are willing to delegate their own work to them by providing grants, access to their territory, and other support.

But governments and NGOs often do not see eye to eye. In the case of HIV/AIDS, we saw that states are more willing to ignore international legal requirements—or act to restrict them. They also tended to look to their own security interests first and humanitarian needs second. And they were perfectly willing to place the HIV debate in the broader context of on going diplomatic disputes. Ultimately, this situation is likely to continue, with the result that NGO influence is likely only to go as far as states are willing to allow.

DEBATE TOPIC

Should NGOs have greater power in international life?

PRO
NGOs are generally filled with experts who are interested primarily in improving the human condition. These experts are often bound by professional ethics that require that they behave in disinterested ways. As a result, the information and advice NGOs provide has a purity to it that is unmatched in the private sector or governmental sphere. This information will likely provide a better guide for good policy than leaving things to governments and corporations. In addition, NGOs often have a passion and zeal that allows them to remain focused in the face of obstacles. States are inherently inward-looking since they are concerned primarily with their own security and status rather than the global interests as a whole.

CON
There is nothing inherently democratic or noble about NGOs. They have their own agendas, just like any other institution. All NGOs are ultimately self-interested since they also must raise money, get attention, and so forth. Besides, just because experts know a great deal about a topic doesn't mean their values are the best. States, on the other hand—especially democratic ones—represent millions of people. They can speak with authority in their behalf and make binding decisions which are then subjected to legislative approval. States are also interested in balancing numerous issues—not just the single issue the NGO is working on. Thus, states should take NGO advice with a grain of salt and make decisions based on the preferences of all people.

THINKING THEORETICALLY

NGOs do not figure prominently in realist thinking since realists focus almost entirely on states and their quest for security. NGOs, according to realists, fall under the broad category of nonstate actors that lack the capacity to directly influence major policy since they lack military capacity on the one hand or statehood on the other. States are uniquely capable of

(continued)

(continued)

acting and shaping global affairs and can largely manipulate or ignore NGOs. Where NGOs are influential, so realists would say, this is because states seek them out and give them access. Note that where states have chosen to ignore NGOs—as we have seen in the case study—there is almost nothing NGOs can do. Put another way, states decide who will have a microphone.

Constructivists, on the other hand, see NGOs as central to the process of identity-formation and norm-creation—key aspect of international life. NGOs may develop and introduce new principles of international life—such as those NGOs that promoted abolition of the slaves, arms control, economic integration, and so forth. They help to create norms to which, at the very least, states must respond. Even if states choose to ignore NGOs and their ideas, the ideas are "out there" nonetheless. Consider, for example, the influence of Enlightenment philosophers who promoted global cooperation and democracy. While governments generally ignored their ideas for one hundred years, the ideas thrived in spite of this and have since moved to the top of major powers' priorities.

Questions to Consider

1. What type of relations have developed between states and NGOs in the area of HIV/AIDS? Have states embraced the NGOs' advice or have they rather manipulated the NGOs to serve their own national interests?

2. What resources do NGOs possess that may strengthen their influence in international affairs? What resources do states have?

3. What are the implications of increased NGO engagement in diplomacy for international politics generally? Is this likely to make the world a better place, impede cooperation, or something else?

Websites

UNAIDS: **www.unaids.org**

WHO's HIV/AIDS Department: **www.who.int/hiv/aboutdept/en/**

CDC: **www.cdc.gov/hiv**

Pasteur Institute: **www.pasteur.fr/english.html**

International AIDS Society: **www.iasociety.org/index.asp**

ACT UP: **www.actupny.org**

Treatment Action Campaign: **www.tac.org/za**

References

Amnesty International (AI). Action on HIV/AIDS and Human Rights, May 2006. Available at: **www.ai.org.**

DeYoung, Karen. "Between the Lines: Immune to Reality," *Foreign Policy* 126 (Sept-Oct 2001): 72–73.

Fidler, David. "Fighting the Axis of Illness: HIV/AIDS, Human Rights, and U.S. Foreign Policy," *The Harvard Environmental Law Review* 17 (Spring 2004): 99–136.

Gostin, Lawrence. "Pandemic Influenza: Public Health Preparedness for the Next Global Health Emergency," *Journal of Law, Medicine and Ethics* 32 (Winter 2004): 565–572.

Lobe, Jim. "World Community Gives Bush AIDS Pledge Mixed Reception." Inter Press Service, January 29, 2003.

MAP Symposium. "The Status and Trends of the HIV/AIDS in the World." Durban Monitoring the AIDS Pandemic (MAP) Network Symposium, July 5–7, 2002.

Okigbo, Charles, Carol A. Okigbo, William B. Hall, Jr., and Dhyana Ziegler. "The HIV/AIDS Epidemic in African American Communities: Lessons from UNAIDS and Africa," *Journal of Black Studies* 32 #6 (July 2002): 615–653.

Pratt, David. "Lessons for Implementation from the World's Most Successful Programme: The Global Eradication of Smallpox," *Journal of Curriculum Studies* 31 #2 (1999): 177–194.

Spectar, J. M. "The Hybrid Horseman of the Apocalypse: The Global AIDS Pandemic and the North–South Fracas," *The Georgia Journal of International and Comparative Law* 29 (Winter 2001): 253–299.

Spectar, J. M. "The Olde Order Crumbleth: HIV-Pestilence as a Security Issue and New Thinking about Core Concepts in International Affairs," *Indiana International and Comparative Law Review* 13 (2003): 481–542.

TAC. Overview of the Treatment Action Campaign. Accessed July 6, 2006. Available at: **www.tac.org.za/about.html.**

UNAIDS. *2006 Report on the Global AIDS Epidemic* (New York: UN, 2006).

WHO. *Global Outbreak Alert and Response: Report of a WHO Meeting*, April 26–28, 2000, Geneva, Switzerland.

WHO. "Cumulative Number of Reported Probable Cases of SARS." 2003. Available at: **www.who.int/csr/sarscountry/2003_05_08/en/.**

WHO. WHO's involvement in UNAIDS. Accessed July 3, 2006. Available at: **www.unaids.org/en/Cosponsors/who/default.asp.**

Wikipedia. Zidovudine. Wikipedia, the free encyclopedia. Accessed July 4, 2006. Available at: **en.wikipedia.org/wiki/AZT.**

Index